Third Edition

RACISM, SEXISM, and the MEDIA

To those of the past, present, and
future who boldly challenge racism and sexism in
American media, this book is respectfully dedicated.

Third Edition

RACISM, SEXISM, and the MEDIA

The Rise of Class Communication in Multicultural America

Clint C. Wilson II
Howard University

Félix Gutiérrez
University of Southern California

Lena M. Chao
California State University, Los Angeles

SAGE Publications
International Educational and Professional Publisher
Thousand Oaks ■ London ■ New Delhi

For information:

Sage Publications, Inc.
2455 Teller Road
Thousand Oaks, California 91320
E-mail: order@sagepub.com

Sage Publications Ltd.
6 Bonhill Street
London EC2A 4PU
United Kingdom

Sage Publications India Pvt. Ltd.
B-42, Panchsheel Enclave
Post Box 4109
New Delhi 110 017 India

Printed in the United States of America

Library of Congress Cataloging-in-Publication Data

Wilson, Clint C.
Racism, sexism, and the media : the rise of class communication in multicultural
America / by Clint C. Wilson, Félix Gutiérrez, and Lena M. Chao.— 3rd ed.
      p. cm.
Rev. ed. of: Race, multiculturalism and the media. 2nd ed. c1995.
Includes bibliographical references and index.
ISBN 0-7619-2515-5 (cloth) — ISBN 0-7619-2516-3 (pbk.)
   1. Racism in mass media. 2. Sexism in mass media. 3. Mass media-United States.
4. Pluralism (Social sciences)—United States. I. Gutiérrez, Félix. II. Chao, Lena M.
III. Wilson, Clint C. Race, multiculturalism and the media. IV. Title.
P94.5.M552U69 2003
305.8—dc21

                                   2003007207

Printed on acid-free paper

03   04   05   06   07   08   09   10   9   8   7   6   5   4   3   2   1

Acquiring Editor:	Margaret H. Seawell
Editorial Assistant:	Alicia Carter
Production Editor:	Claudia A. Hoffman
Typesetter:	C&M Digitals (P) Ltd.
Indexer:	Molly Hall
Cover Designer:	Janet Foulger

Contents

Preface and Acknowledgments

Before the first edition of this book, *Minorities and Media*, was published in 1985, very little comprehensive academic work had been done on the relationship between the mass media in the United States and the largest segments of its non-White population. In fact, one of our university colleagues—although supportive of the effort we were about to undertake—said he didn't believe that enough material was available to fill a book-length volume on the subject. He suggested that perhaps there was enough substance to construct one chapter in a book.

As we release this third edition, the body of work in the area of "minorities and the media" has grown to encompass dozens of books and anthologies addressing not only specific racial "minorities" but also other groups that have been marginalized in the communications media, including women, homosexuals, and the physically challenged. The issues of multiculturalism and gender have been given broader and more consistent attention than ever before—in both the popular press and academic publications. Many scholars and professionals now recognize that an understanding of diversity is central to an understanding of the field of communication. As the discourse has proliferated, a debate has arisen over whether multiculturalism has been overemphasized to the detriment of sound media practice. Among the critics who believe that it has is William McGowan, author of *Coloring the News: How Crusading for Diversity Has Corrupted American Journalism* (Encounter Books, 2000). However, other scholars and practitioners in media have ably defended the notion of equitable racial, cultural, and gender representation in media workforce and content.

It is the intention of this work not to merely espouse the virtues of racial and cultural diversity in the American media but, rather, to further explore, develop, and refine our original objectives. As the subtitles of our two previous editions have shown, we have pursued the impact of America's burgeoning multicultural population on its media landscape, especially the proliferation of media targeted to audience segments rather than the mass audience. Twenty years ago we saw technological, racial, and cultural diversity as harbingers of "the end of mass communication" in the United States. In the second edition of this book, the subtitle reflected the clear shift "from mass to class communication." In this edition, we see "the rise of class communication in multicultural America" resulting from the convergence of new media technologies and the continued demographic segmentation of audiences as people of color grow as targets of and markets for media.

The most important of the many changes in structure and content that we have made in this third edition is that we have added Lena Chao as a coauthor. Her contributions to earlier versions were recognized in those editions and we are very pleased that she was able to become a full partner in creating this edition. This enables us to provide better insight into the media experiences of Asian and Pacific Island cultures in the United States and to widen our scope to include the perspectives of women of color. The result is that we have added a chapter on women of color and made a more integrated assessment throughout the text of the experiences of women of color in the media.

Limitations

As we noted in previous editions, there are limitations in this work in several respects. This book concerns itself generally with only the four largest racial minority groups in the United States, although some references are made specifically to members of groups from East India and the Middle East. Principally, the work is concerned with Native, Black, Latino, and Asian Pacific Americans. Other cultural or social groups sometimes categorized as "minorities" (the physically challenged, gays, lesbians, and White women in the workforce, etc.) are not subjects of this work, although some parallels may be seen between the groups we examine and these groups with regard to their relationships to the mainstream media. Similarly, this book does not attempt to address every general audience public communications medium. Therefore, music recording, book publishing, magazine fiction, and other media are not within the scope of this work.

Although scholars continue to contribute new knowledge about the relationship of the media to the subject groups, we have found that research material on the various groups remains uneven. Thus, it was not possible to tell the complete story of each group in every chapter. The gaps in the research literature continue to suggest areas for future study by students and scholars who are seriously interested in documenting the role of the media as they have related to racial groups in the United States. We hope that this book encourages further work in this important field so that more gaps in our knowledge will be addressed and filled.

Definition of Terms

In this book, the terms *Asian Pacific American* and *Asian American* are used interchangeably to describe people who trace their origins to the Asian continent, as well as those from the Pacific Islands. In 2000, the U.S. Bureau of the Census listed the following ethnic residents as "Asian" or "Asian Pacific American": Chinese, Japanese, Korean, Filipino, Vietnamese, Asian Indians, Native Hawaiians, Pacific Islanders, Southeast Asians (Cambodian, Hmong, Laotian, Thai), South Asians (Sri Lankan, Pakistani, Bangladeshi), and Hapas (persons of mixed race).

The term *Black* is used here to describe African Americans and others who trace their origins to the sub-Saharan part of the African continent. *Latino* or the feminine form, *Latina,* is used along with *Hispanic* as an inclusive term for people of Latin American or Spanish background, including the Caribbean region. The term *Native American* is used to describe the native peoples of the continent that Europeans and other immigrants have called America. The terms *White* and *Anglo* are used, as they are applied by the U.S. Bureau of the Census, to describe people of European background who are not Latinos. All terms are capitalized in the text when referring to people of different races and cultures. We acknowledge, however, that using terms such as *Asian, Latino, African American,* and *White* to describe a diverse group of people is often inadequate, and that the hyphenation of two ethnicities to create—for example, Asian American—is problematic.

Acknowledgments

We wish to again acknowledge people, with their affiliations at the time, who provided assistance during the preparation of the previous editions of this work. We would like to thank for their efforts graduate research assistants Carey Jue and David Tomsky. We would also like to thank Luther Luedtke, who provided support when he served as Interim Director of the University of Southern California (USC) School of Journalism. Appreciation is also extended to Erwin Kim, a former USC colleague, whose assistance with the historiography of film portions of the text was invaluable. Other colleagues at USC who made important contributions include Stanley Rosen, of the USC East Asian Studies Center, who assisted in translating portions of the first Asian American newspaper along with graduate student Stanley Chung. Students in our courses at USC and Howard University contributed their enthusiasm for the subject of race and the media and were a source of inspiration and encouragement, as was Alice Marshall of Wave Publications.

Important to the development of the historical information in the first edition were Michael Emery and Tom Reilly of the journalism faculty at California State University, Northridge. Hugo Garcia of the Northeast Newspapers in Los Angeles provided much of the stimulation for the sections on audience segmentation. In addition, we would like to thank Don Carson and Edith Auslander of the University of Arizona, who provided speaking opportunities and comments that led to some of the concepts developed in the chapter on advertising and marketing. Carolyn McIntosh, research librarian at the University of Southern California, provided valuable assistance in locating material on topics covered in the book, and staff members at the Margaret Herrick Library, Academy of Motion Picture Arts and Sciences, assisted in obtaining photographs.

We would like to extend our gratitude to those who have been gracious with their time and expertise during the preparation of previous editions of the book. They include Vernon Stone, formerly research director for the Radio and Television News Directors Association; Brenda Alexander of the Howard University Department of Journalism; and numerous colleagues in the Minorities and Communications division of the Association for Education in Journalism and Mass Communications who consistently reinforced the need for this volume. For contributions to the second edition, we would also like to thank Elena Gutiérrez of the University of Michigan for her editing and comments on the first chapter and Bunty Anquoe and Tim Giago of *Indian Country Today* and Mark Trahant of the *Salt Lake City Tribune* for their insights into coverage of Native Americans. Jon Funabiki of San Francisco State University provided good counsel on issues relating to diversity in the media and journalism education, and Aissatou Sidime of Xavier University provided research for the chapter on advertising.

Conversations with a number of people helped advance our understanding of the impact of the new technologies on the issues of multiculturalism and access to and usage of the media in the second edition. They include Jorge Reina Schement of Rutgers University; Armando Valdez of Valdez and Associates; Nancy Hicks Maynard of Maynard Partners; Bruce Koon of the *San Francisco Examiner;* and Adam Clayton Powell III of The Freedom Forum Media Studies Center.

Special thanks for their specific contributions to the third edition go to Ping Lien Chao, Monterey Park, California; Thelma Grayson, Los Angeles; Yumi Wilson, *San Francisco Chronicle;* Rick Mastroianni, Freedom Forum Library; Sandy Close, New California Media; Sandra Ball-Rokeach,

Michael J. Cody, Elisia Cohen, Geoff Cowan, Stella Lopez and Michael Parks, Annenberg School for Communication, University of Southern California; Mercedes Lynn de Uriarte and Maggie Rivas-Rodríguez, School of Journalism, University of Texas at Austin; Monty Roessel, Rough Rock Community School, Chinle, Arizona; Julio Moran, California Chicano News Media Association; Dori Maynard, Robert C. Maynard Institute for Journalism Education; Nicolas Kanellos, Arte Público Press, University of Houston; Kuei Chiu, University of California Riverside Library; Andrea Shepherd, Newseum; Steve Montiel, USC Annenberg Institute for Justice and Journalism; Dennis McAuliffe, School of Journalism, University of Montana; Joellen El-Bashir, Moorland-Spingarn Research Center, Howard University; Bill Wong, Oakland, California; Frank Wood, Frank & Marie-Theresa Wood Print Collections, Alexandria, Virginia; and Helen Zia, Oakland, California.

We also extend our thanks to the manuscript reviewers, although they are unknown to us, who provided valuable editing and constructive comments that enhanced this third edition. Our gratitude also to the staff and editors at Sage Publications for their patience, advice, and encouragement during the preparation of this volume.

Most important, we must again recognize the support, encouragement, and sacrifices made by those closest to us: Mary Julia Wilson and Clint C. Wilson III; María Elena, Elena Rebeca, Anita Andrea, and Alicia Rosa Gutiérrez; and Julian Lee Benedict. Without their sustaining presence and nurturing expressions, we could not have completed the task.

—Clint C. Wilson II
—Félix F. Gutiérrez
—Lena M. Chao

Part I

Majority Rules: "Minorities" and the Media

Diversity in the Land of Majority Rule 1

I n May of 2002, Oakland, California, marked its 150th birthday, a newsworthy event by any standard. Anticipating the public celebration, the *San Francisco Chronicle* assigned reporter Rick DelVecchio to write a story on the city's history. DelVecchio wrote that 4 years after the United States took California following the end of its war with Mexico in 1848, Yankee speculators showed up on the San Francisco Bay's eastern shore and began selling real estate they didn't own. The owners were the Peralta family, Californios who lived and worked on 44,000 acres of land granted to them by Spain decades earlier. The Peraltas confronted the squatters. But shortly thereafter, DelVecchio reported, "The Californios vanished."

After the story was published, one of this book's authors (Félix Gutiérrez), a descendant of Californios, wrote to the *Chronicle's* Reader Representative requesting a correction. Citing books and other research, he pointed out that the Spanish and Mexican Californios had not simply "vanished" when White settlers arrived following the U.S. takeover of California. In fact, the Peraltas successfully defended their title to much of their land in U.S. courts, filed court actions for their land rights as late as 1910, and were still living along the San Francisco Bay in 2002, 150 years after they had, according to the *Chronicle*, disappeared from the area. But the *Chronicle* refused to print a correction to its inaccurate reporting in its regular corrections section.

Instead, a week later the paper printed a one-item "Clarification" along with corrections of three other erroneous reports. The "clarification" admitted that the Peraltas and other California families had not vanished and that they had "defended their land titles in U.S. courts against the squatters and others who illegally claimed their land" ("Clarifications," 2002, p. A2). The clarification reported the story more accurately than DelVecchio's article had, but the newspaper's refusal to print it as a correction of its earlier inaccurate reporting reflected a deeper issue in the newspaper that once proclaimed itself "The Voice of the West"—and perhaps in other news organizations as well.

That deeper issue is news media support of the image of the United States as a nation whose progress was driven by the westward movement of Whites into lands inhabited by native, Hispanic, and mixed-race people who gave up to a superior people without a fight. This "White might was right" attitude is not new to the United States or to California. But neither are stories of people of all colors fighting for their rights or contributing to the development of this country. In fact, in 1781 Los Angeles was founded by a multiracial group of settlers that included Whites, Blacks, Indians, Pacific Islanders, and mixed race mestizos sent north from Central Mexico by Spanish authorities.[1]

Racial and ethnic inclusiveness has become more important as people in the United States have looked for ways to live, and let live, in an increasingly diverse society long governed by majority rule in which one group, Whites, have been the majority. The issue under consideration is how people of color fit into the fabric of America and how the media tell them and others how they fit in. In the 21st century, all the people in the United States will need to find ways to form a majority in a nation of minorities.

"No one wants to return to the days when a Euro-centric culture made many Blacks, Latinos and Asians feel like outer-space aliens in their own nation; but too much emphasis on what separates us can deepen divisions," the *Los Angeles Times* editorialized after the city's massive civil disturbances that followed the 1992 acquittal of four Los Angeles police officers who brutally beat Black motorist Rodney King after a chase on darkened streets. The beating was videotaped by a citizen and broadcast widely, triggering calls for prosecution of the officers.

The newspaper editorial continued by quoting University of California at Berkeley ethnic studies professor Ronald Takaki, who called for people to look beyond their roots to find the commonalities that would enable them to bridge their racial and ethnic identities.

> I think people, especially in the post-Rodney King era, are beginning to realize that we just can't study ourselves as separate groups. . . . We've gone beyond the need to recover identity and roots, and now we're realizing that our paths as members of different groups are crisscrossing each other. ("Really, How Different Are We?" 1992, p. A10)

Calls to seek and find common ground continue as the nation struggles with unresolved issues of race and ethnicity at the beginning of the 21st century. They come at a time when more of the racial and ethnic groups that are often called "minorities" are becoming more numerous, assertive, and visible in the social fabric of the United States. At the same time, the growth of people of all colors is forcing the United States to look beyond its previous mindset of race relations as between Blacks and Whites or between colored minorities and a White majority. This soul searching increases as debates on racial and ethnic issues become more focused, sharper, and divisive.

Who Are the Minorities?

When it is used in its statistical sense, the term *minorities* refers to what is small in number, less than the majority. In the past, the term was often applied to people of color in the United States because the total number of Blacks, Latinos, Asian Pacific Americans, and Native Americans was smaller than the White majority. Over time, "minorities" became a convenient umbrella label under which any group that is not White could be placed.

However, it is a misleading label. It misleads those using and seeing the label into thinking of people called minorities as small not only in number but also in importance. In a democratic nation based on majority rule, such a label can make the interests and issues raised by "minorities" seem less important than those of the majority. What's more, the label increasingly is not statistically accurate when referring to the nation's racial and ethnic mix. In most large cities, and in states such as California and Hawaii, the people of color labeled "minorities" are actually more than half of the population when members of each group are added together. In those cities and states, Whites are a minority, along with Asian Pacific Americans, Blacks, Latinos, and Native Americans. Everyone is a member of a minority group, as there is no single majority.

The United States will continue to grow as a nation of minorities through the next generation. People of color already make up more than one third of the U.S. population and their representation will continue to grow at a faster rate than that of Whites until at least 2050, due to immigration, birthrate, and average family size. As these groups grow in number and percentage of the U.S. population, factors such as intermarriage between groups and generational, gender, and ethnic diversity within each group will make umbrella labels like Asian Pacific American, Black, Latino, and Native American less useful.

These changes continue an evolving racial and ethnic mix that has been part of the land that is now the United States since the arrival of the first European settlers in the early 1600s. It is a natural evolution and one that is more inclusive than the "Whites preferred" policies that earlier governed the nation.

"The region changed from predominantly Native American to predominantly White Anglo-Saxon Protestant (WASP) in large part due to high mortality on the part of the former and high immigration and fertility on the part of the latter group," wrote population analysts Leon F. Bouvier and Cary B. Davis. "In 1800 close to 20 percent of what, by then was the United States of America, was Black—in large part the result of high levels of immigration, albeit forced. By 1900, more significant changes had occurred. Blacks were only 10% of the population, but among Whites the proportion coming from Southern and Eastern Europe had grown substantially" (1982, pp. 1, 3).

As Bouvier and Davis pointed out, the influx of Southern and Eastern European immigrants challenged the nation's WASP (White Anglo Saxon Protestant) identity early in the 20th century. These European immigrants were greeted by hostility and prejudice from many Anglo Americans who were hostile to their homeland, language, culture, and religion. Since there were no racial differences between them and the Anglo Americans, they or their children tried to avoid continued discrimination by shedding their old country ways.

"A popular way of getting hold of the assimilation idea has been to use a metaphor, and by far the most popular metaphor has been that of the 'melting pot,' a term introduced in Israel Zangwill's 1908 play of that name," wrote Peter Salins. He quoted from Zangwill's play:

> There she lies, the great Melting-Pot—Listen! Can't you hear the roaring and the bubbling? . . . Ah, what a stirring and a seething! Celt and Latin, Slav and Teuton, Greek and Syrian, black and yellow . . . Jew and Gentile . . . East and West, and North and South, the palm and the pine, the pole and the equator, the crescent and the cross—how the great Alchemist melts and fuses them with his purifying flame! Here shall they all unite to build the Republic of Man and the Kingdom of God. (Zangwill, 1908, quoted in Salins, 1997)

Although Zangwill included "Latin . . . Syrian, black and yellow" in the melting pot, in practice the process of assimilation into American society was less inclusive of non-White people and some European groups such as Jews, Italians, and Irish, a point reinforced in Nathan Glazer and Daniel Patrick Moynihan's 1963 book *Beyond the Melting Pot*. Nevertheless, the melting pot became an idealized and popular way of describing the assimilation of European immigrants coming to the United States in the early 1900s.

With no major physical distinctions such as skin color or eye shape to separate them, many European immigrants looked for ways to cast aside the identities, cultures, and languages of home countries such as Germany, Poland, Ireland, or Sweden as they either adopted, or were forced to adopt, the loyalties, customs, and language of their new homeland. Some immigrants even changed their last names to appear more Anglo, such as from Cohen to Cowan, hoping it would help them more easily fit into American society and avoid future discrimination.

E PLURIBUS UNUM

Illustration 1.1   When most newcomers to the United States came from Europe, the immigrants were urged to shed their home country language and customs and "melt" into Anglo American society. The Melting Pot graduation ceremony of the Ford English School for immigrant automobile factory workers in Michigan in 1916 idealized this with a steamship background and symbolic melting pot.

Source: Henry Ford Museum and Greenfield Village.

The melting pot theory held that it was necessary to forget, or at least submerge, the language and customs of the homeland to be allowed to participate in the benefits of the United States. Assimilation became the price for participation in U.S. society.[2] It was thought that within a generation or so the children of European immigrants would have "melted" into the United States and would no longer be identifiable by their national origin or homeland.

The melting pot concept was so dominant that The Ford Motor Company in Michigan established the Ford English School in 1913. The goal of the school, which in 3 years had 2,200 students from 33 nationalities studying under 150 English-speaking Ford workers, was to teach the immigrants to read, write, and speak English. The graduation ceremony was staged in front of a huge symbolic melting pot under the Latin words printed on U.S. currency, "E Pluribus Unum" (From Many, One).

The website of the Henry Ford Museum and Greenfield Village in Dearborn, Michigan describes the ceremony as follows:

The commencement exercises for each graduating class included an elaborate ceremony in which each student entered a large cauldron (the "Ford English School Melting Pot") in his foreign "costume," carrying a sign indicating the country he had come from. Minutes later the graduates emerged from the melting pot dressed in "American clothes" and waving small American flags in their hands. Although the primary motivation for the English school was to break the language barriers in the factory to increase production efficiency, the ceremony clearly expressed the interest of the Company in "Americanizing" its foreign-born workers.

Today the melting pot's legacy is found among White Americans who know little of their family history, other than that their ancestors came from Germany, Sweden, Denmark, Poland, or some other European country or countries. Their forebears came to the United States with the hope that if they could set aside their mother country language and traditions, they could be accepted within a generation or two by the dominant White population they already resembled. While the descendents of those who blended into the melting pot may not be able to speak the language or share the customs of their European ancestors, they are increasingly curious about family roots, national heritage, and customs, particularly as political changes and ethnic strife have occurred in Europe.[3]

At the same time, people of color whose ancestors were "beyond the melting pot" are growing in the United States. Because of differences in race, legal status, or geographic proximity to the home country, they never fully blended, or were allowed to blend, into the U.S. melting pot. The people in these groups have experienced the United States not as a melting pot but as a salad bowl or stew pot. In a salad, all the ingredients are mixed together but maintain their separate identities and the flavor of one element does not blend with the flavors of others. In a stew, each element retains its identity and also contributes its own flavor to others while absorbing some of the flavors of the others onto itself. For many years, United States laws prohibiting mixed-race marriages, enforcing racial segregation, and severely restricting immigration from non-European countries strengthened the situation in this country that has often been analogized as a salad bowl. As these laws became history at the national level in the mid-1960s, race and ethnic relations in the United States had the opportunity to become more like a stew pot.

People of all races and ethnicities have participated in the process of contending with and contributing to race relations in the United States. This book focuses on the groups who have had the greatest visibility outside of the melting pot: Native Americans and Alaska Eskimos, Blacks, Asians and Pacific Islanders, and Latinos, also called Hispanics.

NO DOGS NEGROES MEXICANS

20 FEB. 1942

LONESTAR RESTAURANTS ASSN.
Dallas, Texas

Illustration 1.2   People of color were long subject to legal and social segregation that limited their educational, political, and social opportunities in the United States. This 1942 NO DOGS, NEGROES, MEXICANS sign attributed to the Lonestar Restaurant Association in Texas marked such segregation.

Population Projections

As a nation whose population growth has been fueled by immigration, the United States has always had racial, national, and ethnic minorities. But, as noted earlier, the White European immigrants who comprised most of the nation's immigrants for much of this nation's history were encouraged to follow the melting pot model of assimilation. The federal government long recognized, and even enforced, racial and gender distinctions among the nation's people. People whose racial or ethnic groups were not White have been counted separately since the first U.S. census of 1790. From the nation's beginning, they were considered separate and usually unequal to Whites.

The categories in America's first census in 1790 reflect the racial and gender priorities as the new nation began: free White males, age 16 and older; free White males, age 16 and younger; and free White females. Non-Whites were designated as "all other persons" and "slaves." Black slaves counted as three fifths of a White person for purposes of determining representation in Congress (Muschick, 2001a, 2001b). The 1790 census counted 757,000 Blacks, 92% of them living as slaves. They comprised nearly one fifth of the nation's population ("U.S. Population: Where We Are, Where We're Going," 1982). Native Americans were not included in 1790 census figures for Congressional representation because they were considered members of separate nations and thus not entitled to equal rights.

"MOVE ON!"
HAS THE NATIVE AMERICAN NO RIGHTS THAT THE NATURALIZED AMERICAN IS BOUND TO RESPECT?—[See Page 363.]

Illustration 1.3   Laws prohibiting Native Americans from voting at the same time that
immigrants, identified by their European attire, and newly freed Blacks
cast their votes were questioned by *Harper's Weekly* political cartoonist Thomas Nast in 1871. Women were not allowed to vote at that
time.

Building on those early U.S. census racial distinctions, the 2000 census
allowed people to designate their race as White, Asian, Pacific Islander,
Black, American Indian, or Alaska Native. They were asked whether they
were Hispanic, who can be of any race. For the first time they were also
able to mark more than one race, indicating a multiracial background, and
resulting in a possible 126 race and ethnicity combinations (Muschick,
2001a, 2001b).

Although they were counted separately for the first time in the 2000
census, Asians are often combined with Pacific Islanders, putting people
from such disparate nations as Japan, Vietnam, Indonesia, and the
Philippines under the same umbrella. By the same token, Native
Americans—called American Indians by some—are joined with Alaska
Natives, combining people who may appear similar to others but may have

Table 1.1   Population Percentages in the United States From 1970 to 2000

Group	1970	1980	1990	2000
White		83.1%	75.0%	69.1%
Black	11.7%	11.7%	12.1%	12.1%
American Indian/ Alaska Native	.4%	.6%	.7%	.7%
Asian/Pacific	.8%	1.5%	2.8%	3.6%
Other		3.0%	.1%	.3%
Two or More Races*				1.6%
Hispanic**	4.5%	6.4%	9.0%	12.3%

*New category in 2000.

**Can be of any race.

important differences. Hispanics, people who trace their roots to Spain, Latin America, or the Caribbean, can be of any race. The term *Hispanic* was not first used by the people it now describes—it was applied by a census bureau official who looked in the dictionary and decided it could be a useful umbrella category for people of Spanish or Latin American origin. Because the term is unfamiliar to some of the people it is supposed to describe, it can confuse some respondents trying to complete their census forms. It can be used interchangeably with the term *Latino*, which is the term often used in books dealing with Hispanics and the media. Even more important than the changes in terminology are the national trends and projections as the United States continues to become more racially and ethnically diverse.[4]

The census reported that people of color were more than 30% of the U.S. population in 2000, up from 25% just 10 years earlier.[5] As the percentage of non-Hispanic Whites in the United States continues to drop, the growth rates for other racial and ethnic minority continue to grow, a trend going back at least 30 years earlier to 1970. Blacks, American Indians or Alaska Natives, Asian or Pacific Islanders, Hispanics, and those who marked "Other" on the census form all grew in number or percentage of the population between 1990 and 2000. The only group that lost ground was Whites, declining from 75% to 69.1% of the people in the United States. People who indicated that they were more than one race, a category used for the first time in 2000, comprised 1.6% of the population. As people of color continue to increase their share of the national population, what has been called "the browning of America" will continue to transform the nation racially, ethnically, and culturally (Rodríguez, 1992, pp. 60-62).

As steep as this reported growth rate has been, it may be less than the actual growth rate of people of color in the United States. One reason for

H. G. "LET US CLASP HANDS OVER THE BLOODY CHASM."—[See Page 808.]
"A Great Victory has been won in Georgia. .... The verdict in Georgia is certainly conclusive."—*New York Tribune*, October 3, 1872

Illustration 1.4   In some elections, White mobs kept Blacks from the voting, as illustrated by *Harper's Weekly* political cartoonist Thomas Nast's drawing of violence at Atlanta, Georgia polling places during the 1872 presidential election.

this is that the Census Bureau, as they themselves admit, undercounted the nation's people of color for decades.

The Census Bureau announced in 2001 that the undercount rate was lower in 2000 than it was in 1990. Still, a higher percentage of people of color were uncounted than were Whites, who the acting director of the census said may have been overcounted (Elliott & Mason, 2001, p. A29). In 2001, the Census Bureau reported that it missed 2.17% of the Non-Hispanic Blacks, 2.85% of the Hispanics, 4.74% of the American Indians and Alaska Natives on Reservations, 3.28% of the American Indians and Alaska Natives off Reservations, and 4.60% of the Native Hawaiians and other Pacific Islanders (Evans, 2001), all a higher percentage not counted than the national undercount rate of 1.2%, or the approximately 3.2 million people the census failed to count (Elliott & Mason, 2001, p. A29). Despite the admitted undercount of people of color, the Census Bureau has refused to adjust its population figures to more accurately reflect the number of people in the United States and their racial and ethnic mix.

Adding to the census controversies, some people have claimed that the Census Bureau's race, ethnicity, or national origin categories caused their groups to be undercounted. Some Hispanic groups noted that while Mexicans, Puerto Ricans, and Cubans had their own boxes to check, people with roots in other countries were asked to check the "other Spanish/Hispanic/Latino" box and then write in the name of their group. This confused some, especially those whose first language is not English. In addition to having difficulty understanding the language, those asked to write in their group often didn't know the appropriate Census Bureau terms and thus were not correctly counted, a criticism raised by Dominicans, Colombians, Assyrians, Chaldeans, Arabs, and Afghans.

"I've checked 'White' all my life," Dearborn attorney Ziad A. Fadel told *The Detroit News*. "There is no category for who I am," said Fadel, an Arab American (Trowbridge, 2001, p. 1). In California, the San Francisco Bay Area Afghan American community, estimated at between 30,000 and 60,000 people, was reported by the Census Bureau as numbering only 7,000, one sixth of its estimated size. Sohaila Hashimi, an Afghan American living in San Jose, said, "It's going to be a problem for us. Numbers count in order to be effective and to stand up for a statement or a view" (Chang, 2001, p. A1).

Further complicating the task of gathering the racial and ethnic identity figures is the increasing number of mixed-race marriages in the United States. The number of racially mixed marriages, which were once illegal, has been reported as 10 times higher in 2001 than it was in 1960. According to a 2001 Census Bureau report, about 5% of all marriages in the United States are between individuals of different races. Hispanics and Asians are likely to marry someone of a different group at a rate three times that of Blacks and five times that of Whites. There are also gender differences within the groups. Asian women and Black men are more than twice as likely to marry into other groups as are Asian men and Black women (Pugh, 2001, p. A12). The biracial children of these marriages will make the nation's diversity even richer in the future. Even with the short-comings of the census count and increasing racial and ethnic blending, it is clear that the growth rate of Blacks, Asian Pacific Americans, Native Americans, and Latinos has moved steadily upward over the past three decades. There have been many causes cited for the steady "browning of America." One oft-cited reason is that most racial and ethnic minority groups have a younger median age than do Whites and, thus, are more likely to be heading toward or within the childbearing years. Their children are also likely to have their own children and families as they grow up in the foreseeable future.

Another reason given for the steady growth of the non-White population in the United States has been increased immigration from Asia and Latin America, largely due to a 1965 immigration act that removed national preferences for people from certain European nations and put immigrants from all countries on a more equitable level for the first time since Congress passed the Chinese Exclusion Act in 1882. As a result of the

Illustration 1.5   This 1871 *Harper's Weekly* drawing by political cartoonist Thomas
Nast shows a White mob moving from burning a Colored Orphan
Asylum to attacking a Chinese immigrant who seeks protection from
Columbia (a United States symbol) alongside a wall of anti-Chinese
slogans. Eleven years later, the U.S. enacted the Chinese Exclusion
Act, versions of which were in force until 1943.

earlier legislation, Europe supplied large numbers of immigrants to the United States. But following the 1965 law, immigration to the United States from Asia and Latin America increased sharply. Another factor accounting for the growth of such populations in the United States is the warfare and political turmoil in certain countries in those regions, from which people have fled to this country. Other immigrants have been driven to emigrate to the United States by the desire to improve their economic status.

Whatever the reason, the United States continues to be the land of opportunity for these new residents, just as it had been earlier for the Europeans who emigrated to this country. The Population Research Bureau reported that between 1977 and 1979 immigrants from Latin America and Asia constituted, respectively, 42% and 39% of the immigrants admitted to the United States, accounting for 81% of the immigrants. Immigrants from Europe accounted for only 13% of those who emigrated to the United States in that period. In contrast, between 1931 and 1960 Europeans comprised 58% of the immigrants, and Latin Americans and Asians comprised, respectively, 15% and 5% of the immigrants (Bouvier & Davis, 1982, p. 2). The increased immigration from Asia and Latin America continued in the 1980s and 1990s. Although the number of European immigrants grew from 1981 to 1990 and 1991 to 1998, more immigrants came to the United States from Asia and the Americas than from Europe. The number of people who emigrated to the United States from Africa also increased (U.S. Census Bureau, 2001a, p. 11). An immigration law that took effect in 1990 spurred some of this growth.

Another factor spurring the racial and ethnic diversity of the United States has been the difference in the number of children born to White and non-White parents. Blacks, Native Americans, and Asian Pacific Americans all had a higher birth rate than that of Whites through the 1980s and 1990s. In 2001, the Census Bureau projected that those groups and Hispanics would have higher birth rates than Whites through 2010 (U.S. Census Bureau, 2001c, p. 60; 2001d, p. 62). In the past, the Census Bureau assumed that the childbearing rates for all racial and ethnic groups would eventually be the same and that there would be a steady decline in the number of children each woman would bear. However, noting "a dramatic rise in total fertility levels to almost 2.1 births per woman" and finding no historical evidence to support the assumption that childbearing rates would become equal, the Census Bureau abandoned both positions in 1992 (Pear, 1992, pp. A1, D18).

Analysts of population trends have cited other possible causes for the diversity population boom. These include a possible increase in the number of persons designating themselves as members of racial and ethnic groups, a change in the categories used on census forms, and stepped up Census Bureau efforts to accurately count the members of the various groups. Whatever the reason, the bottom line is clear. The number of

PUNCH, OR THE LONDON CHARIVARI.—MAY 26, 1920.

HIS OWN BUSINESS.

UNCLE SAM. "IF I WEREN'T SO PREOCCUPIED WITH IRELAND I MIGHT BE TEMPTED TO GIVE MYSELF A MANDATE FOR THIS."

Illustration 1.6   United States intervention in the affairs of Latin American and Caribbean nations has long been accompanied by people moving to the U.S. from that region. This 1920 political cartoon in the British magazine *Punch* shows Uncle Sam pondering whether to once again intervene as he watches a Mexican revolutionary.

people of color has increased at a substantially higher rate than has the White population. As a result, they comprise a larger percentage of the U.S. population than ever before. Even more important are the projections for the future.

THE IMPACT OF A GROWING
RACIALLY DIVERSE POPULATION

The population of people of color will continue to grow both in actual numbers and as a percentage of the United States population for the fore-seeable future. The projected growth rate of this population and its rela-tionship to the White population's trends are a matter of debate among demographers. But, while they may argue over the slope of the ascending racial diversity growth rate curve, all the demographers agree about its upward direction.

The Census Bureau has long projected a much more racially and ethni-cally rich population by the middle of the 21st century, with people of color making up about half of the population by 2050 (Udansky, 1992, p. 1A). In 2001, Census Bureau projections for 2050 foresaw the non-Hispanic White population dropping to 52.8% of the total population, with the remainder being 24.3% Hispanic, 13.2% Black, 8.9% Asian or Pacific Islander, and 8% American Indian and Eskimo. Census demogra-phers predicted that either Asians or Pacific Islanders would have the steepest growth rate, averaging just under 30% in each decade between 2010 and 2050. The growth rates of the Hispanic population in each decade was projected at just over 25%. The Black, Native American, and Eskimo populations were projected to grow about 10% in each decade. The growth rate for the White population was predicted to be around 2.5% in each decade (U.S. Census Bureau, 2001b, p. 17).

The projected continuation of these trends promises to alter dramati-cally the racial and cultural mix of the United States in the 21st century. But the "new" America should not come as any surprise. Signs of the changes, as well as spirited debate over and discussion of their implica-tions, moved the issues of race and ethnicity into the headlines long before the United States entered the 21st century.

The Racial and Cultural Mix: From
Melting Pot to Minorities to Multiculturalism

The racial and cultural trends making the new and more colorful America made front page headlines when they were released by the Census Bureau, but they had been foreseen for some time and were not news to those tracking the nation's changing racial and ethnic makeup. Two decades earlier, the independent Population Reference Bureau reported roughly the same trends, with only slightly different dates and population numbers. In 1982, Leon Bouvier and Cary Davis commented on what these changes would mean for the United States.

> There are those who would prefer a "status quo" society. That is to say a continuation of the present racial and ethnic composition under an Anglo-conformity umbrella. There are those who see the future demographic changes as marking the onset of a new phase in the ever changing American society—a "multi-cultural" society. In the late 19th century and early 20th century the United States successfully changed identity from WASP to multi-ethnic culture within the White community. In the late 20th and early 21st century, it may once again change towards being the first truly multi-racial society on the planet earth, a multi-cultural society which while still predominantly English speaking would tolerate and even accept other languages and other cultures. (p. 57)

The projected changes have already caused some rethinking among those who had become accustomed to the "melting pot" model of assimilation in the United States. The rise of multiculturalism has raised sharp national and local debates over the issues of race, ethnicity, and culture that had long concerned members of racial and ethnic minority groups and has forced others to reassess their vision of the United States.

In the early 1980s, some demographers saw the nation developing as a "confederation of minorities" from different groups, each demanding to be counted by the census and demanding the attention required to address their needs or redress discrimination against them. Others sounded a more optimistic note, arguing that values long seen as "traditional American values" were also part of the value structure of the nation's newest immigrants, particularly Asians and Latinos. These included a strong work ethic and close family relationships of mutual support. Today's immigrants are able to maintain close ties with the ways of their home country, but they also want to be full participants in the United States.

The debates over the impact of the new America's racial and cultural mix have sharpened during the early 21st century, particularly in education. Universities, colleges, and school systems are debating the best ways to educate students and prepare them for a multicultural world. One important debate centers on whether college admissions officers should place so much emphasis on scores on standardized admissions tests such as the SAT and ACT when evaluating potential students who come from homes where more than one language is spoken, were born in another country, and/or have attended schools that do not focus on preparing students for college. These applicants may have out-of-classroom educational attributes not measured by these tests, such as workplace experience, bilingual language expertise, and familiarity with other cultures. As the nation's school-age population has grown more racially and ethnically diverse, the number of people who are members of groups that have not been prepared for college in the traditional manner has increased. There has also been an increase in the number of legal fights over affirmative action and other educational opportunity programs that have opened the doors to college to members of underrepresented groups by considering a wider range of admissions criteria. In 2003, the United States Supreme Court declared unconstitutional the University of Michigan's practice of awarding additional points to applicants who were members of underrepresented racial groups but said race should still be an admissions consideration.

Along with the admissions issues, educators are discussing the best ways to prepare all students to live and work in a multicultural nation. One group argues for the traditional, Anglocentric approach, contending that other cultures are less important in the United States and, to succeed in this country, everyone should learn the dominant system. A second group recognizes the need for multicultural curricula and supports it, as long as the traditions and influence of England and Europe are acknowledged as having shaped the United States. A third group argues for multicultural curricula, recognizing the contributions of all the groups to the United States and affording special attention to the advances of groups that had traditionally been underrepresented. A fourth group calls for educating students in the learning styles and content of people of their own race and culture, such as in an Afrocentric approach to education.

These debates raise the importance of cultural identity as a part of racial and ethnic identity. The issues of language, food, lifestyle, and values become more important as people of all races reclaim or reinforce the cultural elements of their lives while participating in American society—and in so doing, counter the melting pot ideology. And, as intermarriage continues to become more prevalent, it is clear that exclusive racial categories will be less applicable to future generations of Americans.

Growing Racial and Ethnic Diversity: An International Phenomenon

The United States is not the only country with a substantial and growing racial and ethnic minority diversity. Nor is it the only one that has recently experienced racial and ethnic turmoil. During the late 1980s through the early 21st century, racial, cultural, and religious conflicts between groups tore apart nations on all continents. The contests ranged from disputes that had long had international attention—such as disputes between Jews and Muslims in the Middle East, Catholics and Protestants in Northern Ireland, and Hindus and Christians in India—to smoldering conflicts that flared up after political changes—such as battles between Serbs, Slovenes, and Muslims in what had once been Yugoslavia. Conflicts suddenly flared between groups that had long contended for the same territory—such as between Pakistan and India, who both claimed Kashmir—and new immigration inflamed passions—such as those expressed in demonstrations for and against immigrant workers coming to England, France, Germany, and other European nations from Africa, Asia, and the Middle East. Such racial and ethnic conflicts are part of the continuing contentiousness between groups that has characterized most of the world's history.

Like the United States, most nations have different religious, ethnic, cultural, or racial minority groups within their boundaries. The treatment of the members of those groups varies from nation to nation, depending on the political, religious, and economic systems of the country, as well as on the historical relationship between the dominant and subordinate groups. For instance, in most colonial situations in which one country conquers or colonizes the people of another land, rigid social separations are established based on nationality, class, and race. England, the country to which many U.S. political and social institutions are most linked, colonized much of North America, parts of Africa, Oceania, and Asia. The British colonial system maintained strict lines of distinction between the predominantly White Anglo colonizers and the people of "colour" whose territory they came to occupy.

"The British colonial code draws the most rigid color line of all," wrote Raymond Kennedy in 1945 (p. 320), when Britain still maintained much of its colonial empire. "The British have been in contact for a longer time with more dark peoples than any other western nation, yet they hold aloof from their subjects to an unequalled degree. They refuse to associate freely or make friends with other races, and their exclusiveness had engendered a reciprocal feeling toward them on the part of their colonial peoples" (quoted in Marden & Meyer, 1978, p. 5).[6]

In England and elsewhere, literature, children's stories, movies, news coverage, and other media during the era of the British Empire reinforced images of English colonizers bringing civilization to the uncivilized people they colonized prior to the United States picking up "the White man's burden" in the "third world" towards the end of the 19th century.

Stereotypes in the British media of people of color and discrimination against them outlasted the British Empire, upon which it once seemed the sun would never set. One of the British Broadcasting Company's most popular television programs from 1958 to 1978 was *The Black and White Minstrel Show*, which featured White entertainers in blackface. The program was set in "the Deep South where coy White women could be seen

"THE WHITE MAN'S BURDEN"

Illustration 1.7   During the era of the 1898 Spanish-American War, the United States'
Uncle Sam was pictured in *Judge* as following Great Britain's John Bull
in picking up "The White Man's Burden" by carrying Cubans and other
dark-skinned people up from oppression, barbarism, and ignorance to
civilization.

being wooed by docile, smiling black slaves. The black men were, in fact,
White artists 'Blacked-up,'" wrote British media scholar Sarita Malik. She
noted that the "racist implications of the premise of the programme" were
what "led to the programme's eventual demise" (Malik, 2001).

At the beginning of the 21st century, the media legacies of the British
Empire's images of people of color are still an issue for journalists and
media scholars in England and in other lands that are still part of the
British Commonwealth, such as Australia (Jakubowicz, 1994; Meadows,
2001). A mid-1990s study found only 12 to 20 Black journalists among the
3,000 workers on Britain's national newspapers. A 1998 industry-wide
study found only 2% Arab, Asian, and Black journalists in England, a
nation that is 5.26% people of color. Studies such as these led to charges
that England's news media were "blind to Blacks" and reports that "Black
and Asian faces are rare among Britain's 'news breed', the journalists who
gather and process the nation's news" ("What Colour Is the News?" n.d.).

Spain colonized most of the Caribbean and Latin America, including
what is now the United States from Florida to California and as far north
as Wyoming. In the Spanish and Portuguese colonies of Latin America, the

Europeans imposed racial classifications on the indigenous people who survived the conquest and colonial missions and their mixed race children. Throughout the Americas, the European invaders took over the land and forced the indigenous people to work their ancestral lands as slaves or peons in colonies or imported African slaves to do the hard labor. There were class distinctions between Europeans and native Indians and also elaborate classification systems to label mixed-race offspring.

Mixed racial populations emerged in Mexico and other places where the Spanish blended with native populations to bear children called "mestizos." In contrast to English colonists, who labeled the offspring of a White parent and an indigenous parent "half breeds," the term "mestizo" indicates a mixing and blending of races and cultures. In Brazil and the Caribbean, Spanish and native people mixed with Black slaves brought from Africa to form "mulattos."

Colonialism in Asia and Southeast Asia was shared by several European nations, including Britain, France, the Netherlands, Portugal, and Spain, and each nation had its own policy toward indigenous residents. Like the Portuguese in Brazil, some colonizing nations brought in laborers from other areas (e.g., natives of India to Burma and Malaysians and Chinese to most of Southeast Asia). These colonized areas became stratified on three levels: the Europeans, the immigrant workers, and the natives (Marden & Meyer, 1978, pp. 6-7).

In the African, Asian, and American colonies of European nations, the relationship between the minorities and the majority was the opposite of what racial minorities have experienced in the United States. In the colonial situation, the numerical minority groups were the European colonizers, who conquered and then governed the native people who outnumbered them. In this case, the term *minority* could be applied to the Europeans who, though smaller in number, exerted military, political, economic, and social control over the indigenous people. Thus, while Europeans were a minority in numerical terms, they wielded a majority of the power. A legacy of this relationship, and of the fight of indigenous people to regain their rights, can still be seen (1) in the relationship of Whites over Blacks in South Africa, where Nelson Mandela, the first Black to head the government, was not elected until 1994; (2) in Hong Kong, which was not transferred from British to Chinese rule until 1997; and (3) in Macau, which was held by Portugal until 1998.

The legacy of colonialism and distinctions based on race are still found throughout the world. As Charles Marden and Gladys Meyer (1978) point out, nations as diverse in political and economic structure as South Africa, Israel, and the People's Republic of China have substantial divisions based on ethnic and racial divisions between dominant and subordinate groups (pp. 10-15). The heated conflicts between Blacks and Whites in South Africa and between Jews and Palestinians in Israel and the Middle East have been widely reported. Less well known is what Marden and Meyer call "the virtual destruction of small tribal people in Asiatic Russia" (p. 14) and the annexation of Tibetan people by the People's Republic of China in the late 1940s.

Except for Native Americans, who were subjected to colonization by the Spanish and to extermination by the English, minority groups in the United States have followed patterns that are different from those of other nations. This is because the predominantly White Europeans who were to dominate the country were themselves immigrants who became the numerical majority. Rather than exert their control only through a rigid class system, they exterminated or confined the Native Americans; waged war to take lands held by Native Americans and Mexicans; imported and restricted the rights of Blacks, Asians, Pacific Islanders, and Latinos; and encouraged more Europeans to come, settle, and develop a new society of White immigrants in the United States.

Between 1820 and 1970, about 45 million immigrants entered the United States, 75% from European nations (Marden & Meyer, 1978, pp. 63-64). It is these immigrants, their children, and their grandchildren who consolidated their identity through the melting pot and became the new majority in the United States, leaving people of color to be designated as racial and ethnic minorities. Except for Native Americans, they were all immigrants or descendants of immigrants in a new land. But some immigrants were more equal than others.

The Future of the Multicultural United States

In the United States, when the terms *majority* and *minority* are used in a racial context they usually refer to White Europeans as the majority and people of color as minorities. These have long represented both power and numerical relationships in which the White majority both outnumbered and dominated the more racially and ethnically diverse minority groups. As a result, the word *minorities* became an umbrella term covering any group in the United States that was not seen as White.

But the term, though widely used by people of all races, masks the more complex distinctions between the dominant and subordinate groups and the diversity within and between groups bunched under the "minority" umbrella. It also distorts the reality of the racial situation in the United States and in the world. Use of the term has made it appear that racially diverse non-White people are a minority in the world's population when, as a group, they far outnumber Whites. Thus, people who may have felt that they were permanent minorities in the United States and elsewhere were, in fact, a much more substantial part of the population worldwide.

In addition, the term *minority* no longer accurately describes the situation in many urban areas of the nation. By the early 1990s, "minorities" were actually the majority of the population in 55 of the nation's largest cities. In 1991, New York City Mayor David Dinkins told a convention of

Illustration 1.8   As the 19th century ended, *Puck* showed United States' Uncle Sam trying to teach a class of unruly dark-skinned Filipinos, Hawaiians, Puerto Ricans, and Cubans in the front row, with well-behaved and neatly groomed European immigrants behind them. While one dark-skinned girl reads at her desk, a Black janitor washes the windows, a Native American reads a book upside down by the door, and a Black girl hopefully looks in from outside the classroom.

the National Association of Hispanic Journalists that New York is "a city in which no group can claim to be the majority." California and Hawaii are both states that have no single racial or ethnic majority: All the people are members of a racial or ethnic minority group.

But even if the term *minority* did accurately describe the numerical relationship of non-Whites to Whites, the term would still cause unnecessary problems. The umbrella term minority may be useful in adding focus and emphasis to the issues that have separated people of color from White Americans, such as differences in income, education, and employment. However, it also groups people together who have their own diversity as discrete groups. There are as many differences within each of these groups and between the different groups as there are between these groups and Whites.

Rather than portraying race relations in the United States in terms of a majority and minorities, or dominant and subordinate groups, it is probably more accurate to avoid umbrella labels and speak in terms of racial and ethnic diversity. A focus on racial diversity signifies a nation with a variety of races and ethnicities, each one with similarities and dissimilarities within itself and with other groups in a multicultural society. Rather than masking differences between and within different racial groups designated as majority or minorities, the terms *diversity* and *multiculturalism* describe a society of different and diverse races. This is a more accurate description of the United States in the 21st century.

THE GROWING DIVERSITY: MORE POWER OR MORE PROBLEMS?

Growing racial and ethnic diversity will characterize the nation's population through the foreseeable future. The census and projected growth figures clearly show where the United States is headed. How the media and other institutions react to these demographic changes will, to a large extent, determine whether the United States is still considered the land of opportunity. Although some leaders of organizations representing people of color act as though "more will be better," it is not certain that the people of different races will not continue to suffer the same discrimination that Blacks, Latinos, Native Americans, and Asian Pacific Americans have long faced in the United States as they sought equal access to education, employment, housing, and other rights. More people of color does not automatically translate into more power for these groups. But it does translate into more people facing the problems that have long confronted these groups. For these groups, discrimination continues to be a problem that stands in the way of opportunity. More diversity may mean more people left behind.

At the same time, the growing racial and ethnic diversity is described as either a problem or an opportunity by the rest of American society. Unlike earlier immigrants, today's newcomers are able to maintain close ties with their homeland through telephone calls, e-mail, news broadcasts, entertainment programs, and air travel. They don't necessarily leave their culture, customs, and language behind—they may bring it all with them, in addition to finding expressions of their old in their new land. This increasing diversity of the American people forces changes on schools, government agencies, and businesses that have become used to conducting their affairs in a certain way. Now, as people come to the United States speaking different languages, as well as following different religious practices and bringing different cultural traditions, these institutions must respond. While some may view these changes as a problem, others view them as an opportunity to serve new students and consumers. Whatever the reaction, the trend is unmistakable. The question is how people will adapt to a society in which everyone may be in a minority group.

The answer probably lies in changing the dialogue on race and ethnicity from a focus on sociology to a focus on psychology. Until the early 21st century, our understanding of race and ethnicity in the United States was dominated by the field of sociology, with its numbers, demographics, and statistical analyses of the different groups. In the next era, the discussion should focus more on psychology. While the numbers create a context for the discussion, the importance of these data will be known only as people make individual decisions regarding their attitudes and behavior amid a growing diversity of choices. With more people like them than ever before, will individuals stick with their own group? Will they interact with members of other groups, who are also more numerous than before? Will they inter-marry? Will they learn to appreciate new kinds of music, food, and cultures? How will the media prepare people for the changing society, and how will people use the media that are targeted to them and to other groups?

Are the Media Maximizing the Opportunity Created by the Increasing Racial and Ethnic Diversity?

The growth of racial diversity in the United States has forced the American media to reexamine the ways in which they have traditionally dealt with people of color. As these groups have grown at a rate that outstrips the White population, media executives have looked for new ways to deal with them.

Too often, this growth in population diversity has been portrayed as a *problem* for the media and other institutions, forcing them to change their methods of doing business and making them find ways to reach groups that tenaciously hang on to their cultural roots in a nation in which other immigrants have shed theirs. The groups' differences in language, culture, religion, and lifestyle have been seen as a threat to Anglo American values.

Some media organizations, while professing concern over the changing population, have consciously adopted strategies to avoid dealing with people of color as they moved into the nation's cities. These media moved from building audiences based on *geography*, focusing on the readers, viewers, and listeners who live or work nearest the media outlet, to build-ing audiences based on *demography*, focusing on readers, viewers, and lis-teners who fit a desired age, education, income, racial, or gender profile, even if they lived far away from the major city. This change initially involved general audience media efforts to avoid or bypass growing num-bers of people of color; however, in the long run it has led to more media targeted to people of color.

In the 1970s and 1980s, as inner cities were becoming more racially and ethnically diverse, some big-city newspapers decided to chase suburbanites and to avoid the potential readers in their own central city neighborhoods. Newspaper circulation strategies made it difficult, if not impossible, for residents of ghettos and barrios to subscribe to the papers. Some metropolitan newspapers avoided putting newsstands in inner city areas. At the same time, they launched or expanded editions in the suburbs for the predominately White people in the suburbs. Such strategies were defended as being based on economics, in that low-income Blacks and Latinos were undesirable newspaper readers. Mainstream advertisers, some publishers argued, wanted affluent readers who could afford the products they advertised. Denying any racist intentions, the newspaper managers said that they were merely following more affluent readers to the suburbs.

The strategies used by newspapers to avoid inner city readers and coverage were described by Ben Bagdikian in 1978. He quoted a 1976 memo by an editor of the *Detroit News* ordering staffers to aim their newspaper stories at people who made good salaries and were between the ages of 28 and 40. Such stories, the editor wrote, "'should be obvious: they won't have a damn thing to do with Detroit and its internal problems'" (Bagdikian, 1978, p. 64). Bagdikian continued, "The blackout of news to the central city is usually justified by publishers on grounds that it is harder to sell papers there, that it is harder to hire and keep delivery people on the job and there is a higher rate of nonpayment of bills. That is true, and it has always been true. The difference now is that advertisers don't want that population so now the publishers don't either" (p. 66).

Because advertisers wanted affluent readers, newspapers and broadcast media targeted their content to audiences in the more affluent, and predominately Anglo, suburban areas. Circulation percentages and actual numbers declined in the cities whose names the newspapers proudly wore on their front pages and broadcast stations claimed as their cities of license. Broadcasters, while they could not control who watched or listened to their stations and bore no additional costs for having low-income people tuned into their broadcasts, still tried to target news and entertainment programming to more affluent viewers and listeners. The American Broadcasting Company issued a demographic analysis of its audience in the 1970s titled "Some People Are More Valuable Than Others."

This mentality has apparently continued into the 21st century. In 2002, *San Francisco Chronicle* television critic Tim Goodman wrote a front-page article headlined "Un-reality TV: Few Minority Actors in S.F. Shows," noting the absence of non-White lead characters in the growing number of television programs based in San Francisco, one of the nation's most racially diverse cities (Goodman, 2002, p. A1). After a year-long study of television news practices, in 2001 longtime network news executive Av Westin reported his "project's most sobering discovery: Every week—everyday—stories about African Americans, Hispanics, and Asians are kept off the air . . . I feel confident in declaring that racism is alive and well in many television newsrooms around the country" (Westin, 2001). As in the 1970s, Westin cited broadcaster desires to achieve certain viewer demographics as driving race-based news decisions. One former news executive told him, "[Blacks] don't get the demo" (Westin, 2001).

These strategies continued the line of thinking of earlier media executives. In 1978, *Los Angeles Times* publisher Otis Chandler admitted in a television interview that the paper had "a way to go" in adequately covering Los Angeles's communities of color. However, he added that it "would not make sense financially for us" to direct the newspaper to those readers because "that audience does not have the purchasing power and is not responsive to the kind of advertising we carry." Chandler added, "so we could make the editorial commitment, the management commitment, to cover these communities, but then how do we get them to read the *Times?* It's not their kind of newspaper: it's too big, it's too stuffy. If you will, it's too complicated" (Gutiérrez & Wilson, 1979, p. 53).

In 1979, two of the authors of this book (Clint Wilson and Félix Gutiérrez) published an article in the *Columbia Journalism Review* in which Chandler and other *Times's* executives denied the newspaper approached coverage and circulation from a racial standpoint, although one did admit their strategies meant that the newspaper was directed at a predominately Anglo audience. John Mount of the *Times's* marketing research department said, "'We don't approach marketing from a racial standpoint. It just happens that the more affluent and educated people tend to be White and live in suburban communities.'" Chandler said that the *Times's* major retail advertisers had said to them, "'We want a certain class of audience, a certain demographic profile of reader, whether that person be Black, White, or Brown or Chinese or whatever. We don't really care what sex or race they are. But we do care about their income.'" He was confident that more minorities would read the *Times* "as their income goes up and their educational level comes up and they become interested in a paper like the *Times*. Then they become prospects for our advertisers" (Gutiérrez & Wilson, 1979, p. 53).

As Chandler and his paper were sitting back and waiting for these more affluent minorities to come to them, Los Angeles, and indeed all of Southern California, was growing into one of the nation's most racially and ethnically diverse regions. And the *Times* circulation, whether measured by the numbers of readers or the percentage of Southern Californians who read the paper, did not keep pace with this population growth. Rather than sit back and wait for richer and better educated people of color to "become interested in a newspaper like the *Times*," the newspaper's ownership and management recognized that they would have to compete for readers against strong regional newspapers, broadcast news, and the growing ethnic media. In 1990, the newspaper's parent corporation bought half of *La Opinión,* a Spanish-language daily newspaper. The newspaper experimented with a Spanish-language weekly and other targeted newspapers in the early 1990s and also launched a highly regarded "Latino initiative" to improve coverage of Latinos in all sections of the newspaper in the late 1990s. Other ventures to build circulation included codistributing the *Los Angeles Times* with Chinese, Japanese, and Spanish-language newspapers. Not all of these were successful, and by the beginning of the 21st century, as other print, broadcast, and online media competed for audiences, the *Los Angeles Times* was looking for more ways to keep pace as Southern California continued to grow.

The lesson the *Los Angeles Times* and other media learned is that the development of a racially and ethnically diverse population is not a *problem* for the media but an *opportunity*. Instead of trying to bypass non-White readers and coverage, news organizations that made the greatest gains are those that have seen the growing racial diversity as an opportunity rather than a problem. Some general audience media, such as English-language daily newspapers and television news programs, had a hard time learning that if they wanted more people to pay attention to them, they had to pay better attention to the people.

The media coverage of people of color has often focused inordinate attention on the more bizarre or unusual elements of minority communities, such as youth gangs, illegal immigration, and interracial violence. While these are all legitimate topics, the emphasis on such coverage and the near absence of other news stories or dramatic themes involving minorities resulted in a new stereotype of racial minorities as *problem people*; that is, as groups either beset by problems or causing them for the larger society. Thus, the tendency of the media managers to see minorities as a problem has often been reinforced by the coverage and dramatic portrayals that people of color have been allowed by the media.

There have been other difficulties for those who approach minorities as a problem. A problem needs to be solved, and once it is solved it can be set aside. In the late 1970s and early 1980s, hiring minority reporters or staffers became the quick solution to what was seen as the minority problem. Once a minority reporter or actor was hired, the minority problem was seen as solved. If the reporter did not work out or was hired away, the problem reappeared.

Problems also often beg for single solutions; perhaps this is a throwback to our training in mathematics, in which each math problem has only one solution. Thus, if hiring minorities was seen as the solution to the minority problem, more hiring of minorities would add more solutions if the problem resurfaced. Editors often looked simplistically at changes in coverage to try to find out what the Black, or Asian Pacific American, or Latino, or Native American community "wanted" from the media. Some experimented with Spanish or Asian-language simulcasts of news programs, others inserted special sections geared for minority communities on a regular basis, still others did extensive special reports on the different

Illustration 1.9   As the nation's racial and language mix has become more diverse, so have some newspaper's circulation strategies. This 2002 advertisement shows a cooperative newsstand offering both the *Los Angeles Times* and *Chinese Daily News*. The *Times* has also tried joint ventures with the Spanish-language *La Opinión* and Japanese-language *Rafu Shimpo*.

minority communities in their circulation or broadcast areas. Not all of these efforts were successful in gaining increased readers, viewers, or acceptance by the communities of color. And, as a result, some media managers became discouraged from trying other approaches.

Finally, a problem is, by definition, an obstacle, an obstruction, a puzzle that stands in the way of someone's progress. It is something that must be overcome, surpassed, or eradicated so that the forward movement can continue. Thus, when media managers defined growing diversity as a problem, their approaches, however well intentioned or creative, were geared to overcoming or changing something that was seen as an obstacle. Instead of looking for ways to capitalize on the new opportunities presented by the changing population, media managers tried to overcome the problem of that population because it was seen as a threat to "business as usual."

More recently, some media corporations, spurred by pressure groups, competition from ethnic media, their own employees of color, or even a growing social consciousness, have come to see the growing population diversity as an opportunity rather than a problem. Rather than trying just to overcome a hurdle and put the obstacle behind them, they recognize that the United States is growing as a racially and ethnically diverse nation and that the changing racial demographics are an opportunity for them to gain new audiences and readers. It is this attitude, coupled with the growing racial and ethnic diversity of the nation, which presages the greatest progress for diversity in the media.

As census reports and other data indicate, the current and projected growth of non-White groups in the United States ensure that the nation will be less racially and ethnically homogeneous in the future than it has been in the past. This growth of racial diversity in a land that has largely been populated by immigrants will continue to create new opportunities in a nation that prides itself on being "the land of opportunity." At the same time, as a more racially diverse population challenges the commonly held melting pot theory that once characterized thinking in this country, there will be new stresses and strains.

The media of the United States bear a special responsibility in these circumstances; the media help educate older residents about newcomers. The media also penetrate the homes of all the members of the population and assist everyone by defining the society to newcomers and to others beyond the melting pot. In the past, the media have chosen either to ignore racially diverse populations or to treat them in a manner not equal to their treatment of the White population. However, the growth of the Latino, Native American, Asian Pacific American, and Black populations throughout the country, particularly in urban areas, has forced the media to abandon this reaction and to adopt new strategies. As the media move beyond tokenism in hiring and content, they grapple with ways to reach

Illustration 1.10 Unlike earlier newcomers to the United States, immigrants in the 21st century are able to stay in close touch with home country news, relatives, and friends through use of new communication technologies and media, as illustrated by these pictures taken in New York City and Oakland, California.

audiences, cover news, and provide entertainment programming to a diverse society.

Those media that choose to ignore the clearly marked trends will have an increasingly difficult time in capturing a fair share of the audience in areas where non-White groups comprise a substantial and growing portion of the population. The media that do successfully penetrate those audiences will be the media with the greatest chances for success in the future.

Notes

1. For a sociohistorical analysis of initial race and ethnic relations in California from 1850 to 1900, see *Racial Fault Lines: The Historical Origins of White Supremacy in California,* by T. Almaguer, 1994, Berkeley: University of California Press.

2. For an analysis of this phenomenon, see *Assimilation in American Life,* by M. Gordon, 1964, New York: Oxford University Press.

3. For more information, see *Ethnic Options: Choosing Identities in America,* by M. Waters, 1990, Berkeley: University of California Press.

4. For data describing, comparing, and projecting different racial and ethnic groups in the United States to 2007, see the article by A. S. Wellner in the November 2002 supplement of *American Demographics* titled "Diversity in America."

5. For charts and tables based on the 2000 census and other federal data, see *Statistical Abstract of the United States: 2001,* by the U.S. Census Bureau, Washington, DC: Author.

6. For an analysis of the role of the media in Great Britain and their relationship to racial minorities, see *Racism and the Mass Media,* by P. Hartmann and C. Hubbard, 1974, Lanham, MD: Rowman and Littlefield.

References

Bagdikian, B. H. (1978, October). The best news money can buy. *Human Behavior,* 63-66.

Bouvier, L. F., & Davis, C. B. (1982, August). *The future racial composition of the United States.* Washington, DC: Demographic Information Services Center of the Population Reference Bureau.

Chang, J. (2001, November 21). Bay area Afghan-American members dispute statistics. *Contra Costa Times,* p. A1.

Clarifications. (2002, May 10). *San Francisco Chronicle,* p. A2.

Cohn, D. (1992, December 30). Census bureau won't adjust data for '90 undercount. *Washington Post,* p. A7.

Dinkins, D. (1991). Welcoming remarks. National Association of Hispanic Journalists Convention, New York.

Elliott, J., & Mason, J. (2001, October 18). Democrats say census costs state; Using only raw data affects federal dollars. *Houston Chronicle,* p. A29.

Evans, D. L. (2001, March 28). Prepared Testimony of Honorable Donald L. Evans Secretary of Commerce Before the Senate Committee on Commerce, Science and Transportation. Washington, DC.

Glazer, N., & Moynihan, D. P. (1963). *Beyond the melting pot: The Negroes, Puerto Ricans, Jews, Italians and Irish of New York City.* Cambridge: MIT Press.

Goodman, T. (2002, July 24). Un-reality TV: Few minority actors in S.F. shows. *San Francisco Chronicle,* p. A1.

Gutiérrez, F., & Wilson, C. C., II (1979). The demographic dilemma. *Columbia Journalism Review* (January/February), 53.

Henry Ford Museum and Greenfield Village. (n.d.). *The Ford English school.* Retrieved from www.hfmgv.org/education/smartfun/modelt/highlandpark/fordschool/fordschool.html

Jakubowicz, A. (Ed.). (1994). *Racism, ethnicity and the media.* St. Leonards, Australia: Allen & Unwin.

Kennedy, R. (1945). The colonial crisis and the future. In R. Linton (Ed.), *The science of man in the world crisis.* New York: Columbia University Press.

Malik, S. (2001). *Representing Black Britain: Black and Asian images on television.* Thousand Oaks, CA: Sage.

Meadows, M. (2001). *Voices in the wilderness: Images of Aboriginal people in the Australian media.* Westport, CT: Greenwood.

Muschick, P. (2001, March 30). Understanding the data. *The Orange County Register.*

Muschick, P. (2001, April 16). Census raising new racial questions. *Greensboro News & Record,* p. B1.

Pear, R. (1992, December 4). New look at the U.S. in 2050: Bigger, older and less White. *New York Times,* pp. A1, D18.

Pugh, T. (2001, March 25). Mixed marriages on the rise in U.S.: Racial, ethnic barriers abating as country becomes more diverse. *Houston Chronicle,* p. A12.

Really, how different are we? (1992, December 3). *Los Angeles Times,* p. A10.

Rodríguez, R. (1992, May 7). The browning of America. *Black Issues in Higher Education,* pp. 60-62.

Salins, P. D. (1997). Assimilation, American style. Retrieved from reason.com/9702/fe.salins.shtml. (Excerpt from P. D. Salins, *Assimilation, American Style,* New York: Basic Books)

Trowbridge, G. (2001, March 26). Arab Americans lose out in census: No ethnic box costs political, economic clout. *Detroit News,* p. 1.

Udansky, M. (1992, December 4-6). Minorities are headed toward the majority. *USA Today,* p. 1A.

U.S. Census Bureau. (2001a). No. 7. Immigrants by Country of Birth: 1981-1998. In *Statistical Abstract of the United States: 2001* (p. 11). Washington, DC: Author.

U.S. Census Bureau. (2001b). No. 15. Resident population by Hispanic origin status, 1980 to 2000, and Projections, 2005 to 2050. In *Statistical Abstract of the United States: 2001* (p. 17). Washington, DC: Author.

U.S. Census Bureau. (2001c). No. 70. Births and birth rates by race, sex, and age: 1980 to 1999. In *Statistical Abstract of the United States: 2001* (p. 60). Washington, DC: Author.

U.S. Census Bureau. (2001d). No. 74. Projected fertility rates by race, origin and age group: 2000 and 2010. In *Statistical Abstract of the United States: 2001* (p. 62). Washington, DC: Author.

U.S. population: Where we are, where we're going. (1982). *Population Bulletin, 37*(2), 6.

Westin, A. (2001, April). The color of ratings. *Brills Content.*

What colour is the news? (n.d.). Chronicle World: Changing Black Britain. Retrieved from www.thechronicle.demon.co.uk/archive/colnews.htm

Do the Media Matter? 2

How much do you know about the people who first lived on what is now called the North American continent? Think about it. How much do you know about the people who lived in nomadic tribes and permanent villages across what is now the United States? Do you know what languages they spoke? What they liked to eat? Can you describe how they dressed? Or what their villages looked like? Or how they defended themselves against the Europeans who came to their land? How about their lives today? What are their prospects for the future?

If you're like most people in the United States, you probably know some but not all the answers to those questions. You know some things about Native Americans but not as much as you might think you should know. And, unless you're Native American yourself, much of what you know you probably learned from the media. At some time or another, you've seen a movie, viewed a television program, or read a book about Native Americans.

Now, try to remember what you learned about Native Americans from these media: from movies, television, newspapers, and magazines. Chances are, you won't remember much factual information. Aside from their presence in Westerns and an occasional news report, Native Americans are an invisible minority in the media of the United States. The squaws, warriors, and chieftains featured often are images from the 19th century that portray Native Americans as they were seen by Whites, not as they saw themselves. Movies and television programs have traditionally treated Native Americans as savages vanquished by a superior civilization whose people now tell the stories. Even movies that more accurately portray the lives and contributions of Native Americans often tell the stories through White characters with whom the audience can identify, such as Kevin Costner's role in the 1990 movie *Dances With Wolves* or Nicholas Cage's character in the 2002 movie *Windtalkers*.

When Native Americans are covered by the news media, the stories often fall into one of two categories: "zoo stories" or "problem people stories." The zoo stories feature colorful pow-wows with costumed Native American drummers and dancers displaying images of people who are apparently frozen in the past. The problem people stories show Native Americans either as overburdened by their own problems, such as poverty and alcoholism, or as the source of problems for others, such as the casinos on reservation lands. Although both types of stories merit some coverage, neither provides adequate coverage of Native Americans today.

All of us depend on the media to portray and define those things that we have not personally experienced. We "learn" about others through radio, websites, television, movies, video games, newspapers, and magazines. The portrayals and news coverage of Native Americans and other groups in those media can become reality in our minds, especially if we have no direct experiences to balance them against. The impact of media images of people of color and other underrepresented groups on society has been amply described and documented by scholars who have examined how the media affect society.[1]

The Functions of Media in Society

Over the years, many scholars have described the functions of the media in modern society. While they disagree on some details, they all agree on the media's pervasive influence on American society. In a 1948 essay that is often cited by other researchers, Harold Lasswell described the three major functions of communication as:

1. *Surveillance* of the environment, disclosing threats and opportunities affecting the value position of the community and of the component parts within it;

2. *Correlation* of the different parts of society in responding to environment, and

3. *Transmission* of the social heritage from one generation to the next. (quoted in Schramm & Roberts, 1971).

Examined as part of a society with many racial and ethnic minority groups and a majority group that, to a large extent, controls the dominant media, Lasswell's *surveillance* function of the media assigns to the media the lookout role of scanning the society to define and describe the different groups within it. The *correlation* function of the media helps the consumers of the media take stock of the different groups and determine how and where they fit into the society. Finally, the *transmission* function of the media both defines what the social culture and heritage of the society are and transmits it to other members of the society. This process, whether those with the power to do so have consciously engineered it or not, includes some cultures, excludes others, and redefines all the cultures for the audience.

Although the United States prides itself on being a democratic society built on rational public opinion formed through broad dissemination of information, Lasswell (1948) noted that communication can be altered when the ruling elements of the society sense a threat from an inside or outside group.

> In society, the communication process reveals special characteristics when the ruling element is afraid of the internal as well as the external environment. In gauging the efficiency of communication in any given context, it is necessary to take into account the values at stake, and the identity of the group whose position is being examined. (quoted in Schramm & Roberts, 1971, p. 99)

Lasswell reinforces the importance of the fact that the media behave differently when leaders perceive a threat, especially when a particular group is linked to that threat. The group could be identified by its politics, religion, race, ethnicity, age, gender, or any other characteristic linked to it by the media. In these cases, the media must provide a consistent message that communicates a cohesive opinion of that threat or group to others in the society.

If we apply Lasswell's media functions to portrayals of Native Americans, it is not surprising that most people in the United States have little accurate information about native people. The news media have historically treated native people through the surveillance function, watching the horizon and reporting on them as heathen savages when they defended their lands, people, and culture from European intruders. As part of their correlation function, the media defined Native Americans as primitive people who stood in the way of the progress of the Whites who were fulfilling their Manifest Destiny to "civilize" and populate North America. Native people were often portrayed as unable to adapt to the ways of the Whites and worthy only of annihilation, subjugation, or consignment to reservations. Finally, the transmission function of the media defined the culture of the continent as the culture developed by and for European settlers rather than Native American people.

Most of us may have limited knowledge about the cultures and civilizations of Native Americans, but not because what we know about them is derived from the way they were covered in the newspapers and magazines published during the White westward expansion of the 19th century. For the most part, our images of the people the Europeans called "Indians" have been shaped by the movies, television programs, and Western novels we have seen or read. These media are primarily designed not to be informative but to entertain. That is why in 1959 Charles Wright added a fourth

Illustration 2.1   In times of uncertainty, the news media's surveillance function often labels groups of people seen as potential threats, as illustrated in this World War II *Life* layout reporting "U.S. Uproots Jap Aliens." Six decades later, federal officials similarly ordered men from 25 predominately Arab or Muslim countries to report for interrogations following attacks in the U.S.

dimension to Lasswell's three functions: the *entertainment* function, which emphasized that communication can also entertain the society (cited in Schramm & Porter, 1982, p. 27). The entertainment images and portrayals of Native Americans have become reality in the minds of many who have seen Native Americans in movies and on television but nowhere else.

Later, others noted that in addition to these four functions, the media also perform an important *economic* function in society. Communication scholars Wilbur Schramm and William Porter wrote in 1982 that although no economist had as yet outlined the economic functions of the media with the specificity of Lasswell's functions, it was possible to describe the economic roles of the media.

> For one thing, communication must meet the need for an economic map of the environment so that each individual and organization can form its own image of buying and selling opportunities at a given moment. For another, there must be correlation of economic policy, whether by the individual, the organization, or the nation. . . . Finally, instruction in the skills and expectations of economic behavior must be available. (p. 27)

Other scholars took a more bottom line approach to describing the economic role of the media. In a 1972 textbook, Peter Sandman, David Rubin, and David Sachsman described the economic function of the media as "to make money" (p. 14). In another edition of the book 10 years later, they broadened their description to read "to serve the economic system" and emphasized its central role in the operation of media in the United States.

> The fundamental economic purpose of the mass media in the United States is to sell people to advertisers. Economically, the articles in your newspaper and the programs on your radio and TV sets are merely "come-ons" to catch and hold your attention. Advertisers buy that attention from the media, and use it to sell you their products and services. In the process, both the media and the advertisers earn substantial profits. (Sandman, Sachsman, & Rubin, 1982, p. 9)

Today, almost all the media, including those that do not depend on advertiser support—such as movies, compact discs, videocassettes, DVDs, many Internet websites, and some cable television channels—also serve the economic system. Increasingly, corporations pay to have their products placed in movies, push advertising e-mail to World Wide Web users, and copromote their products with movie and music productions. Most media are owned and operated by corporations that sell a product to an audience or advertisers, are privately held, issue stock, and generate profits or losses for their shareholders.

This role of the media in the economy has become even more important in the last two decades as media have been bought, sold, and merged in multibillion dollar deals. In some cases, such as the *Chicago Tribune's* parent company buying Times-Mirror and its daily newspapers in Los Angeles, Baltimore, and Long Island, it was one media chain buying another. In other cases, such as AOL's acquisition of Time-Warner and CNN, it was a new media company buying older media companies. And, in still other cases, such as in General Electric's purchase of NBC, it was a corporate conglomerate buying a media giant.

As the United States has developed into an information economy, these mergers and purchases have served the economic system by concentrating media ownership in fewer corporations, all positioning themselves to become more profitable by creating, buying, selling, and distributing news, entertainment, and information. Some of what they provide is fresh, such as the contents of daily newspapers and prime time network television programs. But other content is taken off the shelf, recycled, and sold over and over again, such as many cable programs, videocassettes and DVDs of movies, and compact discs featuring actors and artists who are no longer alive.

The media must serve the economic system because they are private businesses, rather than publicly supported institutions such as public schools or libraries. Because they are part of the private enterprise system, the media must behave as other corporations and businesses do, seeking income and profits by maximizing the number of people consuming their products while lowering the costs of production and distribution.

Thus we find that scholars have described five central functions for the media in the United States.[2] These are as follows:

1. *Surveillance*: the sentinel or lookout role of the media, that is, watching the society and horizon for threats to the established order and information on people or places of public interest and reporting these to the audience

2. *Correlation*: the interpretation and linking function of the media, which helps the audience to understand, interpret, and comprehend what is happening in and out of the society (and how these events affect each other) and to stay in touch with others in the society

3. *Transmission*: the socialization function of the media, in which the media define the society, its norms and values, to the audience and through their portrayals and coverage assist members of the society in adopting, using, and acting on those values

4. *Entertainment*: the function of the media for diversion and enjoyment, in which the media provide stories, features, music, and films designed to make the audiences laugh, cry, relax, or reflect rather than gain information

5. *Economic Service*: the role of the media within the economic system of the society, which in the United States means that most media function

as businesses serving the needs of shareholders and other corporations by selling a product that they either produce or attract.

The Mass Media

THE MASS MEDIA AND THE MASS AUDIENCE

The U.S. media could fulfill all these functions without treating members of racial and ethnic minority groups any differently from the majority. However, in the early 19th century the development of communication media changed course as the American political, economic, and racial identity was being formed. Earlier, the framers of the U.S. Constitution foresaw a system in which the media would operate in a free marketplace of ideas. They hoped for a society in which every political group, every interest group, or anyone else with the money, message, and motivation would print and disseminate newspapers, books, and pamphlets to promote their views.

It was hoped that the new republic's voters, at that time limited to White males, would choose from the wide variety of diverse media and, after weighing different versions of information and opinions, would make an informed choice at the polling place. The media were seen both as the public's watchdogs on the government and as important communication links on which the new democratic society would depend for information. For this reason, the First Amendment to the U.S. Constitution prohibits Congress from making laws limiting the freedom of the press—the only private business sector with constitutional protection from government.

But in freeing the press from governmental restraints, the framers of the Constitution also withdrew the government licenses and subsidies that had been given to official government or sanctioned media in Europe and America. The press, while freed from the laws of Congress, was forced to function as a business within the unwritten economic laws of capitalism governing business in the United States. For several decades after the First Amendment was ratified in 1791, newspapers and magazines focused on specialized content for targeted audiences. Political parties subsidized their own partisan newspapers, ethnic media in different languages targeted non-English language readers, and commercial publications were published for merchants. But in the 1830s, there emerged a new formula that dominated the development of the media in the United States through the end of the 20th century: the penny press.

The penny press first gained success with the *New York Sun*, which appeared in 1833 and sold for only one cent. The newspaper made a profit through a new form uniquely adapted to the free enterprise system. Unlike competing newspapers, its primary income did not depend on subsidies from a political party, government placed public notices, or reader subscriptions. Benjamin Day, founder of the *New York Sun,* envisioned the penny press as a newspaper for the mass audience of city residents who would be drawn by the newspaper's lively content, low price, and the *Sun*'s promise that "It Shines for ALL."[3] The newspaper's formula, which was widely imitated, was successful in attracting readers. But readers were not the only ones interested in the penny press.

> Another person began to take a special interest in the newspaper for the masses. This was the advertiser, who was impressed by the amazing circulation of the new medium. Putting an ad in every publication bought by small splinter groups was expensive and ineffective sales promotion. The large circulation of the penny papers now made it feasible to publicize articles for sale that formerly would not have warranted advertising expense. (Emery & Emery, 1996, p. 102)

Given the successful formula developed by the penny press, the most successful media in the United States were not *class* communication media, attracting audience segments for many competing views, but *mass* communication media, attracting a large audience to a few mass circulation media outlets. The space for the advertisement in the newspaper or time on the television screen has no economic value by itself. Its worth is based on the size of the audience attracted by the news or entertainment content of the print or broadcast media. As media strove to accumulate larger and larger audiences, they developed content that would attract the widest audience possible and offend the fewest people.

Rather than class media, a variety of small outlets addressing the needs of segments of the society, the media in the United States became mass media seeking a large audience drawn from all groups. As a result, media serving political, national, or racial and ethnic minorities were consigned to a second-class status because they did not attract a mass audience. The activities of those groups, as well as of women, were either ignored by the mass media or portrayed in a way that made them palatable to the mass audience. That the media in the United States were mass media meant not that the media served all the groups in the masses but that they amassed people into a large audience for advertisers.

In an effort to amass the largest possible audience in a nation of immigrants and their descendents, the mass media tried to cultivate broad common interests and address the media content to those interests, whether it be in news, entertainment, or information. The media that most successfully attracted the mass audience could charge the highest rates to print and broadcast advertisers or, in the case of records, CDs, and movies, sell the most products. The advertisers, with their seemingly insatiable appetite for larger audiences for their advertisements, fueled the media's chase of the mass audience. But advertising's important role in shaping mass media content was not always appreciated by scholars describing how the U.S. media developed.

Historian David Potter wrote in 1954 that

> histories of American periodicals and even of the mass media deal with advertising as if it were a side issue. Students of the radio and of the mass-circulation magazines frequently condemn advertising for its conspicuous role, as if it were a mere interloper in a separate, pre-existing, self-contained aesthetic world of actors, musicians, authors, and script-writers; they hardly recognize that advertising created modern American radio and television, transformed the modern newspaper, evoked the modern slick periodical, and remains the vital essence of each of them at the present time. (pp. 167-168)

Although the variety of media has greatly increased in the five decades since Potter wrote, and the media now offer a wider range of content for different segments of American society, the fundamental relationship that he described between advertising and the media has not changed. In the era when the mass media dominated all the media, this relationship dictated that racial and ethnic minority groups were treated in ways that did not challenge but, rather, reflected and reinforced the majority society's attitudes toward these groups.

THE MASS MEDIA AND THE COLLECTIVE CONSCIOUSNESS

As advertisers demanded mass audiences for their products, media corporations responded by adopting news and entertainment strategies that would attract the largest numbers of people. At that time, the people targeted by the mass media in the United States were White, many of them European immigrants looking to the media to learn about the people of their new nation. Men and women of color, such as Blacks, Latinos, Native Americans, and Asian Pacific Americans, were treated by the media as fringe audiences, not large enough in number to influence the content directed to the mass audience. If the media offended people of color by omitting or misrepresenting them, the favorable response of the majority White audience more than made up for the dissatisfaction of the minority.

However, the mass audience was by no means homogeneous, especially in a nation of immigrants from different countries and with different religions. In fact, the people in the predominately White mass audience were not identical to each other. The mass audience included rich and poor, young and old, city and country, men and women: all with different needs and interests. The challenge facing the mass media was to find common themes and content that would attract people from all the desired groups and to look for things they could share.

The media thus shaped and reinforced the collective consciousness needed to attract large numbers of people in a heterogeneous society. The mass media's mission was to find common interests among members of the audience: themes, images, interests, and ideas that would attract the mass audience. To draw the largest possible audience, the media developed content that would attract the lowest common denominator of shared interests in the audience. This meant that the mass media reinforced, rather than challenged, the attitudes and practices of the society. If they would have done otherwise, they would have risked offending significant audience segments and losing the mass audience demanded by the advertisers.

Most immigrants came from Europe in varying shades of White and could be expected to blend together within a generation or two without physical differences separating them. Driven by a melting pot mentality, the U.S. media often treated as outsiders the members of groups that had not assimilated or had not been allowed to assimilate. Racial and ethnic minorities identifiable by color or facial features were placed beyond the melting pot, unable to completely blend because of physical characteristics.

People who could not easily melt into society often were not targeted as audiences by the mass media. Movies, broadcast programs, newspapers, and news magazines generally overlooked the daily issues confronting people of color in the United States, as well as their culture and traditions. Instead, people of color became targets of the media. When they did appear in the media, it was often in stereotypic roles that catered to White society's images of people of color, such as the Black mammy, Indian chief, Mexican bandito, and Polynesian maiden. Although all stereotypes usually have some elements of truth, these gross characterizations were based on the preconceptions outsiders had of the groups rather than on the realities of the groups themselves. They were pictures filtered through Anglo eyes, rather than honest reflections of the people portrayed.

SYMBOLS, STEREOTYPES, AND THE MASS MEDIA

The mass media came to rely on symbols and stereotypes as shorthand ways of communicating to the diversity of people in the mass audience through newspaper headlines, movie characterizations, and television pictures. Images of rich bankers, heroic cowboys, or old spinsters were used so that audiences would understand the character the first time he or she appeared on the screen or in the story. Newspapers used terms such as *right wing*, *leftist*, and *moderate* in headlines as symbols that characterized people or groups along different points of the political spectrum.

These symbols were a useful shorthand for the mass media, since they allowed the entertainment and news media to portray even complex

Illustration 2.2   Exotic, stylized pictures of people of color in early 20th century travel stickers and food product labels appealed to the stereotypes held by many of the predominately White consumers in the United States and reinforced false images of the people portrayed.

personalities and issues with a shortened character or term. Thus, when the audience at a Western movie saw a man come on the screen wearing a white hat, they knew that he was the hero. Or when the term *leftist* was used in a headline, it meant that the group that the term symbolized was on the liberal extreme, bordering on communist. The terms became symbols that made complex matters easier to handle by triggering recall of what Walter Lippmann, in his 1922 book *Public Opinion,* described as "pictures in our heads" (Lippmann, 1922/1997).

   Media symbols are like computer screen icons. When using a computer, we have learned that when we see an icon and point to it, a click of the computer mouse will bring something we want to the screen. The symbol is the icon we see on the screen, and the stereotype is the function the computer brings to the screen when we click on the icon. In the same way, media images of people of color, such as fat Mexican maids, fast-talking Black street hustlers, noble Indian chiefs, and karate-chopping Asians, have become symbols that trigger stereotypes of the people portrayed and of others who share those characteristics.

Racial and ethnic minorities have been among the people portrayed by symbols and stereotypes in mass entertainment and news media through much of this nation's history. As discussed in subsequent chapters, through the 1960s, unrestricted stereotypes of Native Americans, Blacks, Asian Pacific Americans, and Latinos made up nearly all of the portrayals of the people in these groups in the entertainment media of movies, radio, fiction, and television.

Similarly, news media rarely covered the activities of the people in these communities unless, in accordance with their surveillance function, they perceived them as *problem people* who were posing a threat to the established order or, in accordance with their correlation function, they covered them in *zoo stories* during colorful cultural festivals. Thus, the predominately White mass audience saw only a slice of minority communities, one that did not jar their preconceptions of these groups and probably helped legitimize and reinforce their lower social and economic standing. The people on both sides of this biased coverage were shortchanged. People of color were denied accurate representation and Whites were denied the opportunity to become better acquainted with groups different than their own.

In the absence of personal contact, alternative portrayals, and broadened news coverage, such one-sided stereotypes and news coverage could easily become reality in the minds of the White mass audience. Whites were seen in a wide range of roles in movies, ranging from villains to heroes. In contrast, until the late 1960s there were no government or industry-wide efforts to provide alternative media portrayals and coverage to counteract the mass media stereotypes of people of color in a society where they had less than equal standing with Whites.

Do the Media Matter?

It was once thought that the mass media were a "magic bullet" that entered the minds of the audience and could convert them to any opinion or attitude. However, scholars who have examined the effects of the media on members of society have found that the influence of the media is much more limited and complex. Instead of being a mere target for a bullet, the audience is more accurately described as a complex set of groups and individuals who actively make decisions about which media to use, what to remember from the media, and how to interpret what they remember. The media have their greatest effect when they reinforce and channel existing attitudes and opinions consistent with the psychological makeup of individuals and the social structure of the groups with which they identify, not when they try to change opinions.

While the "magic bullet" theories saw the audience as a target for media messages, researchers established later that media audiences are active not passive. Rather than sit back and take whatever the media offer, people seek out the media that fulfill their needs and gratify their desires. In today's world of multimedia, people have more choices of media than ever, quickly change channels, and at the same time may be reading, listening to music, and have the television on.

Because of the wide range of social and psychological factors that affect how a person thinks and acts, it is difficult to pinpoint the specific effects of the media on individuals. However, what we know of the reinforcement and channeling effects of the media, when coupled with the content analyses of coverage and portrayal of minorities in the news and entertainment media, provide insight into the negative effects of one-sided media images on both Whites and the members of the racial and ethnic groups portrayed.

Media effects research is less definitive than other areas of communication research. Nevertheless, studies have shown that negative, one-sided, or stereotyped portrayals and news coverage in the media very often reinforce racist attitudes in prejudiced members of the audience and can channel mass actions against the group that is portrayed stereotypically. The studies also show that bigots watching television programs that ridicule bigotry interpret the program to reinforce their pre-existing beliefs. Children in both minorities and the majority are particularly affected by entertainment characters portraying minority groups. In contrast to the effects of negative portrayals, programs portraying better interracial understanding and cooperation among people of different races can stimulate positive attitudes and behavior, especially among children.

To better understand the different ways news and entertainment media can affect racial attitudes and behavior, it is helpful to examine the findings of three studies examining at different points over the past 60 years.

News Coverage and Mob Violence

THE ZOOT SUIT RIOTS OF 1943

In the midst of World War II, the streets of downtown Los Angeles were the scene of violent attacks by mobs of battle-trained American servicemen on Mexican American, Black, and Filipino youths. The attacks

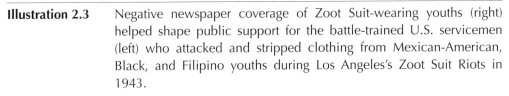

Illustration 2.3   Negative newspaper coverage of Zoot Suit-wearing youths (right) helped shape public support for the battle-trained U.S. servicemen (left) who attacked and stripped clothing from Mexican-American, Black, and Filipino youths during Los Angeles's Zoot Suit Riots in 1943.

Source: Bettmann/CORBIS.

targeted civilians with well-greased hair wearing "zoot suits," which were suits with long coats and pants with deep pleats at the waist that were pegged at the cuff. The servicemen cut off their clothing, whether they were wearing zoot suits or not. The police officers, who responded to reports of the violence, arrested and jailed the civilian youths, not the servicemen who attacked them. The attacks followed and were accompanied by a campaign in the news media that characterized the zoot suited youths, most of them of Mexican origin, as antisocial elements whose dress was out of step with the nation's war effort.

In 1956, sociologists Ralph Turner and Samuel Surace analyzed the press coverage of Mexicans in the Los Angeles press to see if it might have affected the violent attacks on the predominately Mexican American zoot suiters (pp. 14-20). Turner and Surace hypothesized that the period before the riots would be characterized by steady negative news coverage of Mexicans in Los Angeles and studied the portrayal of Mexicans in the *Los Angeles Times* from 1933 to 1943.

Articles covering persons of Mexican descent were categorized five ways:

1. *Favorable*: stories which emphasized the area's Old California tradition; the romantic, brave, dashing image of Mexicans, religion in the Mexican community, or Mexican culture

2. *Unfavorable*: articles on delinquency and crime or Mexicans as a public burden

3. *Neutral*: miscellaneous articles including people with Spanish-surnames, but not identified as Mexicans in the article

4. *Negative-Favorable*: articles that stated and then refuted accusations against Mexicans, such as "Not all zoot suiters are delinquents"

5. *Zooter Theme*: articles identifying the zoot suit dress with crime, sex, violence, or gangs.

Turner and Surace (1956) thought that crowd behavior, such as the organized attacks by military personnel stationed in the area, would be preceded by newspaper coverage in which the term *Mexican* was used as an unambiguous negative symbol. They also hypothesized that because of the negative behavior ascribed to Mexicans by the newspaper, the mass society would sanction mob violence that would not be tolerated in other circumstances.

The sociologists felt that both favorable and unfavorable feelings toward people of color could be triggered by ambiguous symbols, noting that "even the most prejudiced person is likely to respond to the symbol 'Negro' with images of both the feared invader of white prerogatives and the lovable, loyal Negro lackey and 'mammy.'" But unambiguous negative symbols representing people outside the boundaries of normal, accepted behavior would trigger "the dictum that 'you must fight fire with fire' and the conviction that a person devoid of human decency is not entitled to be treated with decency and respect." Turner and Surace wrote that when the media symbol of a group triggers a strictly negative stereotype, the people associated with it can become targets for mob violence.

Therefore, in looking at the news coverage, Turner and Surace (1956) expected to find a decline in the number of times the term *Mexican* was used in favorable news coverage in the period preceding the zoot suit riots. This would result in the development of a clearly negative image for the predominately Mexican zoot suiters.

Their hypothesis was only partially supported by the *Los Angeles Times* coverage for the 10 years before the 1943 riots. In fact, between 1933 and 1943, favorable Mexican themes (primarily those romanticizing Mexican culture) made up between 80% and 90% of the stories in which the term *Mexican* was used. However, in taking a closer look at the data, Turner and Surace discovered the importance of an unambiguous negative symbol in news coverage before the mob violence against Mexican youths.

While the percentage of favorable mentions of *Mexican* in the 3-year period preceding the 1943 riots did not decrease, there was a sharp decline in the number of articles using the term *Mexican* at all. The term was used in 27 articles sampled between January of 1933 and June of 1936, and it was used 23 times in articles between July of 1936 and December of 1939. But it was used in less than half that number, only 10 articles, between January of 1940 and June of 1943. Turner and Surace (1956) found what they described as "a shift away from *all* the traditional references to Mexicans during the period prior to the riots." This shift was not the result of less news coverage of those of Mexican descent in the *Los Angeles Times*—in fact, the number of articles about this group rose steadily in three periods studied between 1933 and 1943. However, there was a decline in the number of articles using the term *Mexican* and an increase in the percentage of articles classified as neutral, negative-favorable, and zooter theme. In the first period, articles coded as favorable constituted 80% of the articles coded, but in the last period those coded as favorable accounted for only 25% of the articles. The percentage of articles coded as neutral increased sharply to 32%, and Turner and Surace (1956) noted that the category "actually consists chiefly of unfavorable presentations of the object 'Mexican' without overt use of the symbol 'Mexican.'" The percentage of articles in the negative-favorable category also increased, although it was smaller than the others, and also was based on an overall negative image of Mexicans, such as reporting that not all Mexicans are lazy.

The most startling shift was the sharp increase in the *Los Angeles Times's* use of the term *zoot suit* as a strictly negative symbol. The zoot suit theme, which was not used before 1940, accounted for one third of all the articles from 1940 to June of 1943. The authors concluded that the introduction of the term and its heavy use in unfavorable circumstances resulted in a strictly negative symbol that triggered no unambiguous or positive stereotypes. It was the association of that symbol with Mexican American youths portrayed as having antisocial behavior that helped spur the indiscriminate attacks of servicemen on them, including those not wearing zoot suits.

Turner and Surace (1956) wrote that

> unlike the symbol " Mexican," the "zoot-suiter" symbol evokes no ambivalent sentiments but appears in exclusively unfavorable contexts. While, in fact, Mexicans were attacked *indiscriminately* in spite of apparel (of two hundred youths rounded up by the police on one occasion, very few were wearing zoot suits), the symbol "zoot-suiter" could become a basis for unambivalent community sentiment supporting hostile crowd behavior more easily than could "Mexican."

The researchers found that in the period just before the violent attacks on Mexican teenagers, the newspaper's coverage of the Mexican American community in the issues sampled was dominated by the zoot suiter theme in unfavorable coverage, less use of the term *Mexican* in favorable coverage, and increased coverage of Mexicans in articles in which the term *Mexican* was not used but the community was portrayed unfavorably. In the month just before and during the attacks by servicemen on Mexican youths, 74% of the 61 articles on the Mexican community concerned zoot suiters, 23% were negative-favorable, and 3% were neutral. While not holding the *Los Angeles Times* entirely responsible for the violent attacks on civilian youths, the researchers felt that news coverage contributed to the violence and general public support of the servicemen by introducing a new symbol, the zoot suiter, and using it in a strictly unfavorable context. Turner and Surace wrote that the new symbol

> provided the public sanction and restriction of attention essential to the development of overt crowd hostility. The symbol "zoot-suiter" evoked none of the imagery of the romantic past. It evoked only the picture of a breed of persons outside the normative order, devoid of morals themselves, and consequently not entitled to fair play and due process. The"zooter" symbol had a crisis character which mere unfavorable versions of the familiar "Mexican" symbol never approximated. And the "zooter" symbol was an omnibus, drawing together the most reprehensible elements in the old unfavorable themes, namely, sex crimes, delinquency, gang attacks, draft-dodgers, and the like and was, in consequence, widely applicable.

Turner and Surace's research is valuable because of the link it makes between the symbols that trigger commonly accepted stereotypes in the minds of the mass audience, which are used often in news coverage of Latinos and other racial and ethnic groups, and the psychological, social, and even physical damage caused those being stereotyped. Symbols are often used at a time when the surveillance and correlation functions of the media are called on to describe a change in the environment posed by minorities or to define how and where members of minorities fit into the society.

A survey of national magazine coverage of Mexicans in the United States from 1890 to 1970 revealed an almost complete absence of news coverage—except when elements of the Mexican population were seen as a threat to society, which then triggered discriminatory acts by the public or law enforcement officials. In these periods, terms such as *zoot suiters*, border-crossing *wetbacks*, and militant *Chicanos* dominated the headlines of national magazines.

More recently, the term *illegal alien* has been used to symbolize a person who enters the country illegally and is said to constitute a burden on public resources. A survey of 114 randomly selected articles from California newspapers on undocumented immigration from January of 1977 through March of 1978 found that nearly half used the term *alien* or *illegal alien* in the headlines. The largest categories of headlines treated the immigrants as a law enforcement problem or drain on public resources (Gutiérrez, 1978). Use of the term *illegal alien* continued in news headlines and coverage through the 1990s, most often referring to Latino immigrants. In the mid-1990s, Los Angeles police chief Willie Williams surprised a national audience of journalists when he reported that the second largest group of undocumented people in his city came not from a Latin American country but from Canada (Williams, 1994).

The news media have used terms—such as *savages* during the 19th century battles against Native Americans, *Japs* in World War II, and *Black Power militants* in the 1960s—as shorthand symbols to trigger stereotypical images in the minds of readers, listeners, and viewers. Following the September 11, 2001 hijacked airliner crashes that destroyed New York City's World Trade Center towers and damaged the Pentagon, the news media used images of Arabs, Muslims, and other Middle Easterners as symbols triggering stereotypes of terrorists.

The Influence of the Media on Bigotry

BIGOTRY AND ARCHIE BUNKER

When the situation comedy program *All in the Family* hit the airwaves in 1971, it immediately triggered a debate over its barrier-breaking use of racial and ethnic humor on network television. The story line of the program pitted Archie Bunker, a rascally but hardworking bigot, against his liberal son-in-law, Mike, a graduate student living in the Bunker household with Archie's daughter. Mike engaged in lively and humorous debates with Archie, who had dropped out of high school and had a blue-collar job. Archie's lines in the show's script featured derogatory racial, ethnic, religious, and gender slang terms that were not then used in polite company or on television. Some lauded the program for tackling racial prejudice and exposing the foolishness of bigotry through the use of comedy. Others argued that the program, by portraying Archie as a lovable bigot, had the effect of sanctioning and even encouraging prejudice.

Norman Lear, the producer of the program, answered critics by arguing that the comedy's story line countered bigotry because Mike effectively rebutted Archie and that Mike was the one "making sense." Lear wrote in 1971 that the audience saw Archie as an advocate of "convoluted logic" (Lear, 1971). He contended that the program's dependence on racial themes would bring bigotry out into the open and would allow parents to answer children's questions about bigotry. CBS, which aired the program, commissioned a study that showed that the program could lessen racial bigotry by humorously exposing its shortcomings. Others defended the

Illustration 2.4   Archie Bunker's use of racial slurs and bigotry when arguing with son-in-law Michael in the 1970s television situation comedy *All in the Family* were shown by researchers to reinforce prejudice in some viewers. The program continued to be seen in syndication and on cable into the 21st century.

Source: Bettmann/CORBIS.

program for using a comedy format to belittle those with prejudiced opinions. The Los Angeles chapter of the National Association for the Advancement of Colored People (NAACP) gave its 1972 Image Award to *All in the Family* for contributing to better race relations.

The program appeared on network television for more than a decade and continued on local and cable stations for more than 30 years. Although several research projects examined the impact of the program on viewers, one of the most important studies was one of the first. In 1974, psychologist Neil Vidmar and sociologist/psychologist Milton Rokeach published a study analyzing the impact of *All in the Family* on viewers in the United States and Canada. Noting the debate then taking place over the effect of Archie Bunker on bigotry and prejudice, the researchers tested the audience reaction to the program in terms of previous studies showing how audiences use selective perception and selective exposure when using media.

Under the selective perception hypothesis, Vidmar and Rokeach theorized that viewers with different degrees of prejudice or racism would have different reasons for watching the program, would identify with different characters, and would find different meanings in the outcomes of the programs. Under the selective exposure hypothesis, the researchers proposed that low prejudiced and high prejudiced viewers would not watch *All in the Family* to the same extent.

To test these hypotheses, Vidmar and Rokeach (1974) surveyed 237 high school students in a small Midwestern town in the United States and 168 adults in London, Ontario, in Canada. Those surveyed were asked to respond to a questionnaire with eleven items designed to probe their reactions to the program and six items designed to measure their ethnocentrism or prejudice. The initial data showed that more than 60% of the respondents liked or admired Archie more than they did Mike, 40% of the American respondents felt Archie won at the end of the show, 46% named Mike as the one most made fun of, and 35% saw nothing wrong with Archie's use of racial and ethnic slurs. The responses of the Canadians who were surveyed followed the same pattern.

The researchers then compared the exposure to and interpretations of the program of respondents who were rated as high prejudiced and low prejudiced on the six items measuring ethnocentrism and prejudice. While both groups enjoyed the program equally, people at different levels of prejudice drew different conclusions from watching the same television characters. Vidmar and Rokeach (1974) wrote that "high prejudiced persons in both the U.S. and Canadian samples were significantly more likely than low prejudiced people to admire Archie over Mike and to perceive Archie as winning in the end" (p. 42). High prejudiced American adolescents were also more likely to report that Archie made better sense than Mike and to report that in 20 years their attitudes would be similar to Archie Bunker's. High prejudiced Canadian adults also condoned Archie's racial slurs more often and saw the show as poking fun at Archie less often than did low prejudiced viewers.

Vidmar and Rokeach (1974) summarized that the findings "tend to support the selective perception hypothesis—namely, that prejudiced persons identify more with Archie, perceive Archie as making better sense than Mike, perceive Archie as winning." Furthermore, high prejudiced viewers noted things they disliked about Mike and low prejudiced viewers noted things they disliked about Archie.

Vidmar and Rokeach (1974) also found support for the selective exposure hypothesis, but in a different direction than that proposed by CBS. Network researchers, assuming that the program would be interpreted as satirizing bigotry, speculated that low prejudiced people would be the most avid viewers. But Vidmar and Rokeach found that American teenagers who were in the high prejudice group were *All in the Family*'s most frequent viewers. The study showed that the most frequent viewers admired Archie more than Mike and condoned Archie's ethnic slurs more than infrequent viewers did. The researchers concluded that the selective exposure meant that "*All in the Family* seems to be appealing more to the racially and ethnically prejudiced members of society than to the less prejudiced members."

Vidmar and Rokeach (1974) wrote that

> the findings surely argue against the contention that *All in the Family* has positive effects, as has been claimed by its supporters and admirers. We found that many persons did not see the program as a satire on bigotry and that these persons were even more likely to be viewers who scored high on measures of prejudices. Even more important is the finding that high prejudiced persons were likely to watch *All in the Family* more often than low prejudiced persons, to identify more often with Archie Bunker and to see him winning in the end. All such findings seem to suggest that the program is more likely reinforcing prejudice and racism than combating it.

The findings of Vidmar and Rokeach, as well as those of subsequent scholars who examined the impact of *All in the Family*, were consistent with previous studies showing that pre-existing social and psychological factors influence people's choices of which media to use and how to interpret what they see, hear, or read. In the classic "Mr. Biggott" studies in the late 1940s, prejudiced individuals were shown cartoons in which the bigoted attitudes of Mr. Biggott were portrayed unfavorably. However, instead of seeing the shortcomings of bigotry, the respondents reinterpreted the cartoons to reinforce their existing prejudices or to avoid ridiculing Mr. Biggott (Cooper & Jahoda, 1971).

These and other studies have shown that the impact of the media is to reinforce attitudes already held by members of their audience rather than to convince people to change them. When the content of the media play on negative racial images, even if these themes are ridiculed, prejudiced persons interpret the message as supporting their bigoted attitudes rather than rejecting or changing them.

BLACKS ON TV: WHAT DO CHILDREN LEARN?

Children are particularly vulnerable to images and portrayals in the media, especially because they are learning about themselves and the society in which they live. Images in the media are often the first impressions children have of their own and other racial groups—and there are not always parents or other adults to help young children understand what the media offer.[4] For these reasons, researchers and education groups have been focusing on the impact of television images on children.

The late-1960s and 1970s witnessed an increase in the percentage of minority characters, particularly Blacks, in prime time network television programming on ABC, CBS, and NBC. In the 1969 to 1970 television season, half of the dramatic programs had a Black character, and from that season through the early 1980s, annual surveys of Blacks in network programming showed that 6% to 9% of all television characters were Black. However, the increase in the number of characters did not necessarily mean that Blacks were treated equally with characters of other races.

Research cited by Charles Atkin, Bradley Greenberg, and Steven McDermott (1983) revealed that television's Blacks in that period were more often in more minor roles and less prestigious jobs than White characters, but they were just as industrious, competent, and physically attractive as Whites. Blacks were portrayed as more kind, moral, and altruistic. They also were more often crime victims and involved in violence and killing than Whites. In addition, Blacks tended to be dominated by Whites in crime dramas, although they dominated Whites in situation comedies. By the late 1970s, most of the Black characters were found in situation comedies, where they typically played characters lower in social status and more beset by problems than did Blacks in integrated programs (Atkin et al., 1983).

A study of the 2001 to 2002 broadcast season showed that the television picture had become more diverse, but not as much as the population had. With the addition of Fox, WB, and UPN, there were more major English-language broadcast networks and their program casts were more diverse. Still, according to a 2002 study by Children Now, prime time television programs were still pretty much cast in Black and White, with members of those two groups making up 90% of the casts and an even greater percentage of lead characters. Whites were 80% and Blacks 15% of the prime time primary recurring characters for 95% of the major roles on prime time network television. Moreover, the study showed that 8 p.m., the hour with potentially the most young viewers, was the least racially diverse and most segregated period in terms of all White or all Black casts. As in earlier studies, Children Now (2002) found that every series with all Black opening-credit casts was a situation comedy, whereas Whites dominated drama, real life, comedic drama, and other television genres.

Illustration 2.5 Researchers have found that television programs, such as *The Bernie Mac Show* that feature African American characters, can influence both how young Black viewers see themselves and how others view African Americans.

Source: Copyright © Fox Broadcasting Company.

To determine how television portrayals and interracial interactions affect children, psychologist Sherryl Browne Graves (1999) examined data on racial and ethnic television content, the ways that television content affects viewer attitudes and beliefs, and whether television could be used to alter stereotypes, prejudice, and discrimination. Her study cited research showing that television provides a "window on the world" that is "a key socializing agent" for children of all races.

Graves wrote that "television could influence children by providing examples of people with or without prejudice, diverse social groups that stimulate positive or negative effect, and settings in which racial discrimination is endorsed or rejected." Noting that this could be done by either *inclusion* or *exclusion* of diverse groups, she cited studies showing that "the limited inclusion of visible racial/ethnic groups in television programming and advertising conveys to children and youth the relative lack of power and importance of these groups in the larger society." Although different racial groups are portrayed differently, the most visible non-White racial and ethnic groups on television "are more likely to be presented as criminals or as crime victims and in limited occupational roles."

Looking at how these images affect children, Graves found that most studies focused on the effects portrayals of Blacks had on White and Black children and that few studies were concerned with the effects of Asian, Latino, or Native American characters on children's attitudes. She cited studies showing that seeing Blacks on television could trigger positive or negative attitudes in Black children toward their own group and that Black children's positive attitudes were especially strong when Black cartoon characters were shown in integrated settings. However, when Black characters in prime time programs were seen as unattractive or untrustworthy, they produced negative attitudes in Black children.

Turning to White children, Graves cited research showing that White children, especially those in rural areas, use television as a primary source of information on the various racial and ethnic groups. Whites with more contact with Blacks are less likely to see Black television portrayals as realistic. In addition, Graves (1999) wrote, "the nature of the African American portrayals, positive or negative, generally predicts attitude change" in White children. But, whatever the portrayals, researchers have found that (1) seeing people like themselves on television is important for children of all races and (2) when people of color are presented attractively on television, it leads to more positive viewer attitudes toward members of those groups.

These findings are consistent with earlier studies. Alexis Tan concluded in a 1979 study that steady exposure to television programs that either ignore Blacks or relegate them to low-status roles could lead to low self-esteem among Black viewers (Tan, 1981, p. 261). In addition, other researchers have shown that media portrayals may have a greater influence on the development of minority children than on that of White children.[5]

Television portrayals also affect teenagers of color. In a 2000 article, Gordon Berry wrote that television confers status on the "storytellers" who appear on it. When television programs do not portray members of certain groups, or portray them negatively or unrealistically, it has a negative effect on the ability of teenagers who are members of these groups to believe in themselves and their own capabilities.

How Do the Media Matter?

The findings of the studies cited above and of other studies show that the coverage and portrayal in the media of minorities have an effect on members of both minority and majority groups. But it is a complex effect, one that is mediated by each person's psychological makeup, social status, age, and use of the media. It is unlikely that scholars will ever be able to make definitive conclusions regarding the effects of the media on racial and ethnic minority groups or on any other segments of society.

Communication, unlike chemistry or physics, is a behavioral and social science. It involves human beings and society, not physical elements in laboratory experiments. The role and effect of the media are not as predictable as the outcome when the same chemicals are repeatedly mixed in the same proportions in a laboratory. Furthermore, laboratory findings do not always reflect reality. While the laboratory may be the best setting to observe physical experiments under controlled conditions, it may be the worst setting for observing social happenings. People encounter the media not in a sterile setting but in homes, waiting rooms, bars, and so on. They may watch a television program alone one week, then see the same show the next week with a group. What they see, hear, and read in those settings is influenced by the people around them and by their own psychological makeup.

Although it is difficult to assess the effects of mass communication on society, the research findings make it clear that certain types of people, including the young, those with predispositions to view members of racially different groups in a certain way, and members of minority groups that are not well integrated into the coverage and programming of the media, are affected to a greater extent than others.

From Mass Media to Class Media

The increased racial and ethnic diversity in the United States and the increased diversity in technologies available for the public to use have radically changed the nation's landscape of communication media. As people have more choices of media, they are able to select from more media targeted to their own interests, age, race, or sex. With more choices of media, people go to more places for media. More people are spending more time with media, but less than before with mass media such as general circulation newspapers and prime time network television. The television audience, once divided among only three networks and a few local channels, now chooses from a wide range of cable and broadcast outlets, DVDs, and videos. The media are moving from mass media to class media, with the sharpest growth in class media that target segments of the population rather than catering to a general audience. More media target more subgroups in the population with news and entertainment for their specific interests. As this occurs, the system of diverse media voices envisioned by the authors of the First Amendment to the Bill of Rights over 200 years ago is coming close to reality.

In a multimedia and multicultural society, people pay attention to the media that pay attention to them. In the past, the mass media often ignored or stereotyped people of color, who were too insignificant in number to matter. Now that both the media and society offer more diversity in content than ever before, more people of more races have more media to choose from that target them as an audience class. Whether more choice leads to a better understanding of ourselves and those not like us is not yet known. What is known is that people of color have not been treated adequately or accurately in the mass audience media that have been the dominant mass media in the United States for almost 200 years.

Notes

1. For books with readings on racial, ethnic, and gender issues in the media, see *Facing Difference: Race, Gender and Mass Media*, S. Biagi and M. Kern-Foxworth (Eds.), 1997, Thousand Oaks, CA: Pine Forge; *Ethnic Minorities and the Media*, S. Cottle (Ed.), 2000, Buckingham and Philadelphia: Open University Press; *The Media in Black and White*, E. E. Dennis and E. C. Pease (Eds.), 1997, New Brunswick, NJ: Transaction; *Gender, Race and Class in Media: A Text-Reader*, G. Dines and J. M. Humez (Eds.), 1995, Thousand Oaks, CA: Sage; and *Cultural Diversity and the U.S. Media*, Y. R. Kamalipour and T. Carili (Eds.), 1998, Albany: State University of New York Press.

2. For a further elaboration of these functions in contemporary media, see *The Dynamics of Mass Communication* (pp. 33-49), by J. P. Dominick, 1983, Reading, MA: Addison-Wesley.

3. For more on the *New York Sun* and its influence, see *The Sun Shines for All*, by J. E. Steele, 1993, Syracuse, NY: Syracuse University Press.

4. For readings on children and the media, see *Children and the Media*, E. E. Dennis and E. C. Pease (Eds.), 1996, New Brunswick, NJ: Transaction.

5. For a review and analysis of the early literature on the effects of television on minority children, see *Television and the Socialization of the Minority Child*, G. L. Berry and C. Mitchell-Kernan (Eds.), 1982, San Diego, CA: Academic Press.

References

Atkin, C. K., Greenberg, B. S., & McDermott, S. (1983). Television and race role socialization. *Journalism Quarterly, 60*(3), 408.

Berry, G. L. (2000). Multicultural media portrayals and changing demographic landscape: The psychosocial impact of television representations of the adolescent of color. *Journal of Adolescent Health: Youth and Media, 27*(2, Suppl. 1).

Children Now. (2002, April). *Fall colors 2001–02: Prime time diversity report.* Oakland, CA: Children Now.

Cooper, E., & Jahoda, M. (1971). The evasion of propaganda: How prejudiced people respond to anti-prejudice propaganda. In W. Schramm & D. F. Roberts (Eds.), *The process and effects of mass communication* (pp. 287-299). Urbana and Chicago: University of Illinois Press.

Emery, E., & Emery, M. (1996). *The press and America* (8th ed.). Boston: Allyn and Bacon.

Graves, S. B. (1999). Television and prejudice reduction: When does television as a vicarious experience make a difference? *Journal of Social Issues, 55*(4), 707-727.

Gutiérrez, F. (1978). Making news-media coverage of Chicanos. *Agenda, 8*(6), 21-22.

Lasswell, H. (1948). The structure and function of communication in society. In W. Schramm & D. F. Roberts (Eds.) (1971), *The process and effects of mass communication* (rev. ed.; pp. 84-99). Urbana and Chicago: University of Illinois Press.

Lear, N. (1971, October 10). As I read how Laura saw Archie. *New York Times.*

Lippmann, W. (1997). *Public opinion.* New York: Free Press. (Original work published 1922)

Potter, D. (1954). *People of plenty.* Chicago: University of Chicago Press.

Sandman, P. M., Rubin, D. M., & Sachsman, D. B. (1972). *Media: An introductory analysis of American mass communication.* Englewood Cliffs, NJ: Prentice Hall.

Sandman, P. M., Rubin, D. M., & Sachsman, D. B. (1982). *Media: An introductory analysis of American mass communication* (3rd ed.). Englewood Cliffs, NJ: Prentice Hall.

Tan, A. S. (1981). *Mass communication theories and research.* Columbus, OH: Grid.

Turner, R. H., & Surace, S. J. (1956). Zoot suiters and Mexicans: Symbols in crowd behavior. *American Journal of Sociology, 47*(1), 14-20.

Vidmar, N., & Rokeach, M. (1974). Archie Bunker's bigotry: A study in selective perception and exposure. *Journal of Communication, 24*(1).

Williams, W. (1994, July). Remarks to The Freedom Forum panel on coverage of crime. Unity '94 Convention, Atlanta, GA.

Wright, C. (1959). Mass communication: A sociological perspective. New York: Random House.

Part II

Racialism in Entertainment Portrayals

The Roots of 3
Racial Stereotypes in
American Entertainment

I n 2000, a film by African American director Spike Lee was released and quickly became a center of controversy because of its use of Black stereotypes from a supposedly bygone era. The film, *Bamboozled*, depicted minstrel shows with Black actors in blackface and parodied a cast of stereotypical characters ranging from mammies to pickaninnies and virtually every other vile portrayal of Blacks ever exhibited in the guise of American entertainment. The target of Lee's satire was the network television industry of the 21st century. The message: Even into the new millennium, film and video producers continue to "bamboozle" American audiences with distorted images of people of color and marginalize them as caricatures in society. How and why this came about, and remains an ugly scar on the history of the media that still influences images in the media today, is the subject of this and the following chapter.

Any discussion of the portrayals of people of color in American entertainment must include the concept of *stereotyping*. It is a means of quickly bringing to the audience's collective consciousness a character's preconceived value system and behavioral expectations. Audience members are then able to assess the character against their own value systems and categorize the character as, for example, "the villain" or "the heroine." Stereotypes are therefore shortcuts to character development and are a crucial element of mass entertainment and literary fare.

As noted in Chapter 2, stereotyping and the use of symbols can be useful devices in helping media producers convey complex issues and ideas. However, when stereotypical images are used with prejudice to castigate entire racial or cultural groups as inferior and undesirable beings, they do injustice to the basic tenets of American democracy. In a racially homogenous society, the possibility of racially based stereotyping is negated. For example, a dramatic presentation in a racially homogenous society wherein a villain is brought to justice by a heroine suggests to the audience that "good" (the heroine) overcomes "evil" (the villain). However, the same concept applied in a multiracial society has the potential to transmit a far different message if it is done persistently with prejudice. Thus, if "good" is consistently represented by members of one racial group and "evil" by members of another, the resulting message is that the offending group is evil.

Because the concept of *prejudice* is central to our discussion, let's use the term as James Jones defined it in his 1972 book *Prejudice and Racism*. Prejudice, he wrote, "is a negative attitude toward a person or group based upon a social comparison process in which the individual's own group is taken as the positive point of reference" (p. 3). Thus, while stereotyping per se may have merits in popular literature, the arts, and—under certain circumstances—news reports, when combined with racial prejudice it poses a devastating obstacle to human development and understanding in a multicultural society.

Before examining racial portrayals in American mass entertainment, we should look at the social and historical precedents and attitudes in which the stereotypes in such portrayals were cultivated. This will provide insight into whether the stereotypes resulted from prejudice and the degree to which social and historical factors have been influential in their development and use. We will consider the experiences of four non-White groups in the United States to determine whether a causal relationship existed between their experiences with Europeans and their subsequent treatment in entertainment media.

The History and Stereotyping of People of Color in the United States

NATIVE AMERICANS

Native Americans (Indians) were the first peoples of a different race and ethnicity to confront Europeans on the American continent. (Christopher Columbus mistakenly believed his 1492 expedition from Spain had resulted in discovery of a short sea route to the Indies—which then included India, China, the East Indies, and Japan—thus European immigrants called the indigenous people "Indians.") The Europeans were at once faced with a dilemma of how to coexist with those they called Indians, people they saw as primitive but who also had some qualities they admired. The writings of early settlers referred to what they considered to be the natives' primitive innocence, their willingness to share food and other essentials of life in a communal environment, and their dark, handsome physical appearance. To the White settlers, these attributes were "noble." At the same time, the settlers also made observations of the natives' proclivity for nudity, open sexual relationships, and incidents of cannibalism. These acts were considered "savage." Thus emerged in colonial era literature the concept of the "noble savage."

Initially, the English colonists decided to convert the natives to Christianity in an attempt to assimilate them while the task of creating a European-style society was under way. However, the colonists eventually realized that religious conversion of the natives was impossible, and they rationalized the elimination of the natives as the removal of a barrier to "civilizing" the continent.

By the mid-1800s, the policies for dealing with the "Indian problem" had found their justification in popular literature, which helped to establish the myth of the monolithic "Indian," without regard for distinctions among the more than 2,000 cultures, languages, and value systems the concept represented. The literary stereotype was part of the Western frontier writing formula developed after the Civil War. Writers of this genre included Bret Harte and Mark Twain. Readers were already conditioned to see the natives portrayed in a manner that justified their elimination as a barrier to Western expansion. Twain and others wrote of the picturesque scenery and romantic lifestyles of the frontier, in contrast with the "savages" who occupied the land. In *Roughing It*, Twain described the Gosiute Indians as "scrawny creatures," "treacherous-looking," and "prideless beggars." It remained only for dime novelist Edward Ellis to write during the 1880s and 1890s of the Indian as merely a prelude to a more enlightened White civilization.

Stories of actual and exaggerated atrocities perpetrated by Indians on White settlers, who pushed ever westward into the frontier, firmly encouraged a hatred of Indians. The Indians were portrayed as the settlers' enemy in warfare and as an enemy of the progress of "civilization." Literature during the Indian wars is rife with tales of natives burning, looting, raping, and scalping pioneers who were only fulfilling their "manifest destiny." It was against this backdrop that Frederick Jackson Turner's *Frontier Thesis*, presented in 1893, argued that American (White) character had been molded by the experience of the Western frontier. Turner's ideas were accepted to the extent that they pervaded history textbooks into the middle of the 20th century. The elimination or subjugation of the Native American was seen as merely an evolutionary step in the development of industrial America.

BLACK AMERICANS

In 1619, a year before the arrival of the Mayflower on the shores of the American continent, 20 Africans were brought to Jamestown aboard a

Dutch pirate ship. The ship's captain offered to exchange his human cargo for a supply of foodstuffs. The young Black men and women with Spanish names such as Antony, Isabella, and Pedro were probably originally headed for the West Indies on a Spanish vessel before being intercepted by the Dutch ship (Bennett, 1966, p. 30). The 20 Africans became the genesis of a Black population that was to have a major impact on the development of the future United States.

Although the facts of slavery in America and its legacy of human indignity have been well chronicled, the roots of its underlying psychosis have been less often explored in popular literature. The popular notion regarding the treatment of Blacks and their African ancestors has tended to focus on slavery as a phenomenon of Southern White culture based on geographic and economic factors. What is often overlooked is that slavery was a part of the Northern experience from colonial times on. It is clear that racism against Blacks was a factor in English Calvinist and Puritan religious ideology before those influences were brought to the New World. This imposed two concepts on colonial-era attitudes toward Black people. The first concept was the Anglo Saxon belief that the color white represented things that were pure, clean, and good and that reflected the spiritual light, and that the color black represented impurity, filth, evil, and spiritual darkness. Remnants of this concept persist to this day in common rhetorical usage. Thus Americans refer to certain baked goods as "angel food" (white) and "devil's food" (dark chocolate), to a miscreant relative as the "black sheep" of the family, to characters in dramas who are costumed in white as heroes and in black as villains (as in *Star Wars* and other movies), and so on. The second concept is related to the Puritan idea of predestination, which relied on observation to distinguish the "Elect" from the "damned." Those who seemed relatively prosperous and self-sufficient were deemed superior to those who were enslaved. Against this religiously seated and strongly held attitude, the reaction of the English colonists (including inhabitants of the Northern seaboard) to Blacks in the New World is predictable. In fact, the trading of slaves was the predominant commodity on New York's Wall Street in 1711 partly because Puritan law was ambiguous on the subject. One such law, of 1641, is revealing:

> There shall never be any bond-slavery, villenage or captivitie amongst us; unless it be lawfully captives taken in just warrs, and such strangers as willingly sell themselves, or are sold to us: and such shall have the libertyes and Christian usages which the law of God established in Israel concerning such persons doth morally require, provided this exempts none from servitude who shall be judged thereto by Authoritie. (cited in Jordan, 1969, p. 7)

The Whites in New England were the first to establish what later would be called "Jim Crow" laws in the post-Civil War South as a means of codifying their prejudices against Blacks, although slavery never became a widespread practice in the Northeast for economic reasons. In the South, the mythology of the "happy slave," who was content to serve his or her master as the ultimate fulfillment of life, grew as a justification for the exploitation of Blacks. Much of the post-Civil War literature paints a negative image of Blacks that was designed to reinforce institutional and social racism. Many of the accusations against Black integrity that emerged during Reconstruction are now too familiar: laziness, slow-wittedness, loose standards of morality, fondness for alcoholic beverages, and so on. Lynching and other acts of violence against Blacks and those sympathetic to them were ample evidence of the attitudes held by Whites toward Blacks in the United States at the dawning of the 20th century.

LATINO AMERICANS

There is little mention of colonial Mexico in North American literature until the 19th century. Spain ruled Mexico for 300 years (from 1521 to 1821) before Mexico won its war for independence. In 1803, however, the Louisiana Purchase removed the vast buffer of territory between the United States and Mexico. The expansionist movement by U.S. settlers into the West and Southwest not only precipitated conflict with Native Americans, as discussed previously, but also led to war with Mexico in 1846.

Central to the development of relations between Mexico and the United States was the Santa Fe Trail, which was legally opened as a commercial trade route in 1821. The trail ran from Independence, Missouri, to Santa Fe, New Mexico, and became the focal point of friction between White settlers and Mexicans. When some inhabitants of the newly formed Republic of Mexico became disenchanted with their new government, Anglo American settlers, who were there in significant numbers by the mid-1830s, spurred their movement for independence. In fact, there is much to suggest that American literature of the period was primarily designed to stir up local sentiment for overthrow of the Mexican government in Texas and New Mexico. Thus, Whites engaged in hostilities against Mexicans during the war for Texas independence. At the same time, popular literature vividly portrayed a "cruel" General Antonio Lopez de Santa Anna's massacre of the "gallant" defenders of the Alamo in 1836, who included the White American folk heroes David Crockett and James Bowie. Americans were generally persuaded to visualize the Mexican as an inhuman enemy a decade before war with Mexico was officially declared.

Cruelty was not the only negative trait ascribed to Mexicans. Cecil Robinson, in his 1977 book *Mexico and the Hispanic Southwest in American Literature*, chronicled the origins of several stereotypes that began to appear in Anglo writings before and during the U.S.-Mexican war of 1846 to 1848. During that war, American naval Lieutenant H.A. Wise wrote that Mexicans were "beyond comparison the laziest and most ignorant set of vagabonds the world produces." George Wilkins Kendall wrote, "Give them but tortillas, frijoles, and chile colorado to supply their animal wants for the day, and seven-tenths of the Mexicans are satisfied; and so they will continue to be until the race becomes extinct or amalgamated with Anglo-Saxon stock."

When Mexicans were not being portrayed in Anglo literature as lazy and indolent, they were assailed for uncleanliness. Texas romance writer Jeremiah Clemens gave his version of the origin of the term "greaser" and why he felt it was appropriate: "The people look greasy, their clothes are greasy, their dogs are greasy—everywhere grease and filth hold divided dominion, and the singular appropriateness of the name bestowed by the western settlers, soon caused it to be universally adopted by the American army." In the short story "The Inroad of the Nabajo" by Albert Pike (1934), the women of Santa Fe are described as "scudding hither and thither, with their black hair flying, and their naked feet shaming the ground by their superior filth." It should be noted that several American writers found Mexican women quite charming and wrote at length about their feminine virtues, which contrasted sharply with puritanical customs of American women of the era in dress and social demeanor.

A major factor in the attitude of Whites toward Mexico and its people was the negativity toward Mexican ethnicity. Most of the population was either full-blooded native (Indian) or mestizo (a mixture of Spanish ancestry and Indian). Anglo American writers routinely referred with disdain to Mexicans as "these mixed races." But it was the sizeable body of popular literature that grew out of the lore of the Santa Fe Trail that set the tone for American imagery of Mexicans and the Southwest. Works such as *The Time of the Gringo* by Elliot Arnold, *Anthony Adverse* by Hervy Allen, and *Adventures in the Santa Fe Trade* by James Josiah Webb established the basic stereotypes by 1900.

The subsequent immigration to the United States of many people from Latin American countries has resulted in little difference in the treatment of Spanish-speaking people by the American media. Puerto Ricans, Cubans, Guatemalans, and others are generally accorded the same stereotypical status as Mexicans, and no attention is paid to the cultural, social, and historical differences between Spanish-speaking people.

ASIAN AMERICANS

The Asian experience in America has a short history prior to 1900. Large-scale Chinese immigration to the United States began with the California gold rush in 1848. Japanese people did not come to the United

States in significant numbers until after 1855, when the Japanese government passed laws enabling its citizens to emigrate. We are concerned in this discussion with the Chinese and Japanese because (1) other Asian and Pacific Island peoples were less of a social factor in the United States before 1900, and (2) American attitudes toward the two groups were similar enough as to be virtually indistinguishable. In fact, many Americans never bothered to note any differences between the Chinese and Japanese, lumping them together simply as the "Yellow Peril."

Since the overwhelming majority of Asian immigration was to California and other West Coast states, their social history in America during the 19th century is focused there. By 1870, more than 60,000 Chinese in California had settled into farming, mining, factory work, and domestic labor after railroad jobs became scarce. Whites, who had moved west to seek quick wealth in the gold rush, came to resent the Chinese because they had jobs while many Whites were unemployed. Dennis Kearney, leader of the California Workingman's Party, orchestrated an anti-Chinese movement with the backing of the *San Francisco Chronicle*. Kearney ended every speech with the slogan "The Chinese Must Go." Kearney and his followers stirred prejudice against Chinese workers who were highly visible because of their adherence to traditional customs of dress, pigtail hairstyle, and communal living. After 20 years as a welcome source of cheap labor and of enjoying a reputation for industry, honesty, thrift, and peaceful disposition, the Chinese became objects of scorn. Whites suddenly saw them as debased, clannish, and deceitful. In the 1870s, racially motivated incidents of violence occurred in several Western towns that resulted in the deaths of numerous Chinese inhabitants.

Finally, in 1882, the first Federal Chinese exclusion law was passed. In 1887, only 10 Chinese people immigrated to the United States. Ironically, the Chinese Exclusion Act of 1882 made possible an increase in Japanese immigration to the United States. The decline in Chinese immigrant labor proved that there was White racism against the Chinese, because jobs once held by the Chinese went unfilled and a serious farm labor shortage developed in California and other Western states. Soon there was a demand for Japanese immigrants who had proven farming skills and were willing to work for low wages. To meet the labor demand, nearly 60,000 Japanese came to America between 1899 and 1904.

History soon repeated itself, from 1901 to 1906, during the corrupt administration of San Francisco Mayor Eugene Schmitz and his political boss Abraham Ruef. They used the Japanese as scapegoats when public attention was turned on their own dubious activities. Schmitz's regime was backed by organized labor, which claimed that the Japanese worked for lower wages and were driving Whites out of the job market. At the same time, Japan quickly defeated the Russians in 1904 in the Russo-Japanese War and eventually seized Korea. Japan's military successes created apprehension in America that Asians were a threat to Western civilization.

Once again, it was the *San Francisco Chronicle* that crusaded in front-page articles against immigration, this time of the Japanese. The *Chronicle* urged and supported a citywide boycott of Japanese merchants in San Francisco. The paper charged the immigrants with maintaining loyalty to the Emperor of Japan. Mass meetings were held denouncing Japanese immigrants and soon there followed acts of violence against them. The official reaction to what became known as the "Yellow Peril" was a series of laws restricting Japanese immigrant rights in America. This culminated in the passage of the Immigration Act of 1924 that banned entry to the United States to all aliens not eligible for citizenship, although the legislation clearly targeted the Japanese.

During the height of "Yellow Peril" hysteria, Chinese and Japanese people were viewed as devious and vicious. Popular literature warned of the dangers of intermarriage with Asians and charged that Asian men purposefully sought White women. Those attitudes found their way into entertainment media, as we shall see.

The Beginnings of Mass Entertainment: Racialism on Stage

The historical social relationships between White Americans and people of color demonstrate that White attitudes have been molded negatively toward each of the groups for specific purposes. In each case, our definition of *prejudice* (a negative attitude toward a group resulting from a comparison process using White society as the positive point of reference) has been fulfilled. We have also seen these prejudicial attitudes reflected in popular literature and observed how they affected American political, economic, and social life. Next, we will consider the relationship of those prejudicial attitudes to mass entertainment. To understand that relationship, we must take a look at the developmental highlights of mass entertainment in America.

It is no accident that the rise of American mass entertainment coincided with the populist movement that began in the 1820s and 1830s. The election of Andrew Jackson to the presidency in 1828 marked the ascension of the "common man" to political and social prominence if not to greater economic stature. Cities became population centers, and laborers moved from farms to cities to become wage earners. The genteel, socially elite Americans with refined cultural tastes were inundated by the onrushing tide of the populist movement.

The pivotal year 1833 marked the beginning of the penny press newspaper ushered in by Benjamin Day's *New York Sun* and its symbolic motto

"It Shines for ALL!" As Day's unsophisticated newspaper became the reading fare of an audience that clamored for "news" (i.e., gossip, sensationalism, and crime), live entertainment changed to accommodate the tastes of the working class. It was also in 1833 in New York City's Bowery Theatre when an uninhibited audience shouted down the orchestra's symphonic overture and hollered instead for a rendition of "Yankee Doodle"—the audience got its wish. Just as the penny press made newspapers affordable for the masses, ticket prices for live entertainment plummeted from several dollars to 25 cents or less.

The stage was the first and, from the middle of the 19th century to the 1920s, the primary major mass entertainment medium in America. People in the cities filled large, ornate theaters. Rural dwellers attended traveling shows housed in tents. Theatrical agents quickly came to understand the imperative of catering to the public's taste. Their reward was a full cash box and lusty cheers; agents who failed suffered hostile catcalls, hisses, and financial losses. People of color played a figurative, if not literal, role in the development of mass entertainment because the populist audience demanded their inclusion in theatrical performances. The price of that inclusion, however, was accommodation of the prejudicial attitudes and values of the masses. In general, the audience wanted plays with common people (i.e., themselves) portrayed as heroes. They wanted foot-tapping music and dancing and maintained a strong desire to see anything that fulfilled their perceptions of Black American culture. Perhaps above all, they wanted comedy, and people of color were a convenient foil. "Leave 'em laughing" became an early show business axiom.

One early favorite play had a Native American theme and was titled *The Original, Aboriginal, Erratic, Operatic, Semi-Civilized and Semi-Savage Extravaganza of Pocahontas*. Stereotypical myths of Native Americans, which had been spread by writers such as James Fenimore Cooper and pulp novelists, easily made the transition to the stage. After the Civil War, live entertainment took to the outdoor theater arena, with "Buffalo Bill" Cody and his "Wild West" show leading the way. Cody played out the American myth of the taming of the West and its Indian population to Eastern audiences while the real Indian wars were being fought across the country. Cody legitimized himself by periodically returning to the West to serve as a scout and Indian fighter. His show played to packed theaters in the United States and Europe for several decades. By 1900, other traveling shows, including circuses and variety acts, were spreading racial stereotypes across America.

Minstrel shows featuring Anglo American actors in blackface appeared in the 1830s, after an itinerant White actor, Thomas Dartmouth Rice, borrowed a song-and-dance routine from a little Black slave boy he had seen perform it on a street corner. Billing himself as "Daddy" Rice, he applied burnt cork to his face, dressed in tattered clothing, and performed the borrowed routine as the "jump Jim Crow" dance—to the delight of audiences from New York's Bowery Theatre to the London stage.

Edwin P. Christie, a traveling salesman from Buffalo, New York, launched his career as a show business promoter after his travels took him through the South in the 1830s and 1840s. In Louisiana, Christie saw Blacks perform at a public gathering where they were allowed to gather for the amusement of Whites. Impressed with the musical and dance variations he saw, Christie went back to Buffalo and developed his own caricatures of Black personalities for an entertainment variety act. Thus the minstrel show was born. For decades, Blacks could neither perform in nor attend such shows, which were based on their musical and dance traditions. Ironically, when Black minstrel troupes did become acceptable to White audiences, Blacks were compelled to perform in blackface.

For 80 years, the minstrel show was the most popular form of live American entertainment. In its classic form, the minstrel show consisted of two acts. Part one employed a minimum of 15 men on stage in a semicircular seating arrangement with gaudily dressed comedians in the seats on the ends. A nattily attired "interlocutor" stood in the center and a comedic exchange took place between him and the comedians. Singers and banjo and tambourine players comprised the rest of the troupe. Songs, dances, rapid-fire jokes, and gags came without pause. Part two of the show (often called the "olio") was comprised of recitations, monologues, specialty songs, comedy skits, and burlesque routines. (After minstrel shows faded in popularity, the olio concept was expanded into a separate group of acts and became known as "vaudeville." Vaudeville launched the careers of some of America's most honored performers, including George Burns, Bob Hope, Jack Benny, and Abbott and Costello.) It remained only for White performer Al Jolson to refine the minstrel show affectations to indelibly stereotype Black people in American entertainment. With renditions of "Mammy," "Rockabye Your Rockabye Baby to a Dixie Melody," "Swanee," and other songs, the blackfaced Jolson was called "Mr. Show Business" as early as 1915, but he had been a popular fixture since the turn of the century. Jolson was unquestionably the most popular entertainer in America during the period. By the time motion pictures began to supplant the live stage show in popularity, the quintessential stage musical *Show Boat* opened the Broadway season in 1927 with a favorite White American theme at its core: the interplay of Blacks and Southern Whites set against an idyllic romantic background along the Mississippi River.

Racialism in the Movies

Thomas Edison is generally credited with the development of motion picture technology with his invention of the Kinetoscope in 1889. In 1903, one of his assistants produced the first motion picture with a story line,

Illustration 3.1   Al Jolson was one of many White entertainers who per-
                        formed in blackface makeup on stage and in movies.

Source: CORBIS.

The Great Train Robbery. Movies were projected without sound until 1927,
when Al Jolson starred as a blackfaced entertainer in *The Jazz Singer,* the
first "talking" (and, of course, "singing") movie.

Portrayals of people of color appeared very early in motion pictures.
As early as 1894, one could view the *Sioux Ghost Dance* on one of
Edison's contraptions and, by 1898, Buffalo Bill's Wild West show had
been committed to film—complete with its imagery of the Indians'

collapse before White "civilization." Only a year after *The Great Train Robbery*, Biograph released a one-reel feature (*A Bucket of Cream Ale*) depicting a Black maid employed by a White man. A White actress in blackface played the maid. Between 1910 and 1914, several films projected Mexican stereotypes, including a series of works with the term *greaser* in the titles. Consistent with the treatment of Asian immigrants at the turn of the century, Asians appeared stereotypically as diabolical personalities in such films as *The Yellow Menace* (1916). Interestingly, in *The Yellow Menace*, Asians and Mexicans combine forces in a subversive plot against the United States.

Although there are many differences between and among the racial and cultural groups under consideration here, a close examination of the treatment of these groups in American mass entertainment reveals remarkable similarities. Our review earlier in this chapter of the historical experiences of these groups shows that Whites held negative, prejudicial attitudes against each of them before those attitudes manifested themselves in popular media.

Generally, all the characterizations of people of color in early films projected an attitudinal posture of White superiority. That attitude revealed itself on screen through the portrayal of non-Whites as inferior in two major capacities: intellectual and moral. Virtually every characterization of non-Whites was designed to reinforce the attitude of White superiority. The low socioeconomic status of working class Whites during the heyday of the industrial age resulted in insecurities that movie producers capitalized on by using racial stereotypes to bolster audience members' self-esteem and reinforce their attitude of racial superiority. White insecurities, as reflected in the first 40 years of American popular cinema, were revealed to be a fear of miscegenation and the threat that non-White cultures would have an impact on White social values. Thus, as stage producers and entertainers profited financially by giving the masses what they wanted, movie makers quickly developed a symbiotic relationship with their patrons, often at the expense of Americans of color.

Several basic movie themes derived from the attitudinal premises of White intellectual and moral supremacy (see Table 3.1). They were applied at various times to Native, Black, Latino, and Asian Americans alike.

With the release of the technical epic *Birth of a Nation* by D.W. Griffith in 1915, movies began to institutionalize racial stereotypes. Griffith established a pattern, which would endure for decades, of portraying American Blacks as intellectually and morally inferior to Whites, and his films carried a strong message against sexual contact between the races. Perhaps the first film to openly proclaim the doctrine of White supremacy over Indians was William S. Hart's *The Aryan*, which was released in 1916. One of the titles projected across the screen of this silent movie also played to the fear

Table 3.1 Some Traits Commonly Applied To People of Color in Early Movies	
Intellectual Traits	*Moral Traits*
Preoccupation with simple ideas	Low regard for human life
Inferior strategy in warfare and conflict situations	Criminal behavior
Low or nonexistent occupational status	Sexual promiscuity
Poor speech patterns or dialect	Drug or alcohol abuse
Comedic foil	Dishonesty

of miscegenation and read in part "Our women shall be guarded." As was most commonly the practice in early movies, Whites portrayed all the non-White characters. (It is interesting to note, however, that genuine Native Americans were sometimes employed to play minor Indian roles, but the practice was not without problems. Directors found it difficult to teach them how to act "Indian," prompting one observer to write an article titled "The Dangers of Employing Redskins as Movie Actors.")

An exception to the practice of White actors portraying all the non-White characters was the work of Japanese actor Sessue Hayakawa, who was involved in at least two early films in which he portrayed Asian characters. In the 1914 film *Typhoon,* Hayakawa plays a young Japanese diplomat in Paris who, among other things, becomes romantically involved with a French actress. During the course of an argument, the woman hurls racial epithets like "whining yellow rat" at the diplomat. He kills her. In the 1915 film *The Cheat,* Hayakawa is cast as a deceitful Asian who schemes to obtain the sexual favors of a naive, but married, White socialite. In both *Typhoon* and *The Cheat* the message is clear: Interracial love leads to tragedy.

Latinos fared no better than other non-Whites in the first two decades of American cinema. A series of films denigrating Mexicans appeared, including *Tony the Greaser* in 1911 and *The Greaser's Revenge* in 1914. Mexicans in American film were the vilest of characters and indulged in banditry, pillage, rape, and murder. The portrayals were so severe that the Mexican government banned such films in 1922—after filing a written protest in 1919 that went unheeded. Hollywood's response was to transport the "greaser" role to other nations and to invent locales with pseudo-Latin names. In a perverse manner, these films set the stage for the popularity of the mysterious, forbidden, "Latin lover" role that became a movie staple in the 1920s and 1930s. Rudolph Valentino was Hollywood's biggest star in that role.

The Changes in Racial Stereotyping During Hollywood's Heyday

The fact that stereotypes can, and do, change is evidenced by shifts in racial portrayals during the 15-year period from 1930 to 1945. Although the basic attitudes held by Whites toward people of color did not undergo significant change, the passage of time altered the social relationships between Whites and non-Whites. The result of this was that Hollywood had to make changes to conform to the new realities. Unfortunately, the portrayals did not become more accurate and sensitive to the realities of the non-White experience in America but were merely adjusted to conform to more credible representations. For example, Hollywood could not continue to portray Blacks only or mostly as criminals and undesirables of various types (as movies had from 1900 to 1920), because it was clear that Blacks had other dimensions of character that were easily observed in "real life." The movie industry's response to social reality was simply to shift to new stereotypes that were still consistent with prejudicial notions.

The portrayals of Native Americans changed little between 1930 and 1945—probably because of their unique place in American lore. The Indian symbolized the fulfillment of the American dream—the immigrant's ability to conquer the obstacles presented by a new continent and its existing inhabitants and to harvest its seemingly endless riches as reward. Hollywood adopted the Indian as a living monument to the ideals of manifest destiny and created a stereotype that barely managed to be a facsimile of Native American culture. Examples of this include the 1939 film *Drums Along the Mohawk* and the 1940 film *Northwest Passage*. No distinction was made in the movies between the Native American cultures of the Northeast, the Plains, and the Southeast. Feathers, beads, fringed pants, pinto ponies, and halting English dialects were applied indiscriminately to represent the concept of "Indian" to movie audiences. The notion played well across the United States, as motion picture audiences seemingly could not get their fill of "cowboy and Indian" movies and serials. The Native American's role was to constantly help audiences relive his defeat at the hands of the U.S. Calvary and other assorted "good guys." Thus, from 1930 to World War II, the major change in movie portrayals of the Native American was the crystallization of an image. The Indian became an American cliché. Clichés die hard and the movie Indian remained throughout the heyday of Hollywood cinema.

A more pronounced shift in a stereotype took place in the movie characterization of the Black American. The venomous, hate-filled disparagement of Blacks epitomized in *Birth of a Nation* and other films of its era, such as *The Wooing and Wedding of a Coon* in 1905, *The Masher* in 1907, and *The Nigger* in 1915, evolved into less threatening characterizations. The new stereotype played to White perceptions of Black personalities who, in the vernacular of the era, "knew their place" in American society.

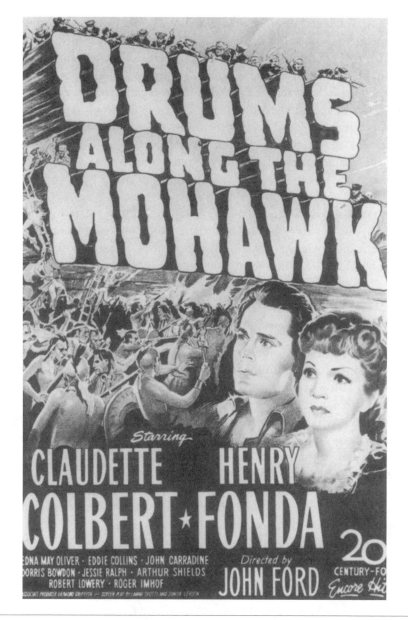

Illustration 3.2   The portrayal of Native Americans as savages was typical Hollywood fare for decades. This poster for *Drums Along the Mohawk* (1939) promised movie viewers action scenes of Indian warriors attacking White settlers.

Source: Academy of Motion Picture Arts and Sciences.

Black actors now appeared in movies for the purpose of entertaining White audiences within the context of actual social limitations. They were cast as domestic workers, waiters, and porters—roles befitting their unequal status as American citizens. In musicals, they demonstrated their "rhythmic" talents as singers and dancers. Meanwhile, the supposed inferior mental capacities of Blacks made for hilarious comedy. The pre-World War II era brought to the screen comedic characters such as Stepin Fetchit, Mantan Moreland, and Willie Best. It also produced the *Our Gang* series, with the characters of Buckwheat, Farina, and Stymie. When the old days of the antebellum South were recalled by Hollywood, as in *Gone With the Wind,* Blacks played the happy, faithful, and sometimes lazy slaves. Hattie McDaniel received the first Oscar awarded to a Black actress or actor for her portrayal of the dutiful and protective mammy to Scarlett O'Hara in the screen classic. Ms. McDaniel's award as best "supporting" actress was, therefore, doubly symbolic.

Perhaps the primary reason for the change in Latino stereotyping during the 1930s was economics. The formal protest and subsequent banning of American movie making and distribution in Mexico by the Mexican government in 1922 did not go unnoticed in other Latin American countries. Although Hollywood intended the "greaser" stereotype to be its vision of Mexicans, Central and South American nations took equal offense when filmmakers began to create euphemisms for the roles in an attempt to placate Mexico. To appeal to the Latin American market, Hollywood eventually imported Latino actors and actresses to star in sizzling romantic features. In the late 1920s and 1930s, filmmakers promoted Latinos to a more sophisticated level of "greasery." The Latino male was yet to attain personal integrity and social acceptability but he did, in the words of one movie critic, at least dress well. At the same time, it was non-Latino actors, such as Noah Beery and Paul Muni, who played the Latino roles in 1928 in *The Dove* and in 1935 in *Bordertown,* respectively. Alas, the "Latin lover" was not always Latino.

One of the traits Hollywood ascribed to Mexicans was a quick temper. Films of this era almost always allowed for a display of irrational Latino temperament. The Latino temperament was soon incorporated into female roles and, by the mid-1930s and into the early 1940s, Hollywood had recruited a number of sensuous, tempestuous leading ladies for the purpose. The idea was to appeal to both U.S. and Latin American audiences. Among the new female stars were Delores Del Rio (*The Red Dance,* 1928) and Lupe Velez (*Hot Pepper,* 1933; *Strictly Dynamite,* 1934; *Mexican Spitfire,* 1940). One concept in the tradition of Hollywood racial portrayals was unchanged, however; interracial movie romances between Latinos and their White lovers were virtually never successful.

By this time, American relations with Latin America were vital for political reasons, because the United States could ill afford to offend potential allies at a time when war was imminent. This circumstance created opportunities for other Latino actors and actresses shortly before the outbreak of World War II. The display of Hollywood goodwill and the profit motive resulted in the successful careers of Carmen Miranda, Cesar Romero, and Desi Arnaz. Film titles began to reflect a Latin American flavor (*Down*

Illustration 3.3   Mantan Moreland provided comic relief in 15 "Charlie Chan" movies as Chan's chauffeur, Birmingham Brown. As shown in this publicity photograph, Moreland often froze in wide-eyed terror when faced with suspenseful situations, a common Hollywood portrayal of Blacks.

Source: RKO photograph courtesy of the Academy of Motion Picture Arts and Sciences.

Argentine Way, 1940; *A Weekend in Havana,* 1941). Concurrently there was a conscious attempt to acquaint American audiences with Latin American history through movies on Benito Juarez and Simòn Bolìvar. Although political and economic pressures combined to accord Latinos the largest degree of change in their stereotype among people of color between 1930

Illustration 3.4   Hattie McDonald earned an Oscar for her portrayal of the faithful mammy to Vivien Leigh in *Gone With the Wind* (1939). Hollywood usually depicted Black slaves as being delighted with their servile roles.

Source: MGM photograph courtesy of the Academy of Motion Picture Arts and Sciences.

and 1945, certain prejudices lingered on screen. In general, Latinos were not seen as people with family values, stable romantic relationships, or honorable careers. Moreover, Latino men still had an uncomfortable (for Anglo American audiences) proclivity for romantic interest in White women.

With the passage of the anti-Japanese Immigration Act of 1924, the presence of the Japanese in American popular films effectively ceased— until the Japanese were brought to the American conscience once again with the arrival of World War II. The "Yellow Peril" previously represented by the Japanese was no longer a threat to White American sensibilities during the 1930s. Instead, China and its people became the center of American attention in the Far East. China was in the midst of civil war and had been since 1911. Negative racial imagery had been popularly established with the appearance around 1910 of Sax Rohmer's fictional

Illustration 3.5   Lupe Vélez, who was born in Mexico, was cast in a series of movies including *Mexican Spitfire* (1940) as the sexy, tempestuous Latina.

Source: The Academy of Motion Picture Arts and Sciences.

Dr. Fu Manchu in several stories and novels. Fu Manchu soon became a diabolical movie villain and provided Hollywood with an entree into new stereotypes based on Chinese warlords. Movies of the genre proved to be highly successful. Among the most profitable of these films that exploited the "mysterious Orient" were *The Bitter Tea of General Yen* in 1933, *Oil for the Lamps of China* in 1935, and *The General Died at Dawn* in 1936. In each of these films, the American audience was given the impression that

Chinese people are prone to violence, anarchy, corruption, vice, and prostitution, even though the central Chinese characters were portrayed in more complex tones. There was no attempt in the movies to explain either why the wars occurred or the role of imperialism in China. Perhaps the only countervailing view was given impetus by Pearl Buck's Pulitzer Prize-winning novel *The Good Earth*, which was published in 1931. The 1938 movie version retained Buck's sensitive account of Chinese peasants as hardworking, loving, and family people. There was, however, a strong anti-communist flavor in films about China during the mid- to late 1930s, with communists depicted most often as the villains.

On the domestic front, the decade of the 1930s belonged to Charlie Chan, who was the Chinese American's cinematic representative, although no Chinese or other Asian actor portrayed him during the series, which, with the release in 1981 of a Peter Ustinov version, had spanned six decades. The White actors who have portrayed the polite, bowing, proverb-spouting detective in the white suit include Warner Oland, Sidney Toler, Roland Winters, J. Carrol Naish, and Ross Martin. Charlie Chan movies were rife with stereotypical affectations. Although Chan seemed the most cerebral of the characters involved in his movie escapades, in addition to his intelligence there were always his "Oriental" traits that enabled American audiences to identify him with his race. Chan was mysterious in his crime-solving techniques; one never knew what thought processes or logic he was employing until the critical moment at movie's end. White America's memories of the diabolical Asian were readily recalled when Chan offered this advise to one of his many sons: "Keep eyes, ears open. Keep mouth shut." His slow gait, drowsy manner, and halting speech suggested that Chan might have spent his private moments with an opium pipe. The character's immense popularity with American movie audiences throughout the 1930s and 1940s may have contributed to the pro-Chinese sentiment that existed then.

While Hollywood tried to temper its stance toward Latinos as World War II approached, it revived and escalated its negative portrayals of the Japanese during that period. Because the Chinese peasant enjoyed favored status among Americans in the afterglow of Pearl Buck's *The Good Earth* novel and subsequent movie, Hollywood had little difficulty resurrecting the theme of the "Yellow Peril" of Japan when Japan became a threat to China. The Japanese attack on Pearl Harbor solidified the fate of the Japanese in American cinema as a negative racial stereotype. But it was Japanese Americans—soon shuttled to "relocation" camps—who immediately felt the sting of attitudes long since implanted in the American psyche and nurtured in movie houses. In films produced between 1942 and 1945, Hollywood dusted off the old images of Japanese duplicity, inhumanity, and lust for White women. Unlike the Germans, who were portrayed as a respectable but misguided people under the influence of the Nazi regime, the Japanese were seen in American theaters strafing Red

Illustration 3.6   Charlie Chan, here played by Sidney Toler, in *The Chinese Cat*. Chan epitomized several stereotypes but was perhaps the most popular Asian character Hollywood has produced.

Source: The Academy of Motion Picture Arts and Sciences.

Cross ships, bayoneting children, and delighting in applying torture techniques presumably handed down from centuries of malevolent practice. Examples of these sorts of portrayals can be found in the films *Wake Island*, 1942; *Guadalcanal Diary*, 1943; and *Objective Burma*, 1945.

The Shameful Legacy of Racial Stereotyping in Entertainment Media

Entertainment stereotypes of non-Whites in American mass media have historical roots in racist attitudes that existed for various social and political reasons against each of the groups prior to their inclusion in the media. The stereotypes were based on traits that, when compared to the traits valued in and by the majority White society, were deemed to be innately inferior traits. The economic success of mass media that have consistently employed such stereotypes reflects the ability of the media to satisfy consumer desires.

Although wide cultural differences exist among the racial groups under consideration, their portrayals in American mass media have been remarkably similar and are the result of the attitudinal premise of White intellectual and moral supremacy. The fundamental concepts of racial stereotyping were applied consistently in each of the American mass media discussed: popular literature, the stage, and motion pictures. This was the shameful legacy with which American entertainment media entered the post-World War II era and the age of television.

References

Bennett, L. (1966). *Before the Mayflower*. New York: Penguin.

Jones, J. M. (1972). *Prejudice and racism*. Reading, MA: Addison-Wesley.

Jordan, W. D. (1969). *White over Black: American attitudes toward the Negro, 1550-1812*. New York: Penguin.

Robinson, C. (1977). *Mexico and the Hispanic Southwest in American literature*. Tucson: University of Arizona Press.

Stereotypes Extend into Television and the Video Age

4

World events and technology combined to alter the treatment of people of color in the American mass media following World War II and into the 21st century. During the five decades after World War II, the United States was involved in wars in Korea, Vietnam, and the Middle East and a "cold war" against the Soviet bloc. Those conflicts and their aftermaths brought major changes in global politics. Domestically, McCarthyism came and went, as did the civil rights movement. By 2001, "terrorist" attacks against U.S. interests abroad had spread to the homeland in devastating assaults on New York's World Trade Center and the Pentagon in Washington, D.C. Meanwhile, theatrical motion pictures were supplanted as the prime mass entertainment medium by television. And new communications technologies have made an impact on popular culture and altered American lifestyles. As a result, this has been a transition period for the movies, as their makers seek to redefine the niche of movies in American mass entertainment. In the context of the transition, racial stereotypes have evolved to reflect the current political viewpoints, popular attitudes, and moods of the White majority audience.

Portrayals of People of Color in American Entertainment Media Since World War II

NATIVE AMERICANS

By the 1950s, Native Americans had become a metaphor used by filmmakers seeking to make political or philosophical statements about other issues. For example, the 1953 film *Arrowhead* was seen by critics as an ultra-right-wing allegory of the McCarthy era, while the 1964 film *Cheyenne Autumn* took a strong stand against the extermination camps in Germany as well as the persecution of Native Americans. In 1970, both *Soldier Blue* and *Little Big Man* made statements about American involvement in Vietnam. At the same time, White America (in the midst of the Black-inspired civil rights movement) was experiencing guilt over the historical and persistent mistreatment of Native Americans. The result was a series of Hollywood productions designed to purge that guilt, including *Hombre* in 1967, *Tell Them Willie Boy is Here* in 1969, and *Jeremiah Johnson* in 1972. Taking matters further, Hollywood reversed itself on portrayals of two Indian tamers it had immortalized in earlier films. In *Little Big Man*, General George A. Custer is characterized as meeting a just end at the Little Big Horn massacre as retribution for atrocities perpetrated against the Indians. Similarly, William Cody is portrayed as a mercenary eagerly exploiting Native Americans for the sake of showmanship in the 1976 film *Buffalo Bill and the Indians*. The 1970s can generally be viewed as the decade when movie portrayals became pro-Native American. Although the image of the violent Indian remained into the 1980s, Hollywood tended to mitigate the violence by placing it in the context of survival, self-defense, or retribution. The 1990s brought more sympathetic, although idealized, portrayals of Native Americans to the big screen. Foremost were those in *Dances With Wolves* and *I Will Fight No More Forever* in 1990, *The Last of the Mohicans* in 1992, and *Geronimo* in 1993. The 1995 animated feature *Pocahontas* continued the mythical "noble savage" portrayals of years past. Adding to the litany of ill-conceived Native American images were such lightly regarded films as *The Brave* in 1997 and *The Homecoming of Jimmy Whitecloud* in 2001. In *The Brave*, director Johnny Depp spins a tale about an unemployed, alcoholic Native American who agrees to submit to a tortuous death during filming of a "snuff" movie for a $50,000 fee to benefit his impoverished family. In *The Homecoming of Jimmy Whitecloud*, a modern-day Native American flees New York City for his reservation with a gang of mobsters in hot pursuit. He reaches the reservation and subsequently rediscovers his tribal heritage there. Under such historically shameful circumstances, the 2002 production of *Windtalkers* merely highlighted the paucity of positive Native American screen portrayals in the modern era by focusing on Navajo code talkers who guided the aim of U.S. artillery fire in World War II.

BLACK AMERICANS

Meanwhile, Black Americans benefited from a shift in White attitudes following World War II, when (under the prodding of the National Association for the Advancement of Colored People, other civil rights

Illustration 4.1   This scene from *Dances With Wolves* (1990) was part of
the movement toward more sensitive but idealistic film
portrayals of Native Americans that emerged in the
1990s.
Source: The Academy of Motion Picture Arts and Sciences.

groups, and the Truman administration) Hollywood began to make films
illustrating the folly and unfairness of discrimination against Blacks. A catalyst of this movement was the manner in which Black military men had
distinguished themselves during World War II in fighting for U.S. freedom. The evils of prejudice against Blacks were denunciated in *Pinky, Lost
Boundaries,* and *Home of the Brave* in 1949, *No Way Out* in 1950,
Blackboard Jungle in 1955, and *The Defiant Ones* in 1958. The sophisticated, heroic Black male character emerged in 1960s films. Actor Sidney
Poitier epitomized the intelligent, cool Black American who harnessed his
hidden rage in tolerance of the prejudice and ignorance found in the
Whites in *Guess Who's Coming to Dinner* and *In the Heat of the Night* in
1967. Poitier won the Best Actor Oscar in 1963 for his portrayal in *Lillies
of the Field* of a handyman who builds a chapel for White European nuns
in a rural American community. Harry Belafonte and Sammy Davis, Jr.
also starred in 1960s films in roles that showed Blacks in nonthreatening
circumstances.

The mid-1960s and early 1970s brought a threatening Black image to the movies in the so-called blaxploitation films. They featured nearly all-Black casts with the assumption of a militant posture. The civil rights movement—led by Dr. Martin Luther King, Jr., who was killed in 1968—was at its zenith. Hollywood portrayed urban Blacks who took revenge against Whites in such movies as *Sweet Sweetback's Baadasssss Song* in 1971 and two detective films featuring Richard Roundtree—*Shaft* in 1971 and *Shaft's Big Score* in 1972. Whites generally showed little box-office interest in blaxploitation movies and the genre soon lost its financial luster. The rest of the 1970s was marked by a trend toward films designed to attract mixed racial audiences. The 1975 film *Cooley High* and 1976 film *Carwash* are examples of this trend. In the early 1980s, with the civil rights movement a distant memory, roles for Blacks in movies became extremely scarce, a circumstance they shared with other non-Whites who worked in the film industry.

The mid- to late 1980s, however, brought a resurgence of African Americans in cinema, due largely to the popularity of two Black comics—Eddie Murphy and Whoopi Goldberg—who had made their marks in television and the stand-up comedy circuit. Murphy proved to have major racial crossover appeal at the box-office following a string of movies, including *Trading Places* in 1983, *Beverly Hills Cop* in 1984, *Beverly Hills Cop II* in 1987, *Coming to America* in 1988, and *Harlem Nights* in 1989. He continued his success into the 1990s with *Boomerang* and *The Distinguished Gentleman* in 1992. Goldberg made her movie debut to critical acclaim in *The Color Purple* in 1985 and followed it with *Jumpin' Jack Flash* in 1986, *Burglar* and *Fatal Beauty* in 1987, and *Clara's Heart* in 1998. In the 1990s, she starred in *Ghost* in 1990, *Sarafina* and *Sister Act* in 1992, and *Sister Act II* in 1993, among others. Goldberg's roles ranged from purely whimsical and comedic to serious and sensitive portrayals of Black Americans.

Black films with a harsher urban ghetto edge also appeared in the 1990s. The release of *Boyz 'N the Hood, Jungle Fever*, and *New Jack City* in 1991 coincided with the emergence of a group of Black film directors who were successful in getting Hollywood to bankroll their efforts. Among the directors were Spike Lee, John Singleton, and Matty Rich. By the 1990s, actor Denzel Washington (who appeared in *Glory* in 1989, *Mo' Better Blues* in 1990, *Malcolm X* in 1992, and *The Pelican Brief* in 1993) had replaced Sidney Poitier as the foremost Black male dramatic actor, closely followed by action adventure specialist Wesley Snipes (who appeared in *Jungle Fever* and *New Jack City* in 1991 as well as *White Men Can't Jump* and *Passenger 57* in 1992 and *Rising Sun* in 1993). In 2002, Washington won the Oscar for Best Actor (in *Training Day*) and Halle Berry won the award for Best Actress (in *Monster's Ball*), the first sweep by performers of color of the top acting categories. Both films were released in 2001, but Washington and

Illustration 4.2   Whoopi Goldberg, shown here in *The Color Purple* (1985), was among the Black performers who moved from night club stand-up comedy ranks to movie stardom in the 1980s.

Source: The Academy of Motion Picture Arts and Sciences.

Berry played roles that were reminiscent of long-standing stereotypes consistent with traditional sensibilities of White racial superiority. The following year, Washington directed and starred in a more substantive film about a Black man's abusive childhood in a Black foster home. But that film, *Antwone Fisher*, was not even nominated for an Oscar—despite widespread critical acclaim for its engaging depiction of a seldom addressed issue within the Black American experience.

LATINOS

The immediate post-World War II period saw a continuation of the relationship established before the war between Latinos and Hollywood, which was built on economic considerations. During the war, U.S.

Illustration 4.3   Halle Berry became the first African American actress to win an Academy Award for best actress for her performance in *Monster's Ball*.

filmmakers could not distribute their wares to European markets. Latin American countries came to represent 20% of Hollywood's total foreign business during the era, resulting in the development of joint movie projects. Many movies were filmed in Latin American nations, with writing

Illustration 4.4   One of the few Hollywood movies produced in the
1980s and 19902 depicting a positive image of Latinos
was *Stand and Deliver* (1988) starring Edward James
Olmos.

Source: The Academy of Motion Picture Arts and Sciences.

and financing provided by Hollywood. Most of the supporting roles were
played by Latino actors and the alliance led to an overly positive image
of Latino characters, as evidenced by such films as *The Fugitive* in 1948
and *Way of the Gaucho* in 1952. In 1953 a precedent was established with
the making of *Salt of the Earth*, in which Latino or Latin American actors
portrayed all of the major roles, although the film was not widely
distributed.

By the 1960s, Hollywood's market in Latin America had withered
because the region had developed its own film industry and screen personalities. Hollywood movies made featuring Latino themes dropped
drastically in number and those that were made reverted to old stereotypes, reintroducing the "greaser" as an urban gang member. Puerto
Ricans were singled out for updated "greaser" treatment in two 1961 films,
West Side Story and The *Young Savages*. The emphasis was on gang violence
in urban America. Hollywood continued the violent "greaser" trend with
Duck You Sucker in 1972, *Bring Me the Head of Alfredo Garcia* in 1974, *The
Warriors* in 1978, and *Boulevard Nights* in 1979. A distorted view of the

Mexican family was presented in *Children of Sanchez* in 1978, but the early 1980s included movies produced and directed by Chicanos (e.g., *Seguín* in 1981 and *The Ballad of Gregorio Cortez* in 1982). The 1981 release of *Zoot Suit* followed the success of the play that had begun its run in 1978. In *Zoot Suit*, which was based on an actual incident, the Mexican American is realistically portrayed during a World War II era race riot in Los Angeles. A series of movies beginning in the 1970s featured the nonthreatening, comedic adventures of "Cheech and Chong" in the Mexican American urban barrio. These films, however, were criticized for their perceived glorification of the drug culture, sexist orientation, and nontraditional lifestyle of the featured characters.

Hollywood offerings did little to portray Latinos as part of the U.S. mainstream during the first half of the 1980s, other than in bit parts. A more positive portrayal appeared with the release of *Stand and Deliver* in 1988, which was based on the true story of a Mexican American high school mathematics teacher. Also receiving critical acclaim were *La Bamba* in 1987 and *The Milagro Beanfield War* in 1988. Generally, however, the late 1980s and early 1990s found Latinos in the story-line background as either street toughs or drug traffickers, such as in *Colors* in 1988, *Tequila Sunrise* in 1989, and *Carlito's Way* in 1993. Better images resulted when veteran actors Jimmy Smits and Edward James Olmos were featured in *Mi Familia* (My Family) in 1995, the story of three generations of a Latino immigrant family, and the film biography of "Tejana" singer *Selena* in 1997 that helped bring Latina singer and actress Jennifer Lopez to stardom. Unfortunately, the 2002 film *Empire* featured a Latino drug king and revisited Puerto Rican stereotypes, evidence that change in Hollywood comes slowly.

ASIANS

Japanese portrayals continued to be negative immediately following World War II. Japanese acts of cruelty and torture were seen in the war movies *Tokyo Joe* in 1949 and *Three Came Home* in 1950. An exception, perhaps inspired by American guilt over Japanese American relocation camps, was *Go for Broke* in 1951. It positively portrayed heroic Japanese American military units that fought in Europe. A major reversal would soon take place, however, between Japanese and Chinese imagery in the movies.

With the coming of the Korean War, the "cold war," and McCarthyism, the issue of communism became the focal point of American fears and anxieties. Synonymous with communism were the Soviet Union and China. China, whose people had been viewed so warmly by Americans only a decade earlier, was once again seen as home of the "Yellow Peril." Japan, on the other hand, was virtually a U.S. satellite and close ally by the late 1950s. Popular movies reflected both attitudes.

Illustration 4.5   Nancy Kwan portrayed Chinese women in the early 1960s movies *The World of Suzie Wong* and *Flower Drum Song*.

The Japanese were portrayed with much more sensitivity than at any time since the Immigration Law of 1924. *The Bridge on the River Kwai* and *Battle of the Coral Sea* from 1959 are examples of the softer treatment given the Japanese by Hollywood. Even the touchy subject of Japanese-White romance was explored in *Sayonara* in 1957 and *My Geisha* in 1962. Although such romances did not have happy endings, they were nevertheless not treated as violations of nature.

In the early 1960s, two Hollywood films explored American visions of Chinese culture. *The World of Suzie Wong* in 1960 portrays a White American businessman, bored with office life, moving to Hong Kong in pursuit of a new career as an artist. He falls in love with a Chinese girl, played by Nancy Kwan, whose cultural circumstance has led to a life of prostitution. Kwan also starred in *Flower Drum Song* in 1961, a musical comedy about the problems of Chinese immigrant assimilation in the United States. It is interesting to note that Kwan's costar, James Shigeta, was a Japanese actor cast in a Chinese role and that Kwan's character had entered the U.S. illegally.

Meanwhile, China (by now commonly referred to as "Red China" or "Communist China") took on movie depictions reminiscent of the early 1930s. The Chinese regime was seen as oppressive and exploitive of its own people in *Satan Never Sleeps* in 1962 and as a devious threat to the American system in *The Manchurian Candidate*, also in 1962. The same period also marked the release of two films, *55 Days at Peking* and *The Sand Pebbles,* which were set in early 20th-century China but reinforced the 1960s image of drug addiction, prostitution, inhumanity, and deceit as staples of Chinese life. From the mid-1970s, following the reopening of diplomatic and trade ties with China, the pendulum swung again in China's favor. Hollywood curtailed its negative portrayals with fantasy characterizations such as *Dr. No* in 1962 and others in the James Bond spy thriller series. A surge of American interest in Oriental martial arts, however, spurred the creation of a series of films featuring almost nonstop violent action scenes showing villains and heroes employing kung fu, karate, and other combative techniques. Chinese American actor Bruce Lee, an acrobatic master of the martial arts, became the catalyst for the motion picture genre that portrayed the Chinese as sadistically violent. Generally, however, his films depicted Chinese characters in both heroic and villainous roles. In terms of popularity with American audiences, Jackie Chan succeeded Lee as the martial arts master. Chan's roles, however, were comedic and he teamed with Black comedian Chris Tucker in a series of movie escapades, including *Rush Hour* in 1998 and *Rush Hour 2* in 2001, that generally played to traditional stereotypes.

In the post-Vietnam war era, American film producers made the Vietnamese their next target of Asian stereotyping. They were portrayed as crafty, devious, guerilla-warfare perpetrators of violence in films in the 1970s and 1980s, including The *Deer Hunter* in 1978, *Apocalypse Now* in 1979, and *Platoon* in 1986, among others. From the mid-1980s into the 1990s, White actors Chuck Norris and Jean-Claude Van Damme assumed the mantle as filmdom's leading martial arts masters, often vanquishing Asian foes in the process. More sensitive portrayals of Asian people surfaced in such movies as *The Killing Fields* in 1984 and *The Last Emperor* in 1987, although the Japanese American community voiced their concerns about the stereotypical characterizations of Asians in *Rising Sun* in 1993. Perhaps the most insightful American film portrayal of Asians in many

Illustration 4.6   Cary-Hiroyuki Tagawa appeared in *Rising Sun*, a film
that drew protests from some Japanese Americans who
objected to its stereotypical imagery.

Source: The Academy of Motion Picture Arts and Sciences.

years was the screen adaptation of Amy Tan's novel *The Joy Luck Club* in
1993. The movie explored Chinese and Chinese American cultural
nuances and the resulting interpersonal conflicts through the eyes of three
generations of Chinese women. A continuation of the trend toward a more
sympathetic view of Chinese culture was manifest in the special effects
triumph of *Crouching Tiger, Hidden Dragon* in 2000.

As U.S. forces were involved in conflicts in the Middle East in the mid-
1990s and early 2000s, racial, cultural, and religious intolerance toward
Arab, Muslim, and Islamic people brought a spate of new negative stereotypes to American movie screens. As early as 1990, the film *Goodfellas* featured a character that matter-of-factly referred to Middle Eastern people
as "sand niggers." It was against this backdrop that the 1995 bombing of a
federal office building in Oklahoma City—later determined to be perpetrated by a disillusioned former U.S. soldier—initially set off public fears
that Arab terrorists were responsible. By 1998, *The Siege*, a story about
terrorism in New York City, featured a government roundup of Arab
American citizens called "towel heads" by a character in the film.

With the dawning of the new century came a revival of the *Star Wars* series and renewed criticisms that certain characters in the science fiction films exhibited stereotypical ethnic minority traits—even though they were not portrayed as "human" figures. The producer, George Lucas, dismissed the criticisms and said the films were merely tales of fantasy (Hinton, 2002).

TV Portrayals: The First 50 Years

Racial images portrayed on movie screens continue to project stereotypical images to both White and multicultural audiences long after their runs in American theaters have ended. The following historical review reveals that most of the vintage films have increased their audience base exponentially via broadcast, cable and satellite television, and video cassette and digital video distribution and may do so for many years to come. Commercial television began to be a major mass medium in 1948, the year Milton Berle's comedy and variety show spurred the purchase of TV sets. People of color were quickly made a part of the new medium, appearing in the traditional roles to which they had been limited in theatrical movies.

THE NOBLE SAVAGE REVISITED

Among the first stereotypical TV characters was Tonto, the Lone Ranger's "faithful" Indian companion, who was played throughout the 8-year run of the series by Jay Silverheels, an actor of Mohawk tribal heritage. *The Lone Ranger* first aired on television in 1949, but it had begun as a radio series in 1933. While the Lone Ranger's mask often made those he encountered in his Western adventures apprehensive, the fact that he maintained a friendship with an Indian made him even more suspect. Tonto's image, however, was positive because he fought for justice in the highest tradition of American folklore. His role as a Native American reflected the established Indian stereotype, including the pinto pony, broken English dialogue, fringed buckskin attire, and secondary status relative to the White hero.

Unfortunately, the historical portrayal of Native Americans on network television differs little from that in Hollywood movies. The list of prime time TV series featuring accurate representations of Native Americans is extremely brief—with regard to both their past and present conditions. Perhaps the only attempt to accurately depict Native Americans was made in the 1955 to 1956 TV season when CBS aired *Brave Eagle.* The show sought to portray the Native American viewpoint of the White expansionist movement during the latter part of the 19th century. The program did feature actual Native American cast members but, ironically, a real Native American (Keena Nomkeena) played the foster son of White actor Keith Larsen who portrayed a Cheyenne tribal chief. There was also an old sage, played by a White actor, who recited tribal history and events. The veracity of the portrayal of Native Americans in the network series *Brave Eagle* has not been equaled into the 21st century, although documentaries and special TV movies with sympathetic themes have appeared from time to time. *Brave Eagle* was followed by ABC's *Broken Arrow* (which ran from 1956 to 1960), another series that featured an all-White cast, which had a story line that centered on the cooperation between Native Americans and Whites in fighting frontier injustice. During the 1960s, when television was dominated by Westerns, Native Americans were mostly relegated to their Indian image in movies, serving as either foils or background characters to stories of how the West was won.

This basic pattern continued into the 1990s. In ABC's *The Young Riders* (which ran from 1989 to 1992), Gregg Rainwater played Little Buck Cross, who was half Kiowa Indian. The story line was about the Pony Express era, but television sensibilities in the early 1990s demanded revisionist history of the Western frontier. So *The Young Riders* spent most of their time protecting the innocent and displaying kindness to any Native Americans who happened to wander into an episode. A unique twist came to Native American TV portrayals with the 1990 arrival of *Northern Exposure* on CBS. In *Northern Exposure*, Elaine Miles portrayed Eskimo medical receptionist Marilyn Whirlwind, an unflappable and down-to-earth personality. The show was a ratings success and continued on prime time into the mid-1990s.

BLACK MAGIC ON THE SMALL SCREEN

Black Americans have comprised the largest non-White racial presence in network television. That fact, however, has not resulted in an altogether satisfactory TV portrayal of the realities of the diversified Black experience in the United States. But recent history shows that there has been improvement over earlier years. In variety programming, Blacks appeared frequently as guest performers almost from the inception of network commercial television. Ed Sullivan featured Blacks as early as 1948 on his CBS *Toast of the Town* variety show (later called *The Ed Sullivan Show*), as did Steve Allen as host of NBC's *The Tonight Show* from 1954 to 1957. In 1950, three network shows went on the air featuring Blacks as cast regulars. They were *Beulah, The Jack Benny Show,* and *The Stu Erwin Show.* Each portrayed Blacks in subservient, domestic roles. The Beulah character was a maid and mammy figure in a White household (played first by

Ethel Waters and later by Louise Beavers) who had a scatterbrained girlfriend (Oriole, played by Butterfly McQueen) and a shiftless Black boyfriend. Eddie Anderson portrayed Jack Benny's valet Rochester on TV for 15 years and Willie Best, who had played imitative Stepin Fetchit roles in numerous movies, brought that character to the Erwin show as the family handyman.

Amos 'n' Andy, the first show with an all-Black cast, made its television debut in 1951, although it had been immensely popular as a radio series since 1929 with its White creators playing the major roles. *Amos 'n' Andy* was awaited with much anticipation across the nation because the show's creators, Freeman Gosden and Charles Correll, held a widely publicized 4-year search for the Black actors who would bring the show to television. A special televised segment was arranged before a studio audience for Gosden and Correll to introduce the handpicked cast prior to the first show. In introducing the male actors, the creators occasionally referred to them as "boys," a term long despised by Blacks as a relic of slavery in the United States. The original series lasted 2 years, but reruns continued into the mid-1960s and continued to stir controversy over the images of Blacks the series projected. Although the show was based on characters with questionable intellects or ethics, some Black characters were seen as attorneys, business owners, educators, and other types of professionals. Nevertheless, pressure from civil rights groups forced the program off the air in 1966 when CBS withdrew it from sale. The advent of videocassette technology made *Amos 'n' Andy* a brisk seller in the home entertainment market into the latter half of the 1990s.

Prior to the civil rights movement of the 1960s, two other significant programs featured Black male vocalists. In 1952, ABC's 15-minute *Billy Daniels Show* was the first national TV program with a Black host. It ran for only 13 weeks, one third of a season by industry standards of the time. A musical variety show hosted by singer Nat "King" Cole, which aired for 59 consecutive weeks from 1956 to 1957, fared somewhat better. Many prominent entertainers, several sponsors, and NBC executives supported Cole and made considerable efforts to keep the show afloat, despite poor ratings throughout its 13-month history. Although Cole was an extremely talented vocalist and successful recording star, his show could not win the ratings competition against the popular mainstream programs in its time slot.[1] From the mid-1960s into the mid-1980s, Blacks were seen on numerous TV series, usually as comedy variety show hosts or as actors in situation comedies. Many shows employed what were seen by critics as a single, "token" Black character. From *Amos 'n' Andy* to the 1984 to 1985 television season, there were only four other shows (all situation comedies) with predominately Black casts that lasted more than one season in regular network television: *Sanford and Son* in 1972, *Good Times* in 1974, *The Jeffersons* in 1975, and *What's Happening!* in 1976. The TV ratings epoch *Roots* aired as a prime time miniseries special in 1977. But many believed

Illustration 4.7   The first network TV show to feature an all-Black cast, *Amos 'n' Andy* debuted in 1951 with (from left) Spencer Williams as Andy, Tim Moore as George Kingfish Stevens, and Alvin Childress as Amos. Protests from civil rights groups forced CBS to drop the series from syndication in 1966.

it served as a catharsis of guilt for Whites over the historical treatment of Blacks in America. An estimated 100 million viewers watched the program over eight consecutive nights, and the miniseries began several trends in television programming.

Into the mid-1980s, the primary roles for Blacks in prime time network television were still in situation comedies rather than serious dramatic programs. However, it should be noted that situation comedies and prime time "soap opera" serials comprised almost all of programming fare on network television in the 1980s. Actress Diahann Carroll, who became the first Black woman to star in a network comedy dramatic series (in *Julia* in 1968), made history again in 1984 when she joined the regular cast of ABC's prime time soap opera *Dynasty.* That same year marked the opening season of NBC's *The Bill Cosby Show,* which became television's top rated program throughout the mid-1980s, proving that a show with an all-Black cast could be an overwhelming commercial success. The success of *The Bill Cosby Show* opened the way for the numerous Black sitcoms that

Illustration 4.8   Bill Cosby (right) starred in the nation's top-rated television program throughout much of the 1980s. His sitcom, *The Bill Cosby Show*, featured an all-Black cast, including Malcolm-Jamal Warner, pictured here, who played his son.

Source: CORBIS.

flooded the airwaves into the early 2000s. Few of them, however, had the production and scriptwriting qualities that characterized the Cosby program.

The most significant Black comedy variety show of the early and mid-1990s was the Fox network's *In Living Color*, which first aired in 1990. The fast-paced show resembled a hybrid of *Laugh-In* and *Saturday Night Live* and its success was due primarily to its multitalented writer, producer, director, actor, and comedian, Keenen Ivory Wayans. By the mid-1990s, advertisers and their television network cohorts had awakened to the fact that Blacks watched more TV than any other racial group. In 1994, the four networks aired 25 programs either starring or featuring Blacks in major roles. Significantly, however, there were major differences in the viewing patterns of Blacks as compared to the general American audience. An article in the *Washington Post* about the most popular shows of the 1993 season revealed that no programs made the top 10 on the lists of both Black and White viewers ("A Television Trend: Audiences in Black and White," 1994). A significant development of the late 1990s and early 2000s was the emergence of the UPN television network that seemed to target the African American audience with all-Black situation comedies such as *The Hughleys* and *The Parkers*.

LATIN THEMES PLAY AGAIN

Latinos were brought to the small screen early in television history when the romantic figure of *The Cisco Kid* rode into American homes in 1950. The Western series aired for 7 years—but only in syndication to independent stations. In 1994, some 37 years after the original series ended, *The Cisco Kid* was revived as a theatrical movie with Jimmy Smits in the lead role. *The Cisco Kid* was the first successful syndicated television program and was among the first TV series shot in color. The Cisco Kid had been an entertainment fixture since his creation in the O'Henry short story "The Caballero's Way." In O'Henry's story, Cisco was a bandito-type character who preyed on the rich to help the poor, a la Robin Hood. The character was brought to the movies in several productions with various leading men, including Duncan Renaldo, who played the role on TV. Cisco and his sidekick Pancho delighted youngsters, who were the key to their popularity. Cisco and Pancho enjoyed a jovial repartee while roaming the Southwest to fight injustice. Renaldo's portrayal was vintage "Latin lover" except that, given his audience's age, he never got romantically involved with the love-stricken ladies. Pancho, played by Leo Carillo, was a rotund, gregarious character who affected the stereotypical speech American audiences had come to expect from movie Mexicans who were not "Latin lovers." Often Pancho would urge his partner, "Hey Cees-ko, let's went!" The next Latino role appeared in 1951 when a White actor, Don Diamond, played El Toro, the Mexican sidekick of the lead in *Kit Carson*.

The biggest Latino television personality of the early days of television was Desi Arnaz, who was Lucille Ball's husband both in life and in the long-running TV show *I Love Lucy*. Although Arnaz played a respectable husband who was a bandleader, he also played straight man to zany Lucy. His Latin temperament, which exploded into a torrent of Spanish diatribe when Lucy's ill-fated activities were revealed, was classic stereotyped imagery. The popular series came to television in 1951 and continued in original production until 1961.

A swashbuckling adventure show, *Zorro*, debuted in 1957. Set in early California, it concerned the political struggles of Spanish settlers. Mexicans, however, served only as villains, buffoons, or backdrops to the affairs of the more cultured Spanish aristocracy. In the 1960s, three television programs stood out for their Latino portrayals. In *The Real McCoys* (which ran from 1957 to 1963), Tony Martinez played farmhand Pepino Garcia, a role consistent with audience expectations. A non-Latino played a simple-minded Mexican on *The Bill Dana Show* (which ran from 1963 to 1965). Dana's opening line with a thick Mexican accent became virtually a national catch phrase because of his night club act and record sales: "My name, Jose Jimenez." In the show, Jimenez worked as a hotel bellhop whose ineptness constantly got him into comedic situations. Perhaps the most unusual prime time TV show centering on Latino characters was *The*

High Chaparral (which ran from 1967 to 1971). It was one of the numerous "adult Westerns" aired during the period and featured an inter-racial marriage between the daughter of a Mexican cattle baron and a wealthy White rancher. Latino actors, however, generally played ranch hands.

In the 1970s, there were two network situation comedies based on the Mexican American barrio of East Los Angeles. The most recognized and criticized of the two was *Chico and the Man*, which starred Freddie Prinze, Sr. It aired for five seasons on NBC, beginning in 1974. Chico was a young, streetwise character who used his savvy to drum up business for the auto repair garage where he worked. The racial "humor" of the White garage owner and the image portrayed by Chico were the subject of controversy throughout the show's network existence. In 1976, another sitcom about an East Los Angeles family was brought to ABC—*Viva Valdez*. It lasted only 4 months. Two other series featuring Latino actors began in the 1970s and continued until 1983. NBC screened the series *CHIPS* for the first time in 1977, which costarred the handsome Latino actor Erik Estrada as a California Highway Patrol officer with romance on his mind. In 1978, *Fantasy Island* starred Ricardo Montalban as the romantic figure host on an idyllic isle. Neither portrayal was very distant from the Latin lover roles that Hollywood had created decades earlier. In 1984, ABC made its second attempt at a sitcom centered on the life of an East Los Angeles barrio family in *a.k.a. PABLO* with Paul Rodriguez. Critics claimed that the show was insensitive because Rodriguez's jokes were seen as ridiculing Mexican American culture. The program lasted only six episodes and did not return in 1985. A Latino flavor was captured in NBC's *Miami Vice* (which ran from 1984 to 1989), which starred Edward James Olmos as Lt. Martin Castillo against a backdrop of drug operatives, many of whom were Latino. A more positive portrayal came in 1986 with Jimmy Smits's role as lawyer Victor Sifuentes on NBC's *L.A. Law*. The show continued its run into 1994, a year in which Latinos filled only 11 of national television's 800 prime time roles.

Some Latino actresses and actors, such as Raquel Welch and Martin Sheen, once took non-Latino roles and subverted their cultural identities to obtain steady employment. Now, they are "able to be ethnically present to the Latino audience but ethnically invisible to a majority audience," said Felix Sanchez, president of the National Hispanic Foundation for the Arts, in a *New York Times* article. Sanchez added, "We need to move it beyond that to where our culture and identity are fully integrated in a character" (Navarro, 2002, pp. B1, B3). Although the multibillion dollar Latino consumer market in the United States has created an expanded presence for Latinos in television, change has been gradual. In 2003, the first network TV series featuring virtually an all-Latino cast aired on NBC. But *Kingpin* merely brought viewers another violence-filled show based on the adventures of a Mexican drug lord and his family of stereotypical characters.

MORE YELLOW PERILS

Asian portrayals came to television in 1949 in an ABC crime show called *Mysteries of Chinatown*, which exploited the old stereotype of the "mysterious" Asian. The show starred White actor Marvin Miller as Dr. Yat Fu. *Mysteries of Chinatown* was set in San Francisco's Chinatown where Miller's stereotyped character was the owner of an herb and curio shop. The regular supporting cast was all White. The next show to surface about Asians was the TV version of *The Adventures of Fu Manchu* in 1956, another crime drama with an all-White cast. The program was vintage "Yellow Peril," with Dr. Fu sending his agents on missions designed to subvert Western civilization. The nefarious and wily Dr. Fu, based in various cities in Asia, recalled old Sax Rohmer stereotypes. In fact, the series was facilitated by Rohmer's sale of rights to his creation in 1955 to Republic Pictures. The show was a nonnetwork syndicated production and aired for only one season. The following year, 1956, Dr. Fu was followed to television by the other venerable Chinese character, Charlie Chan. *The New Adventures of Charlie Chan* was also a syndicated series that lasted only a year. J. Carrol Naish played Charlie Chan, but an Asian actor, James Hong, was cast in the role of Chan's "number one son," Barry Chan. The series was produced in Great Britain and the Chan character operated from London.

In the 1960s, ABC aired an adventure series, *Hong Kong*, which reinforced the Chinese stereotype of intrigue, sexy women, smuggling, and drug peddling. At least two Asian actors were cast as series regulars during its run from 1960 to 1961. The same network brought *The Green Hornet* to prime-time TV from 1966 to 1967. The significance of the series was the casting of Bruce Lee as the Green Hornet's sidekick, Kato. Lee's weekly demonstration of crime-fighting martial arts helped launch the popularity of Asian self-defense techniques in the United States. Interestingly, *The Green Hornet* was the creation of George Trendle, who also developed *The Lone Ranger*. In both shows, a trusty ethnic minority sidekick, perhaps for the purpose of adding fantasy appeal for the mass audience, supports the hero. Bruce Lee influenced another ABC series, *Kung Fu* (which ran from 1972 to 1975), which was a Western starring David Carradine and with supporting Asian actors including Keye Luke and Philip Ahn. Lee was a consultant to those who developed the *Kung Fu* show and labored under the impression that he was to be their choice for the lead role. When Carradine was selected for the part, Lee confided to friends that he had been the victim of racism. *Kung Fu*'s producers told Lee that they didn't believe a Chinese actor could be seen as a hero in the eyes of the American television audience.[5] The show revived the "mysterious" Asian stereotype. With racism standing as a barrier to Bruce Lee's achieving stardom in the United States, he went to Hong Kong and achieved superstardom throughout Asia as a film star. Lee, who died at 33, ultimately became a cult figure in the United States after the release of his final movie, *Enter the Dragon*, in 1973.

The greatest Asian presence in television began in the 1960s and featured an array of supporting police and criminal characters in the long-running CBS series *Hawaii Five-O* (which aired from 1968 to 1980). At least three Asian actors appeared as regulars on the show. In addition, the lead character, Detective Steve McGarrett, pursued his arch enemy, Asian character Wo Fat, periodically throughout the show's 12-year tenure. The portrayals of Asians in *Hawaii Five-O* were varied, although definite stereotypes were projected. The show portrayed White superiority and leadership in a predominately Asian environment.

There have been several prime time shows throughout the history of American television that perpetuated the subservient, humble Asian image. Among them were *Bachelor Father* (which ran from 1957 to 1962), which had an Asian "houseboy" character played by Sammee Tong and *Bonanza* (which ran from 1959 to 1972), which had a Chinese cook, Hop Sing, played by Victor Sen Yung. In *The Courtship of Eddie's Father* (1969 to 1972), Miyoshi Umeki played a housekeeper who was often befuddled by situations that arose in the household.

The early 1980s brought a continuation of Asian supporting roles in sitcoms and dramatic offerings. Two unusual programs using Asian themes came to network TV in 1980. A week-long miniseries, *Shogun*, was based on the exploits of a White adventurer in feudal Japan. Although it provided American audiences with some insight into Japanese culture, *Shogun* emphasized the violence of samurai warriors and the sexual mysticism of Japanese women. NBC brought a variety show called *Pink Lady* to its schedule, which featured a Japanese singing duo of the same name. The two young women were attractive and spoke little English, so comic Jeff Altman served as facilitator. As an attempt to bring the demure yet sexy image of the Japanese woman to network television, *Pink Lady* was a failure. It lasted less than 2 months. That female image, however, returned to prominence in 1983 when actress Rosalind Chao took a costarring role in the CBS series *After M.A.S.H.*, which aired until December 1984. Ms. Chao played the Korean wife of a White ex-G.I. who had served in the Korean War. A different Asian female portrayal came to television in 1994 with the ABC sitcom *All-American Girl* featuring Margaret Cho. Cho's character personified a quick-tongued, modern Asian woman with a distinctly "American" attitude.

Japanese American actor Pat Morita, who had played the role of Arnold in the long-running ABC series *Happy Days* (which aired from 1974 to 1984), became the star of his own ABC series. For two seasons in 1987 to 1988, Morita starred as *Ohara*, a Los Angeles police detective who preferred mystical Asian patience and persuasion to violence in dealing with criminals. Lt. Ohara rarely carried a gun but, true to stereotype, resorted to martial arts when necessary. A similar series using a Chinese actor in the lead role was *Martial Law* (which ran in 1998). The show featured corpulent Sammo Hung Kam-Bo as a Hong Kong detective on loan to the Los Angeles Police Department.

Racial Imagery in the Video Age

The arrival of the 21st century has seen the development of cable and satellite television into major entertainment forces competing with traditional over-the-air networks for viewers. Most Americans—including people of color—now have access to many more channels of programming than were available in even the recent past. Moreover, in what is now called the "video age," visual entertainment is also available to consumers using digital video disc (DVD) technology at home or in portable computers. Executives and producers of video entertainment are using this expanded capacity to bring audiences specialized, "niche" programming, including television channels devoted exclusively to such diverse areas as vintage movies, sports, comedy, shopping, history, gardening, home décor, and so on. Subcategories of all of the above exist to meet virtually every need in every area of human interest. However, the exigencies of providing program content 24 hours a day, coupled with the high production costs of original programming, leads many outlets to rely on reruns of material previously aired. The exceptions to this are the pay cable television channels such as Home Box Office (HBO) and Showtime, which produce and air some original movies and television programs featuring people of color and/or cultural themes. For example, in 2001, Showtime offered *Soul Food*, a Black series based on a theatrical film released a few years earlier, and *Resurrection Blvd.*, a Latino dramatic series. In general, however, situation comedies, dramas, and other programs produced in the 60s, 70s, 80s, and 90s for the original "big three" networks, ABC, CBS, and NBC, constitute much of the fare on cable and satellite television. Even motion pictures from the advent of the sound movie era can be seen virtually every day somewhere on television. Therefore, it is easy to see why the old stereotypes die hard. In essence, the technology of the video age has resulted in the continued conveyance of old stereotypes to new generations of viewers.

In the new millennium, the concepts of *racial diversity* and *multiculturalism* have become part of the fabric of American discourse. Consequently, the television industry faces increased pressure from advocacy groups to better reflect the nation's demographic reality. Many observers of American popular culture believe that multicultural television fare presented when children are most likely to be viewing is critical to advancing acceptance of racial and ethnic diversity in the United States. One such group is Children Now, an Oakland, California, research and advocacy organization that monitors prime time television for racial, gender, and other diversity content. It reports annually on the status of diversity in network programming. Among other findings, its research on prime time programming during the 2001 to 2002 season revealed that the world of American television

- ❖ is primarily populated by white males under the age of 40
- ❖ has few Native Americans, and is a world in which Native American women do not exist
- ❖ shows African American families almost exclusively in situation comedies
- ❖ shows Latinos in secondary and tertiary roles, with nearly half of them in low-status occupations
- ❖ shows family life not serving as a central focus for Asian Pacific Americans, Latinos, or Native Americans
- ❖ portrays only people of color as service workers, unskilled laborers, and criminals (in the top five primary recurring character occupations).[6]

Stereotypes in Video Games

Although video games are not thought of as a traditional segment of the mass media, they have become widely popular entertainment devices for American children and young adults. According to the Interactive Digital Software Association (IDSA), 145 million Americans play interactive video games, and in 2001 the industry had $4.6 billion in sales. IDSA's annual survey in 2002 found that 60% of its customers were between the ages of 18 and 36.

Although the effects of racial stereotypes in video games have yet to be fully explored, a study published in 2002 by Children Now examined how people of color are depicted in video games and how equitable the games are in portraying people of color. Not surprisingly, more than half (56%) of all the human characters in the study were White. Blacks comprised the second largest group (22%), Asians accounted for 9%, and Latinos accounted for only 2% of the depictions. Native Americans and multiracial characters were each represented by only two tenths of 1% of the 1,716 characters studied.

Evidence of racial stereotyping was strong. While 87% of video game heroes were White, only 14% of the heroes were people of color and none were Native American. In sports games, Blacks were most often shown displaying aggressive behaviors. Black competitors (79%) engaged in physical and verbal aggression far more often than did White competitors (57%).

Moreover, Black competitors were the only racial group to use verbal aggression on the field. Among other stereotypes, the study found that 83% of all the Black males depicted were shown in sports-oriented games. Latino males appeared only in sports games, usually baseball. Asians were often depicted as wrestlers or fighters and were more often antagonists (18%) than were Whites (8%).

Depictions of violence also exhibited traditional racial stereotyping. For example, in nonsports games, White characters were most likely to use weapons (31%), while Black characters were most likely to use verbal aggression, which included screaming, ridicule, and insults (23%). Latino characters were most likely to use physical aggression without weapons (36%), and Asian characters were least likely to use weapons when displaying aggressive behavior (11%). Black characters were least likely to have realistic responses to violence. More than half (61%) were "unaffected" by violence and only 15% exhibited both physical harm and pain. In contrast, less than half the White characters (43%) exhibited both pain and physical harm and only 23% were unaffected by violence. Asian characters exhibited both pain and harm (66%), while only 7% were unaffected by violence. And, at the other end of the spectrum, Latinos were shown exhibiting physical harm and pain 83% of the time after being injured, although most Latinos appeared in sports games where athletes are usually unaffected by violence.

Racial gender stereotyping was also prevalent in video games. White female characters (61%) significantly outnumbered female characters of every other racial group. The other depictions were of Asian (11%), Black (4%), and Native American (1%) women. None of the characters in the study were Latina, nor were any Native American males represented. Black females were more likely to be victims of violence (86% of the time) than were the females in any other ethnic group, and they were depicted in that role nearly twice as often as were White females (45%).

The study shows that video games reinforce unhealthy racial and gender stereotypes and messages. People of color are rarely cast in a positive light in video games, thus the images in these games can create negative attitudes in Whites toward people of color. At the same time, children of color may feel devalued or ignored as a result of video games' limited and stereotyped representations of people from their own racial group.

Audience Demand Can Affect Change

The historical overview presented here reveals that stereotyping of non-Whites is contextual within the social, political, and economic realities of the moment and that it changes accordingly. Within any given historical period, the nature of one racial or cultural group's portrayal may be much more positive than another's. A group may get the lion's share of bigoted treatment in the media at times when the United States is in conflict with foreign interests that share the group's racial or cultural heritage. The basic negative portrayals in movies and television of the racial groups considered in this book have never been abandoned totally, although works that seem designed to purge the mainstream conscience of guilt with regard to these groups are exhibited periodically.

Racially prejudicial stereotyping is debilitative in a society, especially one as diverse as that of the United States. Not only does the stereotyping work against groups' recognizing and understanding the common humanity of all people, it also provides succeeding generations of all racial groups—White and non-White—with distorted self-images. The coupling of biased portrayals with the social and psychological power of mass entertainment threatens the maturation of American society into a model of multicultural tolerance and unity. But the attitudinal change must begin with the audience, because producers of popular entertainment are, generally, motivated more by economic incentives than social advancement. For example, in an effort to tap a multibillion-dollar consumer market, television advertisers and network executives began in the mid-1990s to offer more programs aimed at reaching Blacks and Latinos. The programs, however, were almost exclusively situation comedies and continued to reflect many of the stereotypes of the past.

In the early 21st century, the advances of cable, satellite television, and digital video game technology have been used to perpetuate old stereotypes rather than to forge new and more accurate portrayals of the racial groups that comprise the U.S. population. As noted above, if there is to be significant change it will most likely occur only when audiences demand it. The historical incident recounted in Chapter 3 shows that an American concert audience in 1833 demanded—and got—"Yankee Doodle" in place of a symphony. If 21st-century audiences, which are now increasingly comprised of people of color, demand portrayals free of racial stereotypical bias in their entertainment media, they will get them. Collectively, non-White Americans have enough economic leverage to support such demands, but the question is whether they have for so long been exposed to scurrilous portrayals of their kind in the media that they accept the false message that tells them they lack empowerment.

Notes

1. For a comprehensive review of the history of Black Americans as network television performers, see *Blacks and White TV*, by J. F. MacDonald, 1992, Chicago: Nelson-Hall.

2. See the account of Bruce Lee's encounter with the producers of *Kung Fu* in *Giant Steps: The Autobiography of Kareem Abdul-Jabbar* (pp. 188-189), by K. Abdul-Jabbar and P. Knobler, 1983, New York: Bantam.

3. See the complete findings in *Fall Colors 2001–02: Prime Time Diversity Report*, by Children Now, 2002, Oakland, CA.

References

A television trend: Audiences in Black and White. (1994, November 29). *Washington Post*, pp. A1, A20.

Children Now. (2002). Fair play? Violence, gender and race in video games. Oakland, CA: Author.

Hinton, E. L. (2002, May 11). *Star Wars'* Jar Jar Binks is back. . . . Will racial controversy follow? Retrieved from www.DiversityInc.com

Interactive Digital Software Association. (2002). Essential facts about the computer and video game industry. Washington, DC: Author.

Navarro, M. (2002, June 11). Raquel Welch is reinvented as a Latina. *New York Times*, pp. B1, B3.

Part III

Racialism in Public Communication

The Press 5

A Legacy of Exclusion

N ews—which Americans receive every day via newspapers, radio, television, and magazines, and online information services—is a vital commodity. Researchers call news reporting in these media the *surveillance* function of mass communication, the task of surveying the trends and events occurring in society and reporting those that seem to be most important and consequential to its well-being. Without such information, people would be seriously hindered in their ability to participate in the political affairs of the republic or to make business, professional, and personal decisions. Obviously, tens of thousands of events and activities take place daily in the United States and throughout the world, but only a miniscule fraction of them are reported through the major national or local news media.

The most important characteristic of news is its *consequence* (i.e., importance).[1] In other words, those who make decisions about content in news media first consider the importance of the event to the audience. This process is, of course, subjective, but the decision makers (theoretically, at least) stake their professional livelihood on their ability to provide the information that is most desired and needed by society. Another, closely related, social role of news media is the *correlation* function, or the task of analyzing the selected news, offering analysis and opinion to the society concerning its potential impact, and suggesting what should be done about it. Often, leaders formulate social policies using news media as a forum.

Researchers have labeled those involved in the news selection process the *gatekeepers* of information, because they are in position either to let information pass through the system or to stop its progress. Performance of the gate-keeping function results in what some scholars have called "agenda setting" for the society. The process of filtering out huge volumes of information while allowing only a few items to reach the audience is an act that by itself adds credence and importance (i.e., consequence) to the surviving events and issues. The extent to which gatekeepers bear responsibility for the flow of news information and set the agenda in the United States is a topic of discussion among social scientists. It is clear, however, that gatekeepers are vitally influential in the process. The perspectives of American values, attitudes, and ambitions brought to society have largely been those of gatekeepers and others with access to media.

Historically, and continuing into the present, non-Whites have not been gatekeepers in mainstream American mass media. Their near exclusion from the process is the subject of a subsequent chapter, but the effect of that exclusion is our present concern. Coverage of people of color in American news media has been and remains a reflection of the attitudes held by gatekeepers and those who influence them. The frequency and nature of such coverage in news media, therefore, reveal the attitudes of the majority population throughout American history as much as do portrayals in entertainment media. News coverage may be more significant, however, because of its role and function in society: While entertainment is "make-believe," the news is "real." Since news content, in theory, reflects what is really important to society, the coverage of people of color in mainstream news media provides insight into their social status. The gatekeepers of news reveal by their professional judgments precisely how consequential they regard Americans of color to be.

North American newspaper press history began in 1690 with the publication of the ill-fated *Publick Occurrences Both Foreign and Domestick,* which was banned after its first issue because publisher Benjamin Harris failed to get approval for it from the Massachusetts Bay Colony (Boston) authorities. It is significant that Native Americans were mentioned in at least two articles in the small, 4-page newspaper. Throughout the colonial period, references to both Native Americans and Blacks appeared in the press. Native Americans were of interest because of both the French and Indian War and the uneasy relationship between them and White colonials. Blacks were the subject of advertisements for slave auctions and notices for runaway slaves. For most of the first 100 years after the founding of the republic, press coverage of the two racial groups continued to focus on the "Indian problem" and the issue of slavery.

Newspapers, however, did not reach the vast majority of the population until the forces of technology, public education, and the political rise of the "common man" made the penny press in the 1830s the first truly "mass" medium in the United States. Since then, news about people of color in White mainstream news media has been characterized by five developmental phases or patterns that have been experienced by all of the groups under consideration. The five phases are (1) the exclusionary phase, (2) the threatening issue phase, (3) the confrontation phase, (4) the stereotypical news selection phase, and (5) the multiracial coverage phase. These ways of treating non-White groups in news reports are not mutually exclusive and each is evident in contemporary journalism depending on which group and topical issue is being addressed at a given time. In fact, the first four patterns have been so uniformly practiced by news media as to have become virtually established as covert policy. In the early 21st century, American newsrooms implementation of the fifth phase is being met with grudging acceptance and uneven application by journalism practitioners.

Phases and Patterns in the Treatment of People of Color in News Media

THE EXCLUSIONARY PHASE

Although in turn each non-White group contributed to the social and historical development of Anglo American society, none were initially included in the general reporting of news. Insofar as the gatekeepers of public information—and, by extension, their constituent audience—were concerned, people of color were not an important consideration in the conduct of social affairs. In the colonial era this was made clear in such a sacrosanct document as the Declaration of Independence, wherein the phrase "all men are created equal" was understood to exclude women, Native Americans, and Blacks. The point was so obvious that there was no need to insert the word "White" between "all" and "men." Furthermore, the U.S. Constitution specified (Article 1, Section 2) that for the purpose of determining a state's requisite number of members in the House of Representatives, a state could not count the Native American population and each slave counted as only three-fifths of a person. Free Blacks were generally prevented from participating in political affairs by the requirements of extensive property holdings that qualified a person to vote.

Although the policy of virtual exclusion of people of color in news coverage may seem benign, it has had a significant impact on the historical development of race relations in the United States. Its most immediate effect, as noted above, was to signal the status and role Whites accorded other racial groups in society. Lack of coverage of peoples of color in mainstream news media had the effect of asserting their lack of status, a powerful social psychological message delivered to Whites and non-Whites alike. Ultimately, exclusion from coverage in news media signified exclusion from American society, because the function of news is to reflect social reality. For that reason, racial exclusion determined the subsequent phases of the treatment of people of color in news. It established a legacy that permeates American news media into the 21st century.

THE THREATENING ISSUE PHASE

When non-White cultural groups first begin to appear as subjects of news media reports, it is because they have been perceived as a threat to the existing social well-being. Threat is grounded in fear. As may be expected, Native Americans were the first to attract the attention of the news media because of the uneasy relationship between them and the European colonial settlers who referred to them as "noble savages." The ambivalence manifested in the attitude of Whites toward Native Americans was the result of fear of Native American resistance to colonial expansion. Although the European settlers were intruders on the Native Americans' soil, the colonial and early national press began to characterize their Native American hosts in the role of adversary with heavy use of the term "savages." Newspapers, therefore, made it easy to justify the displacement of Native Americans by focusing coverage on acts of Native American violence that reinforced the savagery theme. The "civilized" Europeans were made to seem heroic for any actions, however extreme, that resulted in the overthrow of "uncivilized" savages. By the time the penny press era reached its zenith, the "Indian" wars of the West were fully under way.

Similarly, Blacks were the objects of fears that set the press awash in a flood of articles speculating on the aftermath of emancipation. In the far West, Chinese laborers became the focus of fears that they would displace Whites from the labor market, and the *San Francisco Chronicle* led the press attack against them during the 1870s. In the 1950s, the same fear manifested itself in the California press, as headlines blared against the Mexican immigrant workers the journalists labeled "wetbacks." The 1980s and 1990s saw the press indiscriminately use the terms "illegals" and "aliens" to depict Latinos, who have argued that when used as nouns, the labels are dehumanizing and inaccurate. A 1994 report by San Francisco State University's Center for Integration and Improvement of Journalism explained that "individuals can commit illegal acts . . . but how can a human being be deemed an 'illegal' person?" The report further noted that the term "alien" conjures up images of creatures who are invaders from another planet (p. 44). A 1990 article in New York's *Downtown Express* newspaper characterized the expansion of the Lower East Side Chinatown with a headline reading "There Goes the Neighborhood" (cited in Center for Integration and Improvement of Journalism, 1991, p. 4). In 1991, in *The Daily Breeze* in Torrance, California, the headline of a front-page story about the changing demographics in its circulation area read "Asian Invasion" and rekindled White fears of a "Yellow Peril" ("Asian Invasion," 1991, p. 1).

In early 21st-century America, there remains increasing fear among critics of the media that oversimplifying news coverage of people of color contributes to racial polarization by making them scapegoats for the nation's problems and fueling White fears and hatred of other groups and lifestyles. Little has changed since a 1992 research study titled "The News As If All People Mattered" reported that the media often reduce complex conflicts into simply one side versus another. The study concluded, "The media further stimulate polarization by such actions as treating subgroups within communities of interest differently, repeating inflammatory comments without challenge or balancing statements, omission of relevant news, disregard for certain communities, quoting and referencing sources predominantly from one subgroup" (cited in Gersh, 1992, p. 30).

THE CONFRONTATION PHASE

When a non-White group stimulates fear and apprehension in the general population, the response is inevitably a social confrontation. News media, having already brought the threat to society's attention and exacerbated racial polarization, then proceed to cover the response. The response is often violent, such as the "Indian" wars of the westward expansion, the Mexican War, or the lynchings of Blacks in the South, Mexicans in the Southwest, and Asians in the West. Sometimes the response culminates in legislative action, such as segregation laws, peace treaties, and anti-immigration laws or in the creation of agencies such as the Bureau of Indian Affairs and the Immigration and Naturalization Service. On other occasions, race riots dominate the news with a historical consistency that has involved virtually every non-White racial group.

American news media generally approach confrontation coverage of race-related issues from the perspective of "us versus them." This is a natural progression from the exclusionary phase: News people think of non-Whites as outside the American system, thus, their actions must be reported as adversarial because they are seen as threats to the social order. Until the late 1960s, news headlines and text were filled with racial epithets in reporting on these social confrontations, thereby encouraging conflict instead of conciliation. When the Kerner Commission on civil disorders issued its report in 1968, it condemned this historical trend in news coverage by a press that "has too long basked in a White world, looking out of it, if at all, with White men's eyes and a White perspective" (p. 389). It is during confrontation that news media have the opportunity to exhibit leadership in race relations; unfortunately, their historical track record has been poor and continues so into the 21st century.

An example of this biased reporting is the coverage of civil unrest in Los Angeles following initial verdicts in the 1992 Simi Valley trial of four Los Angeles policemen accused in the beating of Black motorist Rodney King. A report issued by the National Association of Black Journalists (1992) noted that although major news organizations had sufficient representation of Black reporters on their staffs, coverage of the ensuing "riots" was severely flawed. Among the findings was the fact that many Black reporters assigned to the event from mainstream media throughout the United States had their stories filtered through White editors, which resulted in stories skewed toward the preconceived biases and attitudes of White middle-class America. In general, news coverage fixed on the riots as racially motivated—Blacks versus the White "establishment"—when, in fact, they were class motivated. Involvement in the riots transcended race, as Latino, Asian, and Black people joined in the looting and burning. Despair over their common socioeconomic plight, not race-based hatred for each other, explained their participation. Much of the reportage in the media ignored the geographic range of the Los Angeles upheaval, which showed a pattern across ethnic communities and revealed the true common denominator to be poverty. Superficial and oversimplified news reporting distorted isolated events to make them appear in conformity with the existing attitudes and perceptions of Whites.

In 2002—a decade later—events related to the U.S. "war on terrorism" gave rise to another example of racial disparity in conflict coverage by American news media, this time on an international scale. The circumstances involved three persons of different racial heritage: a White American citizen, James Walker Lindh; a dark-skinned French citizen, Zacarias Moussaoui; and a Latino American citizen, Jose Padilla.

Lindh, labeled the "American Taliban," was an enemy combatant captured by the U.S. military in Afghanistan's Mazar-e-Sharif during a prison revolt where his acts directly contributed to the death of an American citizen. Lindh, who had taken the name Abdul Hamid, was brought to the United States, where the news media promptly noted his White middle-class Maryland and California upbringing. The press widely quoted his parents and friends, who believed that he had been "brainwashed" into acts of treason. President George W. Bush told ABC News, "We're just trying to learn the facts about this poor fellow. Obviously he has been misled." News accounts referred to him as John Walker Lindh rather than Abdul Hamid, the emotionally charged name he had taken as a Taliban soldier. Authorities decided that Lindh was to be treated as an American citizen and accorded all the rights guaranteed under the U.S. Constitution. It was rather quickly decided that he would not face the death penalty for acts of treason and he was ultimately allowed to plead guilty to less serious charges.

Zacarias Moussaoui, a French citizen of mixed African heritage, was already in federal custody on immigration charges prior to the September 11, 2001 attacks on the World Trade Center in New York and the Pentagon near Washington, D.C. After an investigation, U.S. authorities charged Moussaoui as a coconspirator in the attacks and he was labeled the "20th hijacker" of the two jetliners used in the attacks. Although American citizens convicted of criminal conspiracy are seldom punished more severely than the actual perpetrators, and although his native France long ago abolished the death penalty, U.S. officials pressed for Moussaoui's death.

Jose Padilla, a Puerto Rican American who was born in Brooklyn, New York, was arrested on charges that he planned to construct a "dirty bomb" device that could spread nuclear radioactive material across a relatively limited geographic area. The press reported him to be a former "Latino gang member" who had taken the name Abdullah Al Muhajir. President Bush—in stark contrast to his sympathetic remarks about Lindh—was widely quoted in the mainstream press as saying, "This guy, Padilla, is a bad guy." Although no damage, and in fact no overt action at all, resulted from Padilla's alleged conspiracy—nor were his coconspirators identified upon his indictment—he was held in military custody as an "enemy combatant" of the United States, a status that deprived him of Constitutional rights usually accorded to U.S. citizens. Nearly 3 months after Padilla's highly reported arrest, the press downplayed an anonymous law enforcement official's admission that Padilla was "small fish" and had no ties to the al-Qaeda network.

Following the lead of federal authorities and the mood of an American public caught up in the emotional issues of "terrorism" and "homeland security," the mainstream press generally ignored the obvious relationship between the racial heritage of the three men and their disparate treatment by the justice system. But some critics, including Wallace L. Walker, a criminal defense attorney and former professional journalist, saw that disparity. He believes that the cases of Lindh, Moussaoui, and Padilla confirm that persons of color are routinely "overcharged" for their criminal conduct, while the reverse is true for White defendants. Walker notes that the news media—many of which employ staff trained in law—could easily have brought the disparity in prosecutors' charges to the attention of the American public. Moreover, the media could have reported the disparity "as a legitimate point of difference that can be objectively noted." By doing so, Walker adds, news organizations could have shined "a ray of light on a possible form of institutional racism." Walker, a criminal defense lawyer for 30 years, believes that the legacy of racial exclusion in news media has parallels in the U.S. system of jurisprudence and may explain why mainstream journalists often parrot the decisions of prosecutors. "Prosecutors who charge defendants with crimes are overwhelmingly White. Their discretion about what criminal charges flow from unlawful conduct is unfettered and generally unquestioned" by news media. Walker concludes that if race is not a factor in these prosecutorial decisions, "the press should assure its readers of this" (W. L. Walker, personal correspondence to Clint Wilson, June 25, 2002).

THE STEREOTYPICAL NEWS SELECTION PHASE

After society has met the perceived threat of a non-White racial group via confrontation, social order must be restored. The transition must be made into the postconflict period to follow. Although conflicts between Whites and other racial groups have been numerous throughout American history, none of the conflict resolutions has resulted in the disappearance of people of color from the American social landscape. Reportage in news media, therefore, moves into another phase, one designed to neutralize White apprehension with regard to non-Whites while accommodating the presence of people of color. Information items that conform to existing White attitudes toward other groups are then selected for inclusion in what is presented by news media, and such items are given repeated emphasis until they reach thematic proportions.

Examples of this process of stereotypical news selection include news stories that ostensibly appear to be favorable to non-Whites, as in the case of "success stories"—people who have risen from the despair of (choose one) the reservation, the ghetto, the barrio, Chinatown, or Little Tokyo. These stories accomplish the two objectives of stereotypical selective reporting: (1) The general audience is reassured that non-Whites are still "in their place" (that is, the reservation, ghetto, etc.) and (2) those who escape their designated place are not a threat to society because they manifest the same values and ambitions of the dominant culture and have overcome the "deficits" of their racial and cultural backgrounds. At such moments of significant personal achievement, people of color have their accomplishments legitimized in the eyes of the Anglo American audience. At the same time, the stories tangentially give credit to the social system that tolerates or praises the upward mobility of people of color without facilitating it.

In the years since the 1968 Kerner Commission report, the news media have responded to the call for better reporting on non-White groups with thematic, stereotypical selective coverage. People of color are now more likely to get past the gatekeepers if they are involved in "hard news" events, such as those involving police action, or in the "colorful" soft news of holiday coverage, such as Chinese New Year, Cinco de Mayo, and Native American festivals. Other reporting in recent years has emphasized non-Whites on "welfare" who live in crime-infested neighborhoods, lack educational opportunity, job skills, and basic language skills; such stories include Latinos and Southeast Asians who are probably not documented as U.S. citizens.

The contrast between two Pulitzer Prize-winning newspaper series suggests that news coverage of people of color may be evolving. In a classic example of stereotypical selective reporting, the *Washington Post* received the 1995 prize for a series titled "Rosa Lee's Story: Poverty and Survival in Washington." The nine-part series focused on the life of a Black family matriarch who lived in an impoverished section of Washington, D.C.

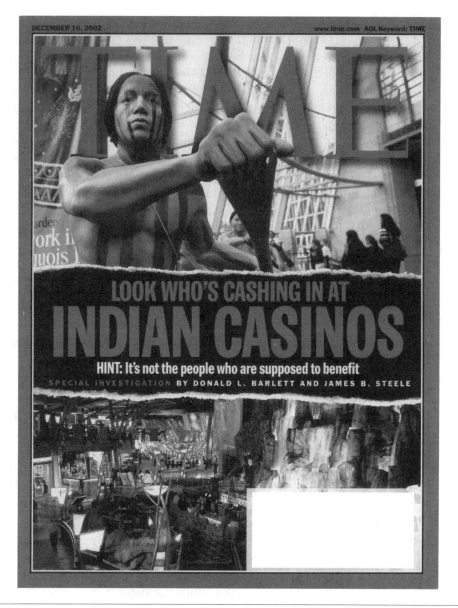

Illustration 5.1   This *Time* magazine cover in 2002 is an example of stereotypical selection in news coverage. Editors used 19th-century imagery to illustrate a 21st-century story about Native Americans.

Written by a Black reporter, Leon Dash, the series was replete with anecdotes that reaffirm every Black racial stereotype held and cultivated by Anglo Americans over the past 300 years. A glance at some of the series headlines is instructive: "Stealing Became a Way of Life for Rosa Lee," "Rosa

Lee Pays a Heavy Toll for Illiteracy," "She [Rosa Lee] Wrestles With Recovery in a Changing Drug Culture," and "A Grandson's Problems Start Early."[2]

In contrast, 5 years later the *New York Times* won a Pulitzer for a 10-part series titled "How Race is Lived in America." The journalists were honored for an honest and probing series that explored racial experiences and attitudes across contemporary America and went beyond the superficial stereotypes usually offered to assuage the consciences of Anglo Americans.[3] Such enlightened and progressive reporting, however, still remains the exception. The old stereotypes of people of color—as violent people who are too lazy to work and who indulge in drugs and sexual promiscuity—remain prominent in 21st century "news" reporting. In fact, the preponderance of such reporting has led some observers to say the news media have offered an image of non-Whites as "problem people," which means that they are projected as people who either *have* problems or *cause* problems for society. The legacy of the exclusion of people of color from the news is that the general audience is led to see people of color as a social burden or problem to solve—the "us versus them" syndrome carried to another dimension.

THE MULTIRACIAL COVERAGE PHASE

Multiracial news coverage is the antithesis of exclusion. If it is to become the goal and policy of American news media, the last vestiges of prejudice and racism must be removed from the gatekeeper ranks. At present this phase is still largely a vision, but it is within the grasp of a society determined to include all Americans in the quest for social equality. This does not mean that all news about people of color will be good news—it means that they will be reflected in all types of news coverage. News will be reported from the perspective that "us" represents all citizens. A major step in the process, of course, is the increased employment of non-Whites as professionals in news media. Equally important is an increased attentiveness in those working in news media to untold stories from non-White communities and the cultivation of news sources there.

The result should be a functional information surveillance system that promotes social understanding and alleviates unwarranted fears based on racial prejudices. In the meantime, major changes must be made in the training of journalists and in applied news philosophy if reporting concerning non-White racial groups is to improve.

Obstacles to Multiracial News Coverage

More equitable employment of people of color as professionals in news media represents an obvious opportunity to effect more accurate reporting of their role in society and merits detailed discussion, which is provided in Chapter 9. For the moment, however, it is important to look at other factors that are currently working against the achievement of culturally integrated news reporting in the United States. Progress toward this phase depends on the ability to overcome two major obstacles. Overcoming the first requires a renewed commitment to the ideals espoused by owners of the media and editors from the inception of professional news reporting standards; overcoming the second necessitates a change in the basic "news values" that journalists apply to their work.

If reporting in news media is to expand to encompass wider representation, it will first have to rededicate itself to the principle that meeting the substantive communication needs of society is its first priority. The obligation of news media to provide information and interpretation of issues and events to society is essential to the development and maintenance of an enlightened citizenry. A major barrier to more racially comprehensive news coverage in the media has been preoccupation with the profit incentive, as "marketing" of the news has led to, among other questionable practices, an increased emphasis on information targeted to high economic profile audiences. Among some major metropolitan daily newspapers, increased circulation among affluent readers has become the primary objective, while broadcast media seek higher audience ratings to attract major advertisers. Because people of color are vastly underrepresented in the upper-middle to upper-class income categories, they have been shortchanged by being underrepresented in coverage by the news media as well.[4] This approach to news reporting has affected both the frequency and nature of their coverage. Although news media, operating under the free enterprise system, have every right to pursue profits, they should not do so at the expense of their responsibility to serve the informational needs of society. The surveillance function of mass communication requires that news media inform society about the perspectives, aspirations, and contributions of all its members.

As noted earlier, the Kerner Commission (1968) provided insight into the nature of a major problem in the news media: the values applied to news judgment. The commission noted that news was determined from "a White perspective." In other words, the importance of news was based solely on an event's significance to the White majority. That notion was instilled in future journalists at the earliest stages of their training in colleges and universities. In the late 1990s and early 2000s, journalism departments and organizations in academia increased efforts to make students aware of the importance of racial and cultural diversity in reporting. But, historically, journalism students were taught that news—by definition—encompassed events of consequence to the majority population audience, which meant Anglo Americans. This concept was easily made practicable because the social system ensured that news sources (those with authority and social standing in the fields of politics, business, education, law enforcement, the military, and so on) were White. Journalism educators

Illustration 5.2   As the United States began to come to terms with the nation's racial diversity in the late 1960s, mass audience media looked for ways to more completely cover all Americans, as illustrated by two *Life* covers featuring journalist Frederick Douglass and The Red Man.

taught their students that the essence of good news reporting was the attribution of facts gathered from authoritative sources. Those news sources, unfortunately, represented in disproportionate numbers the Anglo American ideals and values held in common by the journalists and gatekeepers who reported on their activities. The perspective of non-Whites, therefore, was not "newsworthy." Even in reporting events about people of color, reporters sought news sources to interpret the events who were invariably White. This practice was a primary reason for the alienation and distrust of news media by citizens of color.

Because America's non-White communities generally have not been covered by mainstream news media, their stories have not been told adequately. In the 1970s and early 1980s, news media began to make inroads via special newspaper series and broadcast documentaries on specific issues of concern to people of color. However, the task of integrating people of color into the news requires ongoing inclusion of their views regarding all the major issues confronting society. Attempts to forge a change began in the 1990s and included content audits of news topics and news sources by newspapers; guideline stylebooks for journalists on proper usage of terms and labels; a Multicultural Management Program at the University of Missouri School of Journalism; total community coverage programs of the Robert Maynard Institute for Journalism Education

Illustration 5.3   Dori Maynard, President of Maynard Institute, speaks at
a 2002 Pew Center/Maynard Institute workshop in San
Francisco. The Institute offers programs that seek total
news coverage of America's multicultural population.

Source: Robert C. Maynard Institute for Journalism Education and Pew Center for
Civic Journalism. Copyright © Rebecca Wyhof.

in Oakland, California; and the development of multicultural newsroom
training workshops at the American Press Institute in Reston, Virginia.

As the effects of demographic change gradually alter the racial makeup
of America's opinion leaders, new sources of information must be tapped
from long-neglected racial communities. As the new century unfolds, the
pace of change must be accelerated to provide accurate journalistic
assessments of the non-White experience in the United States. To accomplish that objective, journalism educators and news professionals will
have to redefine news values for future reporters to include the perspectives of a wider spectrum of American citizens. Two results of these
changes may be a change in national priorities and better insight into
global perspectives.

Newsroom Policy and Race

We have observed that the misrepresentation of people of color in news media is partly the result of long-standing policies concerning news values. (Economic incentives—another legacy of the exclusion of people of color from the news—are discussed in Chapter 6.) Change in racial news coverage has come very slowly. Professional news organizations began to publicly address the issues of non-White training, employment, decision making, and coverage in 1968, the year of the Kerner Commission report. In the years since, however, there has generally been an increase in stereotypical selective reporting, notable exceptions notwithstanding. The nearly four decade struggle to provide more racially inclusive coverage suggests the difficulty of changing policy in news organizations. Thus, it is important to understand the fundamental social structure of the newsroom workplace.

In his 1955 study of daily newspapers, "Social Control in the Newsroom," sociologist Warren Breed (1960) characterized the nature of newsroom policy. Breed concludes that every daily newspaper has policies that are covert and that often contravene ethical standards of professional journalism. Such policies involve politics, business, and class considerations. Because the policies are covert and, therefore, not written and codified, new staff members must learn them by other means. New reporters learn such policies by observing the content of the newspaper or news broadcasts, noting which material has been edited from their work, conversing with staff members concerning the preferences and affiliations of their superiors, and noting the priorities assigned to news story ideas discussed in planning conferences.

A common complaint of non-White reporters working in mainstream newsrooms is the application of unwritten policy to their stories and "news angle" ideas. Their ideas are often disregarded because White colleagues define news in terms of the dominant cultural perspective. But both non-White and White reporters face sanctions when policy is violated. Such sanctions include reprimand, loss of esteem among colleagues, and less opportunity for upward mobility in the organization.

A revealing look at how newsroom policy affects news coverage of people of color from the vantage point of a staff newcomer is presented below. This is an exploration of the ways in which new reporters learn the unwritten policies at their papers: content observation, editing by superiors, informal conversation, news planning conferences, and sanctions for policy violations.

Content observation. A contemporary reporter intent on analyzing the news editorial product issued by his or her organization would find reportage of non-Whites ranging from the threatening issue phase to the confrontation phase to the stereotypical news selection phase, depending

Illustration 5.4   Training programs such as the American Indian Journalism Institute may help reduce stereotypical "pow-wow" stories about Native Americans in news coverage.

Source: The Freedom Forum Neuharth Center at the University of South Dakota.

on the historical moment and ethnicity of the group involved. The absence of a fully integrated approach to either individual reports or general coverage would be a strong indicator of organizational policy. Conversely, "zoo stories" about people of color, which focus on special occasions—such as Cinco de Mayo, Chinese New Year, Native American "pow-wows," or Dr. Martin Luther King, Jr.'s birthday—to the exclusion of more substantive reporting is likewise indicative of policy. The inclusion of multiracial views in reporting on environmental issues, alternative energy sources, foreign policy, or the national defense budget would signal to the newcomer that such efforts on his or her part would be welcome. Past performance, therefore, becomes a policy statement as strong as any written or orally expressed edict, perhaps stronger. In certain contexts it is easier to challenge formal than informal policies, because formal policies are often accompanied by a procedure for making changes to them. It is difficult for the newcomer to counter the explanation that conditions exist "because that's the way we do things around here." It is more likely, however, that the force of content observation will not elicit inquiry from a newcomer anxious to "fit in" in the work environment. The compelling instinct of the newcomer is to conform in order to survive.

Editing by superiors. A more direct means of conveying a paper's policy is the editing process. Newsroom editors are gatekeepers and enjoy professional authority over staff reporters. The journalist who produces newspaper or broadcast material that is inconsistent with policy will be edited; that is, what is unacceptable in his or her work will be either altered or deleted by others. As such editing relates to news about non-Whites, the professional explanation—if any is given—is that the item lacks "newsworthiness" or that lack of space or time prevents its inclusion. Since it is the reporter's job to get work into print or on the air, the inability of a newcomer to achieve those objectives reflects on his or her professional competence. Editing is not necessarily a sanction against the newcomer, but it often denotes a policy infringement, and one or two applications are usually enough to convey the message.

Informal conversation. When staff members gather around the water cooler or have lunch together, their conversations often provide insight into policy. When the newcomer's executive superiors mention their political and/or civil affiliations and preferences, it suggests to the astute newcomer which issues and topics to emphasize or avoid. Informal conversation and comments reveal the attitudes held by the newcomer's peers about racial groups and race-related news stories. Policy facilitates the newsroom atmosphere and when consensus is apparent, whatever the issue may be, newcomers quickly get the message.

The informal conversation of a new reporter's newsroom colleagues, however, need not be supportive of the views and attitudes of superiors.

Illustration 5.5   This Institute for Journalism Education workshop (1980) trained journalists of color for newsroom editing jobs in an effort to bring cultural
diversity to the "gatekeeping" process.
Source: Robert C. Maynard Institute for Journalism Education.

For the newcomer's purposes, even negative conversation regarding the
attitudes of superiors is sufficient to convey policy. Staff members need
not agree with policy, only adhere to it.

News planning conferences. Journalists who become privy to news story
planning meetings can observe the hidden force of policy in action. The
priority ranking of news events, activities, and ideas for future reporting
assignments reflects the thinking of executives and editorial gatekeepers.
The reception and "play" given to race-related news as opposed to other
issues reveals policy clearly. It is here where the relative consideration of
values is weighed, where the perception of social consequence is manifest.
Even the decision to do a special series on one racial group or another only
highlights the ongoing neglect of established policy to provide the general
audience with a complete surveillance of the social landscape. The news
perspective is askew, but the newcomer accepts it as "standard operating
procedure."

Sanctions for policy violations. The organizational policy works subtly
but effectively as a barrier to multiracial news coverage, and the sanctions for policy violations are equally subtle. There are four major sanctions that are self-imposed psychologically by the sanctioned reporter
but nonetheless real. An important reason for newsroom conformity
to policy is the reporter's desire for the esteem of his or her peers.

Few journalists, apart from those who attain national prestige, gain consistent recognition for performance. In the absence of letters, phone calls, or e-mails from the public, perhaps the greatest job satisfaction for a journalist is the acknowledgment from fellow staff members of a job well done. Newcomers to a staff arrive with the desire to demonstrate quickly their right to "belong" by earning the respect of their colleagues. Any violation of policy would cast the newcomer as incompetent or, worse, a rebel.

Journalists seek the rewards of career advancement. The fear of not getting the challenging assignments that lead to promotions and recognition by superiors is a strong motivation to learn and conform to policy. And, as in the case of the Black writer of the *Washington Post*'s "Rosa Lee's Story," the possibility of winning the Pulitzer Prize may have precluded any concern that the story was consistent with Black stereotypes. Because policy virtually defines the parameters of news value, policy breaches severely handicap a staff member competing with several peers for promotion. Another major sanction is the desire of journalists to please superiors who have given them employment opportunities. With that desire is a feeling of obligation to submit to the policies and procedures (published or otherwise) established by management.

Finally, journalists can lose their jobs if policy is violated. Although it is rare for a reporter to be fired over misinterpretation of policy, journalists who violate policy may become subject to scrutiny. It is not difficult for an editor or management superior to find other reasons to terminate policy transgressors or to make them feel "uncomfortable" on the job. For example, the continued assignment of routine work that offers no prospect for personal satisfaction or peer recognition denotes a reporter's status as "in the dog house."

It must be understood that newsroom policies and sanctions work against change in news coverage of non-Whites without regard for the racial heritage of reporters. Some reporters of color accept the tenets of racial policy as simply sound journalism: Decades of racially insensitive practice having come to define professional practice. But other journalists of color lament the newsroom atmosphere that forces them to see their profession from an Anglo American perspective. They complain that their colleagues and superiors—who are not so much overtly racist as insensitive or ignorant—evaluate their performance on culturally biased news criteria. If journalists focus too heavily on race-related issues, it jeopardizes their being held in high esteem by their peers, and work on such issues rarely results in the kind of recognition that leads to promotion. Given the nature of the various factors supporting traditional newsroom policy, the slow progress made toward more equitable and accurate news reporting concerning racial groups in American media becomes understandable, although not excusable.

Taking "Time Out" to Improve News Accuracy

Communication media are a vital element that enables a social system to exist and function. The role of news transmission is to reflect the realities of the societal well-being by alerting it to dangers within and without and by providing an agenda of issues for consideration. Individuals involved in that process are called the gatekeepers of information. Because non-Whites began their American experience as social outsiders, they have, by long-standing tradition, been excluded from roles in mainstream news gathering and reporting institutions. Information concerning non-Whites that does get processed through the news media is filtered, almost entirely, through members of the dominant Anglo American culture.

Viewed historically, reporting on non-Whites in news media can be divided into five characteristic phases, which, depending on specific times and circumstances, have been experienced by Native Americans, Blacks, Latinos, and Asians alike. Initially, non-Whites are excluded from news reports because they are not deemed part of the social system. Their continuing and growing presence, however, soon leads to their being reported as threats to "American" society. Official response to the perceived threat leads to conflict and results in confrontation news reporting. Once the confrontation crisis subsides, news media begin reporting stereotypical news items selected to reassure their audience that the non-White group is no longer a threat. Multiracial and multicultural news reporting looms as a promise on the horizon if increased opportunity for people of color to participate in the information gatekeeping process becomes reality.

Obstacles remain, however, in the path leading to multicultural news reporting. The primary obstacle is the placement of the profit motive before the responsibility to inform society accurately about the contributions, ambitions, frustrations, and issues important to all of its racial and ethnic groups—a necessity for its most prosperous survival. The tendency for some media to cater to economically advantaged audiences at the expense of audiences at the lower socioeconomic levels (where a disproportionate number of non-Whites are found) impedes multicultural news coverage. Other media, under the guise of providing news, merely exploit prurient interests to attract the largest audience for profit. In both instances, the result is inadequate and inaccurate reporting of essential information inclusive of all viewpoints.

Another obstacle to racially inclusive reporting in news media is the distorted news values held by many news professionals. Traditional reporting procedures have defined news from a White perspective. Although nationally news media have been cognizant of the need to change their approach since the Kerner Commission report of 1968, progress toward inclusive reporting has been extremely slow. The necessary reorientation of the reporting process has been inhibited by traditional prejudicial news values that have become engrained as matters of newsroom policy.

As sociologist Warren Breed (1955) explained, newsroom policy, however hidden, controls the newsgathering and reporting process. Professional journalistic mores preclude formal written policy and curtail freedom of expression among staff members. A covert system has evolved to teach and enforce this unwritten policy. Newcomers learn policy by observing the organization's news content, by noting which types of their own material are deleted in the editing process, by listening to informal conversation among their peers, and by participating in news content planning conferences. Sanctions, which maintain enforcement of newsroom policy, are also subtle but effective. They include the desire of reporters to earn and maintain the esteem of their peers, to advance up the organizational ladder, to fulfill obligations to their employers, and to protect their jobs. These sanctions affect White and non-White reporters alike.

American society will not achieve the goal of multicultural news coverage that accurately reflects the society until the concept of news is redefined to include non-White perspectives. The failure to do so will result in a nation that falls short of its own vision of itself and the purpose for its existence. Much of the responsibility for change must come from the news media, where dedicated, conscientious efforts must be made by organizations to examine whether outmoded and counterproductive policies are preventing progress toward multicultural reporting.

At the beginning of the 21st century, there are signs that the news industry is acknowledging how vital the issue of multicultural diversity is to its future and credibility. The Society of Professional Journalists (2002) revised its Code of Ethics to reflect that concern and noted in its trade journal that "journalists must avoid the stereotyping and limited vision that corrupt accuracy" (p. 59). It also joined a number of other professional news groups in providing a "Rainbow Rolodex" diversity source listing as a reference tool to assist reporters in identifying non-White news sources that may be used to gain broader perspectives for their stories. Meanwhile, in 1999, a national "Time Out for Diversity" campaign began under the leadership of David Yarnold of the San Jose (California) *Mercury News* and then diversity chair for the Associated Press Managing Editors. The annual project was cosponsored by the American Society of Newspaper Editors and encouraged newsrooms across the nation to devote time during a designated week to reflect on ways to improve the accuracy of reporting America's news in a multiracial and multicultural society. Time Out for Diversity is an example of the type of commitment and effort required by news organizations to overcome the legacy of exclusion that began in colonial America.

Notes

1. For a discussion of the definition of news and news values, see any of several basic news writing texts, including *Basic News Writing*, by M. Mencher, 1989,

Dubuque, IA: William C. Brown and *Newswriting*, by W. Metz, 1985, Englewood Cliffs, NJ: Prentice Hall.

2. The series appeared in the *Washington Post* in 1994, from September 18 to September 25.

3. The series was published in 2000 in the *New York Times*, intermittently from June 4 through June 29.

4. For a report on how socioeconomic factors affected news coverage strategies in the *Los Angeles Times*, see "The Demographic Dilemma," by F. Gutiérrez and C. C. Wilson II, 1979, *Columbia Journalism Review* (January/February), 53-55.

References

Asian invasion: South Bay's Chinese, Japanese, Korean populations swell. (1991, March 24). *Daily Breeze* (Torrance, CA), p. 1.

Breed, W. (1955). Social control in the newsroom. In W. Schramm (Ed.), (1960), *Mass communications* (2nd ed.). Champaign: University of Illinois Press.

Center for Integration and Improvement of Journalism. (1991). *Project zinger: The good, the bad and the ugly.* San Francisco: San Francisco State University and Asian American Journalists Association.

Center for Integration and Improvement of Journalism. (1994). *News watch: A critical look at coverage of people of color.* San Francisco: San Francisco State University.

Gersh, D. (1992, October 10). Promulgating polarization. *Editor and Publisher*, p. 30.

Kerner Commission (1968). *Report of the National Advisory Commission on Civil Disorders.* New York: Bantam.

National Association of Black Journalists. (1992, August). *The L.A. unrest and beyond* (Report). Reston, VA: Author.

Society of Professional Journalists. (2002, June). Source book to launch this month. *Quill*, p. 59.

Advertising 6

The Media's Not-So-Silent Partner

People from Asia and the Pacific Islands can sell you just about anything. At least, that's what advertisers appeared to be saying in the late 1990s and early 21st century as they increasingly used cute Asian toddlers and seductive Polynesian maidens to sell everything from paper towels to pizza. Some images, such as Asian American computer nerds and South Seas warriors, drew on new and old stereotypes of Asians and Asian Pacific Americans. Others portrayed more realistic images of families enjoying a fast food meal, teenagers mixing with a multiracial group of classmates, or Generation Y friends partying. But, whatever the image, the message was the same: Look at these people and then buy the product they are advertising. It's a message central to all advertisements. But when the images used are of people of color, it sometimes sends mixed messages that appeal to some people and offend others.

Alcohol and tobacco companies were among the first to incorporate images of Asians and Pacific Islanders into their advertising. But the reaction the images triggered didn't always favor their products. In 1999, when a Skyy Vodka ad featured a White woman being served by a kimono-clad Asian woman, the advertisement reportedly was pulled after Asian Americans protested. Tobacco giant Philip Morris fielded criticism of a 1999 magazine campaign that urged women of color to "Find your own voice." One advertisement featured an Asian woman made up as a geisha in traditional dress, portraying "Asian women as mysterious and exotic creatures," it was reported (Poblete, 2002, p. 8).

In 2002, clothier Abercrombie & Fitch felt the full force of protest against the Asian images it used in what it hoped would become a trendy line of T-shirts featuring images of Chinese and other Asians advertising hypothetical businesses. "Wong Brothers Laundry Service—Two Wongs Can Make It White," proclaimed one T-shirt advertisement, playing on the stereotypes of Chinese laundries and the families operating many of them. Other T-shirts featured bogus advertising slogans such as "Abercrombie and Fitch Buddha Bash—Get Your Buddha on the Floor" and "Wok-N-Bowl—Let the Good Times Roll—Chinese Food & Bowling" (Kong, 2002, p. 5). After the protests at the firm's outlets drew the attention of Asian Pacific Americans, their supporters, and nationwide news coverage, Abercrombie & Fitch pulled the clothing line from its shelves.

Yet, in doing the right thing, the clothier didn't quite do the thing right. Some of the firm's representatives expressed surprise that the T-shirts were offensive to people they were portraying. "We personally thought Asians would love this T-shirt," said Hampton Carney, a spokesman for the New York public relations agency that handled media calls (Strasburg, 2002, p. A1). Although Carney said "We're very, very, very sorry," after the T-shirts were pulled, he explained, "These graphic T-shirts were designed with the sole purpose of adding humor and levity to our fashion line" (Kong, 2002, p. 5). Asian Pacific American college students were quick to point out why they did not "love this T-shirt" or find "humor and levity" in the images and messages that the T-shirts carried.

"It's really misleading as to what Asian people are," said Michael Chang, vice chairman of Stanford University's Asian American Students' Association. "The stereotypes they depict are more than a century old. You're seeing laundry service. You're seeing basically an entire religion and philosophy being trivialized" (Strasburg, 2002, p. A5). Across the San Francisco Bay, University of California Berkeley professor Ling-Chi Wong compared the image of Buddha with images of figures from other religions, "What would happen if they had put the pope or the prophet Mohammed on those shirts? Would it be so funny then?" (Poblete, 2002, p. D8).

To many observers of race, ethnicity, and the media, the advertisers' adventures with Asian Pacific American images were reminiscent of earlier attempts by advertisers to move from offensive stereotypes of Blacks and Latinos to images that would appeal to people of all races. And, as advertisers looked for ways to effectively catch up with America's growing racial and ethnic diversity, these experiences also reminded people of advertising's pervasive influence in shaping the development of media in the United States.

Advertising and Media in the Land of Plenty

In 1950, historian David Potter was invited by the Walgreen Foundation to prepare six lectures at Harvard University on the American character and the impact of economic abundance on shaping the character of people in the United States. In the lectures, which were later published in revised form in Potter's 1954 book *People of Plenty*, he identified advertising as the "institution of abundance," a unique part of the society "brought into being by abundance, without previous existence in any form, and, moreover, an institution which is peculiarly identified with American abundance" (p. 166). He also noted that media scholars up to that time had not recognized the central role advertising played in shaping and developing media in the United States.

As Potter and later scholars have noted, the development of advertising as a revenue source for print and, later, broadcast media required managers of media to develop news and entertainment content attractive to the largest possible number of people. This gave birth to the term *mass media*, which described the ability of the media to attract a large audience to which advertisers could direct their commercial messages through relatively few channels. The audience circulation and rating figures became the bread and butter of the media, since they translated to increased advertising insertions and higher advertising rates.

Potter emphasized that, far from being an appendage to the mass media, advertising is a force that dictates the editorial and entertainment content of media that depend on advertising dollars for their revenues. The mass media charge artificially low subscription fees to boost their circulation, which forces the media to depend on advertisers even more for their revenues. This, in turn, is accompanied by editorial or programming philosophies that placed a priority on attracting the largest possible audience. News and entertainment content are nothing more than the bait to attract the audience and hold its attention between the commercial messages (Potter, 1954).

> What this means, in functional terms, it seems to me, is that the newspaper feature, the magazine article, the radio program, do not attain the dignity of being ends in themselves; They are rather means to an end: that end, of course, is to catch the reader's attention so that he[or she] will then read the advertisement or hear the commercial, and to hold his[or her] interest until these essential messages have been delivered. The program or the article becomes a kind of advertisement in itself—becomes the "pitch," in the telling language of the circus barker. Its function is to induce people to accept the commercial, just as the commercial's function is to induce them to accept the product. (pp. 181-182)

Potter (1954) explained that the development of content as bait for the mass audience means that the mass media include material that attracts the most people and, at the same time, delete material that could offend and alienate potential members of the audience. This rigidly constrains editorial and entertainment content.

First, a message must not deal with subjects of special or out-of-the-way interest, since such subjects by definition have no appeal for the majority of the audience. Second, it must not deal with any subject at a high level of maturity, since many people are immature, chronologically or otherwise, and a mature level is one which, by definition, leaves such people out. Third, it must not deal with matters which are controversial or even unpleasant or distressing, since such matters may, by definition, antagonize or offend some members of the audience. (pp. 184-185)

The social and legal restrictions historically placed on racial minorities in the United States and the desire of the media to cater to the perceived views of the mass audience had several important racial and ethnic implications. With few exceptions and until legally challenged in the late 1960s, the mass media were characterized by entertainment and news content that largely (1) ignored people of color, (2) treated them stereotypically when they were featured, and (3) avoided tough issues such as racial segregation, discriminatory immigration laws, land rights, and other issues that affected people of color more than they did the White majority. The entertainment and editorial portrayal of non-Whites is amply analyzed in other chapters of this book. Those portrayals were, to a large extent, supported by racial and ethnic advertising images that catered to the perceived attitudes and prejudices of the White majority.

Race and Ethnicity in Advertising

For years, advertisers reflected the place of non-Whites in the social fabric of the nation by either ignoring them or, when including them in advertisements for the mass audience, presenting them as palatable salespersons for the products being advertised. These portrayals in the media largely mirrored the perceived values and norms of the White majority as they saw non-Whites. The images of people of color featured in advertising paralleled and reinforced their entertainment and news images.

The history of advertising in the United States is replete with characterizations that responded to and reinforced the preconceived image that many White Americans apparently had of Blacks, Latinos, Asians, and Native Americans. Over the years, advertisers have employed Mexican bandits like the mustachioed Frito Bandito, Black mammies like Aunt Jemima, Chinese laundry workers, and noble savages like the Santa Fe railroad's Chief to pitch products to a predominately White mass audience of consumers.

In 1984, the Balch Institute for Ethnic Studies in Philadelphia sponsored an exhibit of more than 300 examples of racial and ethnic images

Illustration 6.1   Pigtailed Chinese laundrymen are frightened by a salesman selling Celluloid Waterproof clothing articles that threaten to put them out of business in this 1880s advertising trading card featuring appealing stereotypes of the era.

Source: Donaldson Brothers, Five Points, NY.

used by corporations in magazines, posters, trading cards, and storyboards. In an interview with the advertising trade magazine *Advertising Age*, Balch Institute director Mark Stolarik quoted the exhibit catalog, which recalled the evolution of advertising images of people of color.

> Some of these advertisements were based on stereotypes of various ethnic groups. In the early years, they were usually crude and condescending images that appealed to largely Anglo-American audiences who found it difficult to reconcile their own visions of beauty, order and behavior with that of non-Anglo-Americans. Later, these images were softened because of complaints from the ethnic groups involved and the growing sophistication of the advertising industry. ("Using Ethnic Images," 1984, p. 9)

The advertising examples in the exhibit included positive White ethnic stereotypes, such as the wholesome and pure image of Quakers in an early Quaker Oats advertisement and the cleanliness of the Dutch in a 1900-era advertisement for Colgate soap. But other White ethnics were not treated as kindly. The exhibit featured a late 19th-century advertisement showing an Irish matron threatening to hit her husband over the head with a rolling pin because he didn't smoke the right brand of tobacco. Some products, such as Quaker Oats cereal and Red Man chewing tobacco, went beyond advertising to incorporate racial or ethnic images in the product name or label.

"Lawsee! Folks sho' whoops with joy over AUNT JEMIMA PANCAKES," shouted a bandanna wearing Black mammy in an advertisement for Aunt Jemima pancake mix. A plump Aunt Jemima was featured on the box ("Using Ethnic images," 1984, p. 9). Marilyn Kern-Foxworth, who has studied African American images in advertising, describes how Aunt Jemima has lost weight and her bandanna over the years. But although the image has changed, her legacy continues. A neatly coiffed Black woman wearing pearl earrings is still featured on every Aunt Jemima box. Similarly, boxes of Uncle Ben's rice products still feature a well-groomed Black servant. Although "Aunt Jemima" and "Uncle Ben" may have lived in the same house as the people they served, they were not really considered members of the families for whom the products and advertising were created.

Images of Blacks as friendly servants were for a long time pervasive in the national promotion of products. Early advertisements for Cream of Wheat featured Rastus, the Black servant whose picture is still on the box, in a series of magazine pictures with a group of cute, but ill-dressed, Black children. Some of the advertising ridiculed Blacks, such as an ad in which a Black schoolteacher, standing behind a makeshift lectern made out of a boldly lettered Cream of Wheat box, asks the class, "How do you spell Cream of Wheat?" Others appeared to promote racial integration, such as an advertisement captioned "Putting it down in Black and White," which showed Rastus serving bowls of breakfast cereal to Black and White youngsters sitting at the same table.[1]

Illustration 6.2   In the 1950s, advertisements for Aunt Jemima pancake mix featured romanticized images of relationships between Black slaves and their White owners. Closer to reality were the first images of people of color in American advertising, such as a 1784 newspaper notice of "Negroes for Sale."

Source: For newspaper advertising, CORBIS.

Earlier images of Blacks in servitude were not designed to promote racial equality and, in some, Black slaves were the product being bought and sold. An 1855 Lexington, Kentucky, advertisement featuring a picture of a Black man on the move with his belongings on his back was placed by a slave trader offering to pay "$1200 TO 1250 DOLLARS FOR NEGROES!!" Another newspaper advertised "CASH FOR 500 NEGROES" and on September 7, 1835, a Washington, D.C. newspaper, the *Washington Globe*, offered "FIFTY DOLLARS REWARD" for the return of the "runaway Dennis," a slave.

Racial imagery also influenced the naming and advertising of passenger routes by the Santa Fe railroad. It named its passenger lines the Chief, Super Chief, and El Capitan and featured highly detailed portraits of noble "Indians" in promoting its service through the Southwest. In other advertisements, the railroad featured cartoons of cute Native American children to show the service and sights passengers could expect when riding the Santa Fe line.

These and other portrayals catered to the mass audience mentality by either neutralizing or making fun of the negative perceptions that many Whites may have had of racial minorities. The advertising images, rather than showing people of color as they really were, portrayed them as filtered through Anglo eyes for the mass audience. This presented an out-of-focus image of racial minorities, but one that was acceptable, and even persuasive, to the White majority to which it was directed.

Advertising Images: Protests and Progress

In the mid-1960s, Black civil rights groups targeted the advertising industry for special attention, protesting both the lack of integrated advertisements including Blacks and the stereotyped images that the advertisers continued to use. The effort, accompanied by pressure from federal officials, resulted in the overnight inclusion of Blacks as models in television advertising during the 1967 to 1968 television season and a downplaying of the images many Blacks found objectionable. In 1968, the *New York Times* reported, "Black America is becoming visible in America's biggest national advertising medium. Not in a big way yet, but it is a beginning and men in high places give assurances that there will be a lot more visibility" (quoted in Dougherty, 1982, p. D19).

But the advertising industry did not apply the concerns of Blacks, or the changes made in response to them, to other people of color. Some Black issues were being addressed with integrated advertising in the late 1960s and early 1970s. But other groups were still ignored or experienced continued stereotyped treatment in commercials such as those featuring the

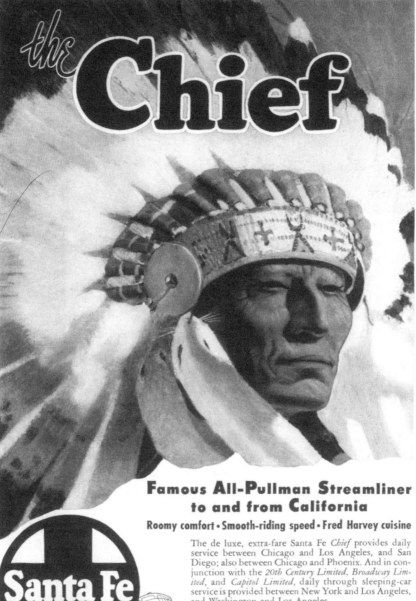

Illustration 6.3   The Santa Fe Railroad attached Native American names and images to trains carrying passengers across Midwestern and Southwestern regions that native people once dominated. This 1940s advertisement for the Santa Fe Chief reinforced the image of Native Americans as a people whose proudest era was in the past.

Frito Bandito, a sneaky Mexican bandido who stole "cronchy" corn chips from unsuspecting homemakers. Although the Frito Bandito campaign was highly effective, it was withdrawn in the early 1970s after it became the target of Latino protests.

Among the Latino advertising stereotypes cited in a 1969 article by Tomás Martínez were commercials for Granny Goose potato chips featuring fat gun-toting Mexicans, an advertisement for Arrid underarm deodorant showing a dusty Mexican bandito spraying his underarms as the announcer intoned, "If it works for him it will work for you," and a magazine photo of a Mexican sleeping under his sombrero against a Philco television set. Especially offensive to Martínez was a Liggett & Meyers commercial for L&M cigarettes, which featured Paco, a lazy Latino who never "feenishes" anything, not even the revolution he is supposed to be fighting. In response to a letter complaining about the commercial, the director of public relations for the tobacco firm defended the commercial (Martínez, 1969, p. 10). "'Paco' is a warm, sympathetic and lovable character with whom most of us can identify because he has a little of all of us in him, that is, our tendency to procrastinate at times," wrote the Liggett & Meyers executive. "He seeks to escape the violence of war and to enjoy the pleasure of the moment, in this case, the good flavor of an L&M cigarette" (quoted in Martínez, 1969, p. 11). Although the company spokesman claimed that the character had been tested without negative reactions from Latinos, Martínez roundly criticized the advertising images and contrasted them with nonstereotypical images of Blacks that were clear evidence of the breakthroughs Blacks were making in advertising in the late 1960s.

> Today, no major advertiser would attempt to display a black man or woman over the media in a prejudiced, stereotyped fashion. Complaints would be forthcoming from black associations and perhaps the FCC. Yet, these same advertisers, who dare not show "step'n fetch it" characters, uninhibitedly depict a Mexican counterpart, with additional traits of stinking and stealing. Perhaps the white hatred for blacks, which cannot find adequate expression in today's ads, is being transferred upon their brown brothers. (Martínez, 1969, pp. 9-10)

A 1970s Brown Position Paper prepared by Latino activists Domingo Nick Reyes and Armando Rendón charged that the media had transferred the negative stereotypes it once reserved for Blacks to Latinos, who had become "the media's new nigger" (Reyes & Rendón, 1971). The protests of Latinos soon made the nation's advertisers more conscious of the portrayals that Latinos found offensive.

As with Ambercrombie & Fitch more than 30 years later, it took protests on the part of offended members of the groups portrayed for advertisers to understand the potential harm embedded in the racial and ethnic advertising stereotypes others found so appealing. National advertisers

Illustration 6.4 Latino activists in the late 1960s protested the Mexican bandit imagery of Frito-Lay's Frito Bandito advertising campaign, illustrated by this wanted poster using both visual and language stereotypes (1968). The campaign was withdrawn in the early 1970s after protests intensified.

had withdrawn much of the advertising that negatively stereotyped Blacks and Latinos by the end of the 1970s, but they sometimes replaced the ads with images of affluent, successful people of color that were as far from reality as the negative portrayals of the past. The advances made by those groups were not realized by Asian Americans and Native Americans until they launched their own protests.

Native Americans, no longer depicted either as noble savages or as cute cartoon characters, have all but disappeared from broadcast commercials and print advertising. The major exceptions to this exclusion of Native Americans are the SUVs, trucks, and motor homes that bear the names of indigenous people, such as Jeep Cherokee, Winnebago, Dakota, and Navajo, to evoke a rugged, outdoors, woodsy image. To show their toughness, some professional teams and schools still use Native American racial mascots in the 21st century. The Kansas City Chiefs, Washington Redskins, Florida State University Seminoles, University of North Dakota Fighting Sioux, Atlanta Braves, and Cleveland Indians are names that play on 19th-century stereotypes and images of the First Americans.

After more than 30 years of protests, some schools have dropped the stereotypical images, although most professional teams have held onto their mascots. In the early 1970s, Stanford University dropped its Indians mascot after criticisms of its racist implications were raised. In 2002, the Massachusetts College of Liberal Arts dropped the Mohawks mascot and stern warrior image after a Mohawk tribal officer told college officials the name given to his people by Europeans translates to "maneater" and did not honor them. San Diego State University retired the stereotypical Monty Montezuma and replaced him with Montezuma II, a more historically accurate figure who told school children about the achievements of Mexico's Aztec people ("Mascot Watch," 2002).[2] Native Americans and others have long protested the marketing of these racial team names and images, as well as the pseudo-pageantry and souvenirs that accompany many of them. The prospects for change improved early in the 21st century as governmental groups, such as the United States Commission on Civil Rights and some state education agencies, took positions against the Indian mascots.

Advertisers have also used images of Asian Pacific Americans that cater to the fears and stereotypes of White America. As with Blacks and Latinos, it took organized action by Asian Americans for corporations and advertising agencies to get the message. Following protests in the mid-1970s, a Southern California supermarket chain agreed to remove a television campaign in which a young Asian karate-chopped his way down the store's aisles cutting prices.

Nationally, several firms hard hit by Japanese imports fought back in the 1980s through commercials, if not in the quality or prices of their products. One automobile company featured an Asian American family carefully looking over a new car and commenting on its attributes in

9 essential nutrients
in every easy-to-open
bottle.

got milk?

Illustration 6.5   Martial arts themes have long been used in some advertising featuring Asians and Asian Pacific Americans, such
as this 21st century "Got Milk?" advertisement showing
actress Zhang Ziyi slicing through a milk bottle with her
hand.

heavily accented English. Only after they bought it did they learn that it
was made in the United States, not Japan. Another automobile company,
which markets cars with an English name that are manufactured in Japan,
showed a parking lot attendant opening the doors of the car to find the car

speaking to him in Japanese. Sylvania television ran a commercial in which the announcer boasted that its picture had repeatedly been selected over competing brands, while an off-screen voice with a Japanese accent repeatedly asked, "What about Sony?" When the announcer responded that the Sylvania picture had been selected over Sony's, the off-screen voice trailed off shouting what sounded like a string of Japanese expletives. In 1982, *Newsweek* reported that "attacking Japan has become something of a fashion in corporate ads" because of resentment over Japanese trade policies and sales of Japanese products in the United States. Motorola's advertising manager was quoted as saying, "We've been as careful as we can be" not to be racially offensive (Treen, 1982, p. 69).

But, like Abercrombie & Fitch's fake advertising on T-shirts, many of the television and print advertisements with Asians featured themes that were racially insensitive, if not offensive. And these advertisements were for real. One commercial featured a Chinese family laundry that used an "ancient Chinese laundry secret" to get customers' clothes clean. Naturally, the secret turned out to be the packaged product paying for the advertisement. Companies pitching everything from pantyhose to air travel featured women coiffed and costumed as seductive China dolls or exotic Polynesian maidens to promote their products, some of them cast in exotic settings and others attentively caring for the needs of Whites. One airline boasted that those flying with them would be under the care of the Singapore Girl.

Asian Pacific women had an exotic, tropical Pacific Islands look, complete with flowers in their hair, a sarong or grass skirt, and a shell ornament. Asian Pacific men in advertising were often beefy and muscular, with an aptitude for surfing or other water sports. Asian women in commercials were often featured as China dolls—with small, darkened eyes, straight hair with bangs, and a narrow, slit skirt. Asian American women who hoped to become models sometimes found that they must conform to these stereotypes or lose assignments. Leslie Kawai, the 1981 Tournament of Roses Queen, was told to cut her hair into a style with bangs when she auditioned for a beer advertisement. When she refused, the beer company hired a model who had bangs (Kan, 1983, p. 5).

The lack of a sizable Asian Pacific American community, or market, in the United States was earlier cited as the reason that members of the group were still stereotyped in advertising and, except for children's advertising, rarely presented in integrated settings. However, their population and income growth rate in the United States during the 1980s and 1990s made clear their potential to overcome such stereotyping and their lack of visibility in advertising. By the mid-1980s, there were signs that advertising was beginning to integrate Asian Pacific Americans into crossover advertisements designed to have a broad appeal. In one commercial, actor Robert Ito said that he loved to call relatives in Japan because the calls made them think he was rich and successful in the United States. Of course, he added, it was because the rates of his long distance carrier were so low that he was able to call so often.

Integration in Advertising

By the end of the 1970s, mass audience advertising in the United States had become more racially integrated than it had been at any time in the nation's history. Blacks, and to a much lesser extent Latinos and Asians, could be seen in television commercials and major magazines. In fact, the advertisements on network television often were more integrated than the television programs they supported. Like television advertising, general circulation magazine advertising showed an increase in the appearance of Blacks, although studies of both media showed that most of the percentage increase had come by the early 1970s (see, e.g., the studies cited in Culley & Bennett, 1976; Reid & Vanden Bergh, 1980; and Soley, 1983). At that time, the percentage of prime time television commercials featuring Blacks had apparently leveled off at about 10%. Blacks were featured in only between 2% and 3% of magazine advertisements as late as 1978. That percentage, however small, was a sharp increase from the .06% of news magazine advertisements reported in 1960.

The advertising breakthroughs were socially significant, since they demonstrated that Blacks could be successfully integrated into advertisements. But some worried that Blacks in advertising might trigger a backlash among potential customers in the White majority. This spurred research to study reaction among Blacks and Whites as the advertising breakthroughs took place. Both sales figures and research conducted in the late 1960s showed that the integration of Black models into television and print advertising did not adversely affect sales or the image of the product. In fact, while integrated advertisements triggered no adverse effects among Whites, such ads helped sway Black consumers, who responded favorably to positive Black role models in print advertisements (Gibson, 1979, pp. 83-84).

Studies conducted in the early 1970s also showed that Whites did not respond negatively to advertising featuring Black models (Soley, 1983, pp. 585-587). However, one 1972 study examining White backlash did show that an advertisement featuring darker skinned Blacks prominently was less acceptable to Whites than those featuring lighter skinned Blacks as background models (Block, 1972). Perhaps such findings help explain why later research revealed that, for the most part, Blacks appearing in magazine and television advertisements in the 1970s were often featured as part of an integrated group (Culley & Bennett, 1976). In the 1970s and

1980s, people of color who appeared in general audience advertising often played token roles in upscale integrated settings, which the Balch Institute's Stolarik criticized as taking advertising "too far in the other direction and created stereotypes of 'successful' ethnic group members that are as unrealistic as those of the past" ("Using Ethnic Images," 1984, p. 9).

Having established that featuring African Americans would not offend potential White customers, corporations and advertising agencies turned their attention to ways to maximize their profits among all racial segments of society in the 1980s. But still unanswered at that time was how much and how often they would feature non-White models in their advertising. Once again, the answer would come down to dollars and cents.

If it is believed that the presence of Black models in advertisements decreases the effectiveness of advertising messages, only token numbers of Black models will be used," wrote Lawrence Soley in 1983. "Given the consistency of the research findings, more Blacks should be portrayed in advertisements. If Blacks continue to be underrepresented in advertising portrayals, it can be said that this is an indication of prejudice on the part of the advertising industry, not consumers. (Soley, 1983, p. 690)

Two decades later, there were more Asian Pacific Americans, Blacks, and Latinos featured in mass audience advertising. But their numbers were still below reflecting the growth of these groups in the nation's population. And it was this sharp growth that had captured the attention of advertisers.

SPANISH GOLD, THE BLACK
MARKET, AND ASIAN TREASURES

While Soley (1983) stopped short of accusing corporate executives of racial prejudice, he contended that a "counter pressure" to full integration of Blacks into portrayals in mainstream media was that "advertising professionals are businessmen first and moralists second" (p. 690). Thus it was the business sense of marketing executives that led to increasingly aggressive advertising and marketing campaigns to capture people of color as consumers—particularly Blacks and Latinos in the 1970s and 1980s and Asian Pacific Americans in the 1990s.

Long depicted as low-end consumers with little money to spend, Black and Latino customers became more important to those national and regional advertisers of mainstream goods who took a close look at the size, composition, and projected growth of the groups. Although Asian Pacific Americans experienced a sharp percentage growth in the 1970s and were generally more affluent than Blacks and Latinos, they were not targeted to the same extent as were those groups, probably because of their relatively

Illustration 6.6   As the United States has become more racially diverse, some advertising appeals have become more racially inclusive, such as these 2003 advertisements by Verizon Wireless to "Join In" and American Airlines to attract business people of all colors.

small numbers and the differences in national languages in the group. And, except for in regions in which they comprised a sizable portion of the population, Native Americans were still ignored as consumers of main-stream products into the 21st century. A 2003 *American Demographics* article on race, ethnicity, and marketing in the United States included data and charts on Blacks, Whites, Hispanics, and Asians but not on Native Americans.[3]

Although some companies began using "special market" advisors early in the 20th century, the first major breakthroughs in the advertising indus-try's courtship of Blacks and Latinos grew out of the civil rights movement of the 1950s and 1960s, in which consumer boycotts challenged racial seg-regation and helped unionize farm workers. In the 1960s, Black ministers organized the Philadelphia Selective Patronage Program, in which Blacks did business with companies that supported their goal of more jobs for Blacks. In the same era, the United Farm Workers of America effectively organized a nationwide boycott of California table grapes until growers recognized the rights of their largely Mexican and Filipino workers to form a labor union. After union contracts were signed in 1970, the union asked their supporters to buy table grapes. This philosophy of consumers using their purchases to patronize the corporations that recognized the importance of minority communities and causes was replicated elsewhere. It was often accompanied by slick advertising campaigns directed at minority consumers. In 1984, the same line of thinking led to Coors brew-ery attempting to end disputes with Blacks and Latinos by signing contro-versial agreements with the National Association for the Advancement of Colored People (NAACP) and five national Latino groups. The agree-ments committed the brewery to increase its financial support of the orga-nizations as Blacks and Latinos drank more Coors beer.

The second, and perhaps more influential, element of the courtship was the hard selling job of advertising agencies and media targeting Blacks and Spanish-speaking Latinos. Spurred by Black advertising executive D. Parke Gibson's 1968 book *The $30 Billion Negro* and a steady stream of articles on Black and Latino consumers in media trade publications, national advertisers in the 1960s began to see these groups as potential purchasers of a wide range of products, not just ethnic foods and cosmetics. Advertisers were persuaded that the inattention Latinos and Blacks had previously received from mainstream products made them loyal to com-panies that courted them through neighborhood billboards and in their publications and broadcast stations.

The third, and most important, element in advertising's courtship of Latinos and Blacks was a fundamental change in the thinking of market-ing and advertising executives. Witnessing the success they had in adver-tising on radio stations and magazines targeted to specific audience segments following the advent of television as the dominant mass audi-ence medium in the 1950s, advertising agencies advised clients to target

Illustration 6.7   The United States' growing racial and language diversity has led to more advertising targeting different groups with images and language tailored to appeal to them, as illustrated by these 2003 advertisements in ethnic magazines.

potential customers classified by market segments rather than the undefined mass audience. Advertisers found that classifications of race, like differences in sex, residence, education, and age, were easy to target using targeted advertising appeals in targeted media. As the advertisers moved from mass communication to class communication, Black and Latino media produced studies to show their effectiveness in reaching and delivering the desired segments of the mass audience.

In a 1984 article in the advertising trade magazine *Madison Avenue,* Caroline Jones, executive vice president of Mingo-Jones Advertising, wrote

> It is a basic tenet of marketing that you go after markets with rifles, not shotguns. It is foolhardy—and idealistic in the worst way—to try to sell the same thing to everyone in the same way. Good marketing involves breaking down potential markets into homogeneous segments; targeting the most desirable segments; and developing creative programs, tailored for each segment, that make your messages look different from your competitors. All of that should be done with the guidance of thorough research on characteristics, beliefs and preferences of the people in the targeted markets. (p. 53)

Jones, whose agency focused on reaching Black consumers, advised advertising professionals to target Black consumers because "there's money in it." Among the factors she cited in 1984 as making Blacks desirable customers was the group's disposable income, a "high propensity for brand names and indulgence items," a strong sense of "brand loyalty," a young and growing population, improved education and income, population centers in the nation's largest 25 cities, and "its own growing media network" (p. 54).

Although the growth rate of Blacks since 1980 has not been as steep as that of Latinos and Asian Pacific Americans, the Black population has continued to grow as an important segment for marketers and advertisers through the early 21st century. With African Americans' discretionary income estimated at $646 billion in 2002 and their purchasing power projected to increase to $853 billion in 2007, they constitute a significant portion of the U.S. audience. Black-targeted advertising has certainly increased, but it still needs to be approached strategically and carefully through a wide variety of print, broadcast, and digital media. Some appeals to this market have backfired, such as two Toyota ads—one featuring an African American with an SUV etched in gold on one tooth and another in Black-targeted *Jet* magazine promising about the car that "unlike your last boyfriend, it goes to work in the morning." Both advertisements were reportedly pulled by Toyota after protests (White, 2001).[4]

The promise of untapped profits also motivated advertisers to sell to Latinos, who had become a target too good to pass up. A 1965 article in the trade magazine *Sponsor* called Latinos "America's Spanish Treasure," a 1971 *Sales Management* article proclaimed that "Brown is Richer Than

Black," and in 1972 *Television/Radio Age* told readers that "The Spanish Market: Its Size, Income and Loyalties Make It a Rich Marketing Mine" (Gutiérrez, 1976, pp. 312-314). Latinos were depicted as having the characteristics that made Blacks an attractive market and as being especially vulnerable because their use of Spanish supposedly cut them off from English-language advertising. Advertisers were advised to use the language and culture most familiar to their target audience to give their messages the greatest delivery and impact.

"U.S. Hispanics are most receptive to media content in the Spanish language," wrote Antonio Guernica in his 1982 book *Reaching the Hispanic Market Effectively* (p. 5). Guernica and others counseled advertisers to package their commercial messages in settings that reflect Latino culture and traditions. These appeals link the product being advertised with the language, heritage, and social system that Latinos are most comfortable with, thus creating an illusion that the product belongs in the Latino home.

In a 1983 *Advertising Age* article, Shelly Perlman, media buyer for the Hispania division of the J. Walter Thompson advertising agency, was quoted as having said that

> the language, the tradition, the kitchen utensils are different [in a Latino home]. There are ads one can run in general media that appeal to everyone but that contain unmistakable clues to Hispanics that they are being sought. It can be done with models, with scene and set design—a whole array of factors. (Gage, 1983, p. M11)

Corporations seeking the Latino dollar also were told to picture their products with Latino foods, celebrities, cultural events, community events, and family traditions. The goal was to make the product appear to be a part of the Latino lifestyle in the United States.

By the first decade of the 21st century, the amount spent by Latinos in the United States had increased markedly—they had an estimated $581 billion discretionary income in 2002 and purchasing power projected to grow to $926 billion by 2007. The Latino population had also become more complex, including more people from a wider variety of nations, as well as generational, gender, and regional differences (Porter, 2000). Latinos, once a single market segment, were split into more subgroups, each with its own characteristics and vulnerabilities. One 2002 conference, titled "Marketing to U.S. Hispanic Youth," featured panels on such topics as "Marketing to Hispanic Girls and Boys (Ages 2–12)," "Entertainment Tie-ins: Advertising and Promotional Opportunities to Reach Hispanic Youth," and "Taking Cultural Differences into Account: Regional Segmentation in Your Marketing Campaign." Another conference featured sessions on "Marketing to the Hispanic Female Head of Household," "Got Hispanics? Applying the 'Got Milk?' Campaign to Ethnic Marketing," and

Illustration 6.8   Increased advertising targeted to different racial and language groups has spurred a growth of ethnic television stations and programs designed for viewers who will respond to images and language that appeal to them.

"How Miller Brewing Company Appeals to the Hispanic Market with Music" (International Quality and Productivity Center, 2002).

Asian Pacific Americans experienced a 108% growth rate from 1980 to 1990 and, with more growth projected for the future, Asian Pacific Americans became an important market for advertisers in the 1990s. This is the nation's fastest growing racial group, which was long undervalued because of its small size and different languages but grew in significance with growth in both its overall numbers and the size of its various nationality groups, such as Koreans, Filipinos, and Asian Indians.

The increased size of this group led to its having more economic clout—Asian Pacific Americans had an annual discretionary income of $296 billion in 2002 and purchasing power projected to grow to $455 billion by 2007. In addition, their $55,521 average annual income was reported as the highest household income of any U.S. group. While the high figure may indicate that more men, women, and children are working and sharing the same living quarters, some have attributed it to higher levels of Asian Pacific American educational achievement and "the unusually high rates of entrepreneurial activity found in this population" (Gitlin, 2002, p. 10).

Noting the different national origins in this group, some marketers and advertisers have asked whether Asian Pacific Americans have anything in common "beyond rice" and have been advised to be careful to avoid cultural conflicts. For instance, it was reported that for Filipinos white is the color of weddings and happiness, but for Japanese white with black is the color of mourning (Dàvila, 2001). The diversity within the group was further reflected in the Census Bureau's combining people from more than fifteen distinct ethnic groups and nations under the Asian and Pacific Islander label. Still, marketers noted that 88% of those so labeled were found in just six of the fifteen groups. In order of size, these are Chinese, Filipino, Asian Indian, Vietnamese, Korean, and Japanese—many of them living "highly concentrated in tight ethnic communities" (Gitlin, 2002, p. 10). This makes members of the group easily targeted through advertising in print and broadcast media reaching those communities.

"The fact that Asian Americans predominantly speak their native languages yields incredibly high ratings and shares for Asian-language media," wrote Jon Yasuda, president of Southern California Asian format television station KSCI in 2002. He advised marketers to "utilize Asian language media to best influence Asian Americans to make wise and educated purchasing decisions" and noted that "Asian media provides sophisticated marketing tools for advertisers." Although many television and radio stations targeted to Asian Pacific Americans block program different languages in different time slots across the broadcast day, Yasuda predicted that the advent of digital television allowing for "four channels of Asian language programming instead of just one" would offer advertisers new 24-hour Chinese and Korean over-the-air channels (Yasuda, 2002, pp. 29-30).

Like many Hispanics, many Asian Pacific Americans are newcomers to the United States who prefer media in their home country language, which is what advertisers use to reach them. And, like Blacks, they also share physical characteristics that distinguish them from Whites in advertising appeals. Long-term effectiveness in reaching this increasingly important market segment will depend on advertisers becoming acquainted with Asian Pacific Americans on their own terms, not in the way they have long been seen by Whites or as off-shoots of the Black or Hispanic market.

Mining Multicultural Markets

Asian Pacific Americans, Latinos, and Blacks combined for an estimated over $1.5 trillion in 2002 discretionary income and have been projected to grow to represent 20% of the U.S. buying power by 2007, as White purchasing power declines. Marketers and advertisers have intensified their search for ways to ride multicultural images and ethnic media into the hearts and minds of people of color. At one 2002 conference in Chicago, executives from firms as varied as McDonald's Corporation, Motown Records, and Mercedes Benz advised other corporations on such topics as "Revving up Your Latino Automotive Consumer," "Building Loyalty Amongst African-American/Hispanic Shoppers," and "New Growth Opportunities & Trends in the Asian-American Marketplace" (Strategic Research Institute, 2002).[5]

For both Blacks and Latinos, the slick advertising directed to them often has meant that advertisers were trying to sell high-priced, prestige products to people who do not fully share in the wealth of the country in which they live. Blacks and Latinos, who have median household incomes well below national averages, have nonetheless been targeted as consumers for premium brands in all product lines, particularly alcohol and tobacco. In response, Black and Latino community groups and health organizations have protested the aggressive targeting of alcohol and tobacco products to their communities and, in some cases, forced outdoor advertising companies to restrict the number of such billboards in their communities.

Alcohol and tobacco companies have long targeted Latinos and Blacks through ethnic media with the goal of increasing smoking and drinking in these groups as other segments of the population became more aware of the health hazards linked to these substances. A 1968 Philip Morris internal memo boasted of "a series of newspaper ads that will appear in the Negro press in an attempt to capture a larger share of the market for Benson & Hedges 100s Menthol in this sizable segment of the trade" (quoted in Cohen, Cody, & Murphy, 2001, p. 4).

The influx of advertising dollars has also made some ethnic media financially dependent on alcohol and tobacco companies. "Tobacco and alcohol advertising revenues are substantial for Hispanic publications," Tino Duran, president of the National Association of Hispanic Publications, told a congressional subcommittee on hazardous materials in 1990. "For some Hispanic publishers, tobacco and alcohol advertising can sometimes make the difference between staying afloat or going under" (p. 3).[6]

Through advertising, corporations making and marketing products from beer to diapers try to show Blacks, Latinos, and Asian Pacific Americans that consumption of their goods is part of the good life in America. It may not be a life that they knew when they grew up in the ghetto, the barrio, Chinatown, or another country. It may not even be a life that they or their children will achieve, but it is a lifestyle they can share by purchasing the same products used by the rich and famous.

Prestige appeals are used in advertising to all audiences, not just to people of color. But they have a special impact on members of racial and ethnic groups looking for ways to show that they are advancing up the socioeconomic ladder. These consumers are especially hungry for anything that will add status or happiness to their lives and help them show others that they are "making it." These advertisements promote conspicuous consumption, rather than education, hard work, and saving money, as the key to the good life. In 1984, Caroline Jones wrote in *Madison Avenue* that

the Black consumer is not unlike other consumers when it comes to the basic necessities of life-food, clothing and shelter. There is a difference, nevertheless, in the priority the Black consumer adopts in the pursuit of happiness; in other words, in how he[or she] structures the *quality* of his[or her] life. Some differences are by choice. And some differences are because of *lack* of choice. The Black consumer must often react to what he[or she] has *not* been able to enjoy or choose, or what he[or she] must choose from among products that have not overtly invited him[or her] to use them . . . in general the Black consumer all too often has learned to live with his[or her] feelings of being ignored altogether or excluded psychologically. (p. 56)

"In the light of life's uncertainties, Blacks also seek instant gratification more than do Whites, who can enjoy 'the good life' earlier and longer," Jones (1984) added, citing a successful advertising campaign for Polaroid cameras that courted Blacks with the line "Polaroid Gives It To You Now" (p. 56).

Asian Pacific Americans and Latinos, particularly recent immigrants or those who have moved up from the economic level of their parents, share with Blacks the ambition of making it in American society. For people of color, marketing and advertising campaigns targeted to them are corporate America's welcome mat, the happy face that lets them know that they are important and recognized. By showcasing elements of their experience that may have been ignored by Whites, advertisers play on national, cultural, and racial pride to boost sales of their products.

In the 1970s, "The King of Beers," Budweiser, placed glossy advertisements saluting the "Great Kings of Africa." Schlitz beer produced a Chicano history calendar and other breweries annually sponsor promotions honoring the Lunar New Year celebrated by Asian Pacific Americans. These marketing and advertising campaigns provided long overdue recognition of Asian Pacific, Black, and Latino cultures and heritages as they also prominently displayed the corporate symbols of their sponsors. They were designed to boost the sale of beer more than to recognize overlooked historical figures and events. Ethnic marketing professionals stress that, in the long run, such blatant overtures making marketing commodities out of cultural symbols and historical events must be replaced by advertising focused on the quality and price of the product. If not, people of color will see that the racial and ethnic welcome mat did not open the door to good value for their dollars and will turn to products offering more than a cultural fix.

Advertising Ethics and Ethnic Media

Since the goal of advertising is to promote the sales and consumption of products, advertising agencies serve no moral code other than to advocate products so that people will buy them. Print and broadcast media that reach the audiences advertisers wish to cultivate have benefited from increased advertising budgets for media targeting Blacks, Latinos, and, more recently, Asian Pacific Americans. Most surveys show that Blacks and Latinos depend on radio and television for information and entertainment more than they do on print media, a fact probably more related to their lower median level of education and the wide availability of Black and Spanish-language broadcasting than any innate racial preferences. Accordingly, most of the millions of dollars that national advertisers spend to reach these audiences are spent on broadcast media. Although its share of broadcasting has grown, Asians and Pacific Islanders in the United States have long been reached by print media that are local editions of mother-country media chains, such as the *Korea Times,* the Hong Kong-based *Sing Tao* newspaper chain, and the Taiwan-based *World Journal.*

These media targeted to non-Whites have long advocated that they, not general audience media, are the most effective way to reach consumers of color. In 1974, one of New York's Black newspapers, the *Amsterdam News,* vigorously attacked the credibility of a New York *Daily News* audience survey that showed it reached more Black readers than the *Amsterdam News.* In a 1979 *Advertising Age* advertisement, *La Opinión,* Los Angeles's Spanish-language daily newspaper, promised advertisers it could "Wrap Up the Spanish-language Market."

More recently, as the United States has become more racially and ethnically diverse, general audience media launched their own ethnic media or bought existing operations to get a cut of multiracial advertising dollars. Newspaper chains from New York to California have tried their hand at publishing their own Spanish-language newspapers. In California, the *San Jose Mercury* publishes Spanish-language and Vietnamese-language weekly newspapers. Viacom bought BET (Black Entertainment Television) in a $3-billion deal in 2001, which was followed by NBC's purchase of the Spanish-language television network Telemundo for $2.7 billion. While these expansions positioned the media giants to attract advertising for people of color, the economics were different for broadcasters reaching non-White audiences.

In 2001, several Black and Latino organizations challenged the practice of advertising agencies paying broadcasters less for advertising on stations for Blacks and Hispanics than they paid for their general audience counterparts reaching the same sized audience. It was charged some advertisers had a "no urban/no Hispanic" policy in deciding which stations would get their advertising dollars and that "urban" was a code word for Blacks. A 1996 study of 3,745 radio stations for the Federal Communications Commission found that stations targeting listeners of color earned less money per listener than general audience stations and that stations owned by people of color earned less per listener than those owned by Whites (Ofori, 1996).

Advertising is the lifeblood of print, broadcast, and some online media in the United States. But as website advertising, direct mail, telemarketing, and promotional events have become more important in targeting desired audiences, it is no longer necessary for corporations to put their messages on print pages or broadcast airwaves to pitch their products to the people they want to reach. They can reach people in target markets in other ways and, if these new avenues prove to be profitable, the print and broadcast media reaching those audiences will suffer a revenue loss.

HOW LOUD IS THE NOT-SO-SILENT PARTNER'S VOICE?

The relationship between racial minorities and advertising has undergone dramatic changes since the early 1960s. The more frequent appearance of Blacks in general audience advertising is the most visible of the many changes that have occurred. In the 1980s, Spanish-speaking Latinos became more important as a market segment as their print and broadcast media grew. More recently, Asian Pacific Americans have gained recognition from marketers and advertisers after experiencing the greatest percentage growth of any racial group in the years between 1970 and 2000, although much of the attention has been focused on cities or regions where their presence is greatest. Given the projected growth for Asian Pacific Americans, it is a near certainty that they will become an increasingly desirable market segment—especially if their households continue to demonstrate income and education levels above national norms and they respond to advertising in media targeted to them.

Native Americans, divided between the cities and rural areas, have become largely invisible in mainstream advertising, except for the use of their tribal names for automobiles, the stereotypical Indians used as sports team mascots, and in some advertising targeted to areas of high concentration such as reservations. The noble Super Chief has gone the way of the passenger train he once advertised, as have the advertising cartoons that once stereotyped Native Americans.

Native Americans are too small a percentage of the population in urban areas and too dispersed geographically in rural areas to make them attractive to mainstream advertisers looking at potential markets. National publications like *Indian Country Today* and *News From Indian Country* largely carry advertisements for products or activities designed for Native Americans, such as music, festivals, and cultural items. Conspicuously absent from such publications is advertising for food, beverage, automotive, and other general household products used by everyone in the United States, including Native Americans. Newspapers targeting Native Americans are often tribally supported and radio stations are licensed to tribal governments as public stations, making both less dependent on advertising as a source of revenue than are privately owned media. As far as advertising is concerned, it appears that, except for local advertising and goodwill announcements by some major corporations, Native Americans will continue to be advertising's "invisible minority" through the early 21st century.

National advertisers in general audience media appear to be reluctant to learn from the experiences with one group in dealing with other groups. Blacks, Latinos, Asian Pacific Americans, and Native Americans have all had to fight battles against stereotyping and racially offensive advertisements—and each group has been individually "discovered" as it grows in size. Blacks, the most visible racial group in network television and general interest magazine advertising, still comprise only a small percentage of the characters in general audience media. Although Asian Pacific Americans and Latinos have recently become more visible in general audience advertising, there is much room for growth in finding ways to develop crossover advertising that both includes and appeals to people of all races and cultures.

Where gains have been made, they often have been tied to the use of athletes, entertainers, and other celebrities of color, such as basketball superstar Shaquille O'Neal, ice skater Michelle Kwan, and singer Jennifer Lopez. Although Black celebrities have been featured more often than those of other non-White groups, it appears that the integration of Latinos and Asians into mainstream advertising will likely continue to follow the crossover model. Such advertisements afford the advertiser the advantage of reaching and influencing consumers of all races and cultures.

ADVERTISING'S DOUBLE-EDGED SWORD

Ethnic publications and broadcasters have benefited from the increased emphasis on market segmentation by promoting to advertisers the purchasing patterns of the audiences they reach and their own effectiveness in delivering persuasive commercial messages to their readers, listeners, and viewers. But advertising is a double-edged sword: It expects to take more money out of a market segment than in invests in advertising to that segment. Thus media that focus on Blacks, Latinos, and Asian Pacific Americans will benefit from the advertising dollars of national corporations only as long as they are the most cost-effective way for advertisers to persuade their targeted audience to use the advertised products.

This situation places the racial and ethnic media in an exploitative relationship with their audience, who because of language, educational, and economic differences sometimes are exposed to a narrower range of media than are Whites. Marketers will support delivery of their messages in places that deliver the audience with the best consumer profile at the lowest cost, not necessarily in the media that best meet the information and

Illustration 6.9 Entertainment and sports celebrities of color, such as basketball star Shaquille O'Neal, have crossover endorsement appeal for products purchased and used by people of all races.

entertainment needs of their audience. And, given increased competition from digital, telemarketing, direct mail, and other advertising delivery systems, they may not put their messages into advertising-supported media at all.

The slick, upscale lifestyle portrayed by national advertisers is more dream than reality for most Blacks, Asian Pacific Americans, and Latinos. It is achieved through education, hard work, and equal opportunity for employment and housing. Rather than encouraging people to save money to meet long-term goals, advertisers promote their products as the shortcut to happiness and the good life, a quick fix for low-income consumers. The message to people of color is clear: You may not be able to live in the best neighborhoods, have the best educational opportunities, or work at the best job, but you can drink the same liquor, smoke the same cigarettes, and drive the same car as those who do. At the same time, advertising appeals that play on the cultural heritage of people of color make the products appear to be "at home" in those communities.

Recognizing the importance of national holidays and peoples' history, advertisers have actually helped bring recognition to important dates, events, and people in the lives of people of color. But advertisers also make culture a commercial commodity by piggybacking their advertising on the recognition of such events, leaders, and heroes. People or actions that in their time represented protests against slavery, oppression, and discrimination are now used to sell products.

Advertising is an extractive industry. European and American companies went into Africa, Asia, and Latin America to cut timber, mine minerals, and exploit other natural resources to produce profits. Along the same lines, advertising's happy face enters the ghetto, Chinatown, and the barrio to persuade people to transfer money from their pockets to the merchants selling advertised products and services. Advertisers' subsidizing of print, broadcast, and online media is only a by-product of their primary purpose of selling their products, and it is possibly decreasing in importance due to the recent proliferation of advertising delivery systems.

Owners of media targeted to people of color, having benefited from the increased advertising of major corporations, have greater opportunities to use those additional dollars to improve news and entertainment content and, thus, better meet their responsibilities to their audience. Unlike advertisers, who may support socially responsible activities for the purpose of promoting their products, minority publishers and broadcasters have a long, though sometimes spotty, record of advocating the rights of the people they serve. As long as the audiences they serve continue to confront a system in inequality in seeking equal treatment in education, housing, income, health, and other social services, the dependence of ethnic media on major corporations and national advertising should not blunt that edge.

Notes

1. For a comprehensive study of African American images in advertising, see *Aunt Jemima, Uncle Ben and Rastus: Blacks in Advertising, Yesterday, Today and Tomorrow,* by M. Kern-Foxworth, 1994, Westport, CT: Greenwood.

2. For a case study of two efforts to change Native American mascots, see "The Sports Team Nickname Controversy: A Study in Community and Race Relations," by V. S. Holden, W. Holden, and G. Davis, in *Facing Difference: Race, Gender and Mass Media* (pp. 69-75), S. Biagi and M. Kern-Foxworth (Eds.), 1997, Thousand Oaks, CA: Pine Forge, 1997.

3. For a description and comparisons of marketing and advertising to Whites, Blacks, Hispanics, and Asian Americans, see "Race, Ethnicity and the Way We Shop," by R. Gardyn and J. Fetto, February 2003, *American Demographics,* 30-33.

4. For a deeper analysis, see Chapter 7 "Selling Marginality: The Business of Culture," in *Latinos Inc.: The Marketing and Making of a People,* by A. Dávila, 2001, Berkeley: University of California Press.

5. For additional readings on multicultural marketing and advertising, see *Multicultural Marketing: Selling to the New America,* by A. L. Schreiber, 2000, New York: McGraw-Hill, and *Marketing and Consumer Identity in Multicultural America,* by M. C. Tharp, 2001, Thousand Oaks, CA: Sage. For current reports, see the bimonthly newsletter *Multicultural Marketing News* from the Multicultural Marketing Resources website: http://www.multicultural.com.

6. This is from a statement made by Tino Duran, as president of the National Association of Hispanic Publications, before the Subcommittee on Transportation and Hazardous Materials, Committee on Energy and Commerce, U.S. House of Representatives, in Washington, D.C. on March 2, 1990.

References

Block, C. E. (1972). White backlash to Negro ads: Fact or fantasy? *Journalism Quarterly,* 258-262.

Cohen, E. L., Cody, M. J., & Murphy, S. T. (2001). *Industry watch: Targeting African American smokers.* Los Angeles: School of Communication, Annenberg School for Communication, University of Southern California.

Culley, J. D., & Bennett, R. (1976). Selling Blacks, selling women. *Journal of Communication, 26*(4), 160-174.

Dougherty, P. H. (1982, May 27). Frequency of Blacks in TV ads. *New York Times,* p. D19.

Ethnic Marketing (Brochure). (2002, September 25-27). Strategic Research Institute conference, Ethnic Marketing, Chicago.

Gage, T. J. (1983, February 14). How to reach an enthusiastic market. *Advertising Age,* p. M11.

Gibson, D. P. (1979). *$70 billion in the Black.* New York: Macmillan.

Gitlin, S. (2002). The Asian American market: An untapped opportunity for America's marketers. *The source book of multicultural experts 2002-2003.* New York: Multicultural Marketing Resources.

Guernica, A. (1982). *Reaching the Hispanic market effectively.* New York: McGraw-Hill.

Gutiérrez, F. (1976). *Spanish-language radio and Chicano internal colonialism.* Unpublished doctoral dissertation, Department of Communication, Stanford University.

Jones, C. R. (1984, May). Advertising in Black and White. *Madison Avenue,* p. 53.

Kan, A. (1983). *Asian models in the media.* Unpublished term paper, Journalism 466: Minorities and the Media, University of Southern California.

Kong, D. (2002, April 19). Abercrombie & Fitch pulls Asian caricature t-shirts. *Oakland Tribune,* p. 5.

Marketing to U.S. Hispanic Youth (Brochure). (2002, June 18-20). Marketing to U.S. Hispanic Youth Conference sponsored by KidScreen magazine, Los Angeles.

Martínez, T. (1969, Fall). How advertisers promote racism. *Civil Rights Digest,* 10.

Mascot Watch. (2002, May 10). *The Chronicle of Higher Education,* p. A8.

Ofori, K. A. (1996). *When being No. 1 is not enough.* Paper submitted to the Office of Communication Business Opportunities, Federal Communications Commission, Washington, D.C., Civil Rights Forum on Communications Policy.

Poblete, P. (2002, April 23). Blueprint for a PR disaster. *San Francisco Chronicle,* p. D8.

Porter, E. (2000, October 13). All agree the Latin market is hot, but solid statistics are hard to find. *Wall Street Journal.*

Potter, D. M. (1954). *People of plenty.* Chicago: University of Chicago Press.

Reid, L. N., & Vanden Bergh, B. G. (1980). Blacks in introductory ads. *Journalism Quarterly, 57*(3), 485-486.

Reyes, D. N., & Rendón, A. (1971). *Chicanos and the mass media.* The National Mexican American Anti-Defamation Committee, Inc.

Soley, L. (1983).The effect of Black models on magazine ad readership. *Journalism Quarterly, 60*(4), 686.

Strasburg, J. (2002, April 18). Abercrombie & Glitch. *San Francisco Chronicle,* p. A1.

Treen, J. (1982, April 12). Madison Ave. vs. Japan, Inc. *Newsweek,* p. 69.

US Hispanic Marketing 2002. (Brochure). (2002, April 30-May 1). International Quality and Productivity Center conference, US Hispanic Marketing 2002, Los Angeles.

Using ethnic images—an advertising retrospective. (1984, June 14). *Advertising Age,* p. 9.

White, B. (2001, July 29). *Ads for minorities take tact.* Cox News Service.

Yasuda, J. (2002). Asian language media works! *The source book of multicultural experts 2002-2003.* New York: Multicultural Marketing Resources.

Public Relations 7

Influencing the Content of the Media

T he 1990s and early 21st century have been years of discussion, dialogue, and debate on the issues of race, diversity, and multiculturalism. In 1992, the Public Relations Society of America chose "At the Crossroads" as the theme for its annual conference. As public relations professionals and educators met in Kansas City in October of that year, it was noted that the conference theme could well be the theme of their discussions on multiculturalism in public relations as well. This is because in 1992 and for much of the 1990s, both public relations educators and professionals found themselves "at the crossroads" as they met to discuss and map out their own diversity plan.

Setting the stage for some of the discussion was a research paper on career influences, job satisfaction, and discrimination described by people of color in public relations by Eugenia Zerbinos of the University of Maryland and Gail Alice Clanton of the American Trucking Association (Zerbinos & Clanton, 1992). The study, which had been judged the "Top Faculty Paper" by the Association for Education in Journalism and Mass Communications Minorities and Communications Division in 1991, presented one of the most comprehensive analyses of diversity issues in public relations up to that time.

In their paper, Zerbinos and Clanton quickly summarized the demographic statistics and growth projections for people of color that make the subject of diversity a hot topic for more than academic discussion. Having set the stage with population projections, they then turned the spotlight to the issue of diversity in public relations.

Diversity and Room for Growth

In 1990, the Census Bureau counted 167,000 people working as public relations specialists. Of these, 14% were people of color: 7% Black, 4.3%

Hispanic, 1.7% Asian/Pacific Islander, and .3% Native Americans/ Eskimos/Aleuts (U.S. Census Bureau, 1990, p. 3). This was about the same percentage as those in broadcast newsrooms. In 1991, the U.S. Bureau of Labor Statistics reported that there were 173,000 people working in public relations, 8.3% of them Black and 3.1% Hispanic (U.S. Bureau of Labor Statistics, 1992, p. 86).[1]

But a greater number of non-Whites in the population or in public relations does not automatically translate to more power or influence. The most immediate conclusion to be drawn from this is that people of color continue to face more of the reality they already know. The most immediate corporate response has been in market segmentation and penetration strategies designed to tap the purchasing power of these groups rather than to provide long-range services to them.

A growth in the amount spent by African American, Latino, Asian Pacific Americans, and Native American consumers has made them more attractive as targets for advertising and the media that advertisers support. Moreover, these groups are growing at rates faster than the overall population growth in the United States. In fact, these markets now comprise more than 30% of the American population (IWMFWire, 1999).

These figures make people of color attractive as consumers and advertising targets, which is how they were seen by advertising executives and public relations agencies during much of the 1980s and 1990s. But the advantages of diversity extend beyond this expanded market for products to include the positive values that a racially and ethnically diverse workforce brings to an organization's ability to understand and communicate to audiences of different races, cultures, languages, and nationalities. This is a point that has been made by Marilyn Kern-Foxworth (1991a), the most prolific scholar analyzing multicultural trends in public relations.

> Public relations and marketing executives should realize what an asset they have in their own employees of fellow officers who are African American, Native American, Latin American or Asian American. Members of these communities are also valuable assets when companies attempt to communicate and market to other countries . . . by bridging cultural and communication gaps. (p. 30)

It is clear that public relations has a long way to go to narrow the gap between the estimated 10% of minorities in the public relations workforce and the percentage of minorities in the U.S. population, which exceeds 30% even without taking into account that the Census Bureau admittedly undercounted people of color. Until positive steps are taken in that direction, the public relations profession will continue to encounter difficulties in capitalizing on the multicultural and multinational opportunities described by Kern-Foxworth and others.

Women of Color in Public Relations

Without a doubt, women of color are woefully underrepresented in public relations practice. Although research in this area is limited, studies show that both their salaries and status are low compared to their White counterparts. They typically play markedly different roles in the workplace, which in turn may hinder their potential career advancement. Len-Rios (1998) found that there are also distinct gender differences with regard to practitioners' perception of discrimination and the discrimination they actually experienced. In her sample of 13 Black, Asian, and Latino practitioners, she found that men recalled more instances of overt racism than did women. To explain this, she suggested (1) that managers may not feel as threatened by women in the workplace and, consequently, may be less likely to openly discriminate against them than against men; (2) that women of color perceive less discrimination than do men of color because they are used to accommodating to and rationalizing others' behavior; and (3) that women may feel more disadvantaged by their gender than by their race.

In 1980, there were roughly 4,000 minority public relations practitioners of the 70,000 public relations practitioners in the United States. According to Layton (1980), despite the small number they represented, they still had an upbeat attitude about the future and used terms like "promising," "hopeful," "most confident," and "optimistic about career opportunities" to describe the outlook for Black public relations professionals. But by the 1990s Blacks in public relations were using words such as "atrocious" and "horrible" to characterize the underrepresentation of Blacks in the field. In fact, the percentage of minorities in public relations actually declined from 7% to 6% during this period, when the number of practitioners in the field more than doubled to 150,000 (Unger, 1992, as cited in Grunig, Toth, & Hon, 2001).

In addition, minority practitioners are often further disadvantaged by being "pigeonholed" in nonprofit or government jobs. They are commonly hired to fill quotas or serve as "show positions" with little real input into policy making and limited access to upward mobility or the higher paying corporate jobs. Finally, it is not uncommon for minority practitioners to be hired primarily to communicate with minority audiences. According to a 1993 study by Kern-Foxworth, about one third of Black practitioners surveyed indicated that they direct their efforts to minority "markets."

When minority practitioners exclusively handle minority issues, they tend to bear the burden of being the *race representative,* much like the token woman who is expected to serve as the voice for *all* women. Often Black practitioners in mainstream organizations find themselves the sole member of their race in an entire public relations department. They consequently are consulted on issues related to the African American public, and have to interpret—whether directly or indirectly—their culture for non-African Americans.[2]

Blacks in the public relations field have mixed, though somewhat positive, feelings about their professional field. Mallette's (1995) study found that even at the onset of the new millenium, Black practitioners are still commonly pigeonholed in the role of *race representative* or *cultural interpreter* who must serve as the collective Black voice for their European American counterparts. Most believe they are viewed first as African Americans and then as public relations professionals (Mallette, 1995). Mallette deemed this a problem because "any preconceived notions non-African American practitioners have of African Americans have the potential to (and often do) interfere with fair and accurate recognition of the African American practitioners' abilities" (Mallette, 1995, p.123).

Gilliam's (1992) qualitative study of 10 Black women who were public relations managers mentioned the importance of targeting Black women as heads of households, the need for successful Black women to share their experiences, and that the Black participants felt (more than the Whites did) that Whites were uncomfortable working with Blacks. The study cited an Atlanta survey showing that although women outnumbered men two to one in public relations, their earnings were lower and that Black women earned less than White women.

The problems surrounding racial bias against African Americans in mainstream organizations are also experienced in minority public relations firms that handle Black clients. Herbert (1990) found in his study of practitioners in the entertainment industry that White firms represented most African American superstars at the time. However, Terrie Williams, a Black woman who represents celebrities including Eddie Murphy, said that Black agencies such as hers have become more visible, and there are "minorities out here doing PR, and doing it in a big way" (cited in Grunig et al., 2001, p. 153).

Asian American practitioners, on the other hand, have been virtually nonexistent in the public relations field. In the past, even the largest public relations firms may not have employed a single Asian American professional at any level—although they may have an Asian receptionist, an Asian CPA, or an Asian in a lower-level job. The reason for this may partially be explained by Asian culture. As Lynne Choy Uyeda, president of an advertising and public relations firm and founder of the Asian American Advertising and Public Relations Alliance, said during a panel discussion on multiculturalism at the Public Relations Society of America (PRSA) conference in 1993, "[We] stay on the wall. Don't rock the boat. Asians are uncomfortable doing the PR thing" (cited in Grunig et al., 2001, p. 160).

A 1992 study by Yamashita (cited in Grunig et al., 2001) that explored the extent to which Asian Americans participated in the public relations field found that they fell into two distinct groups. The first group was

Illustration 7.1   Some successful Black practitioners, such as Terrie
                        Williams, represent high-profile clients such as Eddie
                        Murphy, pictured above.
Source: Copyright © Lynn Goldsmith/CORBIS.

comprised of the "government type" that worked for government,
government-related, and nonprofit organizations. These practitioners
tended to communicate with the Asian or Asian American public, they

were interested in Asian issues, and they considered themselves responsible for getting Asians involved in American society. Generally, they were fluent in both English and an Asian language. Yamashita referred to these practitioners as either "gap-fillers," who were familiar with both Asian and American cultures and could fill any gaps between an American organization and its Asian clients or public, or "mission-oriented" practitioners, whose Asian identity is strong and thus assume responsibility for making their Asian public aware of social issues and getting them involved in mainstream American society. The second group was comprised of the "firm-type" of practitioner, who typically worked in for-profit organizations or public relations agencies and tended to be younger, earned more money, and rarely could speak a language other than English.

Yamashita (1992) found that Asian women in public relations tended to be very enthusiastic, self-assertive, and eager to gain experience and advance in their organizations. They often felt advantaged by the positive Asian stereotype of being bright and hard working. However, while Yamashita believed that their positive attitude would help them achieve their professional goals, she also warned them about the perils of facing a "double glass ceiling"—being Asian and female. While one of the women admitted to facing "two glass ceilings," another shared a more common experience.

> I've never felt [discrimination as an Asian]. . . . Even when I was in [a Southern state], I think this is probably because I was able to integrate pretty well in different environments and with different people. But I do feel that [discrimination] as a woman. This is a very conservative company, and you are also in a very conservative business community where you still have an "old boys' network." (cited in Grunig et al., 2001, p. 163)

Latinos in public relations have had to overcome some major obstacles to enjoy their modest but growing success in the field today. While Hispanics are among the nation's fastest growing ethnic groups, the National Council of La Raza (NCLR) found that during the last decade only one in ten Hispanics in this country—compared with one in five non-Hispanics—had completed 4 years of college. In 1990, NCLR cited Hispanics' low level of educational attainment as a significant barrier to their success at work (National Council of La Raza, 1991). As a consequence of their lack of education compared to other groups, Hispanic Americans across occupations generally earn less than both Blacks and Whites, and in corporate America they have yet to break through the glass ceiling—making them grossly underrepresented in upper management.

However, according to a study by Ferreira (1993) of Latinos in public relations, respondents felt that they had not been hindered by a glass ceiling and they even tended to earn a higher median salary than practitioners of all ethnic groups. She also found that the majority of practitioners she surveyed headed their department and were actually part of the dominant coalition. They were more likely to engage in managerial than technician roles—or serve dual functions as manager and technician—which is similar to the situation of White women in public relations. However, unlike White women, they tended to head their communication department and were included in the dominant coalition—despite having less formal education in the field than did non-Hispanics.

Ferreira also found that Hispanic practitioners preferred to work as press agents or publicists and were not hired to communicate primarily with the Hispanic public. They were not functioning in the role of cultural interpreter or gap-filler as suggested by Yamashita (1992), although they generally were responsible for dealing with Hispanic issues or were called on when knowledge of the Spanish language was needed.

Ferreira (1993) suggested that Latino breakthroughs into the upper echelons of management were the result of the power elite recognizing the need to have Hispanics in decision-making positions in order to bring to the table issues and perspectives relevant to the organization's Hispanic public. Ferreira summarized that "they worked hard to perform their best and demonstrate their capabilities, not as Hispanic public relations practitioners but as public relations practitioners who happened to be Hispanic" (pp. 151-152).

As the fastest growing ethnic minority population, Hispanic women are making significant strides in the public relations profession. In 2002, Rosanna M. Fiske received the D. Parke Gibson Pioneer Award—named after the pioneer in multicultural public relations who authored two books on African American consumerism. Fiske was the first Hispanic woman named president of the Public Relations Society of America's Miami Chapter and director of account service for JGR & Associates, Florida's largest Hispanic PR agency, where she led all of the agency's public relations efforts for the general, U.S. Hispanic, and Latin American markets. She was recognized for her multicultural understanding and expertise, as well as her development of successful bilingual programs for local, national, and international clients such as Charles Schwab, American Airlines, Wells Fargo Bank, and MCI (Public Relations Society of America, 2002).

Why Public Relations Needs People of Color

The diversity agenda in public relations education involves more than social justice and demography. It involves more than urging others to "Do the right thing" or, as former Newspaper Association of American president Cathie Black said, to "Do the thing right." And it should go beyond copying the efforts of the print, broadcast, and advertising side of the profession to be racially inclusive. It is an initiative that could be driven by the very essence of this country's professed democratic ideals: freedom of speech.

Print journalists and journalism educators are quick to wrap their work in the First Amendment and rightfully proclaim their right to a free press. Similarly, advertisers present arguments for the right of commercial free speech and broadcasters warn against the threats to free press and free speech that they believe are posed by government regulation. The case for the sometimes competing First Amendment rights of print media, broadcasters, advertisers, and new technologies are most often fashioned and focused by public relations professionals.

But where is the public relations profession in this turf battle for the First Amendment high ground? On many campuses, its place in the mass communication curriculum is affected by the same "last hired, first fired" mentality that people of color have faced for many years. Public relations is sometimes seen as an adjunct to other training for working in the media, not a profession that can or should exist on its own. Its place on campus is often argued within and among educators both in and out of schools of journalism and mass communication. Administrators love the public relations enrollment, but many question the value of the curriculum.

But when it comes to the importance of a diversity agenda, public relations should take a back seat to none. If public relations practitioners and educators were to wrap themselves in the First Amendment rights of freedom of expression, the free marketplace of ideas, and the right to both send and receive information, they would find their case parallels the need for diversity raised by other professions in the media.

In many ways, the practice of public relations is like the practice of law. Public relations professionals believe in the free marketplace of ideas, just as lawyers believe in the legal system. Just as attorneys believe that everyone deserves his or her day in court, public relations practitioners believe, or should believe, that every viewpoint deserves to have its best case made in the court of public opinion. Just as attorneys are skilled in presenting legal arguments in court, public relations professionals are skilled in shaping the public presentation of the viewpoints of those they represent to the media and the public. The message is important, as is the right of the message to be expressed and received. The messenger, however, is less important.

The Influence of Public Relations on News Media

This is a lesson that two of the authors of this volume, Félix Gutiérrez and Clint Wilson, learned in the 1960s: We found ourselves with a journalism education but no real opportunity to enter the nearly all-White newsrooms of Southern California general circulation newspapers. So we did public relations for the Black Student Union (BSU) and United Mexican American Students (UMAS), community organizations, and antipoverty agencies to present the issues of Latinos and Blacks to the news media. Much of this work involved gaining coverage for pickets, protests, demonstrations, marches, and all the other activism associated with the 1960s. But it also focused on gaining coverage and understanding of the need for youth job training, community credit unions, neighborhood beautification efforts, and drug diversion programs.

In these efforts, we learned two important lessons that we had not been taught in the process of earning our journalism degrees. First, we learned that public relations workers are critical to the selection and presentation of the day's news. Second, we learned that journalists too often file inaccurate stories about non-Whites because they are influenced by biases and misunderstandings about who the racial and cultural groups are, what they believe, and what they want.

In the 1960s, this meant that news professionals often portrayed stories from the Black and Latino communities in terms of conflict, activism, and militancy. Too often journalists covered a demonstration by focusing on the demonstrators rather than the issues behind the demonstration. In the 21st century, journalists too often focus on people of color as "problem people," either beset by problems or causing them for the larger society, and as the source of "zoo stories," that is, stories about colorful observances such as the Chinese New Year, Kwanzaa, Mexican Independence Day, and Native American pow-wows. Once again, the journalists see these communities through a lens that filters out certain elements of the story and allows others to pass through to the audience.

Racial diversity in public relations can help lead journalism students and news professionals. Public relations expertise and experience is needed to forcefully, effectively, and accurately present the reality of the multicultural groups in the United States to the news and information media. Public relations professionals are also needed to help journalists overcome their misunderstandings of racially and culturally diverse communities so that they can accurately report on those communities.

The need for multiculturalism in public relations is no less strong today than it was in the 1960s. In fact, with increased racial diversity in this country—and the proliferation of targeted, segmented, and micro media—the need for people of color to learn and practice public relations is greater than ever before. Similarly, students of all races and backgrounds in every field of study need to learn to appreciate and understand cross-cultural communication if they are to be effective in whatever profession they enter. These skills will be even more important over the next generation as more people from racially diverse backgrounds are in a position to speak about their issues and to be heard.

Diversity in Public Relations

No doubt the opportunities will be there for people of color in public relations: The increasing diversity of the population translates into a diversity of messages and messengers and creates multiple opportunities for public relations practitioners and educators. Ketchum Public Relation's Senior Vice President and Director of Media Services, Jonathan Schenker, cited increased demographic diversity as one of 10 key trends affecting the media in the foreseeable future. He noted that demographics will continue to have a huge influence on the media and that consequently people of color will be featured as a matter of fact, not as exceptions to the rule, in media in the future (J. R. O'Dwyer Co., 1992).

"Consider these audiences when creating press kits, and hiring spokespeople," Schenker wrote. "Multiple spokespeople might be necessary for some national campaigns." Schenker forecasted continued diversity and predicted a continuation of the trend away from media for the masses and toward narrowcasting and media targeted to special audiences. He noted, "Expect more of these [targeted] publications and an equal, if not higher, number of them to fail" (J. R. O'Dwyer Co., 1992). Although some ethnic publications, such as *Jet* and *Latina*, have met with long-term success, others, particularly those such as *Jade* and *A.* that targeted Asian Pacific American audiences, have folded after only a few years. Despite the growing ethnic and racial diversity in the American landscape, there are still only a handful of ethnic publications in business today, including the magazines *Jet*, *Latina*, and *Yolk*.

People of color working in public relations share a professional and personal commitment to their work as well as concerns about the field's commitment to diversity. Of the 140 public relations professionals of color who responded to Zerbinos and Clanton's (1992) survey, nearly two thirds (63.6%) were women, average age 37, about half were married, nearly a quarter had undergraduate degrees in journalism, and 11% had graduate degrees in journalism or communication. Of these public relations professionals, 70% had titles indicating managerial or supervisory responsibilities, but only 64% supervised a staff. These practitioners reported that with regard to their careers, they were most satisfied with the networking opportunities and their present job function. They were least satisfied with their interaction with other non-White practitioners and with the limited participation in public relations of people of color. Nearly half (48%) said that they had considered leaving the field. Those in corporations were less satisfied in general than those in public relations firms and were also less satisfied with networking opportunities. Those in public relations firms were most satisfied with networking opportunities.

Many practitioners thought that the race-based discrimination they perceived manifested itself in terms of non-Whites having less access to projects and public relations positions and fewer promotions and salary increases than did Whites. A moderate relationship was perceived between leaving the field and perceived discrimination. The overall high satisfaction level with their career choice indicates that public relations professionals of color have developed coping mechanisms to endure what they perceive as a hostile environment (Zerbinos & Clanton, 1992). Even at the outset of the 21st century, a student entering the public relations workforce would be likely to find that he or she was the only person of color in the public relations department and one of only a few people of color in the entire organization.

In a study of successful African American professionals around the country, Cose (1993) found that their encounters with racism, prejudice, and cultural insensitivity affected their careers, their lives, and even their children's lives. Most admitted to being pigeonholed into "Black jobs" and experienced such discriminatory practices as exclusion from the club, low expectations, faint praise, presumption of failure, self-censorship and silence, mendacity (the lies corporate executives tell them when they claim their companies are color-blind), and the guilt by association that caused others to treat them like drug addicts, thieves, or thugs. This, in turn, led to their having shattered hopes, identity troubles, and coping fatigue. For these reasons, Cose concluded that for many Black professionals, race remains the primary feature that dictates their treatment within the organization and influences their ability for success in their careers (Cose, 1993, as cited in Grunig et al., 2001).

In a 1999 report by the International Women's Media Foundation titled *Women Journalists of Color: Present Without Power*, the majority of women surveyed believed that they faced barriers to their professional advancement that their white and male colleagues did not. Of these women of color, 29% claimed that this was "always" the case, 32% said that it was "frequently" the case, 29% said that it was "occasionally" the case, 8% said that it was "seldom" the case, and 2% said that it was "never" the case (p. 31). In addition, "discrimination in promotion" was perceived by 51% of these women to be the most common barrier to their professional advancement. Other reasons those surveyed frequently cited for lack of advancement were "not having a mentor" (47%), "no access to high visibility projects" (47%), and "lack of role models of same race/ethnic group" (p. 32).

Kern-Foxworth's earlier survey of 196 non-White public relations professionals found the typical respondent to be a Black female, age 38, who had worked for 9 years in public relations, attained a middle-level position, and earned $38,337 per year. More than half the respondents had degrees in journalism, public relations, or communications. Having a journalism degree was a more important determinant of the respondent's role than was having a degree in another area. Those with journalism degrees were more likely to be responsible for writing, editing, and producing material to present management's position, but they were less

Table 7.1   Questionnaire Results from Women Journalists of Color Report

Which of the following do you perceive as possible barriers to your professional advancement? (Check those that apply)

47%	Not having a mentor
35%	Lack of networking opportunities
44%	Lack of role models of same race/ethnic group
47%	No access to high visibility projects
21%	Discrimination in hiring
51%	Discrimination in promotion
28%	No access to professional development programs
22%	Balancing family and work
16%	Other

Which of the following methods do you use to advance your career?

	Always Use	Frequently Use	Occasionally Use	Seldom Use	Never Use
Look for challenging or high visibility assignments	38%	45%	14%	2%	1%
Belong to professional associations	46%	33%	15%	4%	2%
Exceed performance expectations	45%	46%	8%	1%	1%
Relocate	32%	37%	21%	7%	3%
Make an effort to put colleagues at ease	32%	37%	21%	7%	3%
Network	29%	34%	29%	5%	2%
Discuss career aspirations with managers	28%	46%	22%	2%	2%
Outperform colleagues	28%	46%	22%	2%	2%
Master organizational politics	14%	29%	25%	23%	8%
Work hard/put in long hours	51%	38%	9%	1%	1%
Continue advancing education	19%	20%	32%	20%	9%
Seek out influential mentors	19%	26%	29%	17%	8%
Move to another organization	11%	22%	34%	18%	16%

Source: Women Journalists of Color: Present Without Power by Rachel Jones for the International Women's Media Foundation.

likely to guide management through step-by-step planning and program-ming: "The analysis supports the assumption that larger organizations do not allow minorities the opportunity to advance in their careers. The more people employed in the organization for which minorities work, the lower their salaries and the less chance they have to become expert prescribers" (Kern-Foxworth, 1989).

Kern-Foxworth found a gap between the role that minorities assign to themselves (middle-level management) and the role that they actually fill (e.g., communication technician rather than problem-solver). "The misconception indicates that what they perceive perhaps is not the reality of the situation" (Kern-Foxworth, 1989). No doubt the skills of people of color are increasingly needed in developing management strategies and messages for the media. Kern-Foxworth (1991b) asserts that one of the reasons that the R.J. Reynolds $10 million venture to target Uptown ciga-rettes to African Americans went up in smoke is because the company did not use a Black agency to research and assess community and opinion leader reactions in the targeted community.

In 1987, Gloster and Cherrie wrote that

Companies have realized that they must reach all of the racial and ethnic groups in their markets and in their communities. That increasing awareness has led to greater opportunities in the form of growing numbers of minority-owned advertising and public relations firms and in the form of aggressive recruiting of Black, Hispanic, Asian American and Native American professionals by other firms.

But is there an interest in increased diversity on the management side? Maybe not. A 1989 survey of 50 key corporate and agency public relations executives by the Interassociation Council for Public Relations in Atlanta yielded responses from only 18, of which 5 responded they were willing to discuss the issue further (cited in Zerbinos & Clanton, 1992, pp. 7-8). As noted later in this chapter, although some public relations firms have made conscious efforts to recruit minority students through special scholarship and training programs, such programs usually fold after a few years. The problem with these programs seems to be not the programs themselves but the limited resources allotted to them and/or lack of commitment by man-agement to formally integrate such programs into the organizational cul-ture by designating full-time staff to oversee the success of the programs and by hiring student recipients for permanent positions.

Zerbinos and Clanton's 1990 survey offered many and varied reasons for the scarcity of non-White public relations professionals, such as lack of awareness of the opportunities, racism, lack of role models, lack of encouragement, limited growth offered by the field, lack of essential skills, negative reputation of the field, and belief that other fields are more accessible. The most influential factors in people of color making public relations their career choice were an early interest in communication and the opportunity to work with people. The least influential factor was the advice of high school counselors (Zerbinos & Clanton, 1992, pp. 9-15). Today, as target audiences are increasingly segmented and defined by race, ethnicity, gender, and age, public relations firms need to acknowledge as well as meet the growing demand for public relations practitioners of color.

DIVERSITY PRACTICES IN PUBLIC RELATIONS EDUCATION

Public relations educators have an excellent opportunity for both addressing and advancing the diversity agenda in the public relations profession. Some of the obstacles that must be overcome if people of color are to increase their number and power in the public relations field are as follows:

1. Too few non-White students are oriented toward journalism once they reach college. They know little about journalism, and other professions are better known to them. Educators should identify and support high achievers with the motivation and drive to be successful in the public relations field.

2. Professors do not always use racially and culturally inclusive textbooks and classroom materials in their teaching. There has been little research on such inclusiveness in textbooks, which have a great influence in portraying the field, its practice, and its practitioners to aspirants and students of the field.

People of color are not newcomers to the profession, nor are their newspaper histories separate from their public relations history. The first Latino, Black, Native American, and Asian American newspapers in this country were all founded as public relations or public advocacy vehicles: *El Misisipi* to rail against Napoleon's takeover of Spain, *Freedom's Journal* "to plead our own cause," the *Cherokee Phoenix* to advocate a tribal identity and disseminate tribal news to the Cherokees and the native viewpoint to a wider audience, and the *Golden Hills News* to Christianize the Chinese and to gain respect for them among the 49ers in the California gold rush.

An Agenda for Diversity in Public Relations Education

By explaining to their students the economic advantages of working in a corporate environment and stressing the opportunities for community service as part of public relations, professors can help students understand the unique opportunities in the public relations field. Community involvement is encouraged, not discouraged, on the public relations side of the communications profession.

The other professional associations for the media, such as the American Society of Newspaper Editors, offer models of multicultural programs that public relations faculty and professionals can replicate, emulate, and improve on. Similarly, non-White professional associations can also help to establish links for internships, mentors, part-time faculty, and campus speakers. The Los Angeles-based Hispanic Public Relations Association's 80 to 100 members annually raise $10,000 in scholarships and look for contacts on campuses.

Mentoring programs with professionals, internships, early tracking, and a national competition to select, train, place, and track students will help to attract and keep the best students in public relations. Public relations agencies and professional associations can establish contacts with histori-cally Black colleges, schools that are members of the Hispanic Association of Colleges and Universities (HACU), and campuses with large minority student enrollment to help identify and nurture public relations faculty and students. Such contacts should be seen as a two-way street: Public relations agencies and educators who have focused only on general audi-ences can learn from the students and faculty on predominantly non-White campuses as they work with them.

In a multicultural society with a plurality of media rather than mass media, those who are aware of and able to function in more than one cul-ture and to work in more than one medium will be the most advantaged. Public relations students and professionals must know how to communi-cate with people of all cultures and to use all the media at their disposal. Therefore, it is crucial that everyone gain an understanding of the crossover skills necessary to effectively communicate with diverse audi-ences through diverse media.

An Agenda for Diversity in the Public Relations Field

Although specialized public relations agencies were among the first to make corporate America and government agencies aware of effective ways to reach communities of color—through targeted campaigns dating back to the early 20th century—the Public Relations Society of America (PRSA) did not start its own Multicultural Communications Section until 1997, when it began as an outgrowth of PRSA's National Multicultural Affairs Committee begun in 1980.

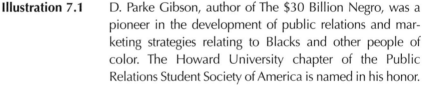

Illustration 7.1   D. Parke Gibson, author of The $30 Billion Negro, was a
pioneer in the development of public relations and mar-
keting strategies relating to Blacks and other people of
color. The Howard University chapter of the Public
Relations Student Society of America is named in his honor.

"From its inception, the Section has been dedicated to championing
multiculturalism and nurturing the careers of ethnically diverse public
relations practitioners," said chair Rhonda Welsh at a 2003 teleconference
on U.S. Hispanics sponsored by the Multicultural Communications
Section. Citing the Census Bureau's projection that by 2040 nearly half of
all Americans will be what are now called minorities, she added that "The
numbers suggest that our organizations in general and our practice specifically must realize the importance of building relationships with all of our
publics" (Public Relations Society of America, 2003).

Some public relations firms, such as internationally renowned
Fleischmann-Hilliard, have recognized the need to add more diversity to
their workforce to meet the shifting demographics of their target audiences, so they offer minority scholarship and training programs. In the

mid-1990s, Fleischmann-Hilliard's Los Angeles office started a Minority Internship Training Program, whereby the firm recruited qualified minority juniors and seniors from regional colleges and universities who were interested in pursuing careers in the public relations field. One candidate, an African American woman who was selected in the second year of the program, said that she was the only person of color in the office. She was subsequently hired full time and transferred to the firm's office in Chicago.[3]

Similarly, THE LAGRANT FOUNDATION in Los Angeles, whose mission is to increase the number of ethnic minorities in the advertising, marketing, and public relations professions, offers graduating high school seniors and undergraduate college students an opportunity to receive a $5,000 scholarship to pursue a degree in these fields. The goal of THE LAGRANT FOUNDATION is "to open the proverbial 'door' for minorities to enter into the fields of advertising, marketing or public relations . . . and provides mentors, career and professional development, enrichment programs, and internships programs" as well.[4]

The 2003 PRSA Multicultural Communications Section conducted several national programs to fulfill its vision to serve "as a link between multicultural issues, practitioners, and the society." The Section's activities included multicultural events at the PRSA convention, multicultural scholarships for promising students, and a quarterly newsletter, as well as increased outreach to leaders of ethnic public relations associations and other professional societies and PRSA accreditation training for ethnic public relations associations.

PRSA's partnering with ethnic public relations associations, such as the Hispanic Public Relations Association (HPRA) and Hispanic Marketing and Communication Association (HMCA), to cosponsor teleseminars has helped general market public relations associations and agencies link with the nation's growing racial and ethnic groups and the media that serve them. In so doing, the ethnic professionals and agencies have been able to go beyond translating press releases into other languages and putting a racial happy face on established campaigns. They have also contributed their creative expertise and knowledge of different racial and ethnic communities to influence the content and focus of public relations campaigns so that the campaigns will be more effective.

The multicultural and multilingual understanding and skills that men and women of color bring into the public relations profession are important in effectively communicating to and with all American communities. As they become more valued by the public relations profession, people of all races and ethnicities who have these skills will also become more valuable to the corporations, nonprofit agencies, and public relations organizations and governments that employ them.

Notes

1. As of this writing, these are the most recent data available in the Census Bureau's EEO Special File.

2. For more details, see Mallette, W.A. (1995). *African Americans in public relations: Pigeonholed practitioners or cultural interpreters?* Unpublished master's thesis, University of Maryland, College Park (cited in Grunig et al., 2001).

3. One of this book's coauthors, Lena Chao, nominated students from California State University, Los Angeles (CSULA) to interview for the program. In the 4 years that CSULA participated in the program, two African American female students were selected in a competitive process and each received a $5,000 scholarship and a full-time summer internship in Fleischmann-Hilliard's Los Angeles-based office.

4. This is from the Call for Applications, THE LAGRANT FOUNDATION, Los Angeles, dated February 14, 2003. For more information, visit their website: http://www.lagrantfoundation.org.

References

Cose, E. (1993). *The rage of a privileged class.* New York: HarperCollins.

Ferreira, J. (1993). *Hispanic public relations practitioners and the glass ceiling effect.* Unpublished master's thesis, University of Maryland, College Park.

Gilliam, J. N. (1992). *Black women in public relations: Climbing to the top.* Unpublished master's thesis, Graduate School of the University of Maryland, College Park.

Gloster, D., & Cherrie, J. (1987, Spring). Communication careers: Advertising or public relations may mean opportunity. *Equal Opportunity*, 36-39.

Herbert, S. J. (1990, August-September). Black public relations movers and shakers in the entertainment industry. *Crisis*, 16, 18-38.

Interassociation Council for Public Relations in Atlanta. (1990). *Report of the Interassociation Council for Pubic Relations Survey.* Atlanta, GA: Author.

IWMFWire. (1999). *Voices for the future: Women of color in the U.S. media* (International Women's Media Foundation report). Retrieved from http://iwmf.org/iwmfwire/Mar99/Voices.htm

Kern-Foxworth, M. (1989, Fall). Status and roles of minority PR practitioners. *Public Relations Review*, 42-44.

Kern-Foxworth, M. (1991a, Spring). Black, brown, red and yellow markets equal green power. *Public Relations Quarterly*, 30.

Kern-Foxworth, M. (1991b, June 6). Advertising and public relations: An educator's perspective. *Black Issues in Higher Education.*

Kern-Foxworth, M. (1993). Minority practitioners' perceptions of racial bias in public relations and implications for the year 2000. In *Diversity in public relations education—issues, implications and opportunities: A collection of essays* (pp. 35-51). Florida International University, North Miami, and University of

South Carolina, Columbia: Diversity Committee, Educators Section, Public Relations Society of America.

Mallette, W. A. (1995). *African Americans in public relations: Pigeonholed practitioners or cultural interpreters?* Unpublished master's thesis, University of Maryland, College Park.

Layton, M. (1980, April). Black in public relations: A growing presence. *Public Relations Journal*, 64-67.

Len-Rios, M. E. (1998). Minority public relations practitioner perceptions. *Public Relations Review, 24*(4), 535-555.

National Council of La Raza (NCLR). (1991). *The Hispanic population 1990. A chartbook "snapshot."* Washington, DC: Author.

O'Dwyer, J. R., Co. (1992, April). *How new media trends affect PR activities.* New York: J. R. O'Dwyer Co., Inc., PR Services.

Public Relations Society of America. (2002, November 11). Retrieved from http://www.prsa.org/_News/press/pr111102a.asp

Public Relations Society of America. (2003, February 5). Retrieved from http://www.prsa.org/_Networking/mc/index.asp?ident=mc1

Unger, T. (1992). Minority hiring debate heats up. In L. A. Grunig, E. L. Toth, & L. C. Hon (2001), *Women in public relations: How gender influences practice.* New York: Guilford.

U.S. Bureau of Labor Statistics. (1992, January). Employment and earnings. *Monthly Labor Review*, 186.

U.S. Census Bureau. (1990). *1990 census of the population special report 1-1, detailed occupation and other characteristics from the EEO file for the United States.* Washington, DC: Author.

Yamashita, S. H. (1992). *The examination of the status and roles of Asian-American public relations practitioners in the United States.* Unpublished master's thesis, University of Maryland, College Park.

Zerbinos, E., & Clanton, G. A. (1992, August). *Minority public relations practitioners: Career influences, job satisfaction and discrimination.* Top faculty paper, Minorities and Communications Division, Association for Education in Journalism and Mass Communication, Montreal.

Part IV

Women of Color in the Media

Women of Color 8

Two Strikes and . . . ?

In the baseball game of American communications media, women of color have two strikes against them before getting to bat. They must confront—and overcome—the dual challenge of sexism and racism. They typically are personified in media as objects of sex and violence and as powerless subjects to a male-dominated society. This persists despite the significant political and economic strides made by American women over the past 30 years.

According to 2000 census data, women still have a slight edge over men as the majority of the U.S. population, 51% to 49%. Yet, they are still not moving into leadership positions in the media at a rate reflecting their numbers in society. The overall lack of women decision makers in the organizations that control the media affects how women are portrayed in entertainment media and covered in the news. A report by the International Women in Media Foundation (1999) showed that women are the focus in only 26% of entertainment and arts media and in only 7% of stories on politics and government.

For women of color, the lack of representation in the media is even bleaker. Not only do they face the obstacles of gender discrimination, but they must also overcome the hurdle of tokenism in an industry notorious for its lack of performance in achieving diversity goals. As was noted at a 2002 conference on Empowering Women of Color in the Media:

> The universes of "media" and "women of color" have a strained relationship borne out of absence and misrepresentation. We may think of the tokenized Asian character in an otherwise completely white T.V. sitcom, of the newspaper articles that unequivocally state it is young Latina and African American girls that are predominantly unwed and uneducated mothers, or of the ongoing portrayals of Middle Eastern women as utterly oppressed and uneducated victims. It can seem that the face of mainstream media in

the United States has, in some ways, changed very little; our articulate, authentic, and ever-evolving voices are simply unheard. (Lewis, 2002)

This chapter offers some historical and contemporary perspectives on the roles and portrayals of women—and women of color—in the media and on how their lack of a voice in management helps to perpetuate stereotypical, sexist, and classist images that continue to undermine the credibility and value of women in the larger society. However, because there is a limited amount of information available that specifically addresses women of color, the following discussion will provide a broader overview of the status of women in the media, with an emphasis on minority women where data are available. Our discussion begins with an overview of the relationship between non-Whites and the American motion picture and television industry.

Breaking the Barrier: Black Women Rise to the Top

It was a historical night for African American performers when Halle Berry and Denzel Washington won Oscars for best actress and best actor, respectively, at the 74th Academy Awards in 2002. Not only was it the first time that two African Americans won Hollywood's highest award for acting, but, for her performance in *Monster's Ball,* Berry also became the first African American woman to win the best actress Oscar. Three years earlier, she won an Emmy for her portrayal of Dorothy Dandridge in the cable television film *Introducing Dorothy Dandridge.* Coincidentally, Dandridge was the first African American woman to receive a best actress Oscar nomination—for her 1954 role in *Carmen Jones.* Upon receiving her award, an emotional Berry acknowledged the magnitude of the moment.

> This moment is so much bigger than me. This moment is for Dorothy Dandridge, Lena Horne, Diahann Carroll. It's for the women who stand beside me, Jada Pinkett, Angela Bassett, Vivica Fox, and the nameless, faceless women of color who now stand a chance tonight because the door has been opened. (cited in Welkos & King, 2002, p. A1)

The groundbreaking evening trumpeted a new era in which women of color not only could break racial barriers but also could play leads in non-traditional—though often stereotypical—female roles in mainstream films. While lead roles that feature African American women, such as Whitney Houston's role in *The Bodyguard* in 1992, are still few and far between, a number of women of color have been cast in high-profile supporting roles, such as Whoopi Goldberg in *Ghost* in 1990 and Beyonce

Illustration 8.1   Actress Diahann Carroll broke racial and cultural barriers in her nonstereotypical role as nurse Julia Baker in the weekly series *Julia*, which ran from 1968 to 1971 on NBC.

Source: CORBIS.

Knowles in *Austin Powers in Goldmember* in 2002. Indeed, African American women have come a long way since the days when they were cast as affable servants content to serve their White masters, as in *Gone With the Wind* in 1939; or as subservient buffoons, as in the 1950s ABC television show *Beulah;* or even as tough femmes fatales like those that made Pam Grier the queen of blaxploitation in films like *Coffey* in 1973, *Foxy Brown* in 1974, and *Friday Foster* in 1975.

It was Diahann Carroll who really broke down the racial barriers in the 1960s with her role as earnest nurse Julia Baker in NBC's *Julia*, which ran from 1968 to 1971. In response to the social movements and racial reforms of the 1960s, television began to present "respectable" images of Blacks that more closely reflected America's newfound sense of racial morality. Consequently, Carroll became the first African American actress, who was not playing a servant, to star in her own TV series (UCLA Center for African American Studies, 2002b).

But the drawback of "assimilationist" shows like NBC's *Julia,* which featured African Americans in middle-class lifestyles, was that Blacks were positioned as tokens in a White world and were disconnected from the stark realities of a largely economically disadvantaged Black community. By contrast, during the 1970s a series of Black-oriented sitcoms featuring African American women emerged on network television. Shows like *Good Times* (CBS) and *The Jeffersons* (CBS) exposed the gritty realities of inner city and/or urban life—albeit sanitized with humor and comic relief. However, while the shows were firmly set in the Black world with Black characters, they were still developed by White writers and producers to appeal to the predominantly White television audience. In fact, some critics have suggested that in the 1970s depictions of Blacks in the medium had actually regressed back to the buffoonish portrayals of Blacks that were common in the 1950s (UCLA Center for African American Studies, 2002a).

Of all the groups of people of color, African Americans have experienced the greatest career success both on screen and behind the scenes. According to a study by the UCLA Center for African American Studies (2002a), both Black and White Americans were overrepresented on the screen in 2001, accounting for about 16% and 76%, respectively, of all "featured" characters (i.e., those characters who have speaking roles or who are explicitly highlighted by the words or actions of other "featured" actors). Combined, these two groups represented 92% of all prime time characters, while they comprised only 82% of the nation's population. In contrast, Latinos were grossly underrepresented in prime time, constituting only 2% of all characters, while Asian Americans approached appropriate representation at roughly 3% of all characters. Native Americans were the most underrepresented group, at 0% of all characters. When the genders were compared, it was found that Black men significantly outnumber Black women on the screen, at 59% versus 41%. The percentages are identical for White men and women (UCLA Center for African American Studies, 2002a).

In the 2001 to 2002 and 2002 to 2003 television seasons, African American women enjoyed the greatest amount of exposure on their own prime time shows—although they were essentially "ghettoized" on the two least-watched networks (UPN and WB) in a handful of Black-oriented sitcoms. In the 2002 to 2003 fall line-up, Tracee Ellis Ross, Golden Brooks,

Illustration 8.2   Successful talk show host, actress, broadcasting execu-
                       tive, author, and founder and editorial director of her
                       own magazine, Oprah Winfrey is one of the most pow-
                       erful women of color in television.

Source: Copyright © Rufus F. Folkks/CORBIS.

Persia White, and Jill Marie Jones reprised their roles in UPN's *Girlfriends.*
Although there were no plans for singer-actress Brandy to return in UPN's
Moesha, her show was responsible for the spin-off show *The Parkers,*

featuring the popular actress Mo-Nique. And Rachel True, Essence Atkins, and Telma Hopkins were featured in UPN's new show, *Half and Half* ("Fall TV Preview," 2002).

Television, considered by many to be the most powerful medium, has historically been resistant to racial diversity in the power at the top. However, there have been a number of African American women who have risen through the ranks to hold real power positions that influence projects and determine what we see and don't see on the small screen. In 2001, Pamela Thomas-Graham was named president and CEO of CNBC and was responsible for overseeing the company's $500 million domestic operations—including programming, advertising sales, and ensuring brand synergy across CNBC's TV and Internet platforms. Broadcast veteran Lana Corbi is president and CEO of Crown Media United States. Prior to becoming CEO, she was executive vice president and COO of the holding company, which owns the $114 million Hallmark Channel, and had held several top-level executive positions at Fox Broadcasting Company. In 2002, Christina Norman was named executive vice president and general manager of VH1, a subsidiary of Viacom that reaches more than 82 million U.S. households. She also supervises VH1's sister channels, VH1 Classic, VH1 Mega Hits, VH1 Soul, VH1 Country, and VH1 Uno. Paula Madison, who began her journalism career as a print reporter and moved to television news in 1984, is president and general manager of NBC4 (KNBC), the station NBC owns and operates in Los Angeles. She was the first African American woman to become general manager at a network-owned station in a Top 5 market ("10 Most Powerful Blacks in TV," 2000).[1]

Arguably the most prominent, powerful woman of color in television is Oprah Winfrey, who is chairman and CEO of Harpo Productions and cofounder of Oxygen Media, which includes a women's cable network. She became a television icon when her television program, *The Oprah Winfrey Show*, debuted in 1986 and became an enormous success—attracting 26 million American viewers. In fact, her influence was so far reaching that when a book was featured on Oprah's Book Club, it instantly hit the bestseller list. Her development deals with ABC through Harpo Productions resulted in the award-winning TV movie *Tuesdays with Morrie*, and she produced and starred in the Oxygen Network show *Use Your Life* ("10 Most Powerful Blacks in TV," 2000).

Sex, Servants, and Stereotypes: Latinas in the Media

Historically, Latinas have been portrayed in the media either as the fiery, passionate, tempestuous sexpot or as the domestic help. Mexican film stars such as the glamorous Maria Felix, whose perfect beauty got her

Illustration 8.3   Born Raquel Tejada, a shapely Raquel Welch became one of the most famous sex symbols of all time after appearing scantily clad in the 1967 movie *One Million Years B.C.*

Source: CORBIS.

discovered as she was walking down the street and catapulted her to international stardom, portrayed a collection of fierce women over several decades in such films as *Enamorada* in 1946 and *La Generala* in 1970 (cited in *Time,* April 22, 2002).

One of the most recognizable Latina actresses is the former Raquel Tejada, better known as Raquel Welch. When Welch broke into movies in the mid-1960s with such hits as *One Million Years B.C.* and *Fantastic*

Voyage, the studios never promoted the fact that she had a Latina background. Today, she trumpets the fact and has reinvented herself as a Latina actress who boasts of her cultural roots. This is evidenced by her having chosen a role in the PBS series *American Family,* created by Gregory Nava (director of *Selena*), which premiered in 2002 and was billed as the first drama series on broadcast TV featuring a Latino cast. The series is about a Mexican American family and deals with the serious—and often comedic—aspects of life in East Los Angeles (Brady, 2002). Welch plays Aunt Dora, the drama queen of the family, who is a passionate, romantic woman who might have become a Hollywood star if she had vigorously pursued an acting career. As one television critic noted, Welch infuses the role with her trademark sultriness and smoky voice.

As for getting beyond the role of the maid or sex kitten, actress Lupe Ontiveros has played roles that counter traditional media stereotypes, such as that of Hispanic heroine and union organizer Dolores Huerta, who founded the United Farm Workers, and the 17-century Mexican poet and nun Sor Juana Inez de la Cruz, who is often viewed as the first feminist of the Americas (Navarro, 2002).

Despite the headway some Hispanic actresses have made by acting in nonstereotypical roles, most Latinas are still portrayed by the media in ways that connote sex and sexuality. For instance, the Winter 2002 issue of *Sports Illustrated* featured bikini-clad model Yamila Diaz-Rahi on the cover, with the subtitle "Red Hot in Latin America. . . . Yamila sizzles in Mexico." Even the cover of the Spanish-language publication *TV y Novelas* had two Latina actresses posing in swimsuits—despite the fact that the issue has nothing to do with swimwear. In a 2001 *New York Times* article titled "Latino Style Is Cool. Oh, All Right: It's Hot," author Ruth La Ferla described 17-year-old Lisa Forero, of the La Guardia High School of Performing Arts in Manhattan, as perched on 4-inch platform boots, playing up her curves in a form-fitting gray spandex dress, sporting outsized gold hoop earrings, and having pink and ivory airbrushed fingernails. Did La Ferla think that the teenager fretted that her image—that of a saucy bombshell—bordered on self-parody? Not in the least. In fact, La Ferla concluded that dressing up as a familiar stereotype was Lisa Forero's pointedly aggressive way of claiming her Latino heritage.

In "Will the Real Latina Please Stand Up?" the July 2002 issue of *Latina* magazine profiled three nonstereoypical Latina authors to show how in reality Hispanic women are many different shades and sizes. Latinas comprise a broad range of people from various ethnicities and nationalities, including but not limited to the variations the public may immediately think of, such as those represented by tall, blond, blue-eyed Cameron Diaz; petite, brunet, olive-skinned Salma Hayek; and statuesque, curly haired, dark-skinned Gina Torres. For example, profiled author Veronica Chambers hails from Panama and may look African American but has Latin roots. When people see author Michele Serros's straight black hair,

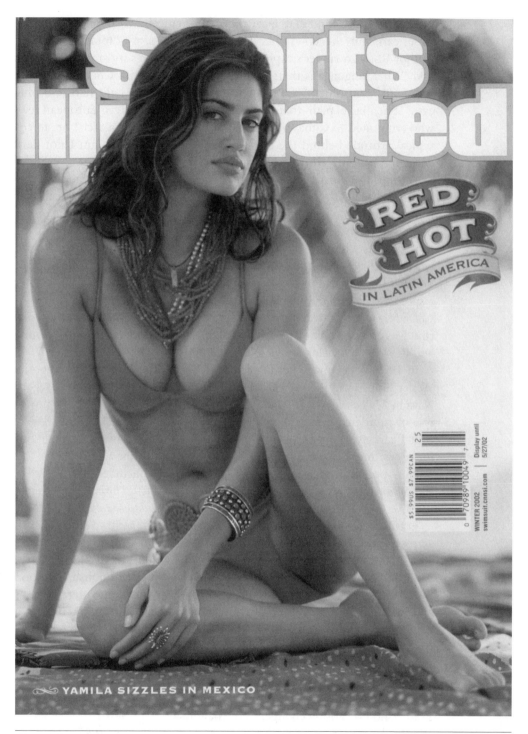

Illustration 8.4   Sexy, sizzling, bikini-clad Latinas perpetuate the "fiery" stereotype in the Winter 2002 edition of Sports *Illustrated* magazine.

prominent nose, and flat face, they automatically assume she's Native American, but she is—as her Latina friends assert—"totally Mexican." Author Rosa Lowinger's rapid-fire Spanish perplexes most people, who'll ask, "What language is that?" When she replies that it's Cuban, they look astounded and blurt, "How can you be Cuban with light hair and blue eyes?" She may explain that her grandparents were Eastern European Jews who emigrated to Cuba in the 1920s, but if she detects a racist or stereotypical attitude behind the question, she'll retort: "What, am I not dark enough to call myself *cubana?*" (p. 83).

Perhaps the most visible and successful Latina actress to emerge in the 1990s and make the transition into nontraditional, nonstereotypical roles is the multitalented Jennifer Lopez. She not only appeared in a string of box office hits with some of Hollywood's leading men but also topped the music charts with her CDs *On the 6, J.Lo.,* and *This Is Me . . . Then.* Lopez, who is of Puerto Rican descent, was born in the Bronx, New York, and got her first big break in 1990 when she won a dance audition that landed her a spot as a Fly Girl on Keenan Ivory Wayan's Fox television series *In Living Color.* She went on to appear in the series *Second Chances* and *Hotel Malibu* (but was credited on both as Melinda Lopez), the short-lived *South Central,* and the 1993 television movie *Nurses on the Line: The Crash of Flight 7.*

In 1995, Lopez made her big screen debut in *The Money Train* opposite Wesley Snipes and Woody Harrelson, before working with director Gregory Nava in *My Family, Mi Familia* (1995). This led indirectly to the high-profile role of murdered Tejana star Selena Quintanilla in the 1997 biopic *Selena,* which garnered Lopez Golden Globe and MTV Movie Award nominations for best actress. By 2002, Lopez had become the first Latina actress to earn $12 million per film. Her long list of movie credits includes *Jack* in 1996, *Anaconda* in 1997, *Out of Sight* in 1998, *The Cell* in 2000, *The Wedding Planner* in 2000, *Angel Eyes* in 2001, *Enough* in 2002, and *Maid in Manhattan* in 2002.[2]

Future roles for Latinas may be best illustrated by the experience of actress Salma Hayek, who moved to Los Angeles in 1991 to make movies after being Mexico's most popular soap opera star at age 21 on *Teresa.* After enrolling in a Shakespearean acting class to learn English, she soon found out she did not need it to play the parts she was being offered: extras and maids. Although she eventually landed a recurring role in 1993 as a neighbor on the sitcom *Sinbad,* Hayek found that work remained scarce for Latinas. "I came here and had to start at the bottom," said Hayek. "There were no parts for Latinas. It was very painful, but the hardest part about staying was that I was constantly offered soaps in Mexico. The temptation to take the work was great. Then I got the part in *Desperado* [in 1995], and everything changed" (Buchalter, 2002, pp. 9-10).

After landing roles in such movies as *Fools Rush In* in 1997, *Dogma* in 1999, and *Wild, Wild West* in 1999, she founded her own production company, Ventanarosa (Pink Window) and starred in several films the company produced: *No One Writes to the Colonel* in 1999, *In the Time of*

Illustration 8.5   Multi-talented Jennifer Lopez dazzled audiences in her role as a working-class, single mom who falls for a high-profile politician in the 2002 film *Maid in Manhattan*.

Source: Copyright © Neal Preston/CORBIS.

the Butterflies in 2001, and *Frida* in 2002—a film both Madonna and Jennifer Lopez tried to make about the life of the innovative Mexican artist and freethinker Frida Kahlo, but which Hayek succeeding in making due to her pure passion for it and after a 7-year struggle to produce and star in the film. Her performance in the film earned her an Academy Award nomination. Reflecting on her success, Hayek said, "I used to be a whiner . . . Now, instead of whining that there are no parts for women, no parts for Latinas, I am creating them" (Buchalter, 2002, pp. 9-10).

From Geisha Girl to Woman Warrior: Cashing In on the Asian Mystique

Over the past two decades, there has been an unusual proliferation of Asian women news anchors in major markets, spurred by Hollywood's stereotypical images and the success enjoyed by such high-profile newscasters as Connie Chung. Hollywood's portrayals of the Asian woman as a submissive, subservient "geisha" girl, in such 1950s films as *Sayonara*, and as an exotic, sexual object, in such 1960s films as *The World of Suzy Wong*, have created in the American audience a favorable perception of the Asian woman as being beautiful, docile, and sensual.

San Francisco news anchor Wendy Tokuda believes the profusion of Asian women newscasters reflects the fascination that Americans have with the geisha girl—or Singapore Girl—and is rooted in the experiences U.S. servicemen had with Asian women while overseas in China, Japan, Korea, the Philippines, and Vietnam. Those experiences, however, were primarily with prostitutes, "a very select strata of the society overseas, and they bring those images home," says Tokuda. This, in turn, has contributed to—if not created—the "Suzy Wong Syndrome," or distinct impressions about the exotic Asian female that still linger today (Chang, 1984).

This archetype of the Asian woman is vividly illustrated in a 1979 *Oakland Tribune* feature article titled "East meets West," in which the author describes a 48-year-old divorced man who found the ultimate gift to the American male in a 23-year-old "Oriental" servant.

> She would be required to be a complete housekeeper. She would prepare meals on the evenings when he dines at home. She would do laundry. She would keep the apartment immaculate because he's a "nutsy clean." . . . Naturally, she would do the grocery shopping and the cooking from a marketing allowance of $90 a week.
>
> And the understanding went beyond that. He liked to be bathed. He told her all of his requirements in advance. And he would like on occasion more than just massage. She understood. And about every 10 days or so he would be entertaining. He likes to give dinner parties for three couples, and the young maid would be expected to prepare and serve, with NO indication she was other than hired help. No twinges of jealousy were to cross her eyes; no hints to the lady he'd brought as his date to one of his dinner parties.
>
> "You couldn't believe," he said. "She's only 23, but with the wisdom of a woman much older. That's the Oriental mind. And she doesn't get demanding. She's grateful for what I've given her—her privacy when she wants to go into her own room and shut the door, her $100 a month which she can save, her uniforms which she seems proud to wear. It's working out very well." (Fiset, 1979, p. 68)

Asian actresses have also been typecast in roles that perpetuate the Asian mystique. In the 1957 to 1959 film *Sayonara,* Miyoshi Umeki portrayed the stereotypical coy, subservient geisha, and in the 1960 film *The World of Suzy Wong,* Nancy Kwan defined the "Suzy Wong" sex-object image as a young Asian woman with long hair, long legs, and a slit dress. Later, Joan Chen perpetuated these images in her role as the sensual, submissive Asian Pacific woman in the 1986 movie *Taipan.*

Comedienne Margaret Cho's 1994 prime time network comedy *All American Girl* departed from portraying Asian women stereotypically, as had been the norm in earlier movies and television programs, but the series's attempt to convey a genuine sense of Asian America within a U.S. television comedy framework was unsuccessful. *All American Girl* featured

Illustration 8.6   Comedienne Margaret Cho at the American Comedy
                        Awards.
Source: CORBIS.

a predominantly Asian American cast, but its tone—hip 20-something
California "Valley Girl" meets the Borscht Belt—was the work of mostly
White writers and producers. In addition, her TV Asian family was largely
parodied, which wasted the talents of accomplished actors such as B. D.
Wong. In short, what the show revealed to America was not an emerging

Asian subculture but, rather, watered-down stereotypes of Asian Americans. As of 2002, no prime time network television series with an Asian emphasis had aired since the short-lived *All American Girl* was cancelled (Wong, 2001, pp. 233-239).

While Asian women have also historically been depicted as dragon ladies, domestic workers, gang molls, and hookers, or in subservient, overexoticized images, more contemporary roles for Asian women have launched a new genre that typecasts them as "women warriors." Whether it's Zhang Ziyi performing gravity-defying stunts in the academy award-winning *Crouching Tiger, Hidden Dragon* in 2002, Lucy Liu kick-boxing as a femme fatale in the 2001 remake of *Charlie's Angels,* or Kelly Hu storming soldiers and tyrants in *The Scorpion King* in 2002, a contemporary woman's strength and independence these days is measured by her ability to master her maneuvers in the martial arts. As film critic Leonard Maltin has noted,

> People like action nowadays, and it has crossed over the gender line. . . . I'd prefer to see a woman who's "strong" in the more organic or cerebral sense of the word, but that doesn't seem to sell tickets. Many of the young women I know believe it's about time that we see women kicking butt on screen. (cited in Whipp, 2002, p. 6)

Newswomen of Color

NEWSWOMEN WHO PAVED THE WAY

In the late 1800s, at a time when women were fighting for their basic rights in American society, a few Black women were emerging as important voices in the Black press. One of the most prominent was Lucy Wilmot Smith, who eloquently commemorated her fellow "Negro" women writers in the following passage in the Indianapolis *Freeman* on February 23, 1889.

> The Negro woman's history is marvelously strange and pathetic. Unlike that of other races, her mental, moral, and physical status has not found a place in the archives of public libraries. From the womb of the future must come that poet or author to glorify her womanhood by idealizing the various phases of her character, by digging from the past examples of faithfulness and sympathy, endurance and self-sacrifice and displaying the achievements which were brightened by friction. Born and bred under both the hindrance of slavery and the limitations of her sex, the mothers of the race have kept pace with the fathers. They stand at the head of the cultured, educated families whose daughters clasp arms with the sons. The educated Negro woman

occupies vantage found over the Caucasian woman of America, in that the former has had to contest with her brother every inch of the ground for recognition, the Negro man, having had his sister by his side on plantations and in rice swamps, keeps her there, now that he moves in other spheres. As she wins laurels he accords her the royal crown. This is especially true in journalism. Doors are opened before we knock, and as well equipped young women emerged from the class-room the brotherhood of the race, men whose energies have been repressed and distorted by the interposition of circumstances, give them opportunities to prove themselves; and right well are they doing this by voice and pen.

Other notable Black women journalists include Ida B. Wells, a former slave and prominent African American journalist who spoke out against lynchings in the late 1800s; Lucile Bluford, editor and publisher of the *Kansas City Call*, an African American newspaper at which she worked from her graduation from the University of Kansas in 1932 on; and Marvel Cooke, who worked for the *Amsterdam News* (which in the 1930s was a Black New York newspaper) and who was the only African American and the only woman reporter on the staff of the *Compass*, a liberal New York daily where she worked from 1950 to 1952 (Beasley & Gibbons, 1993).

In the early 1900s, during a tumultuous time for Mexicans in Texas, Jovita Idar became a celebrated "Heroine of La Raza." As the Mexican Revolution was raging, and the Texas Rangers, or "los rinches," were routinely lynching Mexican Americans and Mexican children, Idar wrote about the atrocities—and the extreme discrimination against Mexican children in the public schools—in her father's newspaper, *La Crònica*. She wrote about the lynching and hanging of a Mexican child in Thorndale, Texas, by the Texas Rangers and the brutal burning at the stake of 20-year-old Antonio Rodriguez in Rocksprings, Texas. Of Rodriguez, she wrote that

> The crowd cheered when the flames engulfed his contorted body. They did not even turn away at the smell of his burning flesh and I wondered if they even knew his name. There are so many dead that sometimes I can't remember all their names ("Jovita Idar: 1885-1946," 2000).

In 1911, Idar became the first president of the League of Mexican Women to promote the education of poor Mexican children. The organization also provided free food and clothing for the needy. In 1913, Idar caught the attention of the U.S. federal government and Texas Rangers when she began writing articles supporting the revolutionary forces of Francisco Villa of Mexico and crossed the border to serve as a nurse in the Cruz Blanca on the side of General Villa. When she returned to Laredo in 1914, she wrote an article criticizing Woodrow Wilson's deployment of troops on the border, and the Texas Rangers were dispatched to Laredo to

Illustration 8.7   CNN hoped to capitalize on news anchor personalities with audience recognition to boost its ratings when it launched Connie Chung's own—but short-lived—news program *Connie Chung Tonight* in June, 2002.

Source: Copyright © Bettman/CORBIS.

destroy Idar's printing presses. Although she bravely fended off "los rinches" for a short while, they eventually returned and, in the stealth of night, broke open the doors of *La Crònica* with sledgehammers and destroyed the presses and linotype machines. At that moment, the voice of "La Raza" was silenced.

Although few other women journalists of color have led such a strong and effective campaign for political and social justice as Jovita Idar did, some have made significant steps toward progress in the fight for greater equality and fairer representation in news coverage and employment. In 1965, after Peggy Peterman was hired by the St. Petersburg *Times* to write for the "Negro Page," she concluded that news about the Black community should not be segregated, and she fired off a 14-page memo stating why the page should be abolished. The editors agreed, and she was immediately transferred to the "Women's Page."

SEXISM IN THE NEWSROOM

Although the days are gone when blatant segregation of news content was routine, what remains is an acute perception of physical divisiveness. With few women of color as role models or mentors, many women journalists of color sense a degree of hostility in their newsrooms. Consequently, many minority women journalists have developed a professional strategy for negotiating their careers. They stay focused on their goals, and they do not approach every situation with the expectation of being harassed or discriminated against (International Women's Media Foundation, 1999).

The civil rights movement of the 1960s enabled women of color to successfully wedge themselves into the broadcast industry—albeit slowly. News directors at stations with large ethnic markets sought minority anchors and reporters who reflected the shifting demographics of the local communities, as well as the stations' changing attitudes toward racial and ethnic minorities.

Proportionately, Asian Americans have witnessed the greatest proliferation of on-air jobs than any other racial or ethnic group. In the early 1970s there was only a small number of Asian American broadcast journalists, but a decade later there were more than 30 nationwide—a far higher precentage than their presence in the general population. With the exception of San Francisco, where the numbers of Asian American men and women on-air are roughly equal, women outnumbered men by a 2 to 1 ratio (Chang, 1984). This gender imbalance reflects the residual effect of the stereotype created by the "Suzy Wong Syndrome" in which Asian women are subservient, sexual objects of fantasy. It is perhaps best explained by the following passage from the December 8, 1983 issue of *Far East Economic Review*:

Such stereotypes have made life difficult for women who object to the manner in which Hollywood, pornography and popular fiction continue to stereotype the "Oriental doll" as a sexually submissive slave. The many Asian American women who are anchoring major national and local news programmes are among the most talented of their profession. But their disproportionately high representation probably reflects the tendency for yellow women to be more acceptable in highly visible jobs in a predominately white society where their ethnic brothers are seen as unattractive. (cited in Chang, 1984)

It appears that television news directors and station managers have determined that the least threatening anchor combination is a White male with a White or Asian female. Often referred to as the "Connie Chung Syndrome," the disproportionate success of Asian women newscasters has garnered them public accolades—but at the cost of driving a wedge between Asian American women and men.

Despite the success of Asian American women in broadcast news, they remain virtually invisible at the national level. Only Connie Chung, the most high-profile Asian American female news anchor, was offered a coveted stint cohosting a network news program. She was paired with Dan Rather on the *CBS Evening News.* Her journalistic credentials are impressive: Since launching her career in 1969, she has become one of the few women of color who has been a correspondent and anchor at three of the network news operations—CBS, NBC, and ABC—as well as a local anchor at Los Angeles' KCBS-TV for 7 years (Jensen, 2002, pp. F1, F12).

In 2002, Chung became CNN's biggest news hire, commanding a $2 million salary to host *Connie Chung Tonight.* Her salary was second only to that of Larry King, who is paid $7 million a year to host his top-rated show *Larry King Live.* Yet, despite Chung's impressive credentials and on-air talent, a reporter from *People* magazine still thought it was appropriate to inquire about who made the suit and shoes she wore to the news conference announcing her jump to CNN from ABC.

Another newswoman who is admired—for her fighting determination, accomplishments, and concern for the role of women and minorities in television news—is Carole Simpson, one of the few African American women to regularly anchor a network news program. In the late 1990s, she commuted from ABC's Washington bureau every Sunday morning to anchor *Sunday World News Tonight* in New York. As the only Black woman to graduate from the department of journalism at the University of Michigan in 1962—and the only one of the 60 graduates who was not offered a job—her road to success was an arduous one laden with battles against racism and sexism. At the peak of the civil rights movement, the head of the journalism department finally arranged an internship for her at Tuskegee Institute in Alabama. Simpson explained what it was like for a girl who grew up in Chicago to go south to a rural town of 5,000 people.

I had to go to segregated things. I had to shop in Montgomery, Alabama. You could not try on clothes. You had to guess at things because black people were not allowed to try on clothes. You couldn't try on hats. I refused to use the water fountains in the bathrooms. I would just hold it rather than go to a colored washroom. But it was an amazing experience. (cited in Marlane, 1999, p. 98)

In 1970, after 5 years of hard news reporting at WCFL radio in Chicago, and after having earned a master's degree at the University of Iowa, Simpson was hired as a television reporter at WMAQ in Chicago, which was where she wanted to anchor. It wasn't long, however, before she once again confronted the all-too-familiar attitudes of racial and sex discrimination.

I was told that White people didn't want to hear news from a Black person. . . . It was patently absurd because I'd always been told I had a good delivery. I had an authoritative delivery. I had the credentials. I had the education. I had the experience. How could somebody say that I would not be able to anchor? And then they said my enunciation was too perfect, that it was too clear and too precise. And I'm going, "Excuse me. Isn't this what this is all about?" Yet other Black reporters in Chicago were told they sounded too ethnic. So, it was all the discriminatory efforts to keep us from the higher paying jobs, the top jobs, the jobs with more visibility. We were kind of window dressing. It became quite clear that we'd been hired so they could say they had one. But that was it. You can come this far but no further. We'll let you report but you can't anchor. So at WMAQ, I fought and fought and fought to be able to anchor and I finally got a chance to anchor on the weekends. It was okay, White people could hear somebody Black give news on the weekend. It was 1972, the beginning of the women's movement. Now everybody's got to try to put a woman up there. Then I was a "two-for." I was Black and a woman so I became a double token. But my emphasis was always to show, "Look, you're not hiring me because of what color I am or what my gender is. It's because I'm good. I'm a good anchor." (cited in Marlane, 1999, p. 98)

Although Latinas may not have saturated the news media to the extent that Asian and African American women have, one who successfully worked her way to the top is Emmy Award-winning reporter and anchor Elizabeth Vargas, who joined NBC in 1993 as one of the few Latinas in network news. Not only had she worked for many of the top-rated news programs on ABC (*20/20, World News Tonight/Saturdays, 20/20 Downtown, Good Morning America*) and on NBC (*Now With Tom Brokaw and Katie Couric, Dateline NBC,* and *NBC Nightly News*), but she also had been at the center of our country's biggest news stories. She covered the Middle East conflict, Elian Gonzalez, the JonBenet Ramsey case, and the death of Diane Whipple in San Francisco.

Born in Patterson, New Jersey, to a Hispanic-Italian father and Irish-German-Swedish mother, Vargas has been keenly aware of the benefits and limitations of both her Hispanic heritage and her gender. According to Vargas, being a Hispanic journalist is as much a part of her identity as is being a woman. She has always worked hard to be the best reporter in the newsroom. Although she serves as an inspiration to Hispanic women aspiring to television news careers, she has also been the target of racist attacks. Earlier in her career, she was taken aback when she received "rude letters" suggesting that she "go back to Mexico." She replied, "And by the way, my family [i.e., her paternal grandfather] is from Puerto Rico" (Brecher, 2002, pp. 24-25).

There have been very few women of color delivering the news at the network level and, in general, local stations have been better than national stations at employing on-air talent that is representative of the larger population. Viewers want to see people on the news who look like they do, and network executives should ensure that the people who deliver the news are representative of the audiences watching them.

Newsroom Power and Practices: Perpetuating Inaccurate Portrayals

Despite hints of progress, it would be premature for women to start congratulating themselves for the inroads they have made in dictating news coverage of women's issues and stories. Studies of sex roles in the media continue to show that women are still far from being seen as a major influence either inside or outside the newsroom. The 2002 American Society of Newspaper Editors newsroom census found that only 37% of newspaper newsrooms were occupied by women—despite the fact that roughly 60% of students in college journalism programs are female. Minority women fared even worse: Only 2.99% of all the women in newspaper newsrooms are women of color. And a 2001 survey conducted by the Radio-Television News Directors Association and Foundation showed that women account for less than one quarter (24%) of television news directors and only one fifth (20%) of radio news directors (WENews, 2002).

In his handbook *Best Practices: The Art of Leadership in News Organizations* (2002) former *Los Angeles Times* editor Shelby Coffey III offers insights from the careers of 20 news executives. Only 4 of his interviewees (20%) are women and, of those, only two (10%) are women of color. When addressing the issue of diversity in the newsroom over the past 25 years, Karen Jurgensen, editor of *USA TODAY,* offered the following account based on her own experience:

The industry has failing grades in diversity. Originally, diversity meant a few African-Americans and women in the newsroom. It didn't mean pay much attention to them, it just meant get them in the newsroom. Now I think diversity means that you have to reflect the broad richness of the country, whether it is Latinos or African-Americans or Asian-Americans or whatever. And everyone has a part of the news decisions. Diversity is what the country is. So you have to reflect that in the newsroom or you are not producing something that speaks to large chunks of the population or is accurate. At the same time, those people have to be in a position to make decisions about what is going into the paper or not going into the paper. You can't have (just) one of each. I remember there were times in my history at USA TODAY when I would run the daily news meeting. And it was me and 15 white guys. . . . With all due respect to white guys, the world is not entirely populated by [them]. I would feel that I had to be the one voice for women at the table. (Coffey, 2002)

In "Genderizing Latino News: An Analysis of a Local Newspaper's Coverage of Latino Current Affairs," Lucila Vargas (2002) studied the coverage of Latino news from 1992 to 1995 by *The Raleigh News & Observer* in North Carolina. She found that certain newsroom practices, which she calls "genderization," enable a newspaper to operate as a technology of gender, race, and class—thus relegating Hispanic news as feminine and perpetuating the stereotype of Latinos as an underclass. Vargas asserts that news media are arenas of public speech and that who gets to speak in public spaces is determined by the way power is exercised and social relations are structured.

According to Vargas (2002), the subtle techniques employed by today's journalists obscure the way sexism, racism, and classism are validated in journalistic practices. She has argued that the genderization of journalistic products and texts occurs through the following editorial techniques practiced by reporters and editors: (1) Privileging either men's or women's voices in a story or in the entire coverage of an issue, realm, or group; (2) foregrounding either men or women in photographs and other graphic displays; (3) writing either a "soft" feature or a "hard" news story on a given event or issue; (4) placing a news item in the Home or the Business section; (5) highlighting characteristics of news makers that in Western culture have been traditionally considered either masculine or feminine; (6) positioning stories as subjective and feminine or objective and masculine knowledge; and (7) covering those actions and events of a social group (e.g., Latinos, African Americans, or Asians) pertaining to women's stereotypical domains (education and domestic violence), while neglecting the group's actions and events pertaining to men's traditional domains (e.g., politics and business).

Feminist scholars contend that the genderizing of newsroom practices occurs within the ideological framework of the patriarchy and that the distinction by sex connotes value judgments that have a subtle—yet tremendous—impact on the public's perception of minority groups. Nancy Leys Stepan (1993) has argued that the race-gender comparisons naturalize the subordination of both women and minority groups.

> In short, lower races represented the "female" type of the human species, and females the "lower race" of gender. . . . By analogy with the so-called lower races, women, the sexually deviate, the criminal, the urban poor, and the insane were in one way or another constructed as biological "races apart" whose differences from the white male, and likenesses to each other, "explained" their different and lower position in the social hierarchy. (cited in Vargas, 2002, p. 266)

Because this analogy is embedded in Western ideology, journalists routinely use the race-gender comparison to represent social groups. Thus, by genderizing social or "ethnic" groups as feminine, reporters and editors essentially construct them as an "inferior" other. For women of color, this practice positions them at the bottom of the social order. A good illustration of this positioning is that, over the past six decades, there have been a small number of national rape stories involving African American women, while there have been a large number of rapes of these women. One story that made the national news was a 1959 report of a "Negro coed" who was raped by four lower class White boys; it was called the "Tobacco Roaders' Case." Another story was that of the Tawana Brawley case of 1987, in which the teenager claimed that six white law enforcement officers kidnapped and raped her, and scrawled racial insults on her body. The case was ultimately declared a hoax. And a third and more recent story was that of the rape of Desiree Washington by boxer Mike Tyson. On a smaller, more local level, the director of the rape crisis center in Buffalo, New York, has indicated that 80% of women in the Black community there have been raped, yet to read, listen, or watch the news media you wouldn't know about any of them (cited in Flanders, 1997).

Third world women historically have received inadequate or biased attention in the media—unless they were the victims of some bizarre act or arrived in the United States in a dramatic way. When the *Golden Venture*, a ship carrying roughly 300 Chinese immigrants, ran aground off the coast of New York City in the summer of 1997, the media clamored for an interview with a Chinese illegal immigrant—preferably a woman who had survived the grueling transatlantic ordeal. What the media apparently didn't want to adequately address was the living and working conditions of immigrant laborers. Consequently, no experiences of striking Chinese sweatshop workers ever made it onto the front page of a major newspaper or onto the network evening news (Flanders, 1997).

When the media cover stories of third world women, they tend to portray the women as oppressed victims who are bound by centuries of brutal and barbaric cultural practices. For example, during the height of the global conflict in Afghanistan in 2002, the *Los Angeles Times* reported a story about an 18-year-old Pakistani woman who was ordered to be gang-raped by a tribunal council to punish—or shame—her family after her 11-year-old brother was seen walking unchaperoned with a girl from a higher class tribe. According to the graphic news article, the woman said

> I touched their feet. I wept. I cried. I said I taught the holy Koran to children in the village, therefore don't punish me for a crime which was not committed by me. But [four council members] tore my clothes and raped me one by one. . . . in a mud hut as hundreds of people stood outside laughing and cheering. ("Pakistan Investigating Rape," 2002, p. A4)

Interestingly, the photo that accompanied the *Los Angeles Times* story did not even include a picture of the woman—the subject of the story—but, rather, showed pensive images of her father and younger brother that had been provided by the Associated Press.

This type of problematic coverage might change if women—and particularly women of color—obtain decision-making roles in the newsroom. Their presence should alter the nature of traditional newsroom culture and add a vital perspective that has been absent or overlooked. This perspective not only should widen the scope of news coverage but also could help diminish gender and minority stereotyping in the news. Laura Flanders notes, in her book *Real Majority, Media Minority: The Cost of Sidelining Women in Reporting* (1997), that as more women are hired to report the news, editors are finding that topics historically regarded as "women's news," such as health, family issues, childcare, domestic violence, education, and child abuse, have become stories of general interest to all readers.

NEWS COVERAGE OF WOMEN: VICTIMS, VAMPS, AND VIOLENCE

Helen Benedict, author of *Virgin or Vamp: How the Press Covers Sex Crimes* (1992), has said that "women are more likely to get coverage in the mainstream media as crime victims than in any other role" (cited in Flanders, 1997, p. 58). As one U.S.-based journalist explained, there is so little coverage of women outside of sensationalism that the media often disregard women as leaders and are more likely to portray them as individuals rather than groups, victims instead of heroines, and sexual figures as opposed to thinkers.

Flanders (1997) suggests that this point is perhaps best exemplified by the sensationalized 1993 story that resulted in genital mutilation suddenly being in the headlines—not the kind that affects an entire class of

100 million women in parts of Africa, the Middle East, and Asia who are ritually mutilated prior to adolescence—but, rather, an isolated incident in the United States. The press reported in detail how Lorena Bobbitt hacked off her husband's penis in a fit of fury while he slept and then—perplexed as to what to do with it—drove off in her car and casually tossed it out of the window. News agencies across America picked up the sordid story, and the *New York Daily News* even printed a full-page headline that screamed, "It Really Hurt."

More often than not, news coverage of female victims is associated with sex. And when it comes to sex crime coverage, more is not necessarily better. Given that a woman is raped every 5 minutes in the United States, it is the duty of the press to cover stories of rape—not just from the angle of the victims, but from the angle of the perpetrators as well. Sex crime coverage in the media continues to be both genderized and racialized: The rape of a White woman by a Black man is the most commonly covered type of rape, while the rape of a Black woman by a Black man is the least commonly covered. This practice is not only statistically inaccurate—most rapes are committed by men of the same race and class as the victim—but also reflects and perpetuates the notion that White women are more valued and valuable than Black women.

Women who receive mainstream news coverage as sex crime victims are often categorized in one of two ways. They are presented either as "virgins" or "vamps." In "virgin" rape stories, coverage in the media suggests that a perverted man, usually of a lower class and darker complexion, has attacked a virtuous woman. Examples of the "virgin" victim include beauty pageant winner Desiree Washington, who accused boxer Mike Tyson of rape, and the White woman who while jogging in Central Park was allegedly attacked by non-White youths. The "vamp" categorization suggests that a woman's physical appearance, dress, or behavior drove the perpetrator to commit the rape. An example of the "vamp" victim is Patricia Bowman, who alleged that William Kennedy Smith raped her. News coverage of the court trial emphasized the defense attorneys' position that Bowman had questionable moral values and a history of sexual promiscuity. It is interesting to note that Ms. Washington's case resulted in Tyson's conviction and Ms. Bowman's case resulted in an acquittal for Smith. Framing rape stories in these two extremes not only reflects racism, classism, and sexism but also is grossly inaccurate. Such coverage ignores the fact that most rapists are of the same race and social class as their victims, usually know the victim, and have more normal psychological profiles than any other kind of criminal. Moreover, such coverage makes news media guilty of perpetuating stereotypes and false notions about who rapes and who gets raped, and it ignores the reality of rape as a crime. Coverage in the media tends to focus attention on the victims (women) rather than the criminals (men). News organizations should be looking at why rape is so persistent and prevalent in American society. Editors need to consider whether sexism is a factor in the decisions that are made about such stories. This is unlikely to happen until more women—and women of color—are in decision-making positions and can exert greater influence on how sex crimes are reported (Flanders, 1997).

Power and Positions: Diversity in the Evening News

The absence of women in prominent roles in news media is perhaps no more blatant than in the network evening news anchor positions—still an all-male bastion into 2003. When Tom Brokaw, 62-year-old NBC evening news anchor announced in 2002 that he would be retiring in 2004, Brian Williams was named as his replacement. As this is being written, apparently no women or people of color are being considered to succeed soon-to-be retiring CBS news anchor Dan Rather, 70, or ABC news anchor Peter Jennings, 63. Bonnie J. Dow, associate professor of communication at the University of Georgia and author of *Prime Time Feminism: Television, Media Culture and the Women's Movement Since 1970*, has said that the three network anchor chairs are the last all-male preserve in and of television—notwithstanding Monday Night Football.

In the early 1980s, audience researchers found that viewers—both men and women—believed that women lacked the necessary authority and reliability to fill the coveted evening anchor slots. Some network executives acknowledge that despite the gains that women have made since Barbara Walters appeared on NBC's *Today* show in 1961, many television viewers still want the evening news delivered by a patriarchal figure. Erik Sorenson, president of MSNBC, who was executive producer of the failed CBS newscast that paired Connie Chung with Dan Rather from 1993 to 1995, said in 2002 that the American public is not yet ready to embrace a woman in that role because of a perceived lack of gravitas, or credibility, in women. The breakthrough attempt at CBS in the 1990s abruptly ended when the ratings dropped and the personalities clashed. The pairing of Barbara Walters and Harry Reasoner had met a similar fate 19 years earlier.

With lead anchor posts virtually closed to them, the top female personalities in the news media—Diane Sawyer of ABC's *Good Morning America* and Katie Couric of NBC's *Today*—have moved to morning and prime time positions on such "infotainment" shows as ABC's *20/20*. Although morning programs lack the "hard news" image, these slots have ironically become more lucrative than the evening news, reaping millions of dollars more in revenue. In fact, with a $15 million a year contract, Ms. Couric was the highest paid newsperson in television in 2002.

Some network news executives, like David Westin, president of ABC News, believe that audiences do not care whether the evening news anchor position is filled by a man or a woman, as long as it's the right person for the job. In particular, he praises ABC anchor Elizabeth Vargas, a Latina, who occasionally substitutes for Peter Jennings—and when asked whether she could ever be chosen to become an evening news anchor, he said the network would never put anyone on as a substitute who was not capable of doing the job. As some researchers suggest, what is most important to audiences is that lead anchors have deep experience. However, because of past bias in the workforce, there are simply more men than women who qualify in that regard.

The shortage of women in other aspects of the news industry sadly matches that in anchoring television newscasts. Results from a study reported in 2002 by the White House Project showed that women accounted for only 11% of all guest appearances on Sunday talk shows in 2000 and 2001. The voices of women were virtually unheard on such major public policy issues of the 1990s as North American Fair Trade Agreement (NAFTA) and welfare reform—and even on issues deemed "women's affairs," such as abortion and family leave (WENews, 2002).

When the *New York Times* ran a story on a massive protest against U.S. and U.N. actions in Somalia, the accompanying picture featured a woman at the head of the demonstration. Yet, despite the protest being comprised mostly of women and children, all the sources named in the article were male. As Flanders (1997) noted, the women's faces were seen, but their voices were not heard.

POWER, PERCEPTIONS, AND PROMOTION: DEALING WITH DOUBLE JEOPARDY

Women of color who work in the American media must often confront—or overcome—the dual challenge of sexism *and* racism. Findings from a 1999 report by the International Women's Media Foundation (IWMF) summarized results from recent studies on women and minorities in the news media as follows:

❖ Minorities comprise 26% of the U.S. population but only 12% of the U.S. newsroom workforce.

❖ Minority staff averages 20% in television, 16% in radio, and only 11% at newspapers.

❖ At the management level, the number of minorities drops to 9% in print media and 8% in broadcast media.

❖ In local television news, although women constitute 37% of the
  workforce, only 14% have achieved news director status.

❖ Compared to all U.S. businesses, newspapers hire proportionally
  fewer women at the management and executive levels.

A 2002 Radio-Television News Directors Association (RTNDA) survey
found that the new millennium brought a reduction—*not an increase*—in
minority employment progress in the newsroom. The RTNDA survey
noted that the sharp decline in the percentage of minority journalists
working at radio stations started with the elimination of the FCC's Equal
Employment Opportunity regulations (The National Association of
Hispanic Journalists, 2002).

According to the 1999 IWMF report titled *Women Journalists of Color:
Present Without Power* (1999), minority women journalists have had to
face challenging odds in practicing their craft and getting their messages
heard. As far back as the mid-1800s, ethnic minority groups found a voice
through their own networks of local newspapers and newsletters with
stories about issues affecting their own communities. In the 20th century,
the doors of the mainstream media were slammed shut to people of color
until the social upheaval of the 1960s, when the need to cover civil unrest
forced newsroom managers to find reporters who could enter minority
neighborhoods without being perceived as outsiders.

The shift to greater diversity in the newsroom may also have been
prompted by the release of the Kerner Commission report in 1968, which
sought to analyze and learn from the racial turmoil that defined the civil
rights movement occurring in the 1960s. The commission, appointed by
then-president Lyndon Johnson, found that the mounting frustration
among African Americans reflected how their plight was portrayed—or
ignored—by the media. According to the Kerner Commission report,

> The media report and write from the standpoint of a white man's
> world . . . by failing to portray the Negro as a matter of routine and in the
> context of the total society, the news media have, we believe, contributed to
> the black-white schism in this country.

Over the years, the common thread among women journalists of color
is that they "succeeded in spite of . . ." obstacles, barriers, and outright
exclusion—and these hurdles are not a thing of the past. In the 1980s, an
editor asked aspiring journalist Vicki Torres how she would feel about
having to "leave [her] roots behind" as she advanced in her career. She
responded by saying that as a fourth-generation Mexican American, she
could trace her roots back to *Leave It to Beaver* episodes (International
Women's Media Foundation, 1999). Similarly, when Joaquin Estus was
hired as the first Native American reporter at a Midwestern public radio

station in 1995, her colleagues rebuked her qualifications and claimed that she had only been hired because she was a minority. In her experience, people have felt free to come up to her and complain about Native Americans with complete disregard for the fact that it might be offensive to her. All they ever talked about around her was Native American issues, and she could never get them to really see her for who she was. As a result, Estus challenged herself to work even harder to get ahead (International Women's Media Foundation, 1999).

In a 2002 presentation titled "Racial Constructions and Visual Representations of Blacks in Television News Media," former CBS and NBC television news anchor Libby Lewis explored how racialized perceptions of beauty, such as skin color or hair texture, shape the hiring practices in the television news industry. She discussed how racially constructed images continue to resonate in television news—particularly with regard to selecting in-house anchors and field reporters—and how these images both influence and undermine the broader perceptions of Black identity. As a news anchor and reporter, she found that station management would enforce hair and dress codes that would essentially mute her African American heritage. When she wore her hair naturally, she was told it was "unprofessional" and that she needed to "Anglicize" her hair. No ethnic clothing was allowed. She was astounded when a viewer actually called in to complain about her eyebrows—and that it led to a big discussion with her producer about the shape of her eyebrows. She was finally forced to go to an image consultant to avoid further critique of her hair, eyebrows, or particular choice of sweater (Lewis, 2002).

According to a 1999 IWMF study, the majority of Native American, Hispanic, African American, and Asian American women working in the media today do not feel that they have to overcome insurmountable obstacles based on gender or race. However, while there are now more women of color working in U.S. news media than ever before, the unfortunate reality is that few women journalists of color are in a position in the management hierarchy to make decisions about what becomes news. Consequently, while women may now have greater numbers in the newsroom, they have little influence over news content. They are present without power—and without the voice in the gatekeeping process that would enable them to prevent racist and sexist content from appearing in news stories.

The majority of women of color working in the media say that lingering racial stereotypes and subtle discrimination hinder their professional progress, particularly in terms of promotion opportunities. Women journalists of color often feel they must work "twice as hard" to be perceived as being "half as good" as their White male counterparts in order to get ahead in the industry. In fact, the majority surveyed by the IWMF (61%) said that they face barriers to professional advancement that their White and male colleagues do not face. For these women, it's a Catch-22: On the one hand, they often refuse to assimilate into the White male corporate culture; on the other hand, they continue to face stereotypes regarding their abilities and the perception that they merely got the job as an affirmative action hire. However, the major reason that women journalists of color may face barriers to opportunities is explained in the following rationale:

> Continued concentrations of power in white male hands on a daily basis and throughout the organization. These informal power groupings decide what the paper looks like each day, who get the key assignments, how stories are played and who gets a "hand up" in the organization. No matter how many times our newsroom is reorganized and the systems revamped, those informal power groupings seem to survive and thrive. (International Women's Media Foundation, 1999)

Other obstacles to professional advancement that are encountered by women of color include not having a mentor, the lack of role models of the same race or ethnic group, and the lack of access to high visibility assignments.

In addition, there is an enormous disparity in how managers and women journalists of color perceive cultural diversity in the newsroom and in the news product. While the vast majority (82%) of the managers surveyed by the International Women's Media Foundation said that management respects cultural differences, only 32% of the minority women journalists agreed. When asked whether the news they produce reflects the diversity of the markets they serve, 69% of the managers said that it did, while only 25% of the minority women journalists concurred.

Despite such formidable obstacles and disparities in the newsroom, some younger women journalists of color have enjoyed tremendous success in their careers in the media. For example, Jemele Hill was the first woman—and woman of color—to cover Michigan State University football and basketball for a Michigan newspaper. The 23-year-old African American reporter said that she was fully aware of the "double whammy" she posed in both the newsroom and locker room but had learned to accept those attitudes. Hill believes that being an African American woman in sports has worked to her advantage and helped her to be conscious of the responsibilities inherent in her position. Although she saw that White males were given opportunities more easily than she was, she claimed that it's all part of the game and that she didn't let it discourage her or keep her down (International Women's Media Foundation, 1999).

Creating a productive work environment in which men and women from various racial and ethnic backgrounds can perform their tasks comfortably is a challenge for any manager. Most of the newsroom managers surveyed are aware that diversity plays a critical role in the future and progress of the news media, and they said that women journalists of color make their particular contribution to the news-gathering process as follows:

- ❖ They are able to bridge communities.
- ❖ They challenge assumptions.
- ❖ They cover angles that otherwise might be overlooked.
- ❖ They talk to people who too often are overlooked.
- ❖ They remind us of cultural institutions others are unaware of.
- ❖ They understand cultural differences and their impact on daily life.

To ensure a more equitable work environment in the news media that reflects the diversity of the community they serve, mechanisms need to be developed to allow for more open dialogue between managers and women journalists of color. In addition, better training opportunities, diversity programs, and mentoring relationships need to be implemented that will not only maximize minority female journalists' potential but also prepare them for the crucial decision-making positions that will enable them to exercise their voice within the organizations that control the media.

Notes

1. For more details on the most popular African Americans in television, see "10 Most Powerful Blacks in TV," October 2000, *Ebony*, pp. 86-96.

2. For more on Jennifer Lopez, see the article about her in the December 30, 2002 issue of *People* that is the source of this information (pp. 106-107). See also the following websites: www.mtv.com/bands/az/lopez_jennifer/bio.jhtml; www.askmen.com/women/3c_jennifer_lopez.html; www.vh1.com/artists/az/lopez_jennifer/bio.jhtml; www.jlzone.com/cache/jl_html_jl_html_2_.phtml.

References

Beasley, M. H., & Gibbons, S. J. (1993). *Taking their place: A documentary history of women and journalism*. Washington, DC: American University Press in cooperation with the Women's Institute for Freedom of the Press.

Brady, J. (2002, March 17). In step with Raquel Welch. *Parade Magazine*, pp. 26-27.

Brecher, E. J. (2002, June). Elizabeth Vargas: Tuning in at the top. *Hispanic, 15*(6), 24-25.

Buchalter, G. (2002, September 22). Now, I have found real challenges. *Parade Magazine*, pp. 9,10.

Chang, H. (1984). *Asian Americans in the news.* Unpublished paper prepared for the honors colloquium at the University of California, Berkeley.

Coffey, S. (2002). *Best practices: The art of leadership in news organizations.* Arlington, VA: The Freedom Forum.

Fall TV Preview. (2002, September 13). *Entertainment Weekly,* pp. 29-108.

Fiset, B. (1979, May 2). East meets West. *The Oakland Tribune,* p. 68.

Flanders, L. (1997). *Real majority, media minority: The cost of sidelining women in reporting.* Monroe, ME: Common Courage.

International Women's Media Foundation. (1999, September). *Women journalists of color: Present without power* (Report).Washington, DC: Author.

Jensen, E. (2002, June 24). CNN's new star format put to the test. *Los Angeles Times,* pp. F1, F12.

Jovita Idar: 1885-1946. Por La Raza y para La Raza. (2000, February 27). *La Voz de Aztlan, 1*(5). Retrieved from http://aztlan.net

Kerner Commission (1968). *Report of the National Advisory Commission on Civil Disorders.* New York: Bantam.

La Ferla, R. (2001, April 15). Latino style is cool. Oh, all right: It's hot. *The New York Times on the Web.* Retrieved from http://premium.news.yahoo.com

Lewis, L. (2002, March 2). *Racial constructions & visual representations of Blacks in television news media.* Paper presented at the annual Empowering Women of Color Conference, Berkeley, CA.

Marlane, J. (1999). *Women in television news revisited: Into the twenty-first century.* Austin: University of Texas Press.

The National Association of Hispanic Journalists. (2002, July 30). Retrieved from http://www.nahj.org

Navarro, M. (2002, May 16). Trying to get beyond the role of the maid: Hispanic actors are seen as underrepresented, with the exception of one part. *The New York Times on the Web.* Retrieved from http://premium.news.yahoo.com

Pakistan Investigating Rape Ordered by Tribal Council. (2002, July 4). *Los Angeles Times,* p. A4.

10 Most Powerful Blacks in TV. (2000, October). *Ebony,* pp. 86-96.

UCLA Center for African American Studies. (2002a, June). *The CAAS Research Report,* Vol. 1, No. 1. Los Angeles: Author.

UCLA Center for African American Studies. (2002b, June). *The CAAS Research Report,* Vol. 2, No. 1. Los Angeles: Author.

Vargas, L. (2002, September). Genderizing Latino news: An analysis of a local newspaper's coverage of Latino current affairs. *Critical Studies in Mass Communication, 17*(3), 261-293.

Welkos, R. W., & King, S. (2002). Beautiful historic night. *Los Angeles Times,* pp. A1, A14.

Part V

Strategies for Dealing With Racially Insensitive Media

Access 9

Toward Diversity With (Un)Deliberate Speed

There is an old adage that says that "beauty is in the eye of the beholder." As an observation on American popular media, it is equally appropriate to say that stereotypical, distorted images of non-Whites are the visions of others. Data on employment in the media clearly reveal that non-Whites have little influence in determining how they are represented. The images in the media that result from this are therefore fashioned by White creators and decision makers and represent their perspective on people of color.

People of color have been very aware, of course, of discriminatory hiring practices in media professions and industries for generations. However, very little official attention was focused on the employment of people of color in media prior to the civil rights movement in the 1960s. By the late 1960s, U.S. governmental agencies had been formed to address the question of fair employment practices in American business and labor. Among those agencies were the Equal Employment Opportunity Commission (EEOC) and the U.S. Commission on Civil Rights. In 1968, as a result of the Kerner Commission's strong indictment of mass media culpability in perpetuating racial discrimination, the EEOC, the Civil Rights Commission, and the Federal Communications Commission (FCC) turned their attention to aspects of hiring practices in the media. At the same time, the Kerner report stimulated some news media professional associations to assess their hiring records. These efforts can be summarized by looking at racial employment patterns in two major categories of media—entertainment and news.

Discrimination in the Film and Television Entertainment Industries

In Chapters 3 and 4, we discussed the portrayals of various races in Hollywood movies and television and in the roles the actors played. Here we discover the nature of the participation of people of color in behind-the-scenes stage crafts and in production management roles. In 1969, the EEOC held hearings in Los Angeles on minority employment in the film industry. The commission found that Hollywood's non-White employment rates were well below the average for other industries, which themselves had poor hiring records. Furthermore, the film industry data revealed discriminatory hiring practices in nearly every occupational category, whether it was white collar or blue collar.

The EEOC concluded that

> The motion picture industry reports approximately 19,000 employees, 13,000 of whom are white collar workers. But it is not the raw numbers of people employed that is significant, it is the fact that the industry plays a critical role in influencing public opinion and creating this country's image of itself. In order to portray accurately the nation's minority groups, the industry must employ minority personnel at all levels. . . . The Equal Employment Opportunity Commission's analysis indicates that this is not happening. (U.S. Equal Employment Opportunity Commission, 1969, p. 352)

At that time, a studio official who testified before the commission said that of 81 management level personnel only 3 were people of color—2 were Latino, the single Black manager headed the janitorial department, and there were no Asian or Native American managers. The studio executive also testified that his organization employed 184 workers classified as technicians. Of those workers, only 5 were non-Whites—3 were Latinos, 1 was Black, and 1 was Asian. Generally, in the late 1960s the non-White employment percentage in other industries in the Los Angeles metropolitan statistical area was twice that of the movie industry. People of color comprised approximately 40% of the Los Angeles metropolitan area population, but they made up only 3% of the movie industry labor force.

In 1977, the U.S. Commission on Civil Rights conducted its investigation of the television entertainment industry and also convened a hearing in Los Angeles. Among those called to testify were officials of the various unions representing producers, directors, and writers, as well as non-White craftsmen in the several theatrical trades. One witness, a member of the Cherokee nation, testified about how a trade union "lost" the job application of a highly skilled Native American worker. When a union official was confronted about the incident, he replied, "No one tells us who we have to hire or anything of that matter. We decide that" (U.S. Commission on Civil Rights, 1977). Other testimony revealed a union scheme to systematically phase out Blacks who attained union membership by seeking their suspension without due process hearings. In addition, experienced union members of color were overlooked for job promotion while young Whites, who were sons of union journeymen, obtained superior status directly out of high school and without job experience. These examples of systematic discrimination and nepotism in the television industry were not countermanded by either network executives or union officials. The civil rights commission noted that the television entertainment industry had not assumed equal employment opportunity responsibilities in hiring practices.

Data were compiled over a 3 year period (from 1974 to 1976) on union rosters representing the workers who produced the movies, situation comedies, and variety programs televised to millions of American viewers. Crafts represented in the trade union data included make-up artists, projectionists, prop workers, set designers, script supervisors, story analysts, and camera operators, among others. Even though 8 years had elapsed since the EEOC had investigated the movie industry, the television trade union data presented at the 1977 hearing showed an average of only 8% non-White employment for the period. Not even one person of color obtained work during the 3 years either as a script supervisor or as a story analyst, according to data supplied to the U.S. Commission on Civil Rights. Although attacks on the concept of affirmative action had barely begun, only 50% of non-Whites who applied for union rosters achieved their goal, as compared with 62% of White applicants during the same period.

In August of 1977, the civil rights commission published its findings on racial and female employment in television (U.S. Commission on Civil Rights, 1977b). For historical perspective, it must be noted that in 1969 the FCC had adopted equal employment opportunity guidelines prohibiting job discrimination by broadcast licensees. The implied penalty was loss of license. It was during this period that the term "two-fer" became part of the lexicon of American broadcasting. A "two-fer" was any woman employed in broadcasting who happened to also be non-White. Broadcast executives were able to list such women in their hiring statistics twice, once under the gender category and again under the ethnic category—a "two-for-one" employee. The tabulated result padded the actual affirmative action employment total. The use of "two-fers" and other manipulative measures created some unusual employment data reported by American broadcasters. In an attempt to make the hiring and placement of people of color in upper level job categories seem more equitable, the industry reported an astonishing 45% increase in ethnic managers between 1971 and 1975. At the same time, however, the proportion of all employees in those job categories increased by only 13%. A close look at the broadcasters' figures also revealed a dramatic decline in the number of clerical and service jobs listed. These data prompted a public interest group to ask, "Do more executives need fewer clerks to serve them? Do larger staffs need less janitorial service?" (Jennings & Jefferson, 1975, p. 11). It was obvious that broadcasters had merely reclassified their non-White employees into upper job categories while keeping them on the same old jobs with the same low salaries. Most of these "managers," particularly in television, held jobs with such titles as Community Relations Director or Manager of Community Affairs. Almost without exception, even those people (who were far removed from day-to-day programming decisions) reported to a White male department head.

Among the significant conclusions drawn in 1977 by the U.S. Commission on Civil Rights regarding the employment of non-Whites in television were the following:

❖ There was an underlying assumption by television executives that realistic representation of non-Whites would diminish the medium's ability to attract the largest possible audience.

❖ Broadcasters misrepresented to the FCC the actual employment status of non-Whites and women via reports on FCC Form 395.

❖ People of color were not fully used at all levels of station management or at all levels of local station operations.

❖ White males held the overwhelming majority of decision-making positions.

❖ Non-Whites held subsidiary positions.

❖ Increased multicultural visibility as on-air talent belied lack of representation in managerial and other jobs off camera; in other words, people of color were merely "window dressing."

Employment conditions changed little in the 1980s. FCC statistics released in 1982 showed that non-Whites held about 17% of all jobs in broadcast television and about 14% of jobs in cable TV. Although the FCC reported the number of non-White "officials and managers" to be 9%, that number included lower ranking positions, such as promotion directors and research directors, which were most frequently held by people of color (Alperowitz, 1983). However, those figures also included the small and slowly growing number of TV stations owned by people of color and that had largely non-White management staffs.

Another round of hearings descended on Hollywood and the television industry on June 1, 1983 when the House Subcommittee on Telecommunications, Consumer Protection and Finance heard from a group of Black actors led by Sidney Poitier. Poitier, the first Black to win an Oscar for best actor, urged the committee to instigate a full-scale investigation of the "flagrant unfairness in the hiring practices of producers, the studios and the networks." Poitier's words seemed to echo the testimony of other witnesses who had appeared nearly 15 years earlier before another federal committee. But, by the 1990s, EEOC employment data revealed that people of color had made significant strides in terms of share in the industry workforce. In 1969, non-Whites comprised only 3% of the motion picture

Table 9.1   Non-White Employment in the Motion Picture Labor Force in 2000

	Percentage of Total	Percentage Officials/ Managers	Percentage of White Collar	Percentage of Blue Collar
Blacks	6.6%	1.5%	4.4%	0.7%
Latinos	10.9%	2.0%	6.0%	2.8%
Asians	9.3%	2.3%	6.4%	0.6%
Native Americans	0.5%	0.1%	0.2%	0.1%
Totals	27.3%	5.9%	17.0%	4.2%

Source: U.S. Equal Employment Opportunity Commission.

industry labor force, but by 1991 they were more than 24% of the industry labor force. Over the next decade, people of color experienced only a very modest increase to 27% of the industry workforce, according to EEOC data collected in the Hollywood region (Los Angeles-Long Beach, California statistical area) (see Table 9.1). It should be noted, however, that non-Whites comprised more than half of the resident population in the area. In a reflection of general demographic trends, Blacks had the largest "minority" share of industry jobs in 1991 at 11%, but by 2000 their percentage had been surpassed by the percentages of both Latinos and Asian Pacific Americans in the industry. Significantly, during the same time period the total percentage of persons of color holding jobs in the white collar category of "officials and managers" dropped from 11% to under 6%. A 1998 report by the Writer's Guild noted that approximately 75% of those writing for television and feature films were White males. And the Screen Actors Guild reported that movie and television roles for actors of color in 2001 declined 9.3% from the previous year ("Roles for Minority Actors Declined," 2002). These employment data perhaps suggest why the quantity and quality of racial portrayals in the film industry have stagnated in the early 21st century. Economic motives, rather than social concerns, dictate television and film content and messages.

The Racial Composition of the News Media Workforce

The increase in employment opportunities for people of color in professional journalism progressed at less than half the pace of the motion picture entertainment industry over most of the last 30 years of the 20th century. A 1992 study of journalists working for all forms of news organizations (daily and weekly newspapers, news services, magazines, and radio and television stations) found that non-Whites comprised only 8.2% of the journalistic workforce (Weaver & Wilhoit, 1992). The daily newspaper industry began to assess the racial composition of its labor force in the early 1970s, and it began an annual survey of newsroom racial inclusion in 1978. The American Society of Newspaper Editors (ASNE) reported that only 1.6% of daily newspaper professionals were members of underrepresented racial groups in 1972.

Interestingly, in the same year a Radio and Television News Directors Association (RTNDA) survey found that non-Whites held 14% of commercial television news jobs and 10% of those in radio news, figures that remained basically constant until the late 1980s. In 1988, RTNDA research revealed that television news hiring of non-Whites had increased to 16% but radio hiring of non-Whites had slipped to only 8%. By 1992, the percentage of non-Whites in the television news workforce had grown to 18.5% and radio had reversed its decline, with 11% of its workforce being non-White.

The broadcasting industry initially moved much more quickly on the issue of multicultural hiring in news because radio and television frequencies are licensed by a governmental agency, the Federal Communications Commission. Newspapers, on the other hand, are unregulated private enterprises that must be motivated by conscience, economics, or social pressure to improve their employment practices.

Although the movement toward increased hiring of non-Whites in broadcast journalism lost momentum within 5 years after it began, the industry saw no such decline in its drive for gender equality. The increase in the hiring of women and their advancement to decision-making ranks has far outstripped that of people of color. For example, in 1972 only 4% of the nation's radio news directors were women, but by 1982 the figure had risen to 18% and by 1992 it was 29%. (However, the total had dropped to 22% by 2001.) In contrast, people of color comprised only 4% of radio news directors in 1982 and 8% in 1992 (and remained at 8% in 2001). In 1972, only 57% of the nation's television stations had at least one woman on the news staff, but by 1982 virtually every station (97%) had at least one female journalist and that percentage held constant to 2001. By comparison, non-Whites were in 60% of all TV newsrooms in 1972, but the figure had grown to only 72% by 1982 and 87.5% by 1992. In 2001, the percentage had dropped to 86%.

Daily newspapers lag behind radio and television news organizations in increasing the racial diversity of their workforce. By 1983, non-Whites represented only 5.6% of the journalists working for the nearly 1,750 daily newspapers in the nation. The newspaper industry experienced a 4-year decline in its multicultural employment growth rate from 1979 to 1983, according to the American Society of Newspaper Editors. Economic

Table 9.2   Non-White Employment Rate in Daily Newspapers at 5-Year Intervals From 1978 to 2001

Year	Percentage Non-White	Percentage Increase
1978	4.0%	—
1983	5.6%	1.6%
1988	7.0%	1.4%
1993	9.8%	2.8%
1998	11.5%	1.7%
2001*	11.6%	0.1%

Source: Based on research data compiled by the American Society of Newspaper Editors. As of this writing, this was the most recent available data.

reversals decreased the number of daily newspapers to about 1,550 in 1993 and multiracial hiring did not reach 10% until that year (see Table 9.2). Yet, 1993 was also a year when over half (51%) of all U.S. daily newspapers—mostly smaller circulation publications—still had no journalists of color on their staffs. In 1998, ASNE revised the goal it had established in 1978—that the racial composition of America's newsrooms would reach parity with the nation's population demographics by 2000. A new goal was aimed at newsrooms reflecting the nation's racial composition "by or before 2025." In 2001, with a total of 1,446 daily newspapers being published in the United States, non-Whites still comprised only 11.6% of the journalistic workforce, about the same as in 1998. Meanwhile, the non-White population had grown to about one third of the U.S. population.

A comparison of the numbers of non-White journalists employed in newspapers and English-language television (see Table 9.3) reveals television as the leader. For perspective, it is important to note that 2000 U.S. Census Bureau data showed that people of color comprised about 30% of the nation's population and that the number was growing. None of the news media have achieved racial parity with the U.S. population of color. Table 9.3 shows that in 1992 Black journalists found employment in news media in greater numbers than did Latino, Asian, or Native American journalists. The numerical rank order of the four ethnic groups has been constant since such records have been kept. Latinos, the second largest non-White group employed in the news media, have narrowed the employment gap between them and Blacks, but the gains made by Asians have been proportionally minimal. Native Americans have traditionally been the least represented—and are the least populous in the United States—of the four groups and their employment percentage (about half of 1%) remained virtually unchanged across all media in the two decades between 1982 and 2002.

Table 9.3   Non-White Newsroom Employment in White-Owned Daily Newspapers and English-Language Television Stations in 2001

	Percentage Blacks	Percentage Latinos	Percentage Asians	Percentage Native Americans	Total Percentage
Newspapers	5.2%	3.6%	2.3%	0.4%	11.6%
Television	10.2%	6.7%	4.2%	0.6%	21.8%

Source: Based on research compiled by the American Society of Newspaper Editors and the Ball State University/Radio-Television News Directors Association Foundation survey.

Non-Whites are still scarce in news department decision-making positions. In 2001, the American Society of Newspaper Editors reported that 9% of daily newspaper supervisors were people of color (up from 7% in 1992) and that 19% of all non-White newspaper employees were in supervisory positions (American Society of Newspaper Editors, 2003). Meanwhile, the 2001 Radio-Television News Directors Association/Ball State University survey found that 8% of the nation's TV news directors were people of color in an industry with a total of 21.8% non-White employment ("Up From the Ranks," 2001, p. 35).

The Recruitment and Retention of People of Color

Since the news professions are well aware of the shortage of non-White employees in their industry, the issue of their efforts to recruit and retain a more racially diverse work force deserves attention. There is little mystery concerning the reason daily newspapers have been slow to embrace racial diversity. Some editors have been openly hostile to the idea of hiring non-White staff members. Among the reasons for this hostility cited by editors who responded to the American Society of Newspaper Editors surveys was that they believed hiring people of color would lower the standards of their newspaper. The editor of one of the largest Midwestern daily newspapers said, "Generally, hiring minorities means reducing standards temporarily. Except for one reporter and one news editor, every minority person we've hired in 10 years was less qualified than a concurrently available White" (American Society of Newspaper Editors, 1982, p. 34). The discussion about qualifications of people of color to perform as journalists has been a sensitive one on a number of fronts. Even the 1968 Kerner Commission report noted that officials in the news media complained that too few "qualified" minorities were available for hire. The implications raised the ire of some who observed that people of color have found success in fields ranging from medicine to engineering to law and the arts, but somehow are not "qualified" to be writers, reporters, and editors in the news media. On that issue, one White newspaper editor agreed. He said, "The business isn't magic. Mostly, it's trial-and-error training. If the word skills are adequate, any minority can be trained to do any newsroom task that any non-minority can do" (American society of Newspaper Editors, 1982, p. 35). In 1982, the *Columbia Journalism Review* reported that an angry exchange on the issue took place during a press coverage forum in New York. In a confrontation reminiscent of Breed's study of newsroom policy (see Chapter 5 in this volume), WNBC-TV news correspondent Gabe Pressman responded to the charge of professional racism by invoking the importance of traditional standards of quality in reporting. J. J. Gonzalez, then a reporter for WCBS-TV, rose from the audience to proclaim, "Who passes . . . judgment on competency? Come on, now! Don't tell me 'competency.' . . . When you get the competent person in, he[or she] is not allowed [to do the job.] So stop your bull!" (Massing, 1982, p. 38).

By the early 2000s, however, the debate over the notion that non-Whites were less qualified than Whites as journalists had subsided somewhat in view of the overwhelming evidence of their success nationwide. The emphasis turned instead to whether newsroom and other efforts of the media in the direction of multiracial inclusiveness were "politically correct" in a time when the terms *quota* and *affirmative action* were deemed passé. R.D. Volkman, publisher of the North Sioux City Times in South Dakota, wrote in a trade journal that

> We do not hire minorities merely to achieve a racial mix in our office. We tend not to hire any American-born and schooled minorities . . . we actually practice "red lining" against graduates of certain colleges . . . we advise our newspaper brethren to do as we do, and to even divest themselves of overly [politically correct] staff members. ("Don't Hire Minorities Merely for Diversity," 2001)

The publisher concluded that "America . . . is tired of affirmative action" and that hiring minorities "is dangerous for newspapers who plan for a long future" ("Don't Hire Minorities Merely for Diversity," 2001).

An incident reported in the RTNDA newsletter in 2001 highlights another aspect of the problem—racial insensitivity among newspaper editors. The article described an entertainment event at the ASNE convention in Washington.

> On stage was a white man donning a black wig and Coke-bottle glasses, gesturing wildly and shouting "ching, ching, chong, chong" in a satirical commentary on Chinese-American relations in the aftermath of the U.S. spy plane incident. The audience of mostly white newspaper editors howled

> . . . the issue wasn't simply that white people were using negative stereotypes in an attempt to be funny . . . [but] that hundreds of newspaper editors . . . were hysterical with laughter as the skit went on. By all reports, no one stood up to protest, no one from ASNE ever apologized for the insensitivity of the mostly white editors. (Papper & Gerhard, 2001)

A student intern who witnessed the incident asked on ASNE's website, "Did they think the Chinese American community would have found that skit amusing? Would they have laughed at a white man in blackface if the crisis concerned an African country?" (Papper & Gerhard, 2001).

In the broadcasting and newspaper industries, the gains that have been made must also be considered in view of the sagging U.S. economic fortunes of the early 1990s that forced staff layoffs and resulted in the closing of many newspapers and network television news bureaus. ASNE reported that newspapers hired about one third fewer entry-level journalists in 1992 than in 1991. Thus, new hires of non-Whites during that period reflected more significant ratios of entrance into journalism when compared to that of Whites. Of course, more prosperous times prevailed during the late 1990s and early 2000s. In 1998, the Radio-Television News Directors Association adopted cultural diversity as one of its "core values" by proclaiming one of its purposes is "to diversify the nation's newsrooms and improve the quality of electronic journalism through meaningful coverage of communities and through the advancement of minority journalists to key decision-making and top management positions."

Whereas the industry rationale for the dearth of non-Whites in the workforce had been "we can't find any who are qualified," the issue into the 21st century appears to be "we can't keep the qualified non-Whites we hire." The titles of the following studies and reports issued since 1990 are instructive: *Why Asian-American Journalists Leave Journalism and Why They Stay* (Asian American Journalists Association, 1990); *Employee Departure Patterns in the Newspaper Industry* (Task Force on Minorities in the Newspaper Business, 1991); and *The Newsroom Barometer: Job Satisfaction and the Impact of Racial Diversity at U.S. Daily Newspapers* (Pease & Smith, 1991). In addition, a 1992 study, *The American Journalists in the 1990s*, by Indiana University professors David Weaver and G. Cleveland Wilhoit, revealed that "a serious problem of retention may be just over the horizon," in that "more than 20% of those [journalists] surveyed said they plan to leave the field in five years, double the figure of 1982–83" (Weaver & Wilhoit, 1992). One of the major reasons that the percentage of non-White newspaper journalists has stalled since the 1970s is because of their departure rate from the profession. Weaver and Wilhoit proved prophetic when the ASNE survey found that although newspapers hired 600 entry-level non-White journalists in 2001, 698 left the profession that year. The study by Pease and Smith reveals the reasons underlying the exodus of people of color from newspaper staffs.

Illustration 9.1   The ABC television station in Los Angeles advertised its support for racial and gender diversity by displaying photographs of its on-air news staff in 2000.

The Los Angeles Times - Saluting Diversity and CCNMA

People Make the Difference

Superb. Excellent. Solid. These are just a few of the adjectives supervisors have used to describe CCNMA member Steve Padilla on his rise through the ranks at the Los Angeles Times. From his start as a night police reporter through a variety of beats to his current position as City Editor of The Times' award-winning Valley Edition, Steve is just one of many staff members who prove every day that diversity and excellence go hand-in-hand at the Los Angeles Times.

Los Angeles Times

A Times Mirror Newspaper

Illustration 9.2   This advertisement was produced in 1997 by the *Los Angeles Times* to highlight its promotion of Latino reporter Steve Padilla to City Editor of a suburban edition of the newspaper.

❖ A majority (71%) of non-White journalists said that their papers cover issues of concern to their racial constituency marginally or poorly; 50% of white journalists agreed.

❖ Journalists of color (63%) were twice as likely as their White colleagues (31%) to believe that race plays a role in newsroom assignments, promotions and advancement.

❖ According to 72% of non-Whites and 35% of Whites, newsroom managers and supervisors doubt the ability of journalists of color to perform their jobs adequately.

Pease and Smith (1991) concluded, "These results paint a picture of newsrooms in which journalists of color feel themselves besieged because of their race. It's a picture few whites are aware of."

The issue of retention of non-White journalists is not new, nor is it confined to newspapers. Randy Daniels, a Black journalist, left his job as a CBS correspondent in the 1980s after nearly 10 years because he saw no career advancement opportunities in the network.

> I met with every level of management at CBS News . . . over issues that specifically relate to Blacks and other minorities. . . . When it became clear to me that such meetings accomplished nothing, I chose to leave and work where my ideas were wanted and needed. . . . I have found my race an impediment to being assigned major stories across the entire spectrum of news. (Massing, 1982, p. 39)

Some 20 years later, in 2002, David Honig, executive director of the Minority Media and Telecommunications Council, reported that of 837 job listings posted on the websites of broadcasters from 35 states, 348 (42%) did not contain equal employment opportunity notices. The omission signals a failure to maintain even the pretense that broadcasting employers are committed to fair employment policies.

Another major factor in the quest to improve racial diversity in news media is the preparation and training of future journalists of color. The nation's secondary schools, colleges, and universities share that responsibility. Educational institutions were asked by the Kerner Commission to develop training programs as early as the high school level, with efforts to be "intensified at colleges." However, there have been obstacles facing educators. For example, the small number of non-White students enrolled in journalism education programs partly reflects the historical discrimination against them in the news professions. As noted elsewhere in this book, the often negative and sporadic coverage of non-White racial groups in American media has led to a lack of credibility and distrust of the media. The result has been lessened interest in the field among college-bound high school students of color when compared to that of their White counterparts.

In 1992, non-White students comprised about 14% of the staffs of accredited college and university campus media, excluding those at historically Black institutions and the University of Hawaii, where the student body is predominantly Asian (Kent State University School of Journalism and Mass Communication, 1993). This exceeded the percentage of non-Whites on professional newspaper staffs that year and remained larger than the figure attained by the industry a decade later. A survey released in 2000 projected that about 23% of undergraduate students enrolled in journalism and mass communications programs nationally were non-White. They were categorized as 10.4% Black, 6.6% Latino, 2.8% Asian, and 1.3% Native Amer can (Becker, Kosicki, Lowrey, Prine, & Punathambekar, 2000).

In 1978, the major academic journalism organization, the Association for Education in Journalism, which is now the Association for Education in Journalism and Mass Communication (AEJMC), adopted their Resolution on Minorities. Eight years earlier, the association had created a Minorities and Communication division with a multiracial membership base, but by the time the resolution was adopted the division's membership was almost entirely comprised of academicians of color. In the 1990s, attendance at convention meetings of the Minorities and Communication (MAC) division began to reflect a broader racial spectrum and, in 1991, AEJMC established a Commission on the Status of Minorities. In 1998, only 11.4% of the AEJMC membership was reported to be people of color (Riffe, Salomone, & Stempel, 1998). The efforts of the MAC division have focused on improving the racial and cultural diversity of the journalism and mass communications curriculum and encouraging research by and about people of color and their relationship to media.

The organization charged with setting standards and certifying college journalism education programs is the Accrediting Council on Education in Journalism and Mass Communications (ACEJMC). ACEJMC uses several criteria—called standards—to measure the quality of a program. The most controversial of the criteria has been the one that addresses issues of racial and cultural diversity. It requires accredited academic journalism units to develop and follow a plan for ensuring racial and gender inclusiveness. In 2002, there were 105 journalism programs accredited by ACEJMC. Over the years, the diversity standard has sparked controversy because many units have received accreditation despite not "being in compliance" with the criteria for hiring non-White faculty, enrolling students of color, and/or including multicultural issues in various courses in the curriculum.

Since the late 1960s, there have been a number of training programs established by media organizations and professional groups to augment the journalism education establishment. Several of them owe their impetus to the 1968 Kerner Commission report. Perhaps most well known was the Summer Program for Minority Journalists. The program's history paralleled the interest level and commitment afforded the issue of multiracial inclusiveness by major media corporations and other interested parties. In the wake of the Kerner Commission report, the Ford Foundation supported creation of a training program at Columbia University that was known briefly as the Michelle Clark Program for Minority Journalists. The project trained and placed 70 journalists of color in print and broadcast news jobs from 1968 to 1974. By the time it lost its funding support in 1974, the program had been responsible for 20% of all journalists of color employed in daily newspapers nationally. Although the program was effective, the loss of financial support reflected the short-term commitment of the nation to the cause of integration in its news media. Fortunately, with seed money from the Gannett Foundation (now The Freedom Forum) the program was revived in Berkeley, California, as a newspaper-only training project under the auspices of the Institute for Journalism Education (IJE). A dedicated interracial group of professionals formed IJE to continue the struggle for racial parity in journalism. In 1978, IJE began a similar program at the University of Arizona that also had professionals as instructors training minority editors. In 1993, IJE was re-named The Robert Maynard Institute for Journalism Education in memory of one of its founders, a Black journalist, editor, and publisher who had died earlier that year.

Acting on the belief that the issue of non-White employment is one of "supply and demand," a few newspaper organizations have instituted and maintained in-house training programs for aspiring journalists of color—to buttress what they consider to be an inadequate pool of job candidates. However, researchers at the University of Georgia contend that an analysis of data collected in 2001 refutes the notion that qualified non-White college journalism graduates are in short supply: "The inescapable conclusion from data we have gathered is that large numbers of minorities graduate from journalism programs, large numbers seek media jobs, and large numbers have the basic skills needed for media jobs" (Becker, Daniels, Huh, & Vlad, 2002). Moreover, they noted that had U.S. daily newspapers hired all the college minority graduates who sought jobs with them in 2001, the industry would have added more than 2,500 journalists of color to their staffs. The result would have raised the ASNE reported percentage of such journalists in the industry by about 3%. Thus, the researchers concluded, "The problem isn't supply. . . . The problem is that there is not a suitable link between supply and demand" (Becker et al., 2002).

21st-Century Discrimination

In summary, the hiring records of the motion picture and television entertainment industries in hiring non-Whites was found to be unacceptable by federal agencies that conducted investigations from the late 1960s through the mid-1980s. But by the 1990s, the number of non-White employees in those industries had increased substantially to nearly

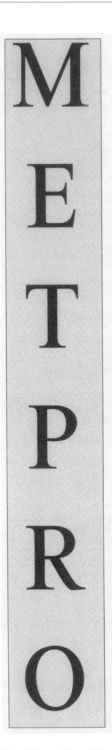

We Train Talent

For a dozen years Times Mirror has offered customized training to some of the nation's most talented entry-level minority journalists, like the 1994-95 class pictured above.

The result? More than 150 METPRO graduates -- including foreign and national correspondents, metro reporters, assignment editors, copy chiefs and news editors -- are working today, most of them at Times Mirror papers.

METPRO programs combine classroom and on-the-job experience in an intensive, individualized course of instruction. For more information, stop by the METPRO booth at the job fair.

METPRO/Reporting	METPRO/Editing	METPRO.biz
Director	Director	Director
Los Angeles Times	Newsday	Times Mirror
Times Mirror Square	235 Pinelawm Road	Times Mirror Square
Los Angeles, CA	Melville, NY	Los Angeles, CA
90053	11747	90053
(800) LA TIMES,	(800) NEWSDAY,	(800) LA TIMES,
ext. 74487	ext. 2637	ext. 73761

Times Mirror
Newspapers

Illustration 9.3   Times Mirror Newspapers was among several media companies that created "in house" training programs for journalists of color.

approximate their percentage in the general population. Broadcasters, particularly in television, were the first to react to federal pressures because of the licensing power of the FCC. But, although their hiring rate initially exceeded those of companion media industries, broadcasters were caught cheating in reporting racial hiring statistics. One example of this is the ploy of counting non-White female employees (so-called two-fers) twice in an effort to pad hiring figures. Generally, broadcast industry hiring of journalists of color took a back seat to the hiring of women in the late 1970s and 1980s. As the hiring of non-Whites slowed, White women made rapid progress in assuming positions in both management and other job categories. In television, people of color were found primarily in visible "on-air" positions, but they were not generally found in decision-making management jobs. Perhaps the most significant indicator of the broadcast news industry's true commitment to cultural diversity is that when legal challenges eliminated FCC equal employment guidelines, the industry's hiring of non-Whites declined dramatically. Juan Gonzalez, president of the National Association of Hispanic Journalists, noted that in 2001 Latino employment in the industry declined by more than 20% from the previous year. Gonzalez, a columnist for the New York *Daily News*, said, "It's deeply troubling to see this kind of backsliding after years of talk from industry leaders about the importance of diversity and the changing face of America." (National Association of Hispanic Journalists, 2002).

Despite television news's disproportionate employment statistics and the protestations of equal rights proponents, some critics believe people of color have gained an unfair advantage in obtaining newsroom jobs. Among them is former Philadelphia television news anchor Rich Noonan, who claimed in 2002 that his contract with the local Fox News station was not renewed because he is White (Bykofsky, 2002). He filed a formal complaint with the Pennsylvania Human Relations Commission seeking more than $300,000 in compensatory and punitive damages. Noonan had been a member of the 10 p.m. news team comprised of three White males and one White female. When his contract expired, Noonan was replaced by a Black male, resulting in a news team with only one non-White anchor. Although people of color comprise a significant percentage of Philadelphia's population, Noonan believed Fox News practiced racial discrimination by not renewing his contract and maintaining an all-White news anchor team. He offered no challenge to his successor's professional qualifications as a television news anchor.

Meanwhile, the nation's daily newspapers have been the most grudging employers of people of color and maintained the lowest non-White employment rate of any media industry segment. In 1970, less than 1% of newspaper journalists were non-Whites and, in 1985, non-Whites in the industry were still short of 6% of journalists and losing ground. What is perhaps indicative of why daily newspapers have lagged in this regard is the attitude expressed openly by some editors that they have neither the desire nor the responsibility to integrate the profession.

In the early 2000s, the collegiate journalism education establishment, some media organizations, well-intentioned individual practitioners, and others interested in accurate news content still want more people of color to enter the profession. But employers are not aggressively tapping the existing talent pool. The slow rate of integration in news media—with little penetration into power management levels—is a precursor to non-White attrition in the workforce. Disillusioned journalists of color are leaving the profession, citing the lack of diverse perspectives in news coverage and charging their superiors with a lack of respect for their skills. Predictably, the result is media that continue to distort the reality of a multiracial United States.

References

Alperowitz, C. (1983). *Fighting TV stereotypes: An ACT handbook.* Newtonville, MA: Action for Children's Television.

American Society of Newspaper Editors. (1982, May). *Minorities and newspapers: A report by the Committee on Minorities.* Reston, VA: Author.

American Society of Newspaper Editors. (2003, April 3). *2001 ASNE census finds newsrooms less diverse: increased hiring of minorities blunted by departure rate.* American Society of Newspaper Editors Newsroom Employment Census. Reston, VA: Author.

Becker, L., Daniels, G., Huh, J., & Vlad, T. (2002, September 12). *Diversity in hiring: Supply is there. Is demand?* Athens: University of Georgia, James M. Cox, Jr. Center for International Mass Communication Training and Research.

Becker, L., Kosicki, G., Lowrey, W., Prine, J., & Punathambekar, A. (2000).Undergrad enrollments level off, graduate education declines. *Journalism and Mass Communication Educator, 55*(3), 68-80.

Bykofsky, S. (2002, August 28). Noonan: Fox didn't want "lily white" cast. *Philadelphia Daily News,* p. A3.

Don't hire minorities merely for diversity, political correctness. (2001, September). *Publishers Auxiliary* (National Newspaper Association newsletter).

Jennings & Jefferson (1975, December). *Television station employment practices: The status of minorities and women, 1974.* New York: United Church of Christ, Office of Communications.

Kent State University School of Journalism and Mass Communication (1993). *Third census of minorities in college media.* Kent, OH: Author.

Kerner Commission (1968). *Report of the National Advisory Commission on Civil Disorders.* New York: Bantam.

Massing, M. (1982, November/December). Blackout in television. *Columbia Journalism Review,* 38.

National Association of Hispanic Journalists. (2002, July 17). Press release. Washington, DC: Author.

Papper, B., & Gerhard, M. (2001, July-August). Up from the ranks: Grooming Women and Minorities for Management. *RTNDA Communicator*, p. 1

Pease, T., & Smith, J. F. (1991). *The newsroom barometer: Job satisfaction and the impact of racial diversity at U.S. daily newspapers.* Athens: Ohio University.

Radio-Television News Directors Association. (1998). Retrieved from www.rtnda.org/diversity

Riffe, D., Salomone, K., & Stempel, G. (1998).Characteristics, responsibilities and concerns of teaching faculty: A survey of AEJMC members. *Journalism and Mass Communication Educator, 53*, 102-119.

Roles for minority actors declined in 2001.(2002, July 1). Retrieved from http://www.diversityinc.com/

Up from the ranks. (2001, July/August). Women and Minority Survey. *RTNDA Communicator*, p. 34.

U.S. Commission on Civil Rights. (1977a, March 16). Hearing before the United States Commission on Civil Rights, Los Angeles.

U.S. Commission on Civil Rights. (1977b, August). *Window dressing on the set: Women and minorities in television* (Report). Washington, DC: Author.

U.S. Equal Employment Opportunity Commission. (1969, March 12-14). Hearings before the Equal Employment Opportunity Commission on utilization of minority and women workers in certain major industries, Los Angeles.

Weaver, D., & Wilhoit, G. C. (1992, November). *The American journalist in the 1990s.* Arlington, VA: The Freedom Forum.

Advocacy 10

Pressuring the Media to Change

The year was 1827 and the words that follow appeared in the first issue of *Freedom's Journal*, the first newspaper published by Black Americans.

> We wish to plead our own cause.... Too long has the publick been deceived by misrepresentations, in things which concern us dearly.... From the press and the pulpit we have suffered much by being incorrectly represented. ("To Our Patrons," 1827, p. 1)

From the beginning, a primary objective of the Black press was to protest and counter the negative and false reportage of the White press. We shall see that Blacks were not alone in early exercising the option of "advocacy" of their own cause as a response to White media. But first, let us put the issue in perspective. We have established in previous chapters the nature of White-owned media and their treatment of non-White and cultural minority groups. The social and cultural imperative that people of color communicate en masse is their survival. As the themes of the chapters in Part V of this volume suggest, non-Whites in the United States have three methods or coping strategies by which to address Anglocentric media tainted by racism and insensitivity to their needs: (1) they may seek access into mainstream media through employment and effect change from within; (2) they may advocate for change in the content of mainstream media by applying various forms of pressure; and/or (3) they may develop and maintain their own alternative communications media. Some students and media activists have simplified the approaches by referring to them as the three A's, meaning access, advocacy, and alternative (media). The methods are related and have been used both independently and in combination with each other. For example, people of color who have obtained professional employment in White media often form organizations that work to change the portrayal or news coverage of non-White cultural groups. And a medium owned by people of color may protest inequities it finds in White media, as was the case with *Freedom's Journal*. We have discussed the first option in Chapter 9. In this chapter, we will look at the ways that people of color advocate for better representation in the American media.

Nearly a century after the appearance of *Freedom's Journal,* the Black press was still defending its constituency against the denigrating reporting of the White press. In 1919, the Black weekly *Wichita Protest* complained about the racial coverage of the Associated Press.

> Every newspaper editor of our group in the country knows that the Associated Press, the leading news distributing service of the country, has carried on a policy of discrimination in favor of the whites and against the blacks, and is doing it daily now. The Associated Negro Press is in receipt of correspondence from editors in various sections of the country decrying the way in which the Associated Press writes its stories of happenings where Colored people are affected. (Detweiler, 1922, p. 149)

Even renowned Black spokesman Booker T. Washington spoke frequently of the poor coverage his speeches received from the White press. A Black journalist reported in 1916 that Washington lamented that his successful speeches before large crowds, normally expected to receive front-page attention in the White press, would be relegated to the last page and given an inch or so of space. The front page would invariably be given instead to considerable reporting of a Black person involved in a minor criminal offense (Detweiler, 1922, p. 150).

There was advocacy for change from the earliest days of the motion picture industry. In 1911, the Spanish-language weekly *La Crònica* of Laredo, Texas, launched a campaign against the numerous movies shown throughout the state that denigrated both Mexicans and Native Americans. The period marked the beginning of the heyday of Western movies. Movie screens were filled with images of Mexican "greasers" and "savage" Native Americans who were brought to justice by White cowboy heroes. Several prominent members of the Native American community wrote protest letters to the Bureau of Indian Affairs in Washington, D.C., about the images such movies projected of their people. The account of this in *La Crònica* read:

> We are not surprised about the complaint of the North American Indians . . . because the Mexicans can make the same complaint . . . and other Latin races, who are generally the only and most defamed in these sensational American movies (such as are seen on the Texas border) . . . that serve only to show the level of culture of the learned makers of films, who have no more ingenuity except to think of scenes with many bullets, horses, 'cowboys' and then it's over. (cited in Limon, 1973, p. 263)

La Crònica proceeded to call for support from other Texas Mexican newspapers in urging an end to the offensive movies. Earlier the paper had addressed the negative effects such movies had on its community.

> We judge these with much indignation and condemn them with all our energy . . . all exhibitions that make ridicule of the Mexican . . . because the showing of these facts are indelibly recorded in the minds of the children and this contributes very much to the development of the dislike with which other races see the Mexican race, who the film company has chosen to make fun of. (cited in Limon, 1973, p. 263)

In addition, the paper sought to persuade Texas theater owners not to acquire and show the films and to follow the lead of two Latinos who wrote letters to filmmakers to cancel further shipments to their theaters. According to the article in *La Crònica*, Latino families often reacted to negative stereotypes by leaving the theaters when they saw such portrayals and roles that "in reality [don't] fit us" (cited in Limon, 1973, p. 263). The paper noted that it would "with pleasure" publish the names of film companies that rejected movies that denigrated Mexicans.

The first generation of Chinese immigrants who settled primarily in California were, for the most part, unsophisticated laborers whose immediate concern was survival in a new and hostile Anglo Saxon world. Chinese immigrants were not made to feel a part of American culture, but because they came from the uneducated working class in China, their displeasure with their treatment by Whites was not often found in printed form aside from the English-language protestations in *The Golden Hills' News*. As small "Chinatown" enclaves developed in settlements in California and the Far West, Chinese immigrants sought internal refuge and protection from the ravages of racism. They dared not, given their small numbers and immigrant status, publicly protest too vociferously against their hosts, whose image of them as inferior precluded tolerance of criticism.

However, the second wave of Chinese immigrants included a number of representatives from China's upper classes. They were educated and were not affected by the anti-Chinese immigration laws passed prior to 1900. Among them were diplomats, scholars, and prosperous merchants and, despite their interest in promoting closer economic and political ties with the United States, some expressed in writing their disapproval of White racism against the Chinese. One such writer was Wu Tingfang, a Chinese diplomat who lived in America for nearly a decade. Wu wrote his book *America Through the Spectacles of an Oriental Diplomat* in 1914. By that time, Sax Rohmer's fictional and diabolical Chinese character, Dr. Fu Manchu, had been around for 4 years. The stereotype was readily embraced by White Americans prone to harbor prejudices against Chinese. Ever the diplomat, Wu asked forgiveness if his "impartial and candid" book caused offense.

American readers will forgive me if they find some opinions they cannot endure. I assure them they were not formed hastily or unkindly. Indeed, I should not be a sincere friend were I to picture their country as a perfect paradise, or were I to gloss over what seem to me to be their defects. (cited in Kim, 1982, p. 31)

Despite this early warning in his book, Wu's criticisms were generally innocuous. He made it clear, however, that he opposed the racism against Blacks and Chinese that he had observed in America. He tried to appeal to the rationality in his White readers by arguing that they could not be racially superior to the Chinese, whose rich culture and intellectual history merited the world's respect.

There are numerous other incidents throughout American history in which people of color expressed their disfavor with White media as a means of advocating change in their treatment by the media. Such activity has included every non-White cultural group and every form of mass communication media. The methods of advocacy have ranged from boycotts to letter-writing campaigns and from monitoring the content of the media to seeking legal redress of grievances. The use of a legal strategy, however, received a major boost when the Federal Civil Rights Act was enacted in 1964. Previously, it was difficult to convince people of color that changes could be made in the media through legal channels. The legal establishment—law enforcement agencies, prosecutors, lawyers, and judges—was seen by many non-Whites as a major contributor to the problems they faced. In fact, sit-ins, street rallies, marches, and picket lines were tactics employed to change unjust laws and challenge those who supported such laws. The notion of working through the legal system to change communications media was an unlikely proposition before the civil rights act. But passage of the law added legal clout to activists who sought change in the employment practices in and content of the media.

As we have noted elsewhere in this book, people of color were able to effect changes more rapidly in broadcasting than in print media because Federal Communications Commission (FCC) employment guidelines for broadcast licensees were more stringent than those of the Equal Employment Opportunities Commission (EEOC), the federal body to which newspapers are answerable. In addition, other social, economic, and political forces began to affect the institutions that control the mass media. Although he was referring to the political process, futurist John Naisbitt captured the essence of why people of color were able to exert considerable leverage to improve their lot in the media. The issue is related to racial pluralism and the trend toward decentralization in the United States. According to Naisbitt in his 1982 book *Megatrends*,

The key to decentralization of political power in the United States today is local action. Localized political power is not delegated from the federal level to the state, municipal, or neighborhood levels. Rather, it stems from the initiatives taken by the state or neighborhood in the absence of an effective top-down solution. . . . Successful initiatives hammered out at the local level have staying power. Local solutions are resistant to top-down intervention and become models for others still grappling with the problems. (p. 112)

The effect of decentralization, as a result of technology and economics, on American mass media is more thoroughly discussed in the last chapter. Here, we will examine how multicultural advocates, working at the local level and using the force of law, began making an impact on mass media in the late 1960s. In some respects, their successes are reminiscent of how the populist movement of the 1830s that was discussed in Chapter 3 drastically altered communications media and entertainment in the United States. The difference this time, however, is that meaningful change often had to be fought for in legal venues.

Challenging Bias in Broadcasting

The advocacy success story for non-Whites in broadcasting began with the United Church of Christ's Office of Communication. The United Church of Christ (UCC) has had a long-standing interest in civil rights, freedom of religion, and other forms of expression. It has committed its resources to such efforts in the United States and in other nations. The organization, a coalition of Protestant denominations, has generally dedicated itself to the proposition that the communications media should operate under Judeo-Christian principles. It considers the mass media to be a missionary sphere of interest. UCC's Office of Communication is the organizational entity assigned to the task of media advocacy. It is responsible for landmark legal decisions that changed the American broadcasting industry and its regulatory agency, the Federal Communications Commission (FCC), in ways even beyond the scope of racial concerns.

The first major race-related case the UCC took on involved television station WLBT in Jackson, Mississippi, in the 1960s. WLBT had incurred the wrath of Jackson's Black community for a number of years because of its discriminatory racial practices, which included on-air references to Black people as "niggers." WLBT also refused to carry a network television show on race relations by airing a sign that read, "Sorry, Cable Trouble" during the scheduled time slot. The station openly advocated racial segregation in a region where Black people comprised 45% of the station's service area. The UCC became involved because, among other reasons, it had a congregation in nearby Tougaloo, Mississippi, and Blacks comprised a significant portion of its membership. When WLBT began to attack local civil rights activities in which church members were involved, UCC took

Illustration 10.1   The Federal Communications Commission (FCC), headquartered in Washington, DC, has been a focal point for much of the advocacy work on behalf of people of color in broadcasting and other telecommunications industries.

Source: Federal Communications Commission.

up the legal challenge. UCC filed a petition to deny renewal of WLBT's FCC license in 1964. Under the social, political, and economic conditions of the time, local Blacks would have faced reprisal and likely violence had they attempted to challenge WLBT strictly as a local effort. The crux of the legal case was the WLBT's breach of the FCC requirement (established by the Communications Act of 1934) that all licensees broadcast "in the public interest, convenience and necessity." On the surface, it appeared that the Black residents of Jackson and the UCC would have little trouble preventing WLBT from retaining its license, assuming that their well-documented case was adequately presented. But only a miniscule fraction of license challenges had been successfully upheld since the FCC's inception. As subsequent legal developments made clear, the FCC had evolved into a protector of broadcasters instead of the public's rights. When the UCC and representatives of Jackson's Black community appeared before the FCC, the agency denied them "standing" to even present their petition on the grounds they had no "interest" (financial) in the license renewal procedure. The FCC renewed WLBT's license, but the UCC then filed suit in the U.S. Court of Appeals, which granted standing to the complainants and ordered the FCC to hold a full hearing of their case. The court maintained that members of WLBT's audience most certainly had standing because as consumers they had an interest in local broadcasting content over public airwaves. In fact, the court's position was that the FCC could not do its job of determining public interest without the assistance of the public. The UCC was distressed when, despite their participation in the hearing process, the FCC granted a license renewal to WLBT on a 1-year probationary status.

Believing the FCC decision to be improper and unfair, the UCC once again took the issue to the Court of Appeals and found relief. In harsh language that took the FCC to task for its shoddy treatment of the petitioners, the court took matters into its own hands and denied the license to WLBT. It was also significant that the court ruled that public petitioners should not bear the burden of proof in such cases but, rather, that the licensee must be able to show it handled its license privilege in a responsible manner. Moreover, the court ordered the denial on the grounds that the Fairness Doctrine had been violated and that WLBT practiced racial discrimination in their programming and hiring—extremely important issues for non-White groups. Another important right, the right of standing in FCC license hearings was, as noted, won in the initial phase of the case.

The UCC was also instrumental in a case involving Native Americans in Rosebud, South Dakota (Ward, 1980). Rosebud is a Sioux reservation whose inhabitants undertook a legal action against two South Dakota television stations, KELO and KPLO, that combined reached 90% of the broadcast audience in the state during the 1950s and 1960s. KPLO became a virtual satellite to KELO and by the mid-1960s neither station was originating much local programming to serve the interests and needs of the Rosebud Sioux. The UCC assisted in filing a petition to deny an FCC license to KELO, which resulted in the negotiation of agreements with both stations. The agreements called for program changes and the full-time employment of five Native Americans.

The concept of advocacy groups and potential broadcast licensees reaching negotiated settlement on matters of nondiscrimination in employment and program content set the stage for another major UCC-inspired milestone. In a 1968 case involving local citizens' groups in Texarkana, Texas, with support from UCC, the license of KTAL television was challenged by a petition to deny its renewal. The station's owners negotiated a settlement that resulted in withdrawal of the petition. Part of the agreement called for reimbursement to UCC of legal expenses incurred during the process. The FCC, however, refused to pay the stipulated reimbursement, citing the possibility of encouraging frivolous lawsuits and the potential for overpayment of such expenses. The FCC also feared that the public interest merits of petitions to deny cases could be overshadowed by the financial aspects of such situations. Again, UCC took the issue before the appeals court and was granted a ruling, which held negotiated reimbursements to be valid in instances where the petition to deny case is bona fide and the public interest has been served. The ruling gave advocacy groups added bargaining power and encouraged challenged licensees to negotiate settlements more quickly to avoid the more lengthy and expensive process of a fully litigated case.

Multicultural advocacy groups (or other local citizens' groups) typically sought changes in broadcasting by using the new legal weapons. If it could be shown that racial discrimination existed in programming, employment, or other areas detrimental to the public interest, a "petition to deny" the station's license renewal would be filed with the FCC. If the petition reached a hearing at the FCC, the licensee bore the burden of showing how its practices were, indeed, in the best interests of the community it served. That was because local citizens' groups had "standing" as interested parties to the license renewal process. If the citizens' advocacy group challenge was upheld, the broadcaster could face loss of its license. If, however, the challenging group and the licensee negotiated a settlement prior to a hearing before the FCC, the challengers could withdraw the petition and seek reimbursement of legal expenses incurred. By the mid-1980s, more than 100 such actions had been initiated, including some by other groups benefiting from precedents established by people of color.

During the late 1980s and throughout the 1990s, government "deregulation" policies—including the 1996 Communications Act—eroded the ability of advocacy groups to challenge the issuance of broadcasting licenses. With deregulation came relaxation of enforcement and the license-challenging tactic became much less of a factor in advocacy efforts. This circumstance led to the 1986 creation of the advocacy group now known as the Minority Media and Telecommunications Council (MMTC). The gains made by people of color during the 1980s and 1990s are apparent in the FCC data, which reveal that in 1978 people of color only owned about 0.5% of all commercial broadcast stations in the United States but that by 1994 the figure had increased to 3%. By 2002, much of the MMTC's work centered on preventing further erosion of the gains made by people of color in the previous three decades. It carried the legal battle for racial and cultural fairness in broadcasting on behalf of 45 or more civil rights advocacy organizations. These efforts became increasingly important in the wake of a 2001 District of Columbia U.S. Court of Appeals ruling that struck down as unconstitutional the equal employment opportunity rules established by the FCC a year earlier. By 2003, the FCC was reexamining its deregulatory policies following reports documenting their negative impact and protests by some industry leaders.

Illustration 10.2   David Honig, Executive Director of the Minority Media and Telecommunications Council, spearheaded legal challenges against racial inequities in commercial broadcasting for more than two decades.

Source: Minority Media and Telecommunications Council.

Expanding Multiculturalism in the Newspaper Industry

Newspapers, as private enterprises, operate under difficult-to-enforce EEO guidelines, and their response to grievances by people of color has been relatively slow. But the advocacy movement has managed to make inroads in assuring that newspapers act on issues that are important to people of color. Some of the progress, however, can be attributed to advocacy efforts being directed toward newspapers owned by large corporations with holdings in media that are subject to regulation. In 1980, for example, the Times-Mirror Company (then owner of the *Los Angeles Times,* Dallas *Times-Herald* and *Newsday,* among other newspapers) reached a negotiated settlement with the National Black Media Coalition (NBMC) over a purchase transaction of several broadcasting stations. The settlement not only addressed rectification of non-White employment and programming shortcomings in the broadcast companies Times-Mirror was purchasing, but it also included the appointment of a Black and a Latino to the Times-Mirror board of directors. The company also agreed to provide scholarships for journalism and broadcasting students attending predominately Black colleges located near the newly acquired broadcast stations. In addition, the agreement led to the funding of several other employment and training programs. (The agreement was made possible because citizen advocacy groups could also intervene when broadcast licenses were transferred, as in a change of ownership, as well as when licenses were considered for renewal.)

In the early 1980s, two lawsuits signaled the beginning of a more committed effort to increase multiculturalism in American newspaper staffs. Legal actions brought against the *New York Times* and the Associated Press forced the two news organizations to hire more people of color in the hope that more culturally sensitive news coverage would follow. Activists believed that successful legal actions—particularly when large, respected institutions were involved—would spur fear of similar lawsuits against other newspapers and thus cause them to increase multiculturalism in their organizations to protect themselves. Individual activists also aimed their efforts directly at newspapers and achieved some success in keeping the issue of multiculturalism before the industry. Among the leaders who emerged in the mid-1970s to mid-1980s were the late Robert Maynard and his wife Nancy Hicks Maynard (who were instrumental in founding the Institute for Journalism Education, which is now The Robert Maynard Institute for Journalism Education, among other efforts); Jay T. Harris (who conducted demographic studies of employment in newspapers for the American Society of Newspaper Editors from 1978 to 1983), and Gerald Garcia (who was then an executive with Gannett Newspapers).

Illustration 10.3   As part of their proactive agenda, professional organizations representing journalists of color conduct an annual "Journalism
Opportunities Conference" to give media recruiters a chance to interview qualified non-Whites for internships and jobs.

Source: California Chicano News Media Association.

Perhaps most influential of all was Gerald M. Sass, a White executive
with the Frank E. Gannett Newspaper Foundation (which is now The
Freedom Forum), who was instrumental in the expenditure of more than
$4 million in "venture capital" grants for multicultural programs in the
newspaper industry between 1975 and 1985. Through the foundation, Sass
helped provide early financial support to the Institute for Journalism
Education, the California Chicano News Media Association, the Asian
American Journalists Association, the Native American Press Association
(which is now the Native American Journalists Association), the National
Association of Black Journalists, and the National Association of Hispanic
Journalists, among others.

Illustration 10.4   The California Chicano News Media Association—with financial assistance from the Dow Jones Newspaper Fund—conducted "Urban Journalism Workshops" for aspiring high school journalists of color. Here, student Chie Kamali Davis works on a story.

Source: Photograph copyright © Rolando Otero, California Chicano News Media Association.

The efforts of these and other advocates for multiculturalism in American daily newspapers were responsible for most of the progress that was made in the 1980s. They prompted the American Society of Newspaper Editors (ASNE) to adopt the goal in 1978 to have the percentage of non-Whites in U.S. newsrooms equal their percentage of the nation's population by the year 2000. Although that goal was not met and the deadline for meeting it was extended to 2025 (see Chapter 9), ASNE has maintained an active institutional commitment to multiculturalism since 1977 through regional job fairs and an annual survey of newsroom employment. From the mid-1990s into the 21st century, the Newspaper Association of America (NAA) and the Associated Press Managing Editors (APME) have been among the professional print media trade associations that maintain a profile of involvement in the move to multiculturalism and "diversity." The Dow Jones Newspaper Fund has several programs for aspiring newspaper journalists of color including efforts aimed at high school students. It is among several endeavors sponsored by corporations or private foundations that focus on various aspects of the issue on behalf of the newspaper industry.

The Impact of Professional
Organizations of People of Color in the Media

A significant advocacy movement of the 1980s involved non-White professionals who had succeeded in mainstream media but who were keenly affected by the biases that non-Whites encounter on the job. They were committed to seeing other people of color join them in the profession. The result was the formation of national professional associations for journalists of color with membership categories open to practitioners in print and electronic media as well as related fields. Among them are the National Association of Black Journalists, the National Association of Hispanic Journalists, the Asian American Journalists Association, and the Native American Journalists Association. They each work separately and cooperatively to improve working conditions, increase job opportunities, and sponsor scholarships for promising students. The organizations hold national and regional conventions where seminars and workshops are presented on issues relevant to news professionals of color. In 1994, the groups cosponsored the first national "Unity" conference in Atlanta where a multicultural gathering of more than 5,000 journalists convened for 5 days to assess progress and strategize on the role of people of color in communications media. The conference was covered nationally by the mainstream press and demonstrated the positive impact that advocates of multiculturalism had made on the media over the previous two decades. An outgrowth was the formation of Unity, an association representing all of the non-White professional media advocacy organizations. Unity held a second convention in Seattle in 1999 and subsequent conventions were scheduled at 5-year intervals.

Advocacy in the Entertainment Industry

As we have documented in previous chapters, anyone critically looking at film and television portrayals of people of color in the early 21st century would find that there is still ample reason for change. Denzel Washington and Halle Berry swept the Oscar awards for best actor and best actress in 2002, but the employment of people of color in the various trades and crafts responsible for movies and television entertainment remains low. The number of strong, meaningful character roles and script plots for people of color is small. However, that state of affairs is not the result of a lack of activism on behalf of multiculturalism among those who are part of the industry. People of color have organized caucuses in the Directors Guild, the Writers Guild, and the Screen Actors Guild. Professional actors and other artisans speak out frequently on the plight of non-White artists, but it is difficult to ascertain their effectiveness. Among the groups historically addressing those issues on the West Coast, where they could apply direct pressure to Hollywood, are The Media Forum, Nosotros, and Asian Americans for Fair Media. Conditions undoubtedly would be worse were it not for the efforts of those who speak out for multicultural inclusion and sensitivity in entertainment.

As technology enables new forms of communication to be brought into use, there will be a need for advocacy voices in public policy to ensure that people of color—particularly those in lower income categories—are able to be active participants in new information delivery systems.

Advocacy in Education

The Association for Education in Journalism and Mass Communication (AEJMC) is the primary organization representing college and university journalism and mass communication education in the United States. Nationally, 90% of all full-time academic instructors in the discipline are White. In 1968, under the prodding of Lionel C. Barrow, Jr. (who had written an "open letter" to the organization's convention urging the journalism education establishment to end its de facto segregation against non-Whites), an ad hoc committee was formed by resolution to bring "minority group members into [the AEJ] pipeline" (Barrow, 1980). A comprehensive set of goals related to multiculturalism was established by AEJMC (which until 1982 was known as the Association for Education in Journalism). The goals included fundraising for 500 non-White student scholarships for the 1969 to 1970 school year and the development of curriculum changes to reflect the contributions of non-White groups in America and the reports of those contributions in the media.

In 1971, the association's Minorities and Communication division (MAC) was created. Barrow, who later became dean of the school of communications at Howard University, was the division's first head. MAC's membership came to reflect multiculturalism and included a number of active White members. Increasingly over the years, the division became the conscience of the larger body, and the ideals and goals under which MAC was founded—to prioritize cultural diversity in journalism faculty hiring, curriculum, and student enrollment nationally—became distant memories. The ambitious goals were never achieved, as the attitude of the journalism education establishment paralleled that of American society once the initial rush of the civil rights movement had passed. Basically, the association's members responded as if it were MAC's job alone to handle multicultural affairs. In 1978, 10 years after the creation of the ad hoc committee that lead to MAC's birth, AEJMC enacted another "Resolution on Minorities," but by 1985 much of its promise, too, was unfulfilled. In 1991, AEJMC elected its first non-White president when Tony Atwater of Rutgers University assumed the leadership mantle for a year. That same year, perhaps in recognition of the unremarkable progress of multiculturalism in the journalism and mass communications academy, AEJMC established the Commission on the Status of Minorities to place additional emphasis on the issue. Meanwhile, the Minorities and Communication division continued to press for a greater multicultural presence in journalism and mass communication education through curriculum revision, expanded research, and the maintenance and development of service programs. In 2000, a fellowship program initiated by Marilyn Kern-Foxworth (AEJMC's first Black woman president) and Shirley Staples Carter (a Black woman and director of the Wichita State University communications school) was created to groom people of color for journalism education leadership positions. The Journalism and Mass Communication Leadership Institute for Diversity (JLID) was a joint effort of AEJMC and the Association of Schools of Journalism and Mass Communication (ASJMC) to bring underrepresented groups into the ranks of college department chairs and deans.

In the mid-1980s—partly spurred by publication of the first edition of this book and an accreditation standard that encouraged racial diversity— a significant number of journalism and mass communication departments in academic institutions began offering courses on the role of non-White groups in communications history and on the response to the treatment of non-Whites in the mainstream media. Other instructional materials, including textbook supplements and videotape presentations, were developed to meet increased interest in the subject. By the late 1990s, more textbooks had broadened the scope of diversity in journalism education to include volumes on gender and other subject areas that expose the inadequacy of the representation of many groups in American media.

The Accrediting Council on Education in Journalism and Mass Communications (ACEJMC) incorporated recognition of multicultural inclusion in faculty hiring in 1982 and multicultural curriculum in 1992 as part of its accrediting standards. Despite the fact that the American journalism academy remained at least 90% White into the 21st century, there is no record of any college or university having lost its accreditation for lack of multicultural representation on its faculty. A few, however, have been afforded one-year provisional accreditation or risk losing accreditation. The number of non-White doctoral graduates in journalism and mass communication in the early 2000s remained less than a trickle for the "pipeline" mentioned in AEJ's 1968 "minorities" resolution, although at the graduate school level there has been a discernable increase in the number of students of color from foreign countries (see Becker, Kosicki, Lowery, Prine, & Punathambekar, 2000).

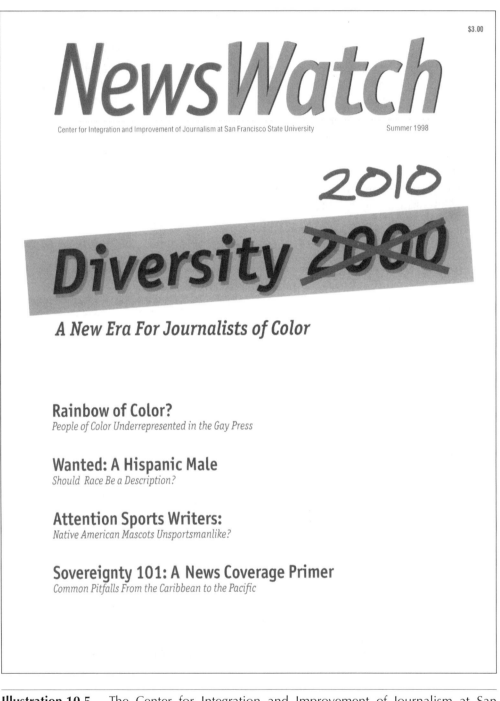

Illustration 10.5   The Center for Integration and Improvement of Journalism at San Francisco State University published "NewsWatch," a periodical focusing on issues of race and gender in news media.

Confronting the Status Quo and
Increasing Multiculturalism in the Media

Throughout their experiences in American society, people of color have expressed their discontent with the treatment they received from White-dominated media. Non-Whites believed it was necessary to protect themselves from the harmful effects of the distorted portrayals and negative news reporting of American mass media. Their responses took several forms but the object was the same—they wanted to change the status quo. Each group found representation in advocates who fought for changes in and reform of the mainstream media. With the passage of the Civil Rights Act in 1964, new legal avenues were opened to advocacy activists. Through the leverage provided by federal regulation of the broadcasting industry, major legal victories were won and some of the worst offenders were driven off the air. Meanwhile, favorable economic conditions and deregulation of media were accompanied by a rise in cross-media ownership. Where broadcast licensees and newspaper groups had common ownership, advocates of multiculturalism had opportunities to affect the slow-to-integrate newspaper industry.

Individual professional activists stimulated the major mainstream media organizations and trade associations to fund newspaper integration efforts. They prodded the industry to increase its multicultural training, hiring, and coverage. Meanwhile, professional journalists of color, who had benefited from the activists' efforts to open doors to employment, began forming their own organizations on the local, regional, and national levels. The organizations, in turn, became strong advocates for change. Although the film and entertainment television industries have multicultural advocacy groups as well as articulate spokespeople among Hollywood actors, little visible progress is apparent in their end products. Technological innovations may create new outlets for non-White expression. The trend toward specialized audience media may force changes in the industry as people of color continue to be desirable target audiences for economic reasons.

College and university educators, who are responsible for the training and ethical development of young professionals in the media, have been slow to meet the challenge of increasing multiculturalism for an increasingly pluralistic American society. But, spurred by internal advocates, the Association for Education in Journalism and Mass Communication has stepped up its efforts to increase racial and ethnic diversity in higher education. While the professorate in American colleges has remained virtually all White and male, course offerings have begun to reflect some progress toward more multiculturalism in the curriculum. The inclusion of multicultural requirements as criteria for the accreditation of journalism and mass communication programs has the potential to lead to greater racial sensitivity and inclusiveness in professionals in the media and in their work.

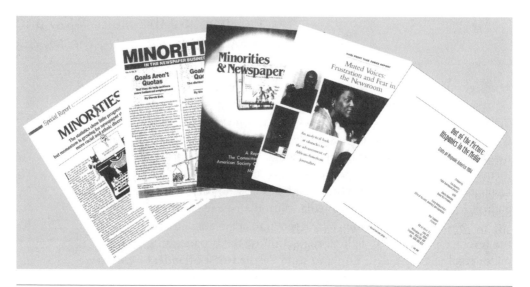

Illustration 10.6   Advocacy efforts over the years have inspired a variety of professional and collegiate media programs aimed at increasing training, hiring, and content images of people of color.

References

Barrow, L. C., Jr. (1980, August). *The Minorities and Communication division—the beginning.* Paper presented to the Minorities and Communication division, Association for Education in Journalism at the 63rd Annual AEJ Conference, Boston University.

Becker, L., Kosicki, G., Lowery, W., Prine, J., & Punathambekar, A. (2000). Undergrad enrollments level off, graduate education declines. *Journalism and Mass Communication Educator, 55*(3), 68-80.

Detweiler, F. G.(1922). *The Negro press in the United States.* Chicago: University of Chicago Press.

Kim, E. H. (1982). *Asian American literature.* Philadelphia: Temple University Press.

Limon, J. E. (1973, Fall). Stereotyping and Chicano resistance: A historical dimension. *Aztlàn, 4*(2), 263.

Naisbitt, J. (1982). *Megatrends.* New York: Warner Books.

To our patrons. (1827, March 16). *Freedom's Journal*, p. 1.

Ward, E. (1980). Advocating the minority interest: Actors and cases. In B. Rubin (Ed.), *Small voices and great triumphs* (p. 250). New York: Praeger.

Alternatives 11

Colorful Firsts in Class Communication

everyone communicates. People of all races and cultures in all parts of the world have all developed ways to share their thoughts and ideas with each other. But when people think about the roots of the media in the United States, they often look to Europe for the beginnings of both the print technology and the political and economic systems that spurred the development of the media. The history of journalism in the United States too often emphasizes the contributions of the general audience mass media and bypasses the contributions of targeted audience class media for population segments, such as people of color. While it is helpful to look to Europe for some roots of the American media, looking there and no where else results in only a partial view of how the media in this country developed.

Communication Before the Europeans

Edwin and Michael Emery (1996) have described some of the earliest forms of communication around the world.[1]

Around 3500 B.C. the Sumerians of the Middle East devised a system of preserving records by inscribing signs and symbols in wet clay tablets using cylinder seals and then baking them in the sun. They also devised a cuneiform system of writing, using bones to mark signs in wet clay. . . . Pictographs or ideographs—drawing of animals, commonly recognized objects, and humans—were popular in the Mediterranean area, China, India, what is now Mexico, and Egypt, where they became known as hieroglyphs. There is evidence that a system of movable type was devised in Asia Minor prior to 1700 B.C., the date of a flat clay disk found in Crete. The disk contained forty-five different signs that had been carved on individual pieces of type and then pressed into the clay. (p. 3)

The Phoenicians created an alphabet in 1500 B.C.E. and used colored fluids to outline its symbols to produce pictographs. About 1,000 years later, the Egyptians began using reeds from the Nile River to make papyrus. Scribes, using brushes or quills, marked the papyrus with hieroglyphic images. The different sheets of papyrus were then joined to form scrolls, which were stored in centers of learning. Sometime close to 100 C.E., parchment made from animal skins was used for special manuscripts or scrolls. But it was the Chinese who made the two greatest advances leading to modern communication: paper and printing.

At about this same time (A.D. 100) the Chinese invented a smooth, white paper from wood pulp and fibres and also discovered a way to transfer an ideograph from stone to paper after inking the surface. . . . Wang Chieh published what is considered the world's oldest preserved book from wood blocks in A.D. 868. Large blocks could be carved so that one sheet of paper, printed on both sides, could be folded into thirty-two pages of booksize. Feng Tao printed the Confucian classics between 932 and 953 and in about 1045 the artisan Pi Sheng was inspired to devise a set of movable clay carvings—a sort of earthen ware "type"—that could be reused. (Emery & Emery, 1996, p. 3)

Wood-block printing was not introduced in Europe until 200 years later when Marco Polo returned from China in 1295. Still the Asian printing advances sped ahead. Emery and Emery wrote that movable metal type of copper or bronze came into use in Korea in 1241, more than two centuries before Germany's Johann Gutenberg, often credited with inventing metal movable type, introduced printing with movable metal type in Europe.

Black Africans south of the Sahara Desert, who were divided into three major groups and many tribes, also developed elaborate systems for recording and communicating information. Like the natives of North America, they used "talking drums" to communicate between villages and transferred information between tribes and with other parts of the world along land and water trade routes. Rock painting was a key activity for the ancient residents of the Kalahari Desert in southern Africa, as well as in the Sahara Desert in the north.

Literature, often in the form of folktales performed with elaborate music and dancing, passed stories and news of important events from generation to generation. In some tribes, special persons known as *griots* memorized tribal history and taught it to younger members of the tribe, as well to future *griots* who would continue the telling of stories of important tribal leaders and developments to the next generation.

In what was to become Latin America, record keeping and communication were important long before the Christopher Columbus arrived in 1492. The native Inca, Mexica (Aztec), and Maya all had elaborate systems of recording, transferring, and storing records, including the work of scribes who wrote on bark tablets and artisans who recorded information and pictures on stone carvings. The Incas, who governed a territory that rose precipitously from the ocean to the mountains, used an elaborate network of runners to transmit messages of importance throughout their empire in what is now Peru. The Mexica apparently used an early form of mass communication by hanging colored banners on the main public square of their capital city of Tenochtitlán, now Mexico City.

Further north, the native people in what became the United States and Canada also developed complex communication systems—before the Europeans arrived. Hollywood movies have popularized the image of Indians communicating through tom tom drums and smoke signals, but Native Americans' actual communication systems were much more sophisticated and systematic than that. A complex network of trails and footpaths spanned the continent and was traversed by special couriers authorized to carry messages between tribes. James and Sharon Murphy (1981) wrote that

> A complex system of native communications covered most of North America before white contact. . . . It was a unique network of trails and footpaths that crisscrossed the continent, passing through dense forests, over rivers and streams, across mountains and meadows. Traversing these trails were Indian runners, known as tribal messengers, who were officially recognized by governing systems such as those of the Iroquois in the East, the Cherokees in the South and Southeast, the Yuroks in the Northwest, and the Eskimos in present-day Alaska. Other tribes, having less complex tribal governing structures, named and trained young men, and sometimes young women, to act as messenger communicators carrying news from tribe to tribe. Their extraordinary strength and endurance, their fleetness of foot, and their intimate knowledge of the land amazed early European immigrants. (p. v)

"Newspaper Rock" is the name given to carvings of figures along one wall in the Navajo's Canon de Chelly and at other sites in Utah and Arizona, thus recognizing the communication role rock carvings, or petroglyphs, may have had. Utah's Newspaper Rock is described as "a four-thousand-year-old 'bulletin board'" in one guidebook (Schaaf, 1996, pp. 53-54).[2] Anasazi, Navajo, Hopi, and other early people developed petroglyphs and elaborate wall paintings, called pictographs, in what is now the Four Corners area of Arizona, New Mexico, Utah, and Colorado. Many images are still visible. One petroglyph in western New Mexico depicts native people driving a buffalo into a huge net trap surrounded by other

Illustration 11.1   Indigenous people developed elaborate methods of recording and reporting their activities before Europeans arrived in America. Newspaper Rock in southeastern Utah contains petroglyphs made by Anasazi, Ute, Navajo, and other Native American people beginning about 1,000 years before Columbus landed in Santo Domingo.

hunters. Another in Canon de Chelly in Arizona was made after the arrival of Europeans and shows Spanish soldiers riding into battle with the Navajo people.

Early Printing in America

Like the history of communication and printing in the world, the history of print media in America started with a group most historians have overlooked—in this case, it was the Spanish colonists. The first printing press in America was sent by Spain to Mexico City in 1535 or 1536, more than a century before the English colonists' first printing press arrived in 1638. The earliest American printing, which was licensed by the Spanish crown to printer Juan Cromberger of Seville, was built on the European languages and the languages of native people. Spain saw the main use of the press as printing government notices and proclamations, as well as catechisms used to convert indigenous people to Catholicism. Therefore, the first booklets printed were bilingual, using a European language such as Spanish or Latin in one column next to text translating the words into the sounds of the native language, such as Nahuatl or Tarascan, in the next column.

The Cromberger press also produced the first printed journalism in America. In 1541, a terrible storm and earthquake struck Guatemala City, south of Mexico City. After the storm, notary public Juan Rodríguez wrote what became the first printed news report in America. Rodríguez's story of the storm and the destruction of Guatemala City was taken to Mexico City, where it was printed as an 8-page booklet by Juan Pablos, the operator of Cromberger's printing house, pressman Gil Barbero, and a Black slave whose name is not known. Giving readers a foretaste of news media to follow, the front page of the news booklet began with an attention-getting headline in large type: "Report of the Terrifying Earthquake Which Has Reoccurred In the Indies in a City Called Guatemala." The article continued, "It is an event of great astonishment and great example so that we all repent from our sins and so that we will be ready when God calls us." A "summary of what happened in Guatemala" began on an inside page with a Guatemala dateline and the story (Gutiérrez & Ballesteros, 1979; see also Emery & Emery, 1978, pp. 5-7; Hester, 1979).

Rodríguez's news report was distributed in Mexico City and was the forerunner of a popular form of news reporting in New Spain, as the Spanish colonies were then called. Based on a European model, the news booklets known as *hojas volantes* (flying pages) or *relaciones* (reports) were issued when major news occurred, when the government had a major announcement, or when ships with news of world events docked at Veracruz. As more presses arrived in New Spain, more printers printed and sold the irregularly issued news booklets. Mexican historian Julio Jiménez Rueda (1950, p. 22) wrote that it was through the *hojas volantes* that "people knew of the death and coronation of kings, wars in Europe, earthquakes and calamities" (cited in Acevedo, 1965, p. 79; our translation).[3]

By 1600, nearly 40 years before a printing press even arrived in the English colonies, the presses of New Spain had produced at least 174 books. An additional 60 books have been identified without dates or verification (Acevedo, 1965, p. 75). In 1693, the news booklet format was used in America's first news periodical, the four volumes of the *Mercurio Volante* published by Carlos de Siguenza y Góngora in Mexico City. One *Mercurio Volante* issue carried news of unsuccessful Spanish battles to reconquer and colonize the native people of what is now New Mexico.

Like the communication advances of Asians, Africans, and Native Americans, the Latino roots of the American media have been overlooked or minimized by many historians of the United States, even though accurate information has long been available. In 1810, the first history of

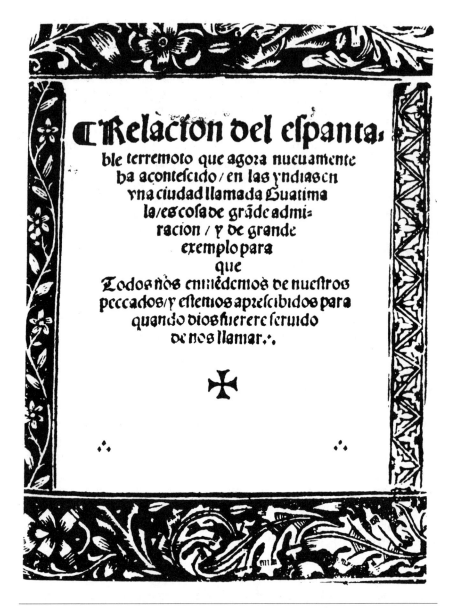

Illustration 11.2   The first printed journalism in America was this 1541 report of an earthquake and storm that destroyed Guatemala City. It was written by Juan Rodríguez and published by Juan Pablos as a news booklet to be distributed in Mexico City.

American journalism, Isaiah Thomas's *History of Printing in America,* correctly began with a 10-page chapter on Spanish America. However, when Thomas's book was reprinted in 1874 and in later editions the first chapter—the chapter on Spanish American printing—was deleted. In

1941, journalism historian Frank Luther Mott relegated America's first printed news, the 1541 Mexico City report of Guatemala City's destruction, to a mere footnote and conveyed the false impression that "no regularly published newspaper on the continent antedated the earliest Boston papers" (cited in Emery & Emery, 1996, p. 615).

More recently, historians have broadened their recognition that Latinos and other groups laid the foundations of American journalism. In its Summer 1977 and Autumn 1979 issues, *Journalism History* devoted the cover and several articles to the contributions of Latinos and the Latino press to news media in America. In the same era, editor Tom Reilly devoted other editions of the journal to the Black press and to Native American media. To their credit, Emery and Emery in the 1980s revised the first pages of their comprehensive history book, *The Press and America,* to include early non-European contributions and a section on the Spanish influence in American journalism, including a picture of the 1541 news booklet.[4] The Latin American press traditions were linked to newspapers published in Texas and New Mexico before those Mexican territories were taken by the United States in 1848 after its war against Mexico.

The focus of this book is people of color and communication media in the United States. Although the general audience mass media have long overlooked news in these communities, each group has long had their own class media focused on the needs and interests of their communities in this country. Spurred by population changes, these racial and ethnic media are growing at a faster rate and are more important than ever. The rest of this chapter describes how the first U.S. newspaper for each group began and explores the experiences they shared.

The first newspapers for people of color were preceded by class media targeted to other ethnic groups and began in a 50-year period around the first half of the 19th century. In chronological order, the four are the first Latino newspaper, *El Misisipí,* founded in New Orleans in 1808; the first Black newspaper, *Freedom's Journal,* founded in New York City in 1827; the first Native American newspaper, *Cherokee Phoenix,* founded in New Echota, Georgia, in 1828, and the first Asian Pacific American newspaper, *Kim-Shan Jit San-Luk, The Golden Hills' News,* founded in San Francisco in 1854. In addition to sharing the same time period for their founding, these first four newspapers all have something more important in common: Each one started as a response to a special crisis their readers faced.

The First Latino Newspaper: *El Misisipí* in 1808

El Misisipí was founded in the midst of the Napoleonic Wars in Europe in the early 1800s, when France had conquered much of the European continent, including parts of Spain, and claimed the extensive Spanish holdings in America. New Orleans, a seaport built where the Mississippi River flows into the Gulf of Mexico, was a major transit point for people traveling between the United States and Europe, as well as to and from the Spanish colonies in the Caribbean, Central America, and South America.

Named after the river that drew ships to New Orleans, *El Misisipí* was a 4-page publication printed primarily in Spanish, but with English translations of many articles and almost all the advertising. It was started by William H. Johnson and Company and was printed on the press of the Louisiana *Gazette.* Not much is known about its founders and only two archived copies remain from its 2-year run.[5]

News stories in the one copy remaining in the United States reveal the crisis under which the newspaper's war refugee readers were living. With Napoleon Bonaparte's French forces conquering most of Europe and establishing a puppet government in Spain, *El Misisipí* is filled with war reports from other newspapers and war news conveyed by sea captains, including a story on the uprising of Madrid citizens against Napoleon's occupying troops. The newspaper also speculated on the possibility of England ending its hostilities with Russia and entering the war on the side of Spain against France.

All the news stories in *El Misisipí* came from outside of New Orleans and almost all covered the war in Europe, including a long commentary on the events. Because there was no wire or electronic communication of news, most of the stories were several months old and at times contradicted each other. In a separate column, the editor commented on the reports and their possible implications for Spain. The newspaper was distinctly pro-Spanish, denigrating Napoleon's puppet regime in Spain.

El Misisipí, like other newspapers of the time, relied on news reports from other newspapers and reports of sea captains and sailors arriving from foreign ports. Among the articles in the October 12, 1808 issue were articles from the Boston *Chronicle* and a newspaper identified as the *Diario de New York* (*New York Daily*). The front page carried the report of the Madrid uprising in all three of its columns, adding only a brief notice of its publication schedule (Wednesdays and Saturdays), its subscription rates ($8 a year, half payable in advance), and its advertising language policy ("in both languages or in the one wanted"), as well as a bilingual advertisement for Don Juan Rodríguez, Abogado (lawyer) in Spanish with an English translation below it. Rodríguez wished "to inform his friends and the public in general that from this date he will reside at his plantation, better than a league below the city," but he added that he would "still continue to keep his office in town, in the house of Doctor Deveze, No. 16 Main Street, where he will execute any business in the line of his profession from ten o'clock A.M. till four P.M."

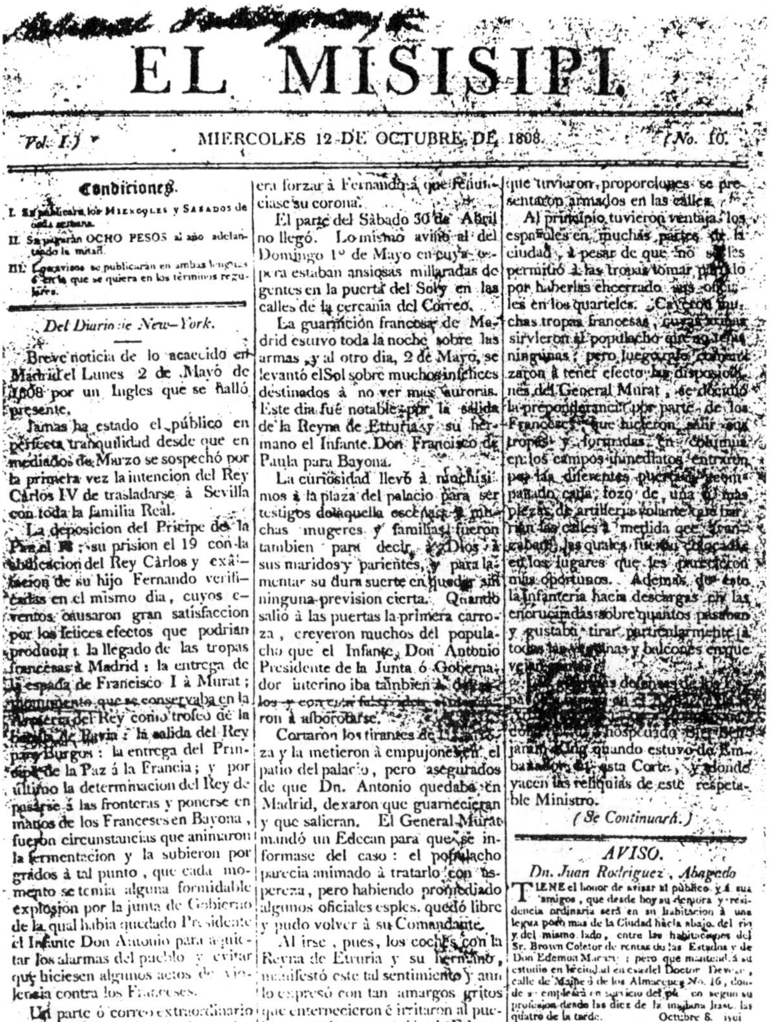

EL MISISIPI.

Vol. I.) MIERCOLES 12 DE OCTUBRE, DE 1808. (No. 10.

Condiciones.

I. Se publicará los Miercoles y Sabados de cada semana.

II. Se pagarán OCHO PESOS al año adelantado la mitad.

III. Los avisos se publicarán en ambas lenguas ó en la que se quiera en los términos regulares.

Del Diario de New-York.

Breve noticia de lo acaecido en Madrid el Lunes 2 de Mayo de 1808 por un Ingles que se halló presente.

Jamas ha estado el público en perfecta tranquilidad desde que en mediados de Marzo se sospechó por la primera vez la intencion del Rey Cárlos IV de trasladarse à Sevilla con toda la familia Real.

La deposicion del Pricipe de la Paz el 18: su prision el 19 con la abdicacion del Rey Càrlos y exáltacion de su hijo Fernando verificadas en el mismo dia, cuyos eventos causaron gran satisfaccion por los felices efectos que podrian producir: la llegada de las tropas francesas à Madrid: la entrega de la espada de Francisco I à Murat; monumento que se conservaba en la Armeria del Rey como trofeo de la batalla de Pavia: la salida del Rey para Burgos: la entrega del Principe de la Paz á la Francia; y por último la determinacion del Rey de pasarse à las fronteras y ponerse en manos de los Franceses en Bayona, fueron circunstancias que animaron la fermentacion y la subieron por grados à tal punto, que cada momento se temia alguna formidable explosion por la junta de Gobierno de la qual habia quedado Presidente el Infante Don Antonio para aquietar los alarmas del pueblo y evitar que hiciesen algunos actos de violencia contra los Franceses.

Un parte ó correo extraordinario acostumbraba venir todas las tardes de Bayona con las noticias de las transacciones: estas jamas se publicaban en la gaceta ... que circulaban en forma de ... cartas privadas de la comitiva del Rey ... los primeros ... una ... cion momentánea ... que ... sistian únicamente en la descripcion de los honores hechos al Principe Fernando con motivo de su llegada ... y en el cordial recibimiento de Bonaparte. Las noticias siguientes ... hicieron ménos satisfactorias ... mero se dieron unos indicios ... curos de que no iba bien todo, y luego se dixo mas ... que la intencion del árbitro de la Francia era forzar à Fernando à que renunciase su corona.

El parte del Sàbado 30 de Abril no llegó. Lo mismo avinó al del Domingo 1° de Mayo en cuya espera estaban ansiosas millaradas de gentes en la puerta del Sol y en las calles de la cercania del Correo.

La guarnicion francesa de Madrid estuvo toda la noche sobre las armas, y al otro dia, 2 de Mayo, se levantó el Sol sobre muchos infelices destinados à no ver mas auroras. Este dia fué notable por la salida de la Reyna de Etturia y su hermano el Infante Don Francisco de Paula para Bayona.

La curiosidad llevó à muchisimos à la plaza del palacio para ser testigos de aquella escena. Muchas mugeres y familias fueron tambien para decir à Dios à sus maridos y parientes, y para lamentar su dura suerte en que ... sin ninguna prevision cierta. Quando salió à las puertas la primera carroza, creyeron muchos del populacho que el Infante, Don Antonio Presidente de la Junta ó Gobernador interino iba tambien ... ron à alborotarse.

Cortaron los tirantes de ... za y la metieron à empujones ... el patio del palacio, pero asegurados de que Dn. Antonio quedaba en Madrid, dexaron que guarneciéran y que salieran. El General Murat mandó un Edecan para que se informase del caso: el populacho parecia animado à tratarlo con aspereza, pero habiendo protegido algunos oficiales esples. quedó libre y pudo volver à su Comandante.

Al irse, pues, los coches con la Reyna de Etruria y su hermano, manifestó este tal sentimiento y aun lo expresó con tan amargos gritos que enternecieron é irritaron al pueblo: entónces volvió el Edecan con una parte de las tropas francesas y comenzó la horrible y sanguinaria escena.

No es fácil atinare si los soldados franceses ó el populacho fueron los primeros agresores, pero es cierto que los franceses comenzaron à ... cargar su mosqueteria contra los que se le oponian, y que caian muchos inocentes espectadores: ... de estos fué un hermoso jóven ... que se hallaba en una ... eran las once ... Las noticias de aquellas ... se esparcieron ... y en ménos de ... todos los de la baxa clase que tuvieron proporciones se presentaron armados en las calles.

Al principio tuvieron ventajas los españoles en muchas partes de la ciudad, à pesar de que no se les permitió à las tropas tomar parte ... por haberlas encerrado ... en los quarteles. ... chas tropas francesas ... sirvieron al populacho ... ningunas; pero luego ... zaron à tener efecto las disposiciones del General Murat, ... la preponderancia por parte de los Franceses ... tropas ... en los campos inmediatos entraron por las diferentes puertas ... pasado cada ... de ... piezas de artilleria volante ... las calles à medida que ... los quales ... en los lugares que ... mas oportunos. Ademas de esto la Infanteria hacia descargas en las encrucijadas sobre quantos pasaban y gustaba tirar particularmente à todas las ventanas y balcones ...

... hospedado ... quando estuvo de Embaxador en esta Corte, y donde yacen las reliquias de este respetable Ministro.

(Se Continuará.)

AVISO.

Dn. Juan Rodriguez, Abogado

TIENE el honor de avisar al público y á sus amigos, que desde hoy su demora y residencia ordinaria será en su habitacion à una legua poco mas de la Ciudad hàcia abajo del rio y del mismo lado, entre las habitaciones del Sr. Brown Coletor de rentas de los Estados y de Don Edemon Macarty; pero que mantendrá su estudio en la ciudad en casa del Doctor Devezé, calle de Mayne ó de los Almacenes No. 16, donde se empleará en servicio del público segun su profesion desde las diez de la mañana hasta las quatro de la tarde. Octubre 8. 1808

Dn. JOHN RODRIGUEZ, Attorney at Law,

HAS the honor to inform his friends and the public in general that from this date he will reside at his plantation, better than a league below the city and on the same side of the river, between the plantation of Wm. Brown, Esq. and that of Mr. Edmond Macarty; but that he will still continue to keep his office in town, in the house of Doctor Devezé, No. 16, Main street, where he will execute any business in the line of his profession, from ten o'clock A. M. till four P.M. October 1. 1808

Pasage para Vera-Cruz ó la Havana.

LAS personas que deseasen pasar à estos puertos lo conseguirán acudiendo à casa de Dn. Leandro Muxo, ó à los editores de esta gaceta.

Septiembre 16.

Blanks for sale at this Office.

Illustration 11.3 *El Misisipí* (1808) in New Orleans was the first Latino newspaper in the United States, publishing news of the Napoleonic Wars and advertising in both English and Spanish.

Source: Wisconsin State Historical Society.

El Misisipí's second page offered the report "of a correspondent" on the problem of separating out the facts in the accounts in newspapers, official news, private reports, and rumors coming from war-torn Europe. *El Misisipí* summarized what its editors felt was the latest factual information and called the Bayonne *Gazette* "an official organ of the usurpers of the thrones of France and Spain." *El Misisipí* then engaged in some interpretation of its own: "Madrid has long been in the possession of the French and the patriots of Spain are not to be duped by the mockeries of Bonaparte, however solemnized by a recreant minister of religion," *El Misisipí* editorialized. Citing uprisings against the French in Spain and Portugal, the paper continued that "we think therefore that nothing has yet appeared to discourage the friends of freedom. To hold their own ground is much for the patriots at the commencement of the struggle. Their armies will increase and improve in a far greater degree than those of the enemy."

The fourth page was devoted entirely to advertising, almost all in a bilingual format, Spanish above English. Everything from ships to hardwood to supplies for sailors was advertised in the two languages. The advertisements reveal the nature of commerce in the sea and river port of New Orleans, which the United States acquired from Napoleon's France 5 years earlier in the Louisiana Purchase. One company, A. & J. M'Ilvain, Grocers, No. 43, on the Levee, offered sugar, coffee, tea, and a "general assortment of groceries" along with "2500 lbs. James River Chewing Tobacco, 1000 bushels Indian Corn, 2000 feet Walnut plank." The firm advised ships' captains preparing to sail "SEA STORES Put up at the shortest notice." Another advertisement announced, "Five or six gentlemen may be accomodated with Genteel Boarding in a private family, at the rate of 20 Dollars per month."

The largest advertisements, taking up nearly all of the second and third columns, were for Mrs. Zacharie, who offered "a handsome assortment of DRY GOODS," and *La Rionda*, a dealer selling two brigantines, the Sophia and the Minerve, each "with all her tackle," two houses on St. Phillip Street, and a long list of goods such as 800 tons of Campeachy Logwood, 40 bales of sassaparilla, and 22 trunks of "Callicoes."

As the first Latino newspaper in the United States, *El Misisipí* exhibited many characteristics found in later media. For one, it was apparently directed to Spanish-speaking readers who came to the United States to escape warfare and political turmoil in their homeland, a consistent theme in immigration from Latin America. Second, it was bilingual, recognizing the importance of both English and Spanish. Third, its news was heavily influenced by events elsewhere, just as much of the news and many programs in Latino media over the years have come from Spain and Latin America. And, fourth, like many Latino publications that followed, *El Misisipí* apparently was a business venture, devoting one fourth of its space to advertising.

The First Black Newspaper:
Freedom's Journal in 1827

A different kind of crisis triggered the founding of *Freedom's Journal*, the first Black newspaper, on March 16, 1827, by the Reverend Samuel E. Cornish and John Brown Russwurm. The crisis was the fight to end slavery, in which Blacks were kept as property in much of the United States. White Abolitionists wanted to abolish slavery and campaigned against it by printing stories of slave life written by freed Black slaves. But the Abolitionists were divided on what should become of former slaves once they gained their freedom. Some argued that they should go back to Africa. Others felt they should be allowed to remain in the United States as citizens. Of course, Anti-Abolitionists, who favored slavery, felt that slaves should not be freed at all.

After an attack on Abolitionists and Black leaders in the New York *Enquirer,* Cornish and Russwurm (the second Black person to graduate from a college in the United States) decided that it was time for Blacks to speak through their own newspaper. In the first edition of the 4-page weekly, the editors wrote

> We wish to plead our own cause. Too long have others spoken for us. Too long has the public been deceived by misrepresentation in things which concern us dearly, though in the estimation of some mere trifles; for although there are many in society who exercise toward us benevolent feelings, still (with some sorrow we confess it) there are others who enlarge upon that which tends to discredit any person of color. (Daniel, 1982, p.184)[6]

Freedom's Journal is often described as an aggressive newspaper that agitated forcefully against slavery and for the rights of free Blacks in the North. All of that is true, but the newspaper was also much more. It built a new consciousness in and community among Blacks and identified their struggle with the struggles of other people of color in America. It was able to do this because the newspaper reflected the broad interests of Blacks, which went beyond slavery, abolition, and freedom. In addition to Abolitionist news and hard-hitting editorials, the newspaper offered information, features, culture, and entertainment.

Its first issue reflected the broad interests of its editors and readers, carrying news from Haiti and Sierra Leone; the first part of a serial on Captain Paul Cuffee, a Black Boston shipper; a poem titled "The African Chief"; and advertising for the B.F. Hughes's School of Colored Children of Both Sexes. In its 2 years, *Freedom's Journal* ran regular columns titled "People of Colour," "Foreign News," "Domestic News," and "Summary." Some of these columns were based on news from other newspapers and were highly sensational. The "Summary" column especially exploited the

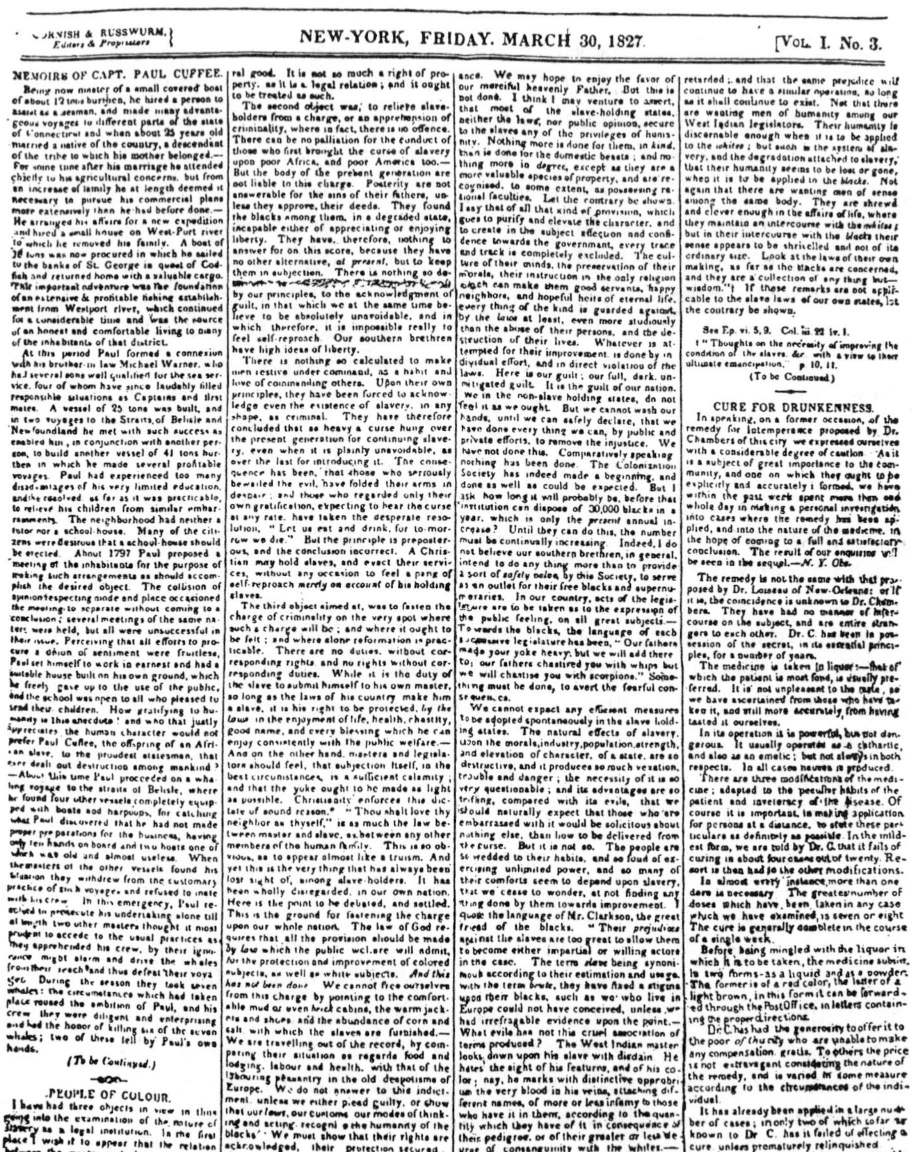

FREEDOM'S JOURNAL.

" RIGHTEOUSNESS EXALTETH A NATION."

CORNISH & RUSSWURM, *Editors & Proprietors* | NEW-YORK, FRIDAY. MARCH 30, 1827. | [VOL. I. No. 3.

MEMOIRS OF CAPT. PAUL CUFFEE.

Being now master of a small covered boat of about 12 tons burthen, he hired a person to assist as a seaman, and made many advantageous voyages to different parts of the state of Connecticut and when about 25 years old married a native of the country, a descendant of the tribe to which his mother belonged.—For some time after his marriage he attended chiefly to his agricultural concerns, but from an increase of family he at length deemed it necessary to pursue his commercial plans more extensively than he had before done.—He arranged his affairs for a new expedition and hired a small house on West-Port river to which he removed his family. A boat of 18 tons was now procured in which he sailed to the banks of St. George in quest of Cod-fish and returned home with a valuable cargo. This important adventure was the foundation of an extensive & profitable fishing establishment from Westport river, which continued for a considerable time and was the source of an honest and comfortable living to many of the inhabitants of that district.

At this period Paul formed a connexion with his brother-in law Michael Warner, who had several sons well qualified for the sea service, four of whom have since laudably filled responsible situations as Captains and first mates. A vessel of 25 tons was built, and in two voyages to the Straits of Belisle and Newfoundland he met with such success as enabled him, in conjunction with another person, to build another vessel of 41 tons burthen in which he made several profitable voyages. Paul had experienced too many disadvantages of his very limited education, and he resolved, as far as it was practicable, to relieve his children from similar embarrassments. The neighborhood had neither a tutor nor a school-house. Many of the citizens were desirous that a school-house should be erected. About 1797 Paul proposed a meeting of the inhabitants for the purpose of making such arrangements as should accomplish the desired object. The collision of opinion respecting mode and place occasioned the meeting to separate without coming to a conclusion; several meetings of the same nature were held, but all were unsuccessful in their issue. Perceiving that all efforts to procure a union of sentiment were fruitless, Paul set himself to work in earnest and had a suitable house built on his own ground, which he freely gave up to the use of the public, and the school was open to all who pleased to send their children. How gratifying to humanity is this anecdote! and who that justly appreciates the human character would not prefer Paul Cuffee, the offspring of an African slave, to the proudest statesman, that ever dealt out destruction among mankind?—About this time Paul proceeded on a whaling voyage to the straits of Belisle, where he found four other vessels completely equipped with boats and harpoons, for catching whales. Paul discovered that he had not made proper preparations for the business, having only ten hands on board and two boats one of which was old and almost useless. When the masters of the other vessels found his situation they withdrew from the customary practice of such voyages and refused to mate with his crew. In this emergency, Paul resolved to prosecute his undertaking alone till at length two other masters thought it most prudent to accede to the usual practices as they apprehended his crew, by their ignorance might alarm and drive the whales from their reach and thus defeat their voyages. During the season they took seven whales: the circumstance which had taken place roused the ambition of Paul, and his crew they were diligent and enterprising and had the honor of killing six of the seven whales; two of these fell by Paul's own hands.

(To be Continued.)

PEOPLE OF COLOUR.

I have had three objects in view in thus going into the examination of the nature of slavery as a legal institution. In the first place I wish it to appear that the relation between the master and slave is a proper subject of legislation. It is a conventional right and depends entirely upon the laws.—as the laws create it they may modify, enlarge, restrain, or destroy it, without any other limitation than is imposed by the general good. It is not so much a right of property, as it is a legal relation; and it ought to be treated as such.

The second object was, to relieve slave-holders from a charge, or an apprehension of criminality, where in fact, there is no offence. There can be no palliation for the conduct of those who first brought the curse of slavery upon poor Africa, and poor America too.—But the body of the present generation are not liable to this charge. Posterity are not answerable for the sins of their fathers, unless they approve their deeds. They found the blacks among them, in a degraded state, incapable either of appreciating or enjoying liberty. They have, therefore, nothing to answer for on this score, because they have no other alternative, *at present*, but to keep them in subjection. There is nothing so de-[illegible] by our principles, to the acknowledgment of guilt, in that which we at the same time believe to be absolutely unavoidable, and in which therefore, it is impossible really to feel self-reproach. Our southern brethren have high ideas of liberty.

There is nothing so calculated to make men restive under command, as a habit and love of commanding others. Upon their own principles, they have been forced to acknowledge even the existence of slavery, in any shape, as criminal. They have therefore concluded that as heavy a curse hung over the present generation for continuing slavery, even when it is plainly unavoidable, as over the last for introducing it. The consequence has been, that those who seriously bewailed the evil, have folded their arms in despair; and those who regarded only their own gratification, expecting to bear the curse at any rate, have taken the desperate resolution, "Let us eat and drink, for to-morrow we die." But the principle is preposterous, and the conclusion incorrect. A Christian *may* hold slaves, and exact their services, without any occasion to feel a pang of self-reproach *merely on account* of his holding slaves.

The third object aimed at, was to fasten the charge of criminality on the very spot where such a charge will be; and where it ought to be felt; and where alone reformation is practicable. There are no duties, without corresponding rights, and no rights without corresponding duties. While it is the duty of the slave to submit himself to his own master, so long as the laws of his country make him a slave, it is his right to be protected, *by the laws* in the enjoyment of life, health, chastity, good name, and every blessing which he can enjoy consistently with the public welfare.—And on the other hand, masters and legislators should feel, that subjection itself, in the best circumstances, is a sufficient calamity; and that the yoke ought to be made as light as possible. Christianity enforces this dictate of sound reason.* "Thou shalt love thy neighbor as thyself," is as much the law between master and slave, as between any other members of the human family. This is so obvious, as to appear almost like a truism. And yet this is the very thing that has always been lost sight of, among slave-holders. It has been wholly disregarded, in our own nation. Here is the point to be debated, and settled. This is the ground for fastening the charge upon our whole nation. The law of God requires that all the provision should be made *by law* which the public welfare will admit, for the protection and improvement of colored subjects, as well as white subjects. *And this has not been done.* We cannot free ourselves from this charge by pointing to the comfortable mud or even *brick* cabins, the warm jackets and shoes and the abundance of corn and salt, with which the slaves are furnished.—We are travelling out of the record, by comparing their situation as regards food and lodging, labour and health, with that of the labouring peasantry in the old despotisms of Europe. We do not answer to this indictment, unless we either plead guilty, or show that our *laws*, our customs, our modes of thinking and acting, recognise the humanity of the blacks.' We must show that their rights are acknowledged, their protection secured, their welfare promoted; and that, in every particular, excepting that of involuntary servitude and its *necessary* attendants, they stand upon the same ground with their masters.—When this is done we shall feel no guilt on the subject. We shall fear no divine vengeance. We may hope to enjoy the favor of our merciful heavenly Father. But this is not done. I think I may venture to assert, that most of the slave-holding states, neither the laws, nor public opinion, secure to the slaves any of the privileges of humanity. Nothing more is done for them, in *kind*, than is done for the domestic beasts; and nothing more in *degree*, except as they are a more valuable species of property, and are recognised, to some extent, as possessing rational faculties. Let the contrary be shown. I say that of all that kind of provision, which goes to purify and elevate the character, and to create in the subject affection and confidence towards the government, every trace and track is completely excluded. The culture of their minds, the preservation of their morals, their instruction in the only religion which can make them good servants, happy neighbors, and hopeful heirs of eternal life, every thing of the kind is guarded against, by the *laws* at least, even more studiously than the abuse of their persons, and the destruction of their lives. Whatever is attempted for their improvement, is done by individual effort, and in direct violation of the laws. Here is our guilt; our full, dark, unmitigated guilt. It is the guilt of our nation. We in the non-slave holding states, do not feel it as we ought. But we cannot wash our hands, until we can safely declare, that we have done every thing we can, by public and private efforts, to remove the injustice. We have not done this. Comparatively speaking nothing has been done. The Colonization Society has indeed made a beginning, and done as well as could be expected. But I ask how long it will probably be, before that institution can dispose of 30,000 blacks in a year, which is only the *present* annual increase? Until they can do this, the number must be continually increasing. Indeed, I do not believe our southern brethren, in general, intend to do any thing more than to provide a sort of *safety valve*, by this Society, to serve as an outlet for their free blacks and supernumeraries. In our country, acts of the legislature are to be taken as to the expression of the public feeling, on all great subjects.—Towards the blacks, the language of each successive legislature has been, "Our fathers made your yoke heavy, but we will add thereto; our fathers chastised you with whips but we will chastise you with scorpions." Something must be done, to avert the fearful consequences.

We cannot expect any efficient measures to be adopted spontaneously in the slave holding states. The natural effects of slavery, upon the morals, industry, population, strength, and elevation of character, of a state, are so destructive, and it produces so much vexation, trouble and danger; the necessity of it is so very questionable; and its advantages are so trifling, compared with its evils, that we should naturally expect that those who are embarrassed with it would be solicitous about nothing else, than how to be delivered from the curse. But it is not so. The people are so wedded to their habits, and so fond of exercising unlimited power, and so many of their comforts seem to depend upon slavery, that we cease to wonder, at not finding any thing done by them towards improvement. I quote the language of Mr. Clarkson, the great friend of the blacks. "Their *prejudices* against the slaves are too great to allow them to become either impartial or willing actors in the case. The term *slave* being synonimous according to their estimation and usage, with the term *brute*, they have fixed a stigma upon their blacks, such as we who live in Europe could not have conceived, unless we had irrefragable evidence upon the point.—What evils has not this cruel association of terms produced? The West Indian master looks down upon his slave with disdain. He hates the sight of his features, and of his color; nay, he marks with distinctive opprobrium the very blood in his veins, attaching different names, of more or less infamy to those who have it in them, according to the quantity which they have of it in consequence of their pedigree, or of their greater or less degree of consanguinity with the whites.—Hence the West Indian feels an unwillingness to elevate the condition of the black, or to do any thing for him as a human being. I have no doubt, that this prejudice has been one of the great causes why the improvement of our slave population *by law* has been so long retarded; and that the same prejudice will continue to have a similar operation, so long as it shall continue to exist. Not that there are wanting men of humanity among our West Indian legislators. Their humanity is discernable enough when it is to be applied to the *whites*; but such is the system of slavery, and the degradation attached to slavery, that their humanity seems to be lost or gone, when it is to be applied to the *blacks*. Not again that there are wanting men of sense among the same body. They are shrewd and clever enough in the affairs of life, where they maintain an intercourse with the *whites*; but in their intercourse with the *blacks* their sense appears to be shrivelled and not of its ordinary size. Look at the laws of their own making, as far as the blacks are concerned, and they are a collection of any thing but—wisdom."† If these remarks are not applicable to the slave laws of our own states, let the contrary be shown.

* See Ep. vi. 5, 9. Col. iii. 22 iv. 1.

† "Thoughts on the necessity of improving the condition of the slaves, &c. with a view to their ultimate emancipation." p. 10, 11.

(To be Continued.)

CURE FOR DRUNKENNESS.

In speaking, on a former occasion, of the remedy for Intemperance proposed by Dr. Chambers of this city we expressed ourselves with a considerable degree of caution. As it is a subject of great importance to the community, and one on which they ought to be explicitly and accurately informed, we have within the past week spent more than one whole day in making a personal investigation into cases where the remedy has been applied, and into the nature of the medicine, in the hope of coming to a full and satisfactory conclusion. The result of our enquiries will be seen in the sequel.—*N. Y. Obs.*

The remedy is not the same with that proposed by Dr. Loiseau of New-Orleans: or if it is, the coincidence is unknown to Dr. Chambers. They have had no manner of intercourse on the subject, and are entire strangers to each other. Dr. C. has been in possession of the secret, in its essential principles, for a number of years.

The medicine is taken in liquor:—that of which the patient is most fond, is usually preferred. It is not unpleasant to the taste, as we have ascertained from those who have taken it, and still more accurately, from having tasted it ourselves.

In its operation it is powerful, but not dangerous. It usually operates as a cathartic, and also as an emetic; but not always in both respects. In all cases nausea is produced.

There are three modifications of the medicine; adapted to the peculiar habits of the patient and inveteracy of the disease. Of course it is important, in making application for persons at a distance, to state these particulars as definitely as possible. In the mildest form, we are told by Dr. C. that it fails of curing in about four cases out of twenty. Resort is then had to the other modifications.

In almost every instance, more than one dose is necessary. The greatest number of doses which have been taken in any case which we have examined, is seven or eight. The cure is generally complete in the course of a single week.

Before being mingled with the liquor in which it is to be taken, the medicine subsists in two forms—as a liquid and as a powder. The former is of a red color, the latter of a light brown, in this form it can be forwarded through the Post Office, in letters containing the proper directions.

Dr. C. has had the generosity to offer it to the poor *of this city* who are unable to make any compensation, gratis. To others the price is not extravagant considering the nature of the remedy, and is varied in some measure according to the circumstances of the individual.

It has already been applied in a large number of cases; in only two of which so far as known to Dr C. has it failed of effecting a cure unless prematurely relinquished.

We have conversed with two respectable gentlemen, entirely disinterested, which have had opportunity to witness its effects on a large number of individuals, and it is their decided opinion that it is a real remedy.

Several persons of good standing in society

Illustration 11.4 *Freedom's Journal* (1827) in New York City was the first Black newspaper in the United States, publishing general news of interest to African Americans, strident opposition to slavery, and advocacy of equal rights for free Blacks in northern states.

Source: Library of Congress.

staples of sensational reporting: blood and sex (Daniel, 1982; Nordin, 1977-1978).[5]

Freedom's Journal strongly opposed slavery and advocated the rights of free Blacks. The newspaper also attacked racism in the White media and reinforced the importance of the alternative viewpoint it presented on African American issues. Walter Daniel (1982) wrote of *Freedom's Journal* that it attacked the editor of the New York *Enquirer*

> as one "whose object is to keep alive the prejudice of the whites against the coloured communities of New York City." Other articles disagreed with the platform of the American Colonization Society which advocated returning Afro-Americans to Africa and reported on lynching. Russwurm believed in universal education as a critical need for Blacks who would be respected by White Americans. (p. 185)

Russwurm left *Freedom's Journal* in 1828 to become an editor and official in Liberia, a part of Africa some Abolitionists established for freed slaves. The newspaper continued to be published by Cornish under the title *Rights of All* until 1829. Lionel Barrow wrote in a 1977 *Journalism History* issue devoted to Black press history that

> *Freedom's Journal* gave Blacks a voice of their own and an opportunity not only to answer the attacks printed in the White press but to read articles on Black accomplishments, marriages, deaths that the White press of the day ignored. Slavery is no longer here, but its vestiges are and today's reporters and publishers—Black and White—could do well to study the *Journal,* adopt its objectives and emulate its content. Blacks still need to "plead our own causes," and will need to do so for sometime to come. (Barrow, 1977-1978, p. 22; see also La Brie, 1977-1978, and Nordin, 1977-1978)

Like many Black newspapers and other racial and ethnic newspapers that followed it, *Freedom's Journal* filled an important void. It did more than take issue with the coverage and editorial positions that were found in the mass audience White press. It presented a class media alternative by reporting events of interest to Blacks with dignity and pride, demonstrating that its Black readers, though targets of slavery and racism, were doing more than was reported in the White press and also wanted to know more about themselves and others.

Along these lines, *Freedom's Journal* identified the struggle of Blacks with the struggles of other people of color fighting for their rights. The April 27, 1827 issue ran a story in its "Summary" section of attempts by Alabama authorities to extend state laws over "territory owned and inhabited by the Indian nations." The editors asked rhetorically, "Is this treating them as they are acknowledged to be an independent nation?" Another story, in the paper's "Varieties" section, was headlined "Indian

Observation" and referred to Native Americans as "our red brethren of the west."

A week earlier, the April 20 issue of *Freedom's Journal* reprinted from the *New York Observer* an article headlined "The Revolt in Texas." The newspapers reported the troubles of "certain slaveholders from the United States" who took slaves to Texas, which was then part of Mexico, "with the expectation of amassing great fortunes by means of the sinews and traffic of slaves." But after Mexico gained its independence from Spain, it adopted a law prohibiting the importation of slaves, which had the potential to end slavery altogether. So the slave owners "set up a government of their own, which they called the Republic of Fredonia." They hoped that nearby Indians would help them, but the Indians "readily took sides with the Mexicans." Unable to hold off the Mexican troops sent to restore order, the article stated, "those advocates for the liberty of enslaving others found plenty of business upon their hands, and are at length either captured or dispersed." The article praised the new Latin American republics for abolishing slavery or "lightening the bar which for centuries had oppressed the poor Indians."

For more than 175 years, Black media have continued to fulfill multiple roles. They have raised the concerns and protests of Blacks when confronted with slavery, segregation, lynching, violation of voting rights, and discrimination—in education, employment, and housing—and other forms of unequal treatment. They have reported on the organizational, social, religious, and other activities and interests within Black communities that have too often been ignored by the White media. And they have built bridges of understanding among all racial groups.

The First Native American Newspaper: The *Cherokee Phoenix* in 1828

Like the first Latino and Black newspapers, the first Native American newspaper was born out of a crisis, in this case the federal government's efforts to displace the people of the Cherokee Nation from the millions of acres of land they held across what are now several states, including North Carolina, Georgia, and Tennessee. During this crisis, the *Cherokee Phoenix* was born to unify and express the opinions of the Cherokee people and counter the portrayal of Native Americans in the White press (LaCourse, 1979).[7]

The *Cherokee Phoenix* was established by the Cherokee Nation in New Echota, near the current site of Calhoun, Georgia, and printed its first edition on February 21, 1828. It appeared weekly, with a few gaps, for 6 years—until 1834. Like *El Misisipí*, it was bilingual, using both English and

Illustration 11.5 *Cherokee Phoenix* (1828) in New Echota, Georgia was the first Native American newspaper in the United States, publishing articles in both English and the Cherokee syllabary developed by Sequoyah.

Source: Library of Congress.

the 86-character Cherokee written language introduced by Sequoyah (who was also known as George Gist) in 1821 after 12 years of work.[8] James and Sharon Murphy (1981) write that the newspaper was started out of two needs: the desire of missionaries to spread Christianity among the Cherokees and the desire of Cherokee Nation leaders to unify Cherokees and others in support of the fight to keep their homelands.

The first editor of the *Cherokee Phoenix* was Cherokee schoolteacher Elias Boudinot (also known as Buck Oowatie), who also was clerk of the Cherokee National Council. To raise funds for the new newspaper, he traveled along the East Coast speaking to philanthropic and religious groups. Financial assistance for the newspaper came both from Cherokee Nation, which approved the building of a newspaper office in 1826 and allocated $1,500 for a printing press in 1827 (before Boudinot began his fundraising trip), and from the American Board of Commissioners for Foreign Missions in New England, which helped finance the casting of Sequoyah's Cherokee syllabary into metal type. Samuel Worcester, a missionary working among the Cherokees, requested the Foreign Mission support. The Cherokee Nation later repaid the mission board for its help.

Boudinot's vision, like that of the editors of *Freedom's Journal*, was of a newspaper to counter the biased accounts in White newspapers by accurately reflecting the lives of his people and mobilizing public opinion in support of their cause. In an 1826 "Address to the Whites" at the First Presbyterian Church in Philadelphia, he proposed a newspaper

> comprising a summary of religious and political events, etc., on the one hand; and on the other, exhibiting the feelings, dispositions, improvements, and prospects of the Indians: their traditions, their true character, as it once was, as it now is, and the ways and means most likely to throw the mantle of civilization over all tribes; and such other matters as will tend to diffuse proper and correct impressions in regard to their condition—such a paper could not fail to create much interest in the American Community, favorable to the aboriginies, and to have a powerful influence on the advancement of the Indians themselves. (cited in Murphy & Murphy, 1981, p. 25)[9]

In its first issue, the *Cherokee Phoenix* reprinted a prospectus prepared by Worcester that promised that the newspaper would cover local happenings, Cherokee laws and customs, and the Cherokees' progress in education, religion, and culture. It would also print news about other tribes and "interesting articles calculated to promote Literature, Civilization, and Religion among the Cherokees" (cited in Murphy & Murphy, 1981, p. 25).

Subscriptions came from as far away as Germany. The newspaper was circulated through Cherokee villages—stretching from present-day North Carolina to Texas—to build the identity of the villages and their inhabitants as part of the Cherokee Nation, even though sometimes only one copy was allocated per village. In the fourth issue, the newspaper carried the first written laws of the Cherokees, with Boudinot's hopes that "our readers will perhaps be gratified to see the first commencement of written laws among the Cherokees" ("Cherokee Laws," 1828, p. 1). Although the newspaper printed articles in two languages, only rarely was the same article published in both English and Cherokee. There were generally three columns in English for every two in Cherokee, because the structure of Sequoyah's written language devised single characters for whole syllables and it took less space to write in Cherokee than in English.

Boudinot has been credited with building the *Cherokee Phoenix* "into a strong and loud voice of the Cherokee people as they struggled against increasingly insurmountable government opposition" (Luebke, 1979, p. 48). But his voice was not always strident. In the first issue, he promised that the paper would "not return railing for railing, but consult mildness" (cited in Luebke, 1979, p. 48). He made it clear that the newspaper would advocate Cherokee positions on issues that brought them into conflict with the encroaching Whites and their governments. Boudinot wrote in the first issue that

> In regard the controversy with Georgia, and the present policy of the Central Government, in removing, and concentrating the Indians, out of the limits of any state, which, by the way, appears to be gaining strength, we will invariably and faithfully state the feelings of the majority of our people. Our views, as a people, on this subject, have been most sadly misrepresented. These views we do not wish to conceal, but are willing that the public should know what we think of this policy, which, in our opinion, if carried into effect, will prove pernicious to us.

Boudinot concluded the editorial by attacking negative symbols Whites and their newspapers often used to characterize Native Americans.

> We would now commit our feeble efforts to the good will and indulgence of the public, praying that God will attend them with his blessings, and hoping for that happy period, when all the Indian tribes of America shall rise, Phoenix like, from their ashes, and when the terms "Indian depredation," "war whoop," "scalping knife" and the like, shall become obsolete, and for ever be buried deep underground. (cited in Luebke, 1979, p. 51)[10]

As Murphy and Murphy (1981) pointed out, in subsequent issues Boudinot used the paper to protest attempts by the state of Georgia to include the Cherokee Nation in its criminal laws, and to fight against federal appropriations to remove the Cherokees from their mineral-laden lands. But, like *Freedom's Journal*, it is unfair to describe the *Cherokee Phoenix* as a newspaper that was concerned solely with the struggles of its audience. The newspaper carried advertising for merchants, a boarding school, and other businesses catering to the needs of its readers. The newspaper also campaigned against alcoholism and argued against the slavery in which Blacks were held, although Cherokee law permitted slaves. The newspaper sent mixed messages on slavery by running advertising by owners seeking return of runaway slaves and occasional anecdotes in Black dialect (Riley, 1979, p. 45).

In 1829, the newspaper enlarged its title and became the *Cherokee Phoenix and Indian Advocate,* which reflected its having broadened its coverage to include the issues faced by other tribes. Over the years, the editor and staff continued to protest the encroachment of Cherokees' legal and civil rights by Whites, including Georgia officials' threats, harassment, and arrests of the newspaper's staff. When the Cherokees came under intense pressure to move from their ancestral lands, the leaders of the nation were divided on the issue. Boudinot resigned the editorship in 1832, after he had been ordered by Cherokee Principal Chief John Ross not to publish reports of the division among the leaders. The new editor was Ross's brother-in-law, John Hicks, who continued to fight against the harassment and land grabbing confronting the Cherokees. The newspaper appeared less regularly and ceased its first run of publication on May 31, 1834.

But, like its namesake, the mythical phoenix bird who died and was born again out of its ashes, the *Cherokee Phoenix* rose again. It was resurrected by the Cherokee Nation and has gone on to publish both print and digital editions. In 2003, the *Cherokee Phoenix* marked its 175th anniversary. The *Cherokee Phoenix,* like the other Native American newspapers that followed, found the bilingual format to be an effective way of communicating with both its Native American and European immigrant audiences. Although the bilingual format is diminishing in print today, it is still used by Native American radio stations that broadcast programs in both English and their native languages. Like the *Cherokee Phoenix,* many newspapers have devoted most of their space to news of specific interest to Native Americans. Tribally affiliated newspapers have had the longest publication runs. But tribal newspaper editors often have clashed, as did Elias Boudinot, with tribal government leaders for editorial freedom.[11]

The First Asian Pacific American Newspaper: *The Golden Hills' News* in 1854

As with the first Latino, Black, and Native American newspapers, the nation's first Asian Pacific American newspaper, *The Golden Hills' News,* was born during a crisis in the lives of its readers. The era was the California Gold Rush of 1849, which drew gold seekers from around the world to what became the Golden State. Among the new arrivals were the Chinese, who crossed the Pacific Ocean to California, which they called Gold Mountain. Although the first Chinese arrivals were welcomed, the Chinese who arrived in San Francisco shortly thereafter were targets of racial prejudice and discrimination. In 1853, a racist Foreign Miners Tax reduced their incomes in the Sierra Nevada gold fields (Takaki, 1989, cited in Zia, 2000, pp. 25-27).

Asians and Pacific Islanders had long been traveling to what became the United States. There are documented, though disputed, reports of Hui Shên, a Chinese Buddhist priest, sailing down what is now the California coast from what is now British Columbia, Canada, in 458 C.E.—more than a thousand years before Christopher Columbus landed in America. Spanish explorers found the wreck of a ship believed to be of Asian construction on the California coast in 1774, and Filipinos worked on Spanish ships sailing to America, including some whose descendants, called Manilamen, settled in Louisiana in the 1760s (Chan, 1991, p. 25; Hansen & Heintz, 1970, pp. 7-8). People from Asia have been reported steadily, but infrequently, in the United States since at least 1785, when several Chinese sailors were stranded in Baltimore. The first enumeration of Chinese by a United States census was in 1820 (Chen, 1971, p. 3).

But it was the need for inexpensive, hardworking labor in the California Gold Rush that brought the first large groups of Asian immigrants to the United States. Almost immediately they drew the attention of San Francisco's White press, although the coverage did little to foster better understanding between San Franciscans and the new immigrants. A leading San Francisco newspaper, the *Alta California,* made what one scholar called "editorial humor" of the Chinese, including its own "Chinese letters" to ridicule Chinese writing. Where there was a profit to be made, English-language newspapers used lithography to insert Chinese characters into advertisements. Chinese characters also appeared in reports on the inscriptions on Chinese graves (Barth, 1971, p. 174).[12]

In 1854, Methodist missionaries in San Francisco's growing Chinatown founded *Kim-Shan Jit San-Luk, The Golden Hills' News* to reach the Chinese in San Francisco and foster a better understanding of them among Whites. The newspaper took its title from the name that the Chinese adopted for California during the Gold Rush—golden hills. Although some sources report that *The Golden Hills' News* began in 1851 (Daggett, 1939, cited in Hansen & Heintz, 1970, p. 45), pioneer California editor Edward Kemble (1858/1962, pp. 117-119) cited a founding date of 1854, a date accepted by Karl Lo and Him Mark Lai in their 1977 book on Chinese newspapers in North America (Lo & Lai, 1977, cited in Chiu, 1996). The 1854 date is also supported by the newspaper's own issue numbers.[13]

Like the other newspapers discussed in this chapter, *The Golden Hills' News* was born at a time of crisis for its readers. The Chinese people had

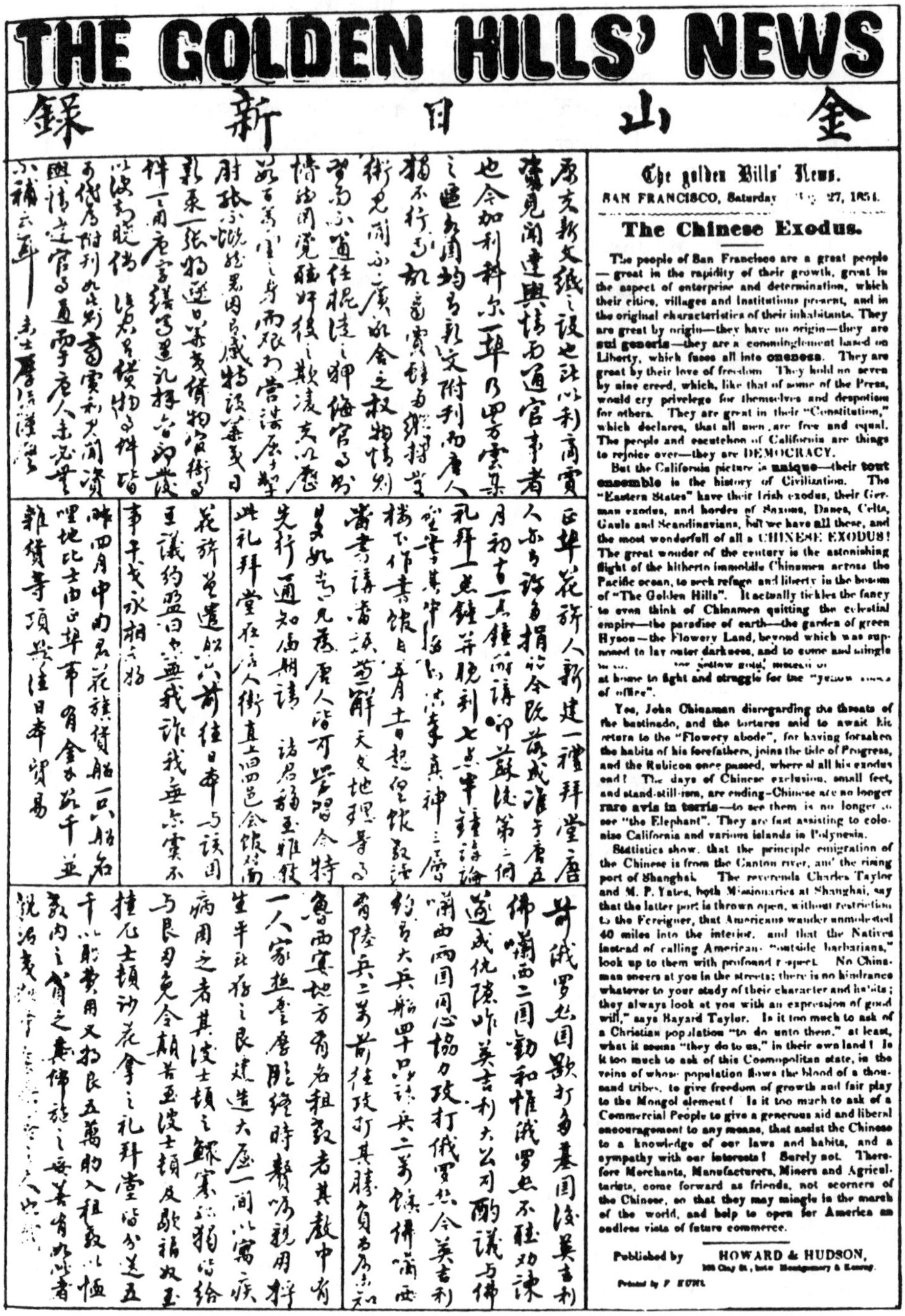

THE GOLDEN HILLS' NEWS

金山日新錄

The Golden Hills' News.

SAN FRANCISCO, Saturday [illegible] 27, 1854.

The Chinese Exodus.

The people of San Francisco are a great people—great in the rapidity of their growth, great in the aspect of enterprise and determination, which their cities, villages and institutions present, and in the original characteristics of their inhabitants. They are great by origin—they have no origin—they are **sui generis**—they are a commingleinent based on Liberty, which fuses all into **oneness**. They are great by their love of freedom. They hold no seven by nine creed, which, like that of some of the Press, would cry privelege for themselves and despotism for others. They are great in their "Constitution," which declares, that all men are free and equal. The people and escutcheon of California are things to rejoice over—they are DEMOCRACY.

But the California picture is **unique**—their **tout ensemble** is the history of Civilization. The "Eastern States" have their Irish exodus, their German exodus, and hordes of Saxons, Danes, Celts, Gauls and Scandinavians, but we have all these, and the most wonderfull of all a CHINESE EXODUS! The great wonder of the century is the astonishing flight of the hitherto immoldile Chinamen across the Pacific ocean, to seek refuge and liberty in the bosom of "The Golden Hills". It actually tickles the fancy to even think of Chinamen quitting the celestial empire—the paradise of earth—the garden of green Hyson—the Flowery Land, beyond which was supposed to lay outer darkness, and to come and mingle [illegible] "yellow gold," [illegible] at home to fight and struggle for the "yellow [illegible] of office".

Yes, John Chinaman disregarding the threats of the bastinado, and the tortures said to await his return to the "Flowery abode", for having forsaken the habits of his forefathers, joins the tide of Progress, and the Rubicon once passed, where al all his exodus end? The days of Chinese exclusion, small feet, and stand-still-ism, are ending—Chinese are no longer **rare avis in terris**—to see them is no longer to see "the Elephant". They are fast assisting to colonise California and various islands in Polynesia.

Statistics show, that the principle emigration of the Chinese is from the Canton river, and the rising port of Shanghai. The reverends Charles Taylor and M. P. Yates, both Missionaries at Shanghai, say that the latter port is thrown open, without restriction to the Foreigner, that Americans wander unmolested 40 miles into the interior, and that the Natives instead of calling Americans "outside barbarians," look up to them with profound respect. No Chinaman sneers at you in the streets; there is no hindrance whatever to your study of their character and habits; they always look at you with an expression of good will," says Bayard Taylor. Is it too much to ask of a Christian population "to do unto them," at least, what it seems "they do to us," in their own land! Is it too much to ask of this Cosmopolitan state, in the veins of whose population flows the blood of a thousand tribes, to give freedom of growth and fair play to the Mongol element? Is it too much to ask of a Commercial People to give a generous aid and liberal encouragement to any means, that assist the Chinese to a knowledge of our laws and habits, and a sympathy with our interests! Surely not. Therefore Merchants, Manufacturers, Miners and Agriculturists, come forward as friends, not scorners of the Chinese, so that they may mingle in the march of the world, and help to open for America an endless vista of future commerce.

Published by HOWARD & HUDSON,
[illegible] Clay St., betw. Montgomery & Kearny.

Printed by F. KUHL

Illustration 11.6 *The Golden Hills' News* (1854) in San Francisco was the first Asian Pacific American newspaper in the United States, publishing both news for Chinese immigrant readers and English-language editorials calling for fair treatment of Chinese coming to the California Gold Rush.

left their homeland, crossed an ocean, and come to the United States with hopes of making their fortune in the gold fields. They found a country vastly different than their own in race, language, and culture. Upon arrival they often were forced into the most undesirable labor, at little or no pay, to repay the cost of their passage. Many of the newly arrived females were poor girls who were sold as slaves into prostitution (Chan, 1991; Yung, 1999).[14] The Chinese people were treated as outcasts by the White world; they were targeted for legal, economic, and social discrimination in a California newly populated by European immigrants. *The Golden Hills' News* was founded by Protestant churches with missionaries in China and outposts in San Francisco's developing Chinatown. The church outposts offered help to Chinese immigrants in the hostile land, hoping to convert them to Christianity in the process.

In his history of the Chinese in the United States from 1850 to 1870, Gunther Barth (1971) notes that the first issue of *The Golden Hills' News*, in April of 1854, promised that the paper would appear twice weekly. It was published by William Howard, with Chinese characters lithographed by F. Kuhl. The day after the first edition appeared, the San Francisco *Herald* compared the newspaper's Chinese characters to the tracks of a spider crawling out of an ink bottle and onto a white sheet of paper.

The paper sold for 25 cents a copy, with a monthly subscription costing 75 cents. Charges for advertising were $1 for less than 25 characters, $2 for between 25 and 50 characters, and three cents apiece for more than 50 characters. Barth (1971) describes most of the content of the paper as being in colloquial Cantonese, with much of the news coming from California (pp. 174-175). By June of that first year, the newspaper had scaled back to weekly publication "until the Chinese generally adopt it, when it will be published semiweekly." In the June 24 issue, the advertisements of Hudson & Co., California Stage Company, Steam Navigation Company, and Miner's Exchange Bank and the want ads filled a full page of advertising targeting Chinese people.

Like *El Misisipí* and the *Cherokee Phoenix,* the newspaper was bilingual, although articles were not translated from one language to the other. The front page of the May 27, 1854 edition featured Cantonese characters on about two thirds of the page on the left-hand side, with an English-language column addressed to the Whites on the right. The Cantonese characters reported commercial news and other community notices of interest to Chinese readers. The English-language column was an editorial directed toward Whites and argued for better treatment of Chinese people in California. The editorial noted that while the Eastern United States was welcoming European immigrants, Chinese coming to California were greeted with discrimination.

The "Eastern States" have their Irish exodus, their German exodus, and hordes of Saxons, Danes, Celts, Gauls and Scandanavians, but we have **all** of these, and the most wonderful of all a CHINESE EXODUS! The great wonder of the century is the astonishing flight of the hitherto immobile Chinamen across the Pacific ocean, to seek refuge and liberty in the bosom of "The Golden Hills." ("The Chinese Exodus," 1854, p. 1)

The writer quoted missionaries in Shanghai who wrote that Americans could "wander unmolested" 40 miles into the Chinese interior and claimed that Chinese who saw Americans would "look up to them with profound respect." That behavior was compared with the racism that Chinese immigrants found in California.

"No Chinaman sneers at you in the streets; there is no hindrance whatever to your study of their character and habits; they always look at you with an expression of good will," says Bayard Taylor. "Is it too much to ask of a Christian population 'to do unto them,' at least what it seems 'they do to us,' in their own land?" ("The Chinese Exodus," 1854, p. 1)

On July 1, 1854 an English-language editorial in *The Golden Hills' News*, "The Government, Press, Public and Chinese," noted that Chinese coming to the United States were "treated with the most rooted prejudice, hatred, and injustice." The newspaper urged that laws be translated and published so that Chinese people could learn the ways of the United States. The editorial stated that

At present each poor Chinese on emerging in our country with Asiatic habits and language is left to himself—a straggler in a strange land—a being, whose efforts are often repulsed—whose chance of employ are limited, and whose conduct is only watched or cared for by Policemen when they are likely to be mischievous to others! They are held responsible for taxes and other duties, but the State or County is responsible for no duties to them in return. (p. 1)

Biased treatment of the Chinese by U.S. newspapers was a special target of *The Golden Hills' News* English-language editorials. On June 10, 1854, an editorial headlined "The Chinese and the Times" charged, "our Conductors of the Press describe them as 'Apes,' 'Brutes,' and 'social lice'!" (p. 1). An editorial in the July 29 issue, "American Preachings versus Practice," argued that the "hypocrisy" of American democracy was "well illustrated in the infamous treatment of the Chinese in this country," especially in newspapers that supported racist practices against Chinese people. The editorial continued, "The Press almost unanimously have spoken against them with bitter contempt, and has excited an aggressive prejudice against them in the public mind" (p. 1).

An editorial that appeared between the two issues of *The Golden Hills' News* mentioned above, in the June 24 issue, was particularly severe in its criticism of the treatment of Chinese in their new homeland. It was titled "Is there no help for the Chinese in California?" and charged that

> The Press has stained its pages with filthy abuse **usque ad nauseam**—hot has been the indignation against their habits; fierce the denunciation against their labor—and fearful the vengeance against their offences. These facts stand recorded in our history and no editorial effrontery can efface it—no "theory of race"-sophistry can wrench it out of its place—that our Press, Legislature, Senate and Municipalities, have done their best, actively or passively, to shut out from the Chinese the light of knowledge of our Institutions and laws, and to stuff bigotry and prejudice against them into every chink of private benevolence or sympathy, which might be shone in upon them. (p. 1)

Other English-language editorials advocated equal rights for the Chinese in America and cited their willingness to participate in the traditions of their new country. Barth (1971) wrote that the English-language editorials set a precedent that was followed by later Chinese newspapers in California. The English-language columns were directed to White readers and were primarily concerned with discrimination and other civil rights violations against the Chinese as well as with pointing to evidence of Chinese adapting to the ways of the United States. The Chinese columns, on the other hand, were filled with commercial notices and other business-related news (Barth, 1971, pp. 175-176). By all accounts, *The Golden Hills' News* did not publish for a lengthy period. Writing in 1858, Kemble concluded his 3-line paragraph on the newspaper with the sentence "It did not live long" (Kemble, 1858/1962, p. 117).

But Asian Studies bibliographer Kuei Chiu (1996) noted that what *The Golden Hills' News* achieved is more important than the length of its existence: "Although this paper was short-lived, it marked the beginning of the Asian language journalism in America" (pp. 2, 4, 5). Like the other newspapers discussed in this chapter, *The Golden Hills' News* established precedents followed by later media directed to its audience. One such precedent was the use of a bilingual format, which continues to be used in Asian Pacific American media today. Another precedent was a column directed to English-speaking readers that argues for fairer treatment of the Chinese while pointing to the contributions of the Chinese to society. A third precedent was coverage of news from Asia. A fourth precedent was the inclusion of advertising by White firms targeting Chinese readers. Finally, a fifth precedent set by *The Golden Hills' News* was its founding in San Francisco, which was also the birthplace of the first U.S. newspapers for people from Japan, *Shinonome (Dawn)* in 1886, and Korea, *Konglip Sinbo (Public News* or *United Korean)* in 1905.

Similarities in the First
Newspapers of People of Color

Identifying the first Latino, Black, Native American, and Asian American newspapers in the United States is important for reasons that extend beyond establishing a chronology for the sake of historical accuracy. As important as the founding of the first printed communication medium for each group was, even more vital are the similarities among the newspapers begun for different groups at different times in different places. All the newspapers were founded, as we have already established, at a time when each group was facing a crisis that was not being experienced by White people. In addition, the founders of each newspaper were men, reflecting the lower status of women across all groups. Three of the newspapers, *El Misisipí*, the *Cherokee Phoenix,* and *The Golden Hills' News,* were bilingual and used both their native language and English. Three of the newspapers had religious roots: The *Cherokee Phoenix* and *The Golden Hills' News* were founded with support of missionaries, and *Freedom's Journal* was cofounded by a minister.

All the newspapers were attuned to the news and information needs of their target audience and, like media for these communities today, offered news that was not well covered by the other newspapers. For example, two newspapers, *Freedom's Journal* and the *Cherokee Phoenix,* were established to provide an alternative voice and a third, *The Golden Hills' News,* appeared when White media were actively ridiculing and disparaging the Chinese. These three newspapers also appeared when the members of their audience were victims of legal discrimination, social subjugation, and violent oppression, and the papers actively took issue with the negative way their people were seen by Whites and portrayed in their press.

Today's newspapers, magazines, broadcast stations, and Internet sites targeted to communities of color are growing rapidly in the United States as class communication becomes more important to all media. Although in most of these media the content has become increasingly commercial and the voice less fiery than in their first predecessors, they continue to provide news, entertainment, and information alternatives to the general audience mass media. There is a longstanding need for people of color to have an alternative to general audience media—a need triggered by the behavior of the first mass circulation newspaper, the *New York Sun.*

In the 1840s, Willis A. Hodges, a Black man, took exception to editorials in the *Sun* that opposed voting rights for Blacks. The slogan of the *Sun* was "It Shines for ALL." So he first tried the access approach and wrote a reply to one of the editorials, which the newspaper printed for $15.

However, when the newspaper published his message, it had been modified and was carried as advertising. When Hodges protested, he was told that "The *Sun* shines for all White men but not for Colored men." So he started his own Black newspaper, *The Ram's Horn,* in 1847 (Penn, 1891, cited in Dodson & Hachten, 1973, p. 25).

As long as all people may produce their own newspapers, magazines, videos, and websites, members of all races will be able to follow Hodges and the founding editors of the first Latino, Black, Native American, and Asian Pacific American newspapers by launching media that reflect their own views and represent their communities. These class media targeting people of color are growing at a steady pace. The list of ethnic media, in a directory published by New California Media, grew from 400 to 600 print, broadcast, and online media from 2001 to 2003. As we make the transition from mass communication to class communication, the media targeted to racial and ethnic groups are becoming an increasingly important force on the media landscape of an increasingly multicultural United States.

Notes

1. For earlier descriptions of communication in non-European cultures, see *Communication in Africa,* by L. W. Doob, 1961, New Haven, CT: Yale University Press; *Mexican and Central American Mythology,* by I. Nicholson, 1967, London: Paul Hamlyn Limited; *Communication and Culture in Ancient India and China,* by R. T. Oliver, 1971, Syracuse, NY: Syracuse University Press; and *Daily Life of the Aztecs,* by J. Soustelle, 1961, Stanford, CA: Stanford University Press.

2. More description and a picture of Utah's Newspaper Rock can be found in "Newspaper Rock," in *Ancient Ruins of the Southwest* (pp. 176-178), by D. G. Noble, 2000, Menomonie, WI: Northland. For more on Southwestern petroglyphs, see *Canyon Country Prehistoric Rock Art,* by F. A. Barnes, 2000, Arch Hunter Books, which includes information on and pictures of the Petrified Forest National Park's Newspaper Rock (pp. 258-262) and Utah's Newspaper Rock State Historical Monument (pp. 244-249).

3. For a description of *relaciones* in Spain, see *The Spanish Press 1470-1966* (p. 72), by H. F. Schulte, 1968, Champaign: University of Illinois Press.

4. For an earlier Eurocentric account of America's journalism heritage, see *The Press and America* (4th ed, pp. 3-27), by E. Emery & M. Emery, 1978, Englewood Cliffs, NJ: Prentice Hall, and for the later more accurate approach, see *The Press in America,* (6th ed., pp. 1-6), by E. Emery and M. Emery, 1988, Englewood Cliffs, NJ: Prentice Hall.

5. All quotes are from *El Misisipí,* October 12, 1808 (pp. 1-4). For a more complete translation of the issue, see "Spanish Language Media in the U.S.," by F. Gutiérrez, January 1984, *Caminos,* pp. 10-12. See also "Spanish-language Media in America: Background Resources, History," by F. Gutiérrez, Summer 1977,

Journalism History, 4(2), 37 and *A History and Bibliography of Spanish Language Newspapers and Magazines in Louisiana, 1808–1949* (pp. 8-9), by R. MacCurdy, 1951, Albuquerque: University of New Mexico Press. For a comprehensive overview and listing of United States Latino periodicals through 1960, see *Hispanic Periodicals in the United States, Origins to 1960,* by N. Kanellos with Helvetia Martell, 2000, Houston, TX: Arte Público Press.

6. For more recent and comprehensive accounts of *Freedom's Journal,* other Black publications, and their editors, see *A History of the Black Press,* by A. Pride and C. C. Wilson, 1997, Washington, DC: Howard University Press; *The Early Black Press in America, 1827–1860,* by F. Hutton, 1993, Westport, CT: Greenwood; and *Black Journalists in Paradox,* by C. C. Wilson, 1991, Westport, CT: Greenwood.

7. See "An Indian Perspective—Native American Journalism: An Overview," by R. LaCourse, 1979, *Journalism History,* 6(2), 34-35, an issue of the journal devoted to Native American journalism.

8. For descriptions of the *Cherokee Phoenix* and Elias Boudinot, see Murphy and Murphy, 1981 (pp. 21-33). See also "The Cherokee Phoenix (and Indian Advocate)," by L. Worthy, and "Elias Boudinot, a North Georgia Notable," in *About North Georgia,* Golden Ink, http://ngeorgia.com/history/phoenix.html. In addition, see "Elias Boudinott, Indian Editor: Editorial Columns from *Cherokee Phoenix,*" by B. F. Luebke, Summer 1979, *Journalism History,* 6(2), 48-53, and "A Note of Caution—The Indian's Own Prejudice, as Mirrored in the First Native American Newspaper," by S. G. Riley, Summer 1979, *Journalism History,* 6(2), 44-47. Elias Boudinot apparently shortened the spelling of his last name to Boudinot from Boudinott early in his career, but he is referred to with his name spelled both ways in writings of the period and in subsequent scholarly works.

9. For more of Elias Boudinot's writings, see *Cherokee Editor: The Writings of Elias Boudinot,* T. Perdue (Ed.), 1996, Athens: University of Georgia Press.

10. For a more comprehensive account of portrayals of Native Americans in the 19th century White press, see *The Newspaper Indian: Native American Identity in the Press, 1820-90,* by J. M. Coward, 1999,Champaign: University of Illinois Press.

11. For more on conflicts with tribal governments over editorial freedom and on Native American journalists, see *Pictures of Our Nobler Selves: A History of Native American Contributions to News Media,* by M. N. Trahant, 1995, Nashville, TN: The Freedom Forum First Amendment Center.

12. For images of the Chinese in California gold rush popular culture, see "The 'Heathen Chinee'on God's Free Soil," by R. G. Lee, 1999, in *Orientals: Asian Americans in Popular Culture* (pp. 15-50). Philadelphia: Temple University Press. For later descriptions and pictures of the Chinese in the media, see *The Coming Man: 19th Century American Perceptions of the Chinese,* by P. P. Choy, L. Dong, and M. K. Hom, 1994, Seattle: University of Washington Press.

13. Chiu cites Lo and Lai (1977). See also *The Golden Hills' News,* No. 7, June 24, 1854; No. 8, July 1, 1854; and No. 10, July 29, 1854.

14. Both Chan (1991) and Yung (1999) cite "Free, Indentured, Enslaved: Chinese Prostitutes in Nineteenth-Century America," by L. C. Hirata, 1977, *Signs: Journal of Women in Culture and Society,* 5(1), 3-29.

References

Acevedo, C. A. (1965). *Breve historia del periodism*. Mexico: Editorial Jus.

American preachings versus practice. (1854, July 29). *The Golden Hills' News*, p. 1.

Barrow, L. C., Jr. (1977-1978). "Our Own Cause": "Freedom's Journal." *Journalism History*, 4(4).

Barth, G. (1971). *Bitter strength*. Cambridge, MA: Harvard University Press.

Chan, S. (1991). *Asian Americans: An interpretive history*. Washington, DC: Twain.

Chen, J. (1971). *The Chinese of America*. New York: Harper & Row.

Cherokee laws. (1828, March 13). *Cherokee Phoenix*, p. 1. Reprinted in the Summer 1979 issue of *Journalism History*, 6(2), 46.

The Chinese and the times. (1854, June 10). *The Golden Hills' News*, p. 1.

The Chinese exodus. (1854, May 27). *The Golden Hills' News*, p. 1. (Translation of Chinese characters by Stanley Rosen.)

Chiu, K. (1996, August 28). *Asian language newspapers in the United States: History revisited*. Paper presented at the Round Table on Newspapers, 62nd IFLA Conference, Beijing, China.

Daniel, W. C. (1982). *Black journals of the United States*. Westport, CT: Greenwood.

Dodson, D., & Hachten, W. A. (1973, May). Communication and development: African and Afro-American parallels. *Journalism Monographs*, 28, 25.

Emery, E., & Emery, M. (1996). *The press and America* (5th ed.). Boston: Allyn & Bacon.

The government, public and Chinese. (1854, July 1). *The Golden Hills' News*, p. 1.

Gutiérrez, F., & Ballesteros, E. (1979). The 1541 earthquake: Dawn of Latin American journalism. *Journalism History*, 6(3).

Hansen, G. C., & Heintz, W. F. (1970). *The Chinese in California: A brief bibliographic history*. San Francisco: Richard Abel.

Hester, A. (1979). Newspapers and newspaper prototypes in Spanish America, 1541-1750. *Journalism History*, 6(3).

Is there no help for the Chinese in California? (1854, June 24). *The Golden Hills' News*, p. 1.

Kemble, E. C. (1962). *A history of California Newspapers 1846-1858*. Los Gatos, CA: The Talisman Press. (Original work published 1858)

La Brie, H., III (1977-1978). Black newspapers: The roots are 150 years deep. *Journalism History*, 4(4).

LaCourse, R. (1979, Summer). An Indian perspective—Native American journalism: An Overview. *Journalism History*, 6(2), 34-35.

Lo, K., & Lai, H. J. (1977). *Chinese newspapers published in North America, 1854–1975*. Washington, DC: Center for Chinese Research Materials.

Murphy, J. E., & Murphy, S. M. (1981). *Let my people know*. Norman: University of Oklahoma Press.

Nordin, K. D. (1977-1978, Winter). In search of Black unity: An interpretation of the content and function of "Freedom's Journal." *Journalism History*, 4(4), 123-124.

Penn, I. G. (1891). *The Afro-American press and its editors*. Springfield, MA: Willey & Co.

Perdue, T. (Ed.). (1996). *Cherokee editor: The writings of Elias Boudinot.* Athens: University of Georgia Press.

The revolt in Texas (Reprinted from the *New York Observer*). (1827, April 20). *Freedom's Journal.*

Schaaf, G. (1996). Newspaper Rock and Canyonlands National Park. In *Ancient Ancestors of the Southwest.* Portland, OR: Graphic Arts Center.

Takaki, R. (1989). *Strangers from a different shore: A history of Asian Americans.* Boston: Little, Brown.

Yung, J. (1999). Unbound voices: A documentary history of Chinese women in San Francisco. Berkeley: University of California Press.

Zia, H. (2000). The pioneers from Asia. In *Asian American dreams: The emergence of an American people* (pp. 25-27). New York: Farrar, Straus & Giroux.

Part VI

The Rise of Class Communication

21st-Century 12
Challenges and
Opportunities

Challenges and opportunities are in the offing for people of color who seek careers in communications in the technology-driven world of the early 21st century. The same is likely to be true for those who wish to reap economic benefits by tapping into any or all of America's multicultural markets. The 1990s saw evolutionary changes in commercial communication. In a whirlwind decade, American communications moved from the era of "mass media" to the era of "class media" with the targeting of specific demographic groups—often on the basis of race—as economic markets. The technologies emerging in the new millennium promise that changes in communication will continue to have a strong impact on a diverse nation and its media. Although obstacles have remained, the steady growth of racial and cultural diversity and the upward mobility of people of color continue to force change on the communications industry. Examples of this include the 2001 acquisition of Black Entertainment Television (BET) by White-owned media conglomerate Viacom and NBC's purchase of Spanish-language television network Telemundo. Viacom executives publicly admitted their need for a presence in the African American marketplace, and both actions illustrated the increased importance of minority audience segments to advertisers and the development of an American media mosaic more racially diverse and inclusive than it has been in the past.

By the mid-1990s, media targeted to minority groups had become increasingly important. The last mass audience media of prime time television and general circulation daily newspapers were losing audience percentages, and the public in general was moving to more personal media in the form of multiple cable television channels, online websites, videocassettes, specialized magazines, and other targeted media made possible by new technology. In order to survive and thrive, media had moved from seeking mass audiences to audience segmentation, from mass communication to class communication, and from a mentality of "one size fits all" to "we do it all for you." To gain and retain audiences in an increasingly competitive market, managers of media found they needed to offer the public more content choices to increase the chance that audiences might find something they would enjoy. In the process, they found that people would pay for media with content that was previously either unavailable to them or subsidized by advertisers and received at little or no cost.

In the United States of the early 21st century, the development of communication media and their relationship to racially diverse groups continues to be influenced by three major forces. They are not the only forces exerting influences in this arena—nor is their impact always predictable. But it is clear that these forces exert great influence on the ways in which media develop and interact with the racially diverse population of the United States. These forces are as follows:

1. The growth of racial diversity in the United States

2. The technological advances in communication media

3. The targeting of audience segments by the media

The Growth of Racial Diversity

As the data on demographic trends in Chapter 1 clearly show, since 1970 the United States has experienced its greatest population growth rate in the non-White populations. The lower median age and slightly larger anticipated family sizes of people of color compared to Whites, as well as continued immigration from Asia and Latin America, point to the development of a society in the United States in which racial "minorities" constitute a much larger percentage of the population than they did in the past. In California and in some of the nation's largest cities, it is statistically incorrect to apply the term "minorities" to the non-White population, since non-Whites make up a majority of the people in that state and those cities.

If current trends persist as forecast, it appears that by the middle of this century the United States will have become a nation in which non-Whites comprise the majority of the population. Because the racial makeup of the nation continues to change in the direction of greater diversity, the media and other institutions in the United States have been responding to racial and cultural diversity at a greater rate than they did in the past. But projections of the available data also clearly indicate that Whites will continue to be the majority during the lifetime of most people born in the 20th century. Even when Whites are outnumbered by the collective strength of individual non-White groups, Whites will continue to be the largest single racial group in the United States for the foreseeable future. In many cities in which racial "minorities" make up the majority, Whites are still the largest single racial group and, in most cases, enjoy the largest share of economic and political power. The numbers a racial group represents in the population of a city, state, or nation do not directly translate into the amount of power that group exercises, particularly with regard to ownership of and policy making in the media. Despite the growth of the population of people of color in recent decades, in 2002 only one metropolitan general circulation daily newspaper (the San Francisco *Examiner*) was owned by members of a racial minority group. The number of major general audience media led by persons of color could be counted on the fingers of two hands.

Also, the growth in racial diversity will have an enduring impact on the nation only if racial minorities remain "beyond the melting pot," that is, bearing physical characteristics that keep them from blending in. Other groups have come to the United States and, after a generation or two, blended into the majority society both culturally and racially. Because of social and legal barriers in the United States, non-Whites have not melted into the mainstream society. In fact, for many years they had their integration severely restricted by laws limiting immigration, legislation and court rulings curtailing their legal rights, and institutional and personal acts of social and economic segregation. Those members of racial minority groups who have succeeded in penetrating predominately White educational institutions, professions, and residential districts are still identifiable by physical characteristics that distinguish them from Whites.

Some members of minority races have achieved upward social mobility through race-conscious educational admissions or hiring policies that placed a special priority on affording them access to previously denied opportunities. It is too early to predict if such advantaged minority people will have the desire or ability to shed the identity, culture, and, sometimes, language they share with others of their race and culture. Intermarriage between members of different races is increasing and the number of persons of biracial parentage is growing. It is clear that the growing racial diversity of the United States will have a long-lasting impact on the media and other institutions only if members of diverse racial and ethnic groups continue to retain a higher degree of racial and cultural identity than did the European immigrants who came to the United States in the past.

The Technological Advances in Communication Media

Perhaps even more important than the racial changes taking place in the society of the United States are the worldwide changes in communication media triggered by technological advances. The past generation witnessed fundamental changes in the technologies used in producing newspapers, television, radio, and video. Technical advances—such as offset printing of daily newspapers in color, satellite transmission of cable television and radio channels, stereo programming on AM and FM radio, and the widespread use of videotape in entertainment and news programming—have become commonplace in only the past two decades. Early 21st century technology has seen the emergence of computer audio and digital video disks (DVDs) and high definition television (HDTV). Previously, the technologies needed to make these products a reality were known to only relatively few people with enough foresight to envision how they could be applied in the future. In the current technological environment, however, "new media" are being linked or "converged" with existing media to provide various personalized communications options to consumers.

In the mid-1990s, the changes wrought by these technological advances were taken as commonplace by most people living in the United States, but many people in communities of color found themselves economically disconnected from these technological advances or able to participate at only the most basic levels. In the early 21st century, however, there are signs that people of color are creatively incorporating the new media into their lifestyles.

A national research study conducted in 2002 found that the urban minority audience was "vastly underestimated" by broadband video (cable and satellite television) executives and advertisers. The Urban Market Report revealed that although the common assumption held by policy makers was that minorities comprised an insignificant portion of marketable viewers, they were actually a viable but largely untapped market. The report noted that people of color highly associate broadband video usage with "quality of life" (W.G. Smith and Associates, 2002). Moreover, minorities with access to such video services were found to have such desirable marketing traits as higher education, occupation, and home ownership status.

Principal researcher Willis Smith noted that Latinos have the highest viewing index for cable television's The Learning Channel than all other minority groups and the general population. And, in a phenomenon Smith termed "self-marketing," many people of color who do not subscribe to pay-per-view TV services access such programming by visiting the homes of their friends and relatives who do. These actions considerably boost the viewing audience of such channels as HBO, Showtime, and ESPN. Smith also noted the implications of this large audience of people of color for Internet usage and policy. He said, "as Internet access and content shifts to a broadband platform, broadband access will become a major policy issue and set the stage as the first new industry of the 21st century that will not grow without [racial] diversity" (W.G. Smith and Associates, 2002).

The Targeting of Audience
Segments by the Media

Market segmentation—the strategy of dividing the potential consumers of a product into identifiable segments and then directing news, entertainment, and advertising through media that reach those audiences—has been an important advertising strategy since the new technology of television emerged as the most effective medium for reaching the mass audience in the early 1950s. Radio and magazines, which once delivered the mass audience to advertisers, were forced to survive by abandoning general audience content and, instead, targeting their media to specific segments within the mass audience. As a result, listeners turning the AM and FM radio dials in most cities find that each station has a different programming format designed to attract a specific group of listeners. By the same token, a visit to the magazine section of a supermarket or convenience store reveals a plethora of magazines, all vying for the attention of potential reader segments with predefined interests. In the early 21st century, the only two mass audience magazines that were still surviving were begun as offshoots of other media: *Reader's Digest* and *TV Guide.*

Market segmentation is a consumer-driven sales approach in which corporations subdivide the total heterogeneous potential market for a product into smaller segments, each of which has its own homogeneous characteristics.[1] Audience segments are broken out a number of ways, by place of residence, socioeconomic status, sex, age, education, and race. Segmentation has become increasingly important for advertisers as they have found that they can increase both their penetration of the audience and the sales of their products if they design advertisements geared to market segments and place them in print and broadcast media reaching those audience segments.

More than population growth and technological advances, however, it is the economic mechanisms of support that control the development of media in the United States. Corporate advertisers largely support print and broadcast media. When advertising is increased for a particular segment of the population, the media that reach and influence that segment gain increased advertising dollars. These dollars also make it more economically profitable for managers of existing media to consider changes to formats and content to try to attract that segment and the advertising dollars that will follow.

Minority-audience media have gained increased advertisement placements and profits because of this change in marketing strategy by major corporations and their advertising agencies. Since such media often reach audience segments that are growing faster than the White majority, they will be even more important with advertisers in the future. Media directed to racial minorities will continue to grow as long as major corporations and advertising agencies divide the mass audience into segments and place

Illustration 12.1   Corporations eager to develop new consumers for their products are drawn to conferences and publications promising to show them how to market their products through promotional campaigns and class communication media targeting different racial, ethnic, and language groups in the United States.

advertising in media that penetrate and persuade the racial minority segments of the overall population. This makes both White and non-White ownership of media directed toward racial minority groups more profitable and stimulates growth in minority media. For instance, by the early 21st century nearly all the major U.S. media corporations—including Tribune Corporation, Knight-Ridder, Gannett, Hearst, New York Times, NBC, CNN, MTV, ESPN, and HBO—had tried publications, programs, or channels directed toward Spanish-speaking audiences in the United States. In the past, Spanish-language media had largely been owned by members of the Latino community.

Moving beyond advertising, the growth of the information society has meant that corporations and entrepreneurs have looked for audiences willing to pay for content not available through the mass audience or advertiser-subsidized media. Thus, videocassette rentals of movies in Spanish and in languages of the countries of Asia and the Pacific Basin have become profitable, as are television channels for these audiences that are sometimes available only via cable television. This "pay to play" mentality moves minority-formatted media beyond advertiser support and into a dependence on the audience's ability to pay for the content.

In addition to the factor of individual minority groups being targeted by the media, the outlook for growth in media for racial minorities is enhanced by the first two factors mentioned in this chapter: the growth of the United States as a racially diverse nation and the advances in communication technology. Together, these three factors point to a racially heterogeneous nation that can be divided and reached by a much wider array of communication technologies. While such an outlook is favorable for the economic success of minority-formatted media, it also represents a fundamental change in the role of the media as they relate to both the racial majority and the racial minorities in the United States.

The Communication Media and the Segmented Society

The development of the media in the United States for many decades was based on mass communication, that is, breaking down differences in sex, age, education, geography, race, and other dissimilarities in the audience and delivering to the mass audience a form of entertainment, news, and advertising that would attract many and alienate only a few. But now the sales approach of advertisers is the opposite. Rather than wanting to address an undefined mass audience, advertisers prefer to target their messages to specific audiences whose demographic profiles are known to them. They want to be able to tailor their advertising to men, women, specific age groups, the affluent, and other definable groups within the mass audience. As a result, the audience strategies of the media that depend on advertising for their revenues have changed. Media must attract the audience that advertisers want to reach if they hope to continue to sell space and time on their stations and in their publications. The commodity they sell to advertisers is not the amount of space or time for the advertising message but the size and composition of the *audience* that will be exposed to the advertising message.

Segmentation can be based on several criteria, such as geography, age groups, sex, and family life cycle. For a portion of the audience to be segmented, it must be

1. identifiable,

2. measurable,

3. accessible, and

4. substantial enough to be potentially profitable.

For many years, minority audiences met the first three criteria, but they were thought to be either too poor or too small to warrant the attention of major advertisers. A 1981 marketing textbook by William and Isabella Cunningham cited race, religion, and national origin as possible bases for segmentation, in addition to the more commonly cited criteria.

> Ethnic and racial factors have been effectively used as a basis for segmenting markets. Although the U.S. is known as a great melting pot, certain groups have not been assimilated into society as quickly as others. In these situations, it has proven beneficial for firms to modify their product and promotion mix to fit the specific ethnic market. (p. 193)

Following the lead of the advertisers, the emphasis in media is now on market segmentation, that is, the ability to define certain segments of the audience, describe their demographic characteristics, and zero in on them through content that will attract members of those segments. Rather than trying to blend all the members of society into a mass audience melting pot, the advertisers have found they can get more impact for their advertising dollars if they can target their messages to specific audience segments and place advertising in media that reach those consumers.

The most immediate implication of audience segmentation in a racially diverse society is that minority groups are being more fully addressed than they were in the mass audience media system. A wider range of minority-formatted media now carry both advertising messages and content to groups that were previously thought to be too small to merit serious attention. Racial minorities no longer have to depend on mass audience media that consider them only a secondary audience—if they consider them at all. To the extent that the minority-oriented media provide entertainment and information content that serves the needs of their audiences, racial minorities benefit from this growth in the diversity of the media.

Even mass audience media, such as general circulation newspapers and prime time network television, are increasingly driven to draw specific audience segments in order to survive as effective advertising vehicles. The television week and day are divided by programming designed to attract different audiences at different times of the day and on different days of the week. Network prime time television is often cited as the last mass audience medium in the United States. But prime time television programs are increasingly dependent on the percentage of men, or women, or city dwellers, or young urban professionals in their audience.

Illustration 12.2   Although many general circulation newspapers reported steady circulation declines as the 21st century began, class communication newspapers directed to audience segments, including people of color, have been a growth area for newspapers.

New Opportunities: The Rise of Class Communication

The new technologies afford new opportunities to racial minorities and other groups that have not enjoyed equal participation or service from existing communication media. But racial minorities will probably take part in the new technologies more as employees or users of the new media rather than as their owners or developers. This is because the major communication conglomerates have invested heavily in developing commercial applications of the new technologies. At the same time, the deregulatory attitude of the Federal Communications Commission and other federal agencies has allowed licenses for some new technologies to be auctioned off to the highest bidder rather than allocated to the owner with the best ideas for using the public resource. In such an environment, the advantage goes to the large corporations that own the technologies of the past—such as print, movies, and broadcast media—who wish to invest in the new technologies.

Most minority investors have neither the seemingly infinite financial resources of large corporations nor the steady income generated by newspapers, movie studios, and broadcast stations. With less breadth of experience and expertise, it is difficult for them to capitalize on the new technologies at a level competitive with the major conglomerates and multinational corporations. Members of racial and ethnic minority groups also have less financial resources to invest in developing commercial applications of the new technologies.

Members of racial and ethnic minority groups do have an advantage in their understanding of minority communities that have not been well served by the communication media in the past. These gaps in telecommunication service provide the best entry point for people of color into the communications opportunities afforded by the new technologies. With knowledge of racially and linguistically different communities, people of color can develop innovative uses of new technologies to serve segments of the audience that have been overlooked by the general audience media. In the past, minority entrepreneurs have succeeded by adapting "new" technologies such as printing and broadcasting to the unique social and economic structure of their communities. There is no reason for the future to be any different, particularly since the technologies vastly expand the opportunities for "narrowcasting" media content to specific audiences. As the range of outlets in radio, in video, in print, on the Internet, and in other media continues to expand it will become increasingly important for the media to compete for audiences by narrowing both their content and their appeal to attract specific segments of the mass audience, including members of racial minority groups.

Controlling the Destiny of Communication Media

The future of communication media in the new century will be determined more by content advances than by technological advances. With a myriad of choices, people will pay attention to the media that pay attention to them. Writers, editors, and producers with an ability to address the tastes and preferences of people in a multicultural audience will do more to shape the future of media than those who design the technologies to transmit those messages. A recent informal poll of communications students at historically Black Howard University revealed that approximately 30% aspire to careers as owners or managers of media targeted to the Black audience. Whether such ambitions ultimately become reality, the concept reflects the sentiment among young people of color toward controlling their own communications agenda and away from roles as traditional content providers for the mainstream media.

Illustration 12.3   As the number of broadcast and cable television channels has grown, so has the number of class communication stations and programs targeting segments of the mass audience, such as people of color.

Based on growth of numbers alone, it would appear that both the mass audience media, which will need to attract an increasing share of a racially diverse population to claim that they are truly mass media, and the media targeted to racial minority groups, which will have a growing target, will continue to evolve as the 21st century unfolds. Mass audience media will have to include more people of color in a wider range of visible roles in entertainment and news content if they hope to attract shares of the growing minority groups. Minority personalities with "crossover" appeal to all races will have the greatest opportunities for success. The media directed toward minority audiences will most likely continue to become more targeted to specific strata within the market segment, such as Black teenagers or bilingual Latinos. As advances in technology make the media more plentiful, they will become more targeted, which will benefit people of color and other segments of the population that are identifiable and potentially addressable.

Illustration 12.4   Magazines directed to people of color grew steadily as the industry changed from magazines designed from mass audience appeal to class audience appeal following the advent of television as the dominant mass medium in the last half of the 20th century.

Not only is the United States becoming more racially diverse, but the divisions that are accompanying its racial diversity are being reinforced by the nation's communication media. Such divisions mean that racial minorities may be more fully served by the expanding media than were racial minorities in the past. But it also means that the socialization function of media in developing and transmitting the common culture of the society may be less important than it has been.

Segmented Media: Are We Losing the Common Culture That Bonds Us?

There are deeper implications of the segmentation of racial minorities in the social fabric of the United States. Audience segmentation can also mean that minorities become further separated and possibly distanced from the rest of society. Segmentation points to a society in which people may be integrated in terms of the products they consume, but they do not

Illustration 12.5 Interactive websites offering digital news, information, and entertainment regarding people of color are among the newest media contributing to the growth of class communication in the United States.

share a common culture based on the content of the entertainment or news media they use. Segmentation means that society will no longer be as strongly bonded together by the media. This is a trend that affects all the people in the United States who use the media, not only minorities. The "Global Village" envisioned by Marshall McLuhan in the 1960s has developed as one in which people are drawn together not so much by the content in the media they read, hear, or watch as by the products they consume. We may all be members of the same Global Village, but we sit at our own campfires.

Market segmentation through the media has even greater implications for society—and particularly for the role of communication media in society. For more than a century, the media of communication were the

Illustration 12.6 The New California Media Expo annually offers booths and exhibits for people to learn more about the importance of the state's growing class communication media targeted to racial and ethnic audiences.

Source: Pacific News Service.

"glue" that helped keep most of the society together. The media built and developed a common culture, albeit a commercial one, that fed a similar diet of news and entertainment to people in different walks of life in different parts of the country. To be sure, this catering to the majority meant that certain segments of the population, such as racial and ethnic minorities, were often either left out of the mainstream content or portrayed in ways that interpreted them through Anglo eyes. But the same media also served to transmit the culture and language of the dominant group to the new immigrants, even those immigrants who, because of geographical proximity to their mother country or physical characteristics such as color, were outside of the melting pot.

The media sometimes built common interests where they did not already exist by developing a surface culture or generating interest in events or personalities that were not of real importance to their readers, viewers, and listeners. And the emphasis on the lowest common denominator often meant that the mass media acted to lower public tastes rather than elevate them.

But the bottom line is that the media sought and built an audience based on common interests rather than differences. And out of this was forged the society that most Americans live in today. Now, with the emphasis on marketing and audience segmentation, the media play a very different role. The media, rather than trying to find commonalities among diverse groups in the mass audience, look for the differences that separate people and groups and for ways to capitalize on those differences through content and advertising. The force in society that once acted to bring people together now works to reinforce the differences that keep them apart.

Notes

1. For general descriptions of market segmentation and market segmentation as applied to racial minorities, see Chapter 4, "Markets and People and Money" (pp. 65-86), in *Fundamentals of Marketing*, by William J. Stanton, 1981, New York: McGraw-Hill and Chapter 7, "Market Segmentation" (pp. 184-203), in *Marketing: A Managerial Approach*, by William H. Cunningham and Isabella Cunningham, 1981, Cincinnati, OH: South-Western.

References

Cunningham, W. H., & Cunningham, I. (1981). *Marketing: A managerial approach*. Cincinnati, OH: South-Western.

Smith, W. G., and Associates. (2002, October 21). *National study finds broadband's impact vastly underestimated among minority groups* (Urban Market Report Press Release). Durham, NC: Author.

Suggested Readings

In addition to considering sources listed at the end of each chapter, those who have a continued interest in the subjects and issues covered in this book may wish to consult the following books.

Ainley, B. (1998). *Black journalists, White media*. Stoke on the Trent, UK: Trentham Books.

Barlow, W. (1999). *Voice over: The making of Black radio*. Philadelphia: Temple University Press.

Bataille, G. M., & Silet, C. L. P. (Eds.). (1980). *The pretend Indians: Images in the movies*. Ames: Iowa State Press.

Berg, C. R. (2002). *Latino images in film: Stereotypes, subversion and resistance*. Austin: University of Texas Press.

Berkhofer, R. F., Jr. (1978). *The White man's Indian: Images of the American Indian from Columbus to the present*. New York: Knopf.

Berry, G. L., & Mitchell-Kernan, C. (Eds.). (1982). *Television and the socialization of the minority child*. San Diego: Academic Press.

Biagi, S., & Kern-Foxworth, M. (Eds.). (1997). *Facing difference: Race, gender and mass media*. Thousand Oaks, CA: Pine Forge.

Bogle, D. (1973). *Toms, coons, mulattoes, mammies, and bucks: An interpretive history of Blacks in American films*. New York: Viking.

Campbell, C. P. (1995). *Race, myth and the news*. Thousand Oaks, CA: Sage.

Choy, P. P., Dong, L., & Hom, M. K. (1994). *Coming man: 19th century American perceptions of the Chinese*. Seattle: University of Washington Press.

Cottle, S. (Ed.). (2000). *Ethnic minorities and the media*. Buckingham, UK: Open University Press.

Coward, J. M. (1999). *The newspaper Indian: Native American identity in the press, 1820-90*. Urbana: University of Illinois Press.

Cripps, T. (1977). *Slow fade to Black: The Negro in American film, 1900-1942*. New York: Oxford University Press.

Danky, J. P., & Hady, M. E. (Eds.). (1998). *African-American newspapers and periodicals: A national bibliography*. Cambridge, MA: Harvard University Press.

Dann, M. E. (Ed.). (1971). *The Black press, 1827-1890: The quest for national identity*. New York: Putnam.

Dates, J. L., and Barlow, W. (Eds.). (1993). *Split Image: African Americans in the mass media*. Washington, DC: Howard University Press.

Dávila, A. (2001). *Latinos inc.: The marketing and making of a people.* Berkeley: University of California Press.

Dawkins, W. (1993). *Black journalists: The NABJ story.* Sicklerville, NJ: August.

Dennis, E. E., & Pease, E. C. (Eds.). (1997). *The media in Black and White.* New Brunswick, NJ: Transaction.

Denzin, N. K. (2002). *Reading race: Hollywood and the cinema of racial violence.* Thousand Oaks, CA: Sage.

Dines, G., & Humez, J. M. (Eds.). (1995). *Gender, race and class in media.* Thousand Oaks, CA: Sage.

Duster, A. M. (Ed.). (1970). *Crusade for justice: The autobiography of Ida B. Wells.* Chicago: University of Chicago Press.

Ely, M. P. (2001). *The adventures of Amos 'n' Andy: A social history of an American phenomenon.* Charlottesville: University Press of Virginia.

Entman, R. M., & Rojecki, A. (2001). *The Black image in the White mind: Media and race in America.* Chicago: University of Chicago Press.

Fisher, P. L., & Lowenstein, R. L. (Eds.). (1968). *Race and the news media.* New York: Praeger.

Friar, R., & Friar, N. (1972). *The only good Indian . . . : The Hollywood gospel.* New York: Drama Book Specialists.

Gandy, O. (1998). *Communication and race: A structural perspective.* London & New York: Arnold.

Graham, A. (2001). *Framing the south: Hollywood, television and race during the civil rights struggle.* Baltimore: Johns Hopkins University Press.

Greenberg, B., Burgoon, M., Burgoon, J., & Korzenny, F. (1983). *Mexican Americans and the mass media.* Norwood, NJ: Ablex.

Gutiérrez, F., & Schement, J. R. (1979). *Spanish-language radio in the southwestern United States.* Austin: The University of Texas at Austin Center for Mexican American Studies.

Hartmann, P., & Hubbard, C. (1974). *Racism and the mass media.* Lanham, MD: Rowman and Littlefield.

Heider, D. (2000). *White news: Why local news programs don't cover people of color.* Mahwah, NJ: Lawrence Erlbaum.

Hill, G. H., & Raglin, L. (1990). *Black women in television: An illustrated history and bibliography.* New York: Garland.

Hogan, L. (1984). *A Black national news service: The Associated Negro Press and Claude Barnett, 1919-1945.* Rutherford, NJ: Farleigh Dickinson University Press; London: Associated University Presses.

Hutton, F. (1993). *The early Black press in America, 1827-1860.* Westport, CT: Greenwood.

Kamalipour, Y., & Carilli, T. (Eds.). (1998). *Cultural diversity and the U.S. media.* Albany: State University of New York Press.

Kanellos, N. (2000). *Hispanic periodicals in the United States origins to 1960: A brief history and comprehensive bibliography.* Houston, TX: Arte Público.

Keever, B. A., Martindale, C., & Weston, M. A. (Eds.). (1997). *U.S. news coverage of racial minorities: A sourcebook, 1934-1996.* Westport, CT: Greenwood.

Keith, M. C. (1995). *Signals in the air: Native broadcasting in America.* New York: Praeger.

Kellstedt, P. M. (2003). *The mass media and the dynamics of American racial attitudes.* Cambridge, UK: Cambridge University Press.

Kelton, E. (1993). *The Indian in frontier news.* San Angelo, TX: Talley.

Kern-Foxworth, M. (1994). *Aunt Jemima, Uncle Ben, and Rastus: Blacks in advertising, yesterday, today and tomorrow.* Westport, CT: Greenwood.

Lee, J., Lim, I. L., & Matsukawa, Y. (2002). *Re-collecting early Asian America: Essays in cultural history.* Philadelphia: Temple University Press.

Lee, R. G. (1999). *Orientals: Asian Americans in popular culture.* Philadelphia: Temple University Press.

Lewels, F. G. (1974). *How the Chicano movement uses the media.* New York: Praeger.

Lo, K., & Lai, H. J. (1977). *Chinese newspapers published in North America, 1854-1975.* Washington, DC: Center for Chinese Research Materials.

Lyle, J. (Ed.). (1968). *The Black American and the press.* Los Angeles: Ward Ritchie.

MacDonald, J. F. (1983). *Blacks and White TV.* Chicago: Nelson-Hall.

Martindale, C. (1986). *The White press and Black America.* Westport, CT: Greenwood.

Martindale, C. (1993). *Pluralizing journalism education: A multicultural handbook.* Westport, CT: Greenwood.

McGowan, W. (2001). *Coloring the news: How crusading for diversity has corrupted American journalism.* San Francisco: Encounter Books.

Miller, R. (1980). *The kaleidoscopic lens: How Hollywood views ethnic groups.* Englewood, NJ: Ozer.

Miller, S. C. (1969). *The unwelcome immigrant: The American image of the Chinese, 1785-1882.* Berkeley: University of California Press.

Nancoo, S. E., & Nancoo, R. S. (Eds.). (1996). *The mass media and Canadian diversity.* Mississauga, Ontario: Canadian Educators' Press.

Newkirk, P. (2000). *Within the veil: Black journalists, White media.* New York: New York University Press.

Noriega, C. (2000). *Shot in America: Television, the state, and the rise of Chicano cinema.* Minneapolis: University of Minnesota Press.

Oak, V. V. (1948). *The Negro newspaper.* Westport, CT: Negro Universities Press.

Owusu, H. (1997). *Symbols of native America.* New York: Sterling.

Pride, A., & Wilson, C., II (1997). *A history of the Black press in America.* Washington, DC: Howard University Press.

Rhodes, J., & Cary, M. A. S. (1998). *The Black press and protest in the nineteenth century.* Bloomington: Indian University Press.

Ríos, D. I., & Mohamed, A. N. (Eds.). (2003). *Brown and Black communication: Latino and African American conflict and convergence in mass media.* Westport, CT: Praeger.

Rivas-Rodríguez, M. (2003). *Brown eyes on the web: Unique perspectives of an alternative Latino online publication.* New York & London: Routledge.

Rodríguez, A. (1999). *Making Latino news: Race, language, class.* Thousand Oaks, CA: Sage.

Rodríguez, C. (Ed.). (1997). *Latin looks: Images of Latinas and Latinos in the U.S. media.* Boulder, CO: Westview.

Rollins, P. C., & O'Connor, J. E. (Eds.). (1998). *Hollywood's Indian: The portrayal of the Native American in film.* Lexington: The University Press of Kentucky.

Ross, K., & Playdon, P. (2001). *Black marks: Minority ethnic audiences and the media.* Burlington, VT: Ashgate.

Rubin, B. (Ed.). (1980). *Small voices and great trumpets: Minorities and the media.* New York: Praeger.

Santa Ana, O. (2002). *Brown tide rising: Metaphors of Latinos in contemporary American public opinion.* Austin: University of Texas Press.

Simon, R. J. (1985). *Public opinion and the immigrant: Print media coverage, 1880-1980.* New York: Lexington Books.

Stephens, L. (1999). *Covering the community: A diversity handbook for media.* Thousand Oaks, CA: Pine Forge.

Streitmatter, R. (1994). *Raising her voice: African-American women journalists who changed history.* Lexington: University Press of Kentucky.

Suggs, H. L. (1983). *The Black press in the south, 1895-1979.* Westport, CT: Greenwood.

Suggs, H. L. (1996). *The Black press in the middle west, 1865-1985.* Westport, CT: Greenwood.

Tovares, R. D. (2002). *Manufacturing the gang: Mexican American youth gangs on local television.* Westport, CT: Greenwood.

Trahant, M. (1995). *Pictures of our nobler selves: A history of Native American contributions to news media.* Nashville, TN: The Freedom Forum First Amendment Center.

Van Dijk, T. (1991). *Racism and the press.* New York: Routledge.

Veciana-Suarez, A. (1990). *Hispanic media: Impact and influence.* Washington, DC: Media Institute.

Vogel, T. (Ed.). (2001). *The Black press: New literary and historical essays.* New Brunswick, NJ: Rutgers University Press.

Waller, L. (Ed.). (1998). *Newspapers, diversity and you.* Princeton, NJ: The Dow Jones Newspaper Fund.

Ward, B. (Ed.). (2001). *Media, culture and the modern African American freedom struggle.* Gainesville: University Press of Florida.

Washburn, P. S. (1986). *A question of sedition: The federal government's investigation of the Black press during World War II.* Charlottesville: University Press of Virginia.

Weill, S. (2002). *In the madhouse's din: Civil rights coverage by Mississippi's daily press, 1948-1968.* Westport, CT: Praeger.

Weston, M. A. (1996). *Native Americans in the news: Images of Indians in the twentieth century press.* Westport, CT: Greenwood.

Wilson, C., II (1991). *Black journalists in paradox: Historical perspectives and current dilemmas.* Westport, CT: Greenwood.

Woll, A. L. (1977). *The Latin image in American film.* Los Angeles: University of California, Latin American Center.

Woll, A. L. (1987). *Ethnic and racial images in American film and television: Historic essays and bibliography.* New York: Garland.

Wolseley, R. E. (1995). *Black achievers in American journalism.* Nashville: James C. Winston.

Online Resources

The following list of media diversity online resources was developed by the Poynter Institute for Media Studies Library in 2002.

ASNE Diversity Resources
http://www.asne.org/kiosk/diversity/index.htm
These are diversity resources from the American Society of Newspaper Editors.

American Women in Radio and Television (AWRT)
http://www.awrt.org
AWRT is dedicated to advancing the impact of women in electronic media and related fields.

Asian American Journalists Association (AAJA)
http://www.aaja.org
AAJA was formed in 1981 to provide support for Asian American journalists.

Asian-Nation
http://www.asian-nation.org/
This is an information source on the historical, political, social, economic, and cultural elements that make up today's Asian American community.

Association for Women in Communications (AWC)
http://www.womcom.org/
AWC champions the advancement of women across all communications disciplines.

Boston Globe Report on Newspaper Minority Employment
http://www.boston.com/asne/
This report was written by Bill Dedman and Steve Doig in 2002.

Columbia Workshop on Journalism, Race & Ethnicity
http://www.jrn.columbia.edu/workshops/
The aim of the Columbia University workshop is to encourage candid and complete coverage of race and ethnicity.

Diversity and Making a Difference (ASNE)
http://www.asne.org/index.cfm?id=3644
This was written by Carolina Garcia and appeared in the June 2002
issue of *The American Editor.*

Diversity Resources (No Train, No Gain)
http://www.notrain-nogain.org/Divers/DIV.asp
These are diversity resources from the No Train, No Gain website.

Diversity Toolbox (Society for Professional Journalists)
http://www.spj.org/diversity_toolbox.asp
These are diversity resources from the Society for Professional
Journalists.

DiversityInc.com
http://www.diversityinc.com/
DiversityInc.com offers information on how diversity affects
companies' relationships with their employees, suppliers,
customers, and investors.

DiversityWeb
http://www.diversityweb.org/
DiversityWeb was designed by The Association of American Colleges
and Universities and the University of Maryland at College Park.

Do We Check It at the Door?
http://www.namme.org/pdfs/FinalReporttotheIND.pdf
This is a McCormick Fellowship Initiative report on media executives
of color written by Keith Woods in 2002.

*The Essence of Excellence: Covering Race and Ethnicity
(and Doing It Better)*
http://www.jrn.columbia.edu/workshops/excellence_intro.html
This report for the Columbia University Graduate School of
Journalism, written by Keith Woods in 2002, was underwritten by the
Workshop on Journalism, Race and Ethnicity.

Freedom Forum: Newsroom Diversity
http://www.freedomforum.org/diversity/default.asp
This website contains links to news, commentary, and analysis.

The Great Divide
http://www.americanpressinstitute.org/curtis/Great_Divide.pdf
This is a 2002 report on female leadership in U.S. newsrooms from
API and the Pew Center for Civic Journalism.

How Race Is Lived in America
http://www.nytimes.com/library/national/race/
This is the 2000 *New York Times* series on race.

International Women's Media Foundation (IWMF)
http://www.iwmf.org/
IWMF was founded to strengthen the role of women in the media.

IWMF: Leadership Report
http://www.iwmf.org/resources/lr.htm
This is a 2000 portrait of where women stand in the international
media.

Journalism and Women Symposium (JAWS)
http://www.jaws.org/
JAWS supports the personal growth and professional empowerment
of women in newsrooms.

Latinos and Media Project
http://www.latinosandmedia.org
This website contains information and resources about a variety of
issues related to Latinos and the media.

Maynard Institute
http://www.maynardije.org/
The Institute is dedicated to increasing racial and ethnic diversity in
news coverage, staffing, and business operations.

MIBTP
http://www.webcom.com/mibtp/
The mission of the Minorities in Broadcasting Training Program is to
ensure diversity in newsrooms at television and radio stations across
the United States.

National Association of Black Journalists (NABJ)
http://www.nabj.org
NABJ was founded with the purpose of promoting and
communicating the importance of diversity in newsrooms.

National Association of Hispanic Journalists (NAHJ)
http://www.nahj.org/
NAHJ is dedicated to the recognition and professional advancement
of Hispanics in the news industry.

National Association of Minorities in Cable (NAMIC)
http://www.namic.com/
NAMIC educates, advocates, and empowers for the cause of diversity
in the telecommunications industry.

National Association of Minority Media Executives (NAMME)
http://www.namme.org/
NAMME is an organization for media managers and executives of
color working in newspapers, magazines, radio, television, cable, and
new media.

National Center on Disability and Journalism (NCDJ)
http://www.ncdj.org/
NCDJ's mission is to educate journalists and educators about
disability reporting issues in order to produce more accurate,
fair, and diverse news reporting.

National Diversity Journalism Job Bank
http://www.newsjobs.com
This job bank is devoted to diversifying newspaper
and other media industries and is primarily aimed at
women and minorities.

National Federation of Press Women (NFPW)
http://www.nfpw.org/
NFPW promotes the highest ethical standards and the professional
development of women.

National Lesbian and Gay Journalists Association
http://www.nlgja.org
NLGJA works to ensure equal benefits and conditions for lesbian and
gay employees in news organizations.

NAA's Diversity and Education Resources
http://www.naa.org/SectionPage.cfm?SID=84&CFID=19996&
CFTOKEN=3262665
This website contains resources from the Newspaper Association
of America diversity department.

Native American Journalists Association (NAJA)
http://www.naja.com/
NAJA was formed to encourage, inspire, enhance and empower
Native American communicators.

News Watch Project
http://newswatch.sfsu.edu/
This is a project of the Center for Integration and Improvement of
Journalism, San Francisco State University
Journalism Department.

People and Product
http://www.naa.org/IndexList.cfm?SID=1154
This is the NAA/*Presstime* supplement on diversity.

Pictures of Our Nobler Selves:
A History of Native American Contributions to News Media
http://www.freedomforum.org/publications/
newsroomtraining/picsnoblerselves/pictureofournoblerselves.pdf
This was written by Mark N. Trahant
(The Freedom Forum, 1995).

Poynter Online's Diversity Resources
http://poynter.org/subject.asp?id=5
This is a broad range of articles and source materials about diversity
from the Poynter Institute.

Poynter Online's Column: Journalism With a Difference
http://www.poynter.org/column.asp?id=58
The featured columnists include Aly Colón, Thomas Huang, Keith
Woods, and Jodi Rave.

RTNDF Newsroom Diversity Campaign
http://www.rtnda.org/diversity/
This website contains links to diversity resources from the Radio and
Television News Directors Association and the Radio and Television
News Directors Foundation.

Reporting Race
http://www.cjr.org/year/99/5/race.asp
This is a September/October 1999 *Columbia Journalism Review* special
report. |FCO|Hyperlink

Richard Prince's Journal-isms|FCC|
http://www.maynardije.org/columns/dickprince/
Richard Prince's column appears on the Maynard Institute website.

South Asian Journalists Association
http://www.saja.org
Their goal is to foster ties among South Asian journalists in North
America and improve standards of journalistic coverage of South Asia
and South Asian America.

Television and Radio News Research
http://www.missouri.edu/~jourvs/index.html
This statistical look at television and radio by Vernon Stone
includes a section on women and minorities.

U.S. Census Bureau Minority Links
http://www.census.gov/pubinfo/www/hotlinks.html
This website contains data on racial and ethnic populations in the
United States.

UNITY: Journalists of Color, Inc.
http://www.unityjournalists.org/
UNITY is a strategic alliance of journalists of color acting as a force
for positive change in the fast-changing global news industry.

Women and Minority Employment Survey
http://www.rtnda.org/research/womin.shtml
RTNDA annual survey about the career progress of women and
minorities in electronic news.

Women in Newspapers: 2002
http://www.mediamanagementcenter.org/
center/web/publications/win2002.htm
This account was written by Mary Arnold Hemlinger
and Cynthia C. Linton, Media Management Center, Northwestern
University.

Index

About the Authors

Clint C. Wilson II is Professor of Journalism and Graduate Professor of Communication at Howard University. He has also held faculty and administrative positions at the University of Southern California, California State University, Los Angeles, and Pepperdine University. He has lectured at other colleges and universities and has been a seminar leader at the American Press Institute. He has written four books on subjects related to the Black press and the relationship between people of color and the general audience media in the United States. His scholarly work has been published in such periodicals as *Journalism Educator, Columbia Journalism Review, Quill,* and *Change.* He is a founder of the Black Journalists Association of Southern California and has written for various news media organizations, including the Associated Press, *Los Angeles Times, The Washington Post, Pasadena Star-News, St. Petersburg Times,* and the *Los Angeles Sentinel. Journalism and Mass Communication Quarterly* cited his book *A History of the Black Press* as among the 35 "most significant books of the 20th century," and he is a recipient of the Honor Medal for Distinguished Service in Journalism from the University of Missouri. Wilson holds an A.A. degree in Journalism from Los Angeles City College; a B.A. degree in journalism and public relations from California State University, Los Angeles; and an M.A. in journalism from the University of Southern California (USC). He also earned a doctorate in higher education administration from USC. In addition, he has completed fellowships with the Freedom Forum Media Studies Center at Columbia University, the Poynter Institute for Media Studies, and the American Society of Newspaper Editors.

Félix F. Gutiérrez is a Visiting Professor of Journalism at the Annenberg School for Communication of the University of Southern California and former Senior Vice President of the Newseum and The Freedom Forum, where he administered journalism education, professional, and diversity programs. Prior to joining The Freedom Forum, he held faculty or administrative positions at the University of Southern California; California State University, Northridge; Stanford University; and California State University, Los Angeles; and visiting appointments at the

325

University of Texas, Austin; Columbia University; and The Claremont
Colleges. His publication credits include five books and more than 50
articles or chapters in academic journals, professional publications, and
books, most focusing on diversity in the media. In addition to writing
freelance articles, he worked during summers and on a weekly basis for
the *Pasadena Star-News* and the Associated Press during the 1980s. His
advocacy on behalf of people of color and their inclusion in the media
has been recognized by the Asian American Journalists Association,
Association for Education in Journalism and Mass Communication,
Black College Communication Association, California Chicano News
Media Association, National Association of Hispanic Journalists, and
others. He is in the National Association of Hispanic Journalists Hall of
Fame and the Stanford University Alumni Association Multicultural Hall
of Fame, received the Honor Medal from the University of Missouri
School of Journalism, and was an inaugural member of the
Northwestern University Medill School of Journalism Hall of
Achievement. He is a trustee of the Freedom Forum Diversity Institute at
Vanderbilt University. His education includes a B.A. degree from
California State University, Los Angeles, an M.S.J. from the Medill School
of Journalism at Northwestern University, and an M.A. and a Ph.D. from
the Department of Communication at Stanford University.

Lena M. Chao is Associate Professor of Communication Studies at
California State University, Los Angeles (CSULA), where she also serves as
Director for the Asian and Asian American Institute. Prior to joining the
faculty at CSULA, she was on the administrative staff of the Media
Institute for Minorities at the University of Southern California and
worked as a Public Service Coordinator at KFWB News radio in Los
Angeles. She also has worked at Radio Español and served as Media
Director for the American Civil Liberties Union of Southern California.
Her areas of scholarly specialization include public relations, mass communication, and intercultural and interpersonal communications. Her
academic work has been published in journals such as *Human
Communication, California Politics and Policy,* and *Feedback,* among
others. She was on the founding board of the Media Action Network for
Asian Americans (MANAA), a watchdog group that monitors the communication media in the United States for fair, balanced, and accurate
portrayals of Asian Pacific Americans. Her public service activities also
include membership on the advisory boards of two nonprofit organizations, The Coalition of Brothers and Sisters Unlimited and the Estelle Van
Meter Multipurpose Center, which are both located in South Central Los
Angeles. She is Faculty Director for Service Learning at California State
University, Los Angeles, promoting curriculum development and faculty
and student involvement in community service learning opportunities.

Dr. Chao received her B.A. in English literature from the University of California, Los Angeles, and her M.S. in print journalism and Ph.D. in communication arts and sciences from the University of Southern California.